The Other Side of Sewanee

by

Patricia Short Makris
Belleville, Illinois

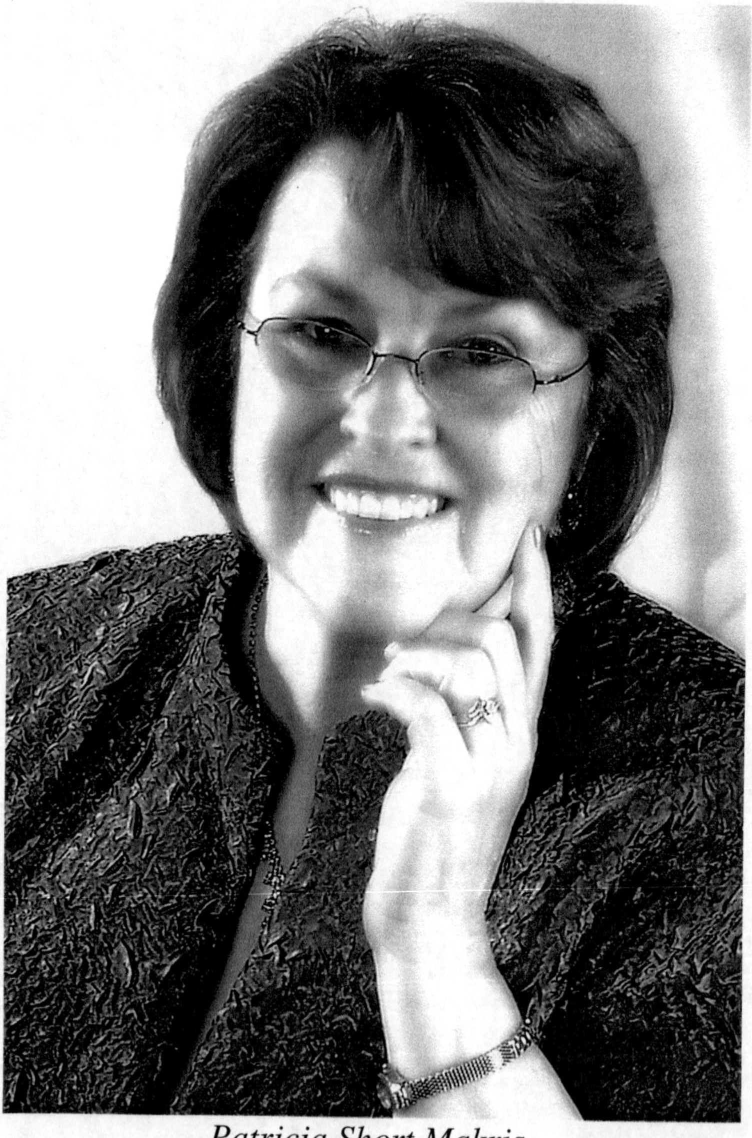

Patricia Short Makris

Printed in the U.S.A. by
Dogwood Printing, Inc.
P.O. Box 716 • Ozark, MO 65721
800-862-8382

This book is dedicated to

my father, Joseph "Reece" Short

1905-1996

and my mother, Lou Sullivan Short

1906-1968

ACKNOWLEDGMENTS:

I would like to thank the following people for providing information, photographs, and reference books. They are: Benton Green, McCord and Lucia Green Yates, William McBee Sr., Una McBee, Polly Green, Paul and Evelyn Mooney, Nancy Taylor, Dr. Harold Jackson, Margaret Garner Short, Louise Terrill, Dorothy and Tommy Andrews, Arthur and Elizabeth Chitty, Sister Kiara, and Mariah Webb. My thanks also to Annie Armour who provided information and photographs from the duPont Library, and for letting me use her notes on the Sewanee Public School. I would like to recognize the late Mary Hamilton for writing the wonderful story about the town of Sewanee, and to Rosie Long and my father, Reece Short, for providing me with a wealth of information before their deaths. They helped me reconstruct Sewanee from the way it was during their childhood. Much of this book could never have been written without the information provided by all the above-mentioned people.

Front Cover Photograph:

The photograph on the front cover was taken around 1910. It was first published in "*One Hundred Years In Sewanee*." I lived on the other side of the railroad tracks from the town of Sewanee, and my first remembrance of the town was from the same view depicted in this photograph. Therefore, the reason my book is titled, "*The Other Side Of Sewanee.*" I thought it was an appropriate title, since it spotlights some of the other places and people that have never been mentioned before in Sewanee's history.

FOREWORD

THE OTHER SIDE OF SEWANEE spotlights the town of Sewanee, Tennessee, and its people. Much has been written about the University of the South, but hardly anything is known about the town, its people, and the adjacent communities.

The first residents on the Sewanee Mountain were the Creek and Cherokee Indians. They lived on the Cumberland Plateau when it was known as "The Nation". The first known white settlers were Jesse Barnes and George Smith who lived on the mountain before 1827. In 1856, the steepest railroad in the country was completed to the coal banks at Midway. The railroad brought the coal miners and railroad workers to the area. By 1860, the Episcopalians built the first log buildings associated with the University of the South. The Civil War soldiers burned all the cabins associated with the University of the South. After the war, the Episcopalians returned to the mountain and built the University of the South, and the town of Sewanee was born in the midst of a wilderness.

By the 1870s, churches, schools, and stores had been built. People came from all over to be apart of the growing population of the mountain town. Even one of Queen Victoria's former guards lived in the village with a group of Confederate Veterans. There were people from all over Europe living on the mountain and operating businesses. 1n 1888, an order of Episcopal Nuns came and established a girls' school. In 1911, President William Howard Taft came to visit the beautiful town perched high upon the Cumberland Plateau.

THE OTHER SIDE OF SEWANEE is about the people who built those magnificent rock masterpiece buildings in the University of the South. It's about a teacher who taught in a one-room schoolhouse, made fires in the stoves to keep her students warm, cooked food for their lunches, and provided them with a good education. It's about soldiers who gave their lives for our freedom. It is mostly about ordinary people who stay in the background, but play an essential part in any success story.

Information from land grants, deeds, and other documents concerning early Sewanee are presented in this book to provide the reader with a better understanding of what it was really like. A list of names and information are provided about the people who were living at Sewanee from 1860 through the 1920 census years. Some land grants were signed by James K. Polk and Sam Houston. This book is also geared to help people find their family roots and ancestors at Sewanee.

ABOUT THE AUTHOR

Patricia "Pat" Short Makris was born and raised at Sewanee, Tennessee. She attended Sewanee Public School, Jump Off Public School, and graduated from Franklin County High School in 1961. After high school, Pat went to work in Miami, Florida for the Webb Realty Corporation as a Secretary. In 1962, she was hired by the F.B.I. After attending their fingerprint school, she was assigned to the fingerprint section of the Identification Building in Washington, D.C. Besides the F.B.I., she has worked for the Lakewood Colorado Police Department in the Crime Lab. Her job included classifying, identifying, and taking fingerprints, creating composites of suspects, booking prisoners, and aided undercover police in various police stings. Pat became a member of the International Association for Identification. Later, she worked in fingerprint positions at the Colorado Bureau of Investigation and Newport News, Virginia Police Department.

Her Barnes family roots at Sewanee go back to the days of the Indians, when the mountain was known as "The Nation." Her Short family roots have been traced from England to Virginia, arriving there in 1634. The Shorts came to Franklin County in the early 1850's to work on the railroad. They helped build the first railroad up the mountain from Cowan. Later, they were among the stonemasons that built the buildings on the domain of the University of the South.

Pat has written four family history books. *MY GREEK CONNECTION* is based on her husband's Greek ancestors. *A JOURNEY THROUGH HISTORY WITH THE SHORT AND BARNES FAMILIES* is about her father's family. *DESCENDANTS OF HENRY SULLIVAN* was written about her Irish roots in America. The *PASSONS' FAMILY CONNECTIONS* is based on her mother's maternal side of the family. Major Passons, the main ancestor in the Passons' book, served in the War of 1812 with Davy Crockett. Major and Davy were part of Major William Russell's Company of Mounted Spies from Franklin County, Tennessee. They fought on horseback, and served as scouts for General Andrew Jackson's Tennessee Volunteers. In 1999, Pat wrote the follow-up *book* called *SEWANEE – ECHOES OF ITS PAST.* This book has additional stories about Sewanee and the families that helped establish it as a community. In 1999, she also published *EARLY EPISCOPAL CHURCH RECORDS*, which are transcriptions of old Sewanee Episcopal Church records from 1872 to 1944. In 2006, Pat wrote her fourth Sewanee book, titled *SEWANEE - PEOPLE, PLACES, AND TIMES.* Besides stories about the people, places and times, she transcribed the 1930 Sewanee census records, to help researchers find their ancestors at Sewanee. This book includes wonderful stories from diaries of union soldiers who were camped at Sewanee in 1863.

Pat married Steve Makris in 1963. Steve retired from the U.S.A.F. as a Lieutenant Colonel in 1992. They have two daughters, Christy who is married to Keith Stern, and Stefanie is married to Chris Hyde. They also have five grandchildren: Zachery Stern; Kyle Stern; Deanna Hyde; Ryan Hyde; and Jared Hyde. Steve and Pat live in Belleville, Illinois, but spend as much time as possible in Sewanee, since her parents' home is still standing in the Bob Town section of Sewanee. The land where her father, grandfather, and great-uncle built their home has been in the family since 1894.

TABLE OF CONTENTS

SEWANEE WAS THE NATION

In the early days of our country, the territory on which Sewanee now sits was known as "The Nation." Creek and Cherokee Indians were living all the way to Jasper.[1] The first white man known to visit "The Nation" was a rather famous frontiersman by the name of Daniel Boone. He stopped on the mountain long enough to carve his name on a rock between the present day town of Monteagle and where the University of the South is now located.[2] Daniel was probably blazing the wilderness trails when he visited the Cumberland Plateau, which was then a part of North Carolina.

In 1779, shortly after the establishment of Fort Nashborough, which is now part of Nashville, the Chickamauga Indians, a tribe of lower Cherokees, attacked the settlers who were living in the fort. The settlers became so irritated at the hostile Indians they started planning revenge attacks against them. Major Orr was chosen to take a group of scouts across the Cumberland Mountains to find a route to the Chickamauga's villages on the banks of the Tennessee River. The route they took was an Indian trail that crossed the Cumberland Plateau. This was the second time white men were known to be on the Sewanee Mountain. Afterwards, Major Orr and his scouts led a group of settlers to the Indians villages of Nickajack and Running Water and burned down their villages. The settlers defeated the Chickamaugas and their power was broken forever

The Indians' defeat at Nickajack and Running Water was important in the settlement of Tennessee. It gave settlers a route across the Cumberland Plateau without fear of being attacked by a tribe of warriors. Settlers were then able to explore the territory west of the Cumberland Mountains in order to establish new settlements.[3] The newly created settlements played an important role in Tennessee becoming a state on June 1, 1796.[4] President George Washington signed legislation making Tennessee the 16th state to be admitted to the union.[5]

In 1800, settlements sprang up at places that became known as Beans' Creek, which was located below the town now known as Winchester, and near the town that became known as Cowan. The Bean family settled on Bean's Creek and Major William Russell brought a group of settlers to the Cowan area around 1806.[6]

In 1807, Franklin County was created from land that was previously part of White County. It was named in honor of Benjamin Franklin. The first courthouse was located in Major William Russell's log cabin near the town of Cowan[7]. Afterwards, Franklin County was buzzing with merchants from all over the state. They would meet at Caldwell's bridge to make the long journey across the Cumberland Mountains to Baltimore, Maryland. Merchants would transport their goods by wagon train, and would bring back enough supplies to last a year.[8] During this time, Baltimore was considered one of the leading market places in the country. Caldwell's bridge is thought to be the last bridge you cross before going up the mountain from Cowan to Sewanee on highway 41A/64.

There were streams of settlers coming to Franklin County between 1813 and 1814. Many came from North and South Carolina and settled in Rowarks Cove just below the Cumberland Plateau. They must have been a rugged bunch of pioneers to choose such a dense wilderness in which to build their settlement. Many settlers including the Richardsons, Perrys, Morrises, Gilliams, Longs, Smiths, Williams, Catchings, Hills, Cherrys, Finneys, Henleys, Roses, Austins, Roarks, Barnes and Gibsons were early settlers in Rowarks Cove.

The settlers at Rowarks Cove built a log fort for protection against the Indian raids and outbreaks that were common during the early days.[9] Indians were still trying to drive white settlers out of their country. The Indians who were attacking the settlers at Rowarks Cove were thought to be a small band of hostile Red Creeks and Chickamauga Indians living on the Cumberland Plateau.

I should say at this point that some history books written about the Cumberland Plateau area say the mountain was only used as a camping ground and migration route by the Indians. Old timers at Sewanee tell a different story of Indians actually living on the mountain and marrying the settlers. My father, Reece Short, found an Indian burying ground inside the gates at St. Mary's. The small mounds are located near a fence on the left side of the road leading into St. Mary's, and not far from the old stage coach road.

My grandmother, Litha Barnes Short, was of Indian descent. Tradition has it that her Barnes family lived among the Indians on the Sewanee Mountain. One of her ancestors was said to have married an Indian squaw living on the Cumberland Plateau.

A present day resident of Sewanee says two Indians were said to be buried on his property. Many times squaws would take English names before marrying white settlers. The name change made it impossible to trace their Indian heritage. Allen Gibson who came to Rowarks Cove in 1814, left written information saying that both the Creek and Cherokee Indians lived all the way to Jasper. Barnes settlers told stories about the mountain Indians attacking the white settlers living in the Crow Creek Valley.

An article that appeared in the Purple Sewanee tells about Mrs. Sally Sewell Hawkins seeing Indians in Hawkins Cove.[10] Another article in the Purple Sewanee told about an Indian making a trip from the West to see the beech grove on the old Lost Cove Road below Natural Bridge. The grove was sacred land in the traditions of his tribe.[11] Mrs. Mary Statem Hamilton who was born at Sewanee in 1899, gave information that in her childhood Indians were still present at Sewanee. Wherever the women would go they would be accompanied by men with guns, and it was a long time before the mountain was free of the Indians.[12]

Mrs. Polly Green, granddaughter of John and Mary Ellen Elliott Pack, remembers that an Indian family lived in a wigwam near her Grandparents' house in the 1920's. The Packs lived near Natural Bridge, where an Indian trail was located. Older residents said the trail lead out of Lost Cove near Natural Bridge, and crossed the mountain to other unknown destinations.

Descendants of students attending St-Paul's-on-the-Mountain reported that Miss Flora Fairbanks and Miss Charlotte Elliott took armed guards when going to the spring because Indians were going there for water. My father, who was born in 1905, told about an Indian living in Lost Cove during his childhood. Unfortunately, no records can be found listing names of Indians who lived on the Cumberland Plateau or in the surrounding coves.

Saint Paul's On The Mountain Episcopal Church and School ca. 1870
(Courtesy of University of the South Archives)

Allan Gibson.

Perhaps the oldest resident of Sewanee at the time, Allan Gibson Died April 12 1896. Born Jan 1st. 1803 in South Carolina — came to Sewanee in 18[illegible]. At 19 he became engaged & at that time came to the conclusion that tobacco in any form was injurious so he then resolved never to use it, & bound his wife over never to make use of it. & neither of them did — Nor did he ever drink whiskey except for medicine — In the early days of Sewanee there was a fort in Rowark's Cove to which the people roundabout resorted in times of threatened Indian raids & outbreaks. The territory on which Sewanee is located was then known as "The Nation" & many Creek & Cherokee Indians lived all the way to Jasper.

Gibson gave to the University the land bounded by what is now known as Gibson's Path down the mountain (on the west), the Hardee Field (on the South) & Chalybeate Spring on the east, the whole of it lying on the northern boundary of the domain along the brow of the mountain — He was a good friend to the University, & his life had many virtues & was in every way exemplary.

Died April 12, 1896.

A copy of Allan Gipson's recollections of early Sewanee mountain (Obtained from University of the South Archives)

SEWANEE'S EARLY SETTLERS AND LAND OWNERS

The first land grants found that were issued by the State of Tennessee to settlers and land speculators on the Cumberland Mountain show that more people had mountain land than has been written about previously. Lanson Rowe built cabins on the mountain to stay in during the Summer months.[13] A road system to and from the mountain and surrounding coves had already been established when land was being surveyed in 1826.[14]

The earliest land grant found by the writer was an application made by Henry M. Rutledge, a land agent and speculator. He filed an application at the entry taker's office in Franklin County Court House on August 24, 1824, for a tract of land containing fifty acres. He paid the State of Tennessee one half cent an acre for land described as being on top the Cumberland Mountain. It crossed the road leading from Caldwell's Bridge to Jasper, north of Grant's improvements. Henry received his land grant on May 21, 1832.[15] There is no mention of him ever living on the Cumberland Mountain.

The second earliest land grant found belonged to William Barnes. His land grant was dated September 27, 1824, in Marion County, Tennessee. William bought fifty acres of land for twelve cents an acre. The description of the land shows it on the Cumberland Mountain adjoining what is called Tally's Fork on the waters of Cove Creek. William's land grant was recorded at Murfreesborough (Murfeesboro) on August 26, 1825. This was not long after the State of Tennessee started selling land grants to settlers for mountain land.[16] Until 1819, the Cumberland Plateau was still Indian territory.[17]

The next land grant found was applied for by Dennis Barnes, brother of William, on February 13, 1826, in the office of the entry taker at the Franklin County Court House. Dennis paid one cent an acre for a one hundred acre tract. The land was located on top a bluff of the mountain and including the five acres where he formerly lived. Dennis received the land grant on May 17, 1830.[18]

One day later on February 13, 1826, John T. Bowers applied for a land grant through the entry takers' office at the Franklin County Court House. He paid one cent an acre for a one hundred acre tract of land. It was described as being at the foot of the mountain and at the bluff of rocks above said Bowers' house. It ran between John and Samuel Tally's land, and up the mountain crossing the Jasper Road. John received his land grant on March 27, 1827.[19]

On October 11, 1826, John Bowers applied for another land grant in the entry taker's office at the Franklin County Court House. He paid one cent an acre for a one hundred and twenty acre tract. It was located on the side of the mountain west of Tally's Cove. It ran north up the mountain to his other fifty acre tract. He received his land grant on October 30, 1827.[20]

Miles Vasser applied for a land grant on October 12, 1826, in the entry taker's office at the Franklin County Court House. He paid one cent an acre for a one hundred and thirty acre tract of land described as being on the mountain on a road leading from Winchester to Jasper. His land was located on both sides of the road west of Edward Harris'. Miles received his land grant on October 30, 1827.[21]

On October 12, 1826, William Bowers applied for a land grant in the entry taker's office at Franklin County. He paid one cent an acre for a two hundred acre parcel of land on the Cumberland Mountain. It was located on a dividing ridge between the head of Boiling Fork and Crow Creek. It continue to a bluff at the head of the Lost Cove and from there ran west crossing the Jasper Road.[22]

Dennis Barnes filed another application for a land grant on April 16, 1827, in the entry taker's office at Franklin County, Tennessee. He applied for a one hundred acre tract of land on the Cumberland Mountain. His land was described as including houses, springs, and plantations where old Jesse Barns and George Smith formerly lived.[23]

Thomas S. Logan and Madison Porter filed an application for a land grant at the entry taker's office in Franklin County, Tennessee, in 1832. Their land grant was for a one hundred acre tract that was on the Cumberland Mountain. It was located on a drain that ran into Rowarks Cove. There was a coal bluff on the west side about one hundred yards from where the wagons recover the coal on the bluffs. It then crossed a large branch that runs through the coal beds. Thomas and Madison received their land grant from the State of Tennessee on August 2, 1849.[24]

Wallis Estill Jr. applied for a land grant in 1832. His two thousand acre tract of land was located at the east corner of William Buchannon's thousand acre tract. It ran south with Madison Porter's line crossing his southwest corner. The south boundary line was by George W. Buchannon's line. Wallis received his land grant on August 25, 1849, from the State of Tennessee.[25]

Wallis Estill, Thomas S. Logan and Madison Porter made an entry for a grant from the State of Tennessee for five thousand acres of land in 1834. The land was on the Cumberland Mountain. It was located near a boundary line where old James Davis had a five thousand acre tract of land. The land included the coal banks of Lost Cove.[26]

Madison Porter, Wallis Estill Jr., and Thomas S. Logan filed another application for a land grant from the State of Tennessee in 1834. The land was for a five thousand acre tract located on the Cumberland Mountain. It was on the first high point above the right side of the coal road going up the point of the mountain above Mrs. Norman's and William Farris' houses. It ran east on the side of the mountain in Rowarks Cove. Then it ran south on the bluff of Tally's Cove and north including the coal banks in Rowarks Cove.[27]

In 1838, another application for a land grant was made by Wallis Estill Jr., Thomas S. Logan and Madison Porter for another five thousand acre tract of land on the Cumberland Mountain. It was located between Rowarks Cove and the Elk River. It ran across the

Jasper Road. Estill, Logan, and Porter each owned a third of all the land from the three five thousand acre tracts.[28] There was no mention of any money being paid to the State of Tennessee for these land grants.

Isaac T. Hines applied for a land grant in the entry taker's office in 1839. It was for a four hundred acre tract of land. The survey showed the land to be at the east corner of an entry made by Paul Williams and near William Barnes and James T. Darnell's line. Isaac was granted the land by the State of Tennessee on July 20, 1842.[29]

Madison Porter made another application for a land grant for one thousand seven hundred acres of land in 1848. The land was on the east corner of Richard P. Holders' and Peter S. Dechard's land. It ran by the Smith, Holders and Decherd's boundary lines to the west bank of Tally's Fork. Madison received a land grant on September 25, 1847, from the State of Tennessee.[30]

Isaac T. Hines made an application for land on the Cumberland Mountain in 1848. His parcel of land contained six hundred acres by survey. It was on the south side of the Cumberland Mountain above Tally's Cove. It begins on the southeast corner of an eighty acre entry made by John W. Holder. Isaac received his land grant from the State of Tennessee on August 25, 1849.[31]

Land Grants from the State of Tennessee and deeds to the University of the South list the names of people who owned land on the Cumberland Mountain. In addition to the before listed land grants, Allen Gipson owned a thousand acre tract on the slope of the mountain facing Rowark's Cove. A fifteen hundred acre tract of mountain land was owned by John W. Holder. James J. Darnell and Lanson Rowe owned two hundred acre tracts of land. John Hendley owned some land that the Sewanee Mining Company gave to the University of the South. John Gilliam had land and Crandley Viases had a cabin. W. B. Shepard sold land to the University of the South that was granted to his father, William B. Shepard Sr. It contained six hundred forty acres.[32] This land may have been given to William Shepard Sr. for service in the Revolutionary War. Grants of six hundred and forty acres were usually given to veterans or widows of veterans who had served in the Revolutionary War. Others may have land that was not found in my research.

In addition to the before mentioned land grants, Hansford H. Roberts, Benjamin Cherry, William Anderson, Henry Garner, D. L. Gipson, John Perry, Edward Harris, Joe and Charley Miller, James Davis, George and William Buchannon, Richard P. and John Holder, Benjamin and Peter S. Decherd, George Smith, Jesse and John Barnes, Abraham Bowers, Paul Williams, J. B. Hawkins, Moses Reynolds, John and James Oliver, John Castleberry, James Kelly, Sherrod Williams, and James O'Dear all owned land or lived on the mountain at one time before the University of the South was located there by 1860. There could be others who were missed in my research.[32]

STORIES OF SOME EARLY SETTLERS AND LANDOWNERS

Henry Rutledge was the first to apply for a land grant, but William Barnes was the first to received one. William was a member of the Barnes family who were the earliest known settlers on the Cumberland Mountain along with George Smith. The exact date of their arrival in Franklin County is still unknown. Jacob Barnes and his wife lived on the Cumberland Mountain with their son, Jesse. They probably settled on a face claim in the beginning. Jesse's sons, William and Dennis, and his brother, John, were also residents of the mountain. George Smith and his family lived nearby. The Smiths and Barnes were kin, but their exact relationship has never been learned. The Barnes came to Tennessee from South Carolina after 1808.

A mountain cabin built by Jesse and Dennis Barnes was later known as Barnes Inn. It was noted as being the place where President Andrew Jackson spent the night while traveling through the area as a circuit court judge.[33] Barnes Inn was also the place where stagecoach travelers spent the night in the 1830's and 40's. The stagecoach road ran by Barnes Inn near St. Mary's and in front of the present residence of Rubin and Margaret Short. One of the stagecoaches that crossed the mountain traveled between Knoxville and Huntsville and the other between Atlanta and Nashville.

William's land was located on a bluff above Tally's Fork. He eventually sold fifty acres of his land to John Perry, an early settler from Rowarks Cove. John built a house on the property and lived there for a number of years. After John's death, his heirs sold the land to Susan Fairbanks, wife of George Fairbanks who was one of the University of the South Trustees. Susan bought the land on March 7, 1867, from Jeremiah Perry, William Hill, Malinda Hill, Lucinda Hill and Nancy Barnes.[34]

Another early land owner was Miles Vasser. He owned a hundred and thirty acres of land on the Cumberland Mountain.[35] His land was located near Edward Harris' property. Miles just seemed to have disappeared. Edward was an early settler from Rowarks Cove who had migrated from New Bern, North Carolina. Edward probably lived on the Cumberland Mountain on a face claim.

The hundred and thirty acre tract of land that was granted to Miles Vasser by the State of Tennessee was given to the University of the South by Henry Garner.[36] Henry probably bought the land from Miles. Henry did live on the Cumberland Mountain at one time, but his main residence was in Lost Cove. He came to Franklin County from North Carolina and settled in Lost Cove, while it was still populated with Indians. Many of Henry's descendants have continued to make their home on the Cumberland Mountain. A section of Sewanee near St. Mary's is known as Garner Town.

Thomas Logan, Madison Porter, and Wallis Estill owned large tracts of land together on the Cumberland Mountain. All three lived in Winchester and were active in affairs there. Madison Porter was a blacksmith and trustee for the Winchester Female Academy. Wallis Estill came to Winchester in 1816, and was a well-known surgeon in Franklin

County for many years. Thomas Logan manufactured carriages and coaches. The wood that he used to build the Logan Carriages came from the Sewanee Mountain. His carriages were mostly sold to wealthy planters. [37] The Logan carriages were well known throughout the South. Logan, Porter and Estill were probably accumulating land on the Cumberland Mountain for an investment, since they never actually lived there.

Isaac T. Hines owned more than a thousand acres of land on the Cumberland Mountain. One tract of his land was located near William Barnes and James Darnell's land above Tally's Cove. According to a deed executed by Isaac in 1859, in which he gave the University of the South the right to quarry stone from his land lying along the Sewanee Railroad tracks. He stated that his residence was on the Cumberland Mountain. [38] It is not known how long he actually lived on the mountain. Some settlers had Summer cabins on the mountain. Isaac was in Franklin County by 1812. He was a Justice of the Peace and a successful farmer.

James Darnell had land by William Barnes above Tally's Cove. [39] A large field that intersects with the old stagecoach road near St. Mary's was always referred to as Darnell's field. This is probably where James' land was located. Old timers at Sewanee say the Darnells did live on the Mountain. Some members of the Darnell family married into the Gibson family and moved to Arkansas.

Peter and Benjamin Decherd owned land on the Sewanee Mountain. They probably accumulated the land for an investment since there is no record of them ever living on the mountain. They were successful merchants in Winchester, and Benjamin was involved in the early Presbyterian Church there[40]. The town of Decherd was named in honor of Peter S. Decherd. [41]

John and Richard Holder owned land on the Cumberland Mountain. The Holders' land faced Rowarks Cove. John owned a fifteen hundred acre tract of mountain land. Richard Holder owned a hundred and twenty-five acre tract with Peter Decherd. [42] There has been no mention of the Holders ever living on the mountain. In 1851, Richard Holder was living in a cabin near the railroad tracks in Decherd, Tennessee. [43]

Arthur M. Rutledge owned land and lived on the Cumberland Mountain. [44] After the University of the South became a reality, the Rutledges lived on the domain. He was probably living near where Rowe's cabins stood by 1860. Point Rutledge was named in his honor. He gave the University of the South five hundred acres of his land.

Woodrow "Wood" C. Moreland owned a two hundred acre tract of land on the Cumberland Mountain. [45] Moreland's land was given to the University of the South by J. B. Hawkins. Mr. Hawkins probably purchased the land from Moreland. There is no record concerning Wood Moreland other than him owning land on the Cumberland Mountain. He, like Miles Vasser, seemed to disappear.

John. B. Hawkins had land on the Cumberland Mountain, too. The University of the South's records indicate that J. B. Hawkins gave the University Trustees eighty-six acres of land in Tally Cove and on a bluff.[46] The Hawkins married into the Miller family who were among the earliest settlers in Franklin County.[47] Many of the Hawkins still live in Franklin County.

Allen Gibson was a settler from Rowarks Cove. His family came to Franklin County from Laurens County, South Carolina in 1814.[48] Allen had large tracts of land on the Cumberland Plateau.[49] He gave seventy-two acres of his land to build the University of the South.[50] Records at the University show that Allen gave another twenty-five acres of land by absolute deed.[51] The Gibsons were early settlers on the mountain, but their date of arrival is unknown. In later years, Allen ran a trading post at a place known as Gibson Switch and a dry goods store in Sewanee.[52] He married into the Long and Garner families. His descendants still live at Sewanee, and throughout Franklin County.

William B. Shepard Sr. owned six hundred and forty acres of land on the Cumberland Mountain. There was a field by the old stagecoach road that was known as Shepard's Field. There were cabins near where Shepard's property was located. William's son sold his land to the University of the South for four thousand five hundred dollars in cash. When the deed was written, William Jr. was living in Nashville, Tennessee.[53] He was said to be a banker in Nashville.

Lanson Rowe was another settler from Rowark's Cove that owned land on the Cumberland Mountain. He had two hundred acres of land where the University domain is now situated. There was a spring on the land that was known as Rowe's Spring. The Stagecoach Inn was located on his property. Lanson built several cabins on his land and would spend the summer months on the mountain. Hansford "Hance" Roberts lived in one of the cabins that Lanson built.[54] When the first people came to start the University of the South, they stayed at Hance's cabin.[55] There was also a cabin on the property that was always known as Rowe's cabin. Some referred to it erroneously as Rose's Cabin.

Joe and Charley Miller had land on the Cumberland Mountain.[56] The only Joe Miller found in Franklin County records of age to have land in 1889, was Joseph Miller that lived in Cowan. Joseph and Charley Miller are thought to be descendants of the Miller family that came to Cowan with Major William Russell in 1806. Joseph's father, Samuel Miller, and his mother, Elizabeth Montgomery Miller, were said to be the first white babies born in Franklin County.[57] Samuel owned one hundred and fifty acres of mountain land.[58] Joe may have inherited the land from Samuel. I was unable to locate information on Charley Miller. The Sewanee Mountain was once known in court records as being in Miller's Tenth District of Franklin County.[59] Cowan was in the same district.

Smith W. Houghton and Robert Hines were early landowners. Together they owned at least eighty acres of land on the Cumberland Mountain.[60] S. W. Houghton lived in Winchester and was in business with the Decherds.[61] His name was always linked to agriculture events in the county. At one time he ran a nursery. Robert Hines was a well to do farmer that lived in Decherd, Tennessee. He was in Franklin County by 1812. [62]

Israel Simpson had a one thousand acre tract of land on the brow of the mountain. All that is known about Israel is that he lived in Rowark's Cove. It is not known if he actually lived on the mountain. There was a branch near Israel's property that was known as Gilliam's Spring Branch. [63] This property is thought to be where coal mines were located.

There was a Kelly, possibly James Kelly, who owned land near St. Mary's. Hance Roberts owned land in the same area. Hance sold ten acres of his land to my great-grandpa, Reuben Short, in 1866. The Kelly house and the Roberts' cabin were identified on a U.S. Engineers' field map during the Civil War in 1863. The Kelly and Roberts' houses were the only ones listed for people living on the mountain. Reuben Short's family has continuously lived on this same land since 1866. [64]

George Reynolds in his book titled, "*Sewanee and the Cumberland Plateau in the Civil War,* " tells of a union chaplain riding his horse up Brakefield Road, and not seeing a log cabin or human being for six miles. A deserted blacksmith shop was finally spotted. [65] This may have been one of Madison Porter's blacksmith shops, since he owned land in the vicinity. He was one of the earliest known blacksmiths in Franklin County. Brakefield Road ran from the direction of Tullahoma up the mountain and past Rowe's cabins and spring, then down the mountain toward Jasper.

SEWANEE COAL BROUGHT THE RAILROAD

Coal was discovered on the Cumberland Plateau before the reported date of 1840. Land grants show that in the 1830's, coal roads were in existence and horse and wagons were being used to recover the coal. [66] Coal beds and coal banks were mentioned in Madison Porter, Thomas Logan and Wallis Estill's applications for land grants in 1834.[67] An Irishman named Leslie Kennedy dug up samples of the coal that he found on the mountain and took them back to his home in Nashville. [68] He peddled his idea of exploiting the coal stone as a resource to interested investors. The blacksmiths in the area were already making use of the coal. They burned it in their furnaces to shape and re-shape irons and other metals.

Samuel Franklin Tracy, a member of a wealthy group of investors in New York City, was interested in the coal found on the mountain. The Tracy investor group bought the land that contained the coal deposits from Madison Porter and Thomas Logan. Mr. Tracy and his investors obtained a charter from the State of Tennessee to mine the coal in 1852. Their Company was known as the Sewanee Mining Company. [69]

At this time, the Cumberland Mountain Plateau was still known as "The Nation." The first mention of the name Sewanee on the mountain only related to the mining company and coal. The town of Sewanee came later. Mr. Tracy eventually became President of the Sewanee Mining Company and Tracy City was named in his honor.

In order to ship their coal to other areas, the Sewanee Mining Company started building a railroad up the mountain in 1853, and it was completed in 1856. It was the first railroad up the Cumberland Plateau, and was an extension of the Nashville and Chattanooga Railroad. [70] It ran to the lower coal banks at Midway and was known as the little mining railroad. At the time, it was steepest railroad in the country. The train engine that hauled the coal down the mountain was called the "Sewanee Mountain Goat."

Construction crews on first railroad line going up the side of Sewanee mountain.
(Obtained from Coulson Studios, Cowan, Tennessee)

Mountain Goat train at Slop Well, Sewanee, Tennessee
(Obtained from Coulson Studios)

Lem Tom Long standing in front of the main railroad depot.
The freight depot is to the left
(Obtained from Coulson Studios)

THE UNIVERSITY SITE

By 1856, the Southern States were more prosperous than ever before in history. The population was growing faster than ever. Rich cotton fields and sugar cane plantations were being cultivated throughout the South. [71] Slave labor was an important commodity to the rich plantation owners who depended on them to cultivate and harvest their crops. The Episcopal Church was a benefactor of the South's prosperity.

Reverend James H. Otey organized the first Episcopal congregation in Tennessee and became its first bishop. He felt that to remove ignorance and prejudice against the Episcopal Church, a church university should be established to train young men in the ministry. [72] Bishop Otey gave birth to the idea of a church university, but it was Leonidas Polk, Bishop of Louisiana, who started the ball rolling.

Bishop Polk was a graduate of West Point and a relative of President James K. Polk. He expanded Bishop Otey's idea of a church university. [73] He felt that it was the duty of the chief ministers of the southern Episcopal churches to provide religious training and education for the young men throughout the southern dioceses. [74]

In order to organize the building of a University, the southern Episcopal bishops created a board of trustees. It was one of their duties to find a suitable site for the proposed church university. In the summer of 1857, Bishop Polk was visiting Beersheba Springs just above Tracy City, Tennessee. At Beersheba, Bishop Polk became acquainted with Colonel Vernon K. Stevenson, President of the Nashville and Chattanooga Railroad Company. He told Bishop Polk about the mountain area and recommended it as a suitable location for the clergy's proposed university. [75]

A group of men consisting of Bishop Polk, Colonel Stevenson, Dr. Wallace Estill of Winchester, John Armfield, owner of a hotel at Beersheba Springs, John Bass, and Dr. Safford took a ride from Winchester up the mountain to examine Colonel Stevenson's claims. Bishop Polk was immediately impressed with the many advantages of the mountain and its pure water supply. He exclaimed that it was the ideal location for a university. George Fairbanks in his "History of the University of the South" relates that Dr. Safford remembered Bishop Polk riding over the ground, up one hill and down another, to this spring and to that one, until, reining up his horse in the midst of a beautiful growth of forest trees and more than satisfied, exclaimed, "Gentlemen, here is the spot and here shall be the University." [76]

This was the first mention of the mountain town now known as Sewanee as a suitable site for the proposed Episcopal University. The other sites proposed were in Huntsville, Cleveland, Atlanta, Chattanooga, and McMinnville. Large donations of land and aid were promised to the clergy from each of the communities under consideration. [77]

After a long debate by the trustees, the Cumberland Plateau was finally chosen as the site for the proposed church University on November 25, 1857, at Montgomery,

Alabama. There were nine votes cast for the Cumberland Plateau; three votes for Atlanta; and two votes for Huntsville. The Cumberland Plateau was the unanimous choice. Bishop Green is the one who proposed the name "The University of the South" and it was accepted. Other considerations were "The Church University" and "The University of Sewanee."[78]

During a Board of Trustees meeting at Beersheba Springs in August 1859, the trustees reported that the Sewanee Mining Company had agreed to donate 5,000 acres of land for the University. However, the mining company stipulated that the University was to be operational within ten years or the land would revert to the mining company. Colonel Arthur M. Rutledge and A. S. Colyer agreed to donate other tracts of land unconditionally. Dr. Wallace Estill from Winchester obtained promises from others in Franklin County to secure 5,000 acres of land if necessary.[79]

In the proceedings of the Executive Committee of the University of the South on July 19, 1860, a list of people who gave land to the University was presented to the committee. They were: Wallace Estill's heirs with a survey of 5,000 acres; Allen Gipson giving 25 acres of land by absolute deed; A. M. Rutledge 410 acres; Lanson Rowe 100 acres; Dennis Barnes 100 acres; Houghton and Hines 80 acres; Bowers tract 250 acres; Henry Garner giving the Vassar tract that included 130 acres; J. B. Hawkins giving 86 acres of land in Tally's Cove and bluff; and a Moreland tract that included 100 acres. There was a total of 6,281 acres of land received from the above listed persons and titles were secured for University.[80]

The Board of Trustees report from 1857 to 1868 made by Bishop James H. Otey shows that Sewanee Mining Company gave the University of the South 5,000 acres; A. Gibson gave 25 acres; A. M. Rutledge 410 acres; L. Rowe 100 acres; D. Barnes 100 acres; Houghton and Hines 80 acres; Bowers Tract 250 acres; H. Garner 130 acres; Moreland Tract 200 acres; W. Estill heirs 2,500 acres; Decherd tract 120 acres; and W. B. Shepard 610 acres for a total of 9,525 acres of land.[81]

The actual deeds to the University of the South show the Sewanee Mining Company giving the University two tracts of land that contained 2,500 acres each. John Hendley owned some of the land that the mining company gave to the University. John did surrender his right to the land and also gave his part to the University on May 26, 1860. Land that the Sewanee Mining Company gave to the University was previously owned by Thomas Logan and Madison Porter. The mining company had purchased the land previously from Logan and Porter.[82]

The Sewanee Mining Company made provisions in its deed to the University of the South. "If the Trustees shall at any time sell or lease any portion of said tract of land, the Sewanee Mining Company shall receive an amount equal to one half of the net proceeds of such sales or leases as may be made by the Trustees. The Sewanee Mining Company expressly reserves four hundred feet on either side of its railroad through the entire five thousand acres according to the map. The four hundred feet on each side shall only be used for railroad and depot purposes or for dwellings for the use of the company. The said dwellings shall be subject to the police regulations of the said University."[83]

"The deed was executed upon further proviso...and conditions that the Trustees of said University have agreed that neither they nor their successors will at any time use any part of the said five thousand acres of land for mining purposes or dig up or mine the same for coal or allow any part thereof to be used by any other person or persons buying or leasing from them."[84]

"Active operation shall be commenced for the construction of the buildings of the University on the land above described within three years from the twenty seventh day of April 1858. And if the said University shall not be put in operation within ten years, the said land be reconveyed by said University to the said Sewanee Mining Company. Or if the buildings at any future time be backed or not used for University purposes in consequences of the removal of the University to some other location, there and in that event the Trustees of the University may upon a fair valuation of the lands at that time without the improvement pay to the said Sewanee Mining Company in money said valuation and keep the land and improvement or the said Trustees may at their discretion reconvey the whole to said company or in case they shall do neither, the said lands shall convert to the said Sewanee Mining Company."[85]

The following people either gave or sold land to the University of the South according to the deeds.

1. W. B. Shepard sold two tracts of land to the University for $4,500. The total amount of land in the Shepard tract was 640 acres more or less.[86]
2. A. M. Rutledge gave two tracts of land to the University containing 500 acres more or less.[87]
3. The number of acres that S. W. Houghton and Robert Hines gave to the University was left out of their deed to the University.[88]
4. J. B. Hawkins gave the University a deed to land granted to Woodrow Moreland. It contained an undivided half of tract of land containing 200 acres.[89]
5. Abraham Bowers sold the University two tracts of land containing 250 acres. The University gave Abraham Bowers $200. and Isaac Hines $100. for the Bower's land. This was with the consent of Abraham Bowers.[90]
6. Allen Gipson gave the University a tract of land containing 72 acres.[91]
7. Henry Garner gave the University of the South a deed to land that was granted to Miles Vasser. It contained 130 acres of land.[92]
8. Dennis Barnes' deed shows that he was paid $75. by the University Trustees for a 100 acre tract of land. The deed was written in 1858, but not recorded until 1895.[93]

The writer was unable to locate deeds from the Decherds, Estill heirs, and Lanson Rowe.

Arthur S. Colyar and Charles Barney probably secured most of the titles to land for the University Trustees. Their names appeared as witnesses on many of the deeds between the local land owners and the University of the South Trustees. Mr. Colyar was a successful lawyer in Winchester. He later owned the Tennessee Coal and Railroad Company. He had a law practice in Winchester with A. S. Marks who later became Governor of the State of Tennessee. [94] Arthur was married to Agnes Estill, daughter of Dr. William Estill. Dr. William Estill and Dr. Wallis Estill were brothers. [95] They were sons of Isaac Estill who was the son of another Wallis Estill. [96] At one time, Isaac Estill was the County Court Clerk for Franklin County. Dr. Wallis was actively involved in promoting the University and securing land for it. He and his family gave a large portion of their land for the University to be located on the Cumberland Mountain. [97] But, later some of the Estill heirs went as far as the State Supreme Count in a dispute with the University of the South over the land.

Charles Barney was a retired military colonel and engineer from Maryland. He had previously worked for the railroad in Franklin County. The Bishops knew him from West Point and hired him to supervise the construction of the University of the South. [98] He surveyed some of the land that was sold or given to the University of the South.

Deeds to the University usually started out with "for and in consideration of the benefits to be derived from the location of the University of the South in Franklin County." The Franklin County businessmen who were promoting and supporting the University's location on the Cumberland Mountain, must have been aware of the many business and educational opportunities the University would bring to their county. The mountain was still a dense forest populated with a few die hard settlers and lots of wild animals. No big settlement or town have sprung up even though settlers had been living on the mountain since at least the 1820's. This was a great opportunity for all concerned with populating the mountain and creating a town in the forest. The Bishops and lay leaders from the Southern Episcopal Dioceses seemed to welcome the challenge of taming the mountain.

On October 10, 1860, the cornerstone was laid to start the "University of the South." At this time, the Cumberland Plateau was known as University Place. A great celebration was held with thousands of people attending from all over Tennessee and other states. It was a religious ceremony with items such as a prayer book and coins placed in the cornerstone. [99] Old timers say there was gambling and horse trading going on before and after the ceremony.

Hansford "Hance" H. Roberts had a cabin and farm on the land that was chosen as the future site of the University of the South. Hance's property was once a part of the Lanson Rowe tract of land. Hance was living in one of the cabins that Lanson built before Bishop Leonidas Polk, Bishop Stephen Elliott, and George Fairbanks arrived on the mountain. [100] Hance married Mary Lynch on March 7, 1851, and in 1860, they were living on the Cumberland Plateau. The date of Hance's arrival on the mountain is unknown. The 1860 census records show Hance and Mary with daughter Ann. Joshua

Roberts was also in the same household. Joshua must have been Hance's brother. Living with Hance was Colonel Charles R. Barney, and his foreman, William Ensign, from New York. Patrick Castleberry from Ireland was also in the same household. Patrick was a station master, possibly for the railroad. Afterwards, Hance became a hack driver and eventually sold his land to the University.

Another local resident on the Cumberland Plateau in 1860, was John Castleberry and his wife, Sarah, along with their children A. J.; Isaac; James M; Benjamin; Malissa E, John, Tim; and Almeda. John came to Tennessee from Georgia. He built a shed for the University to use during the laying of the cornerstone. It was big enough to house 300 people.[101]

In a letter written by Sada Elliott and published in the *Sewanee Sampler,* she tells about where the Castleberrys used to live. She writes, "Beginning from the south end of town, I will give you the families as they come. First the Tomlinson, who live on the same spot where the Castleberrys used to live. A square white house with green blinds, an unlovely porch and not the sign of a shade tree save a few freshly planted saplings. A straight gravel path leading from a fancy gate, set in a rail fence, terminates at the foot of a square pair of steps. This is called Chestnut Hill because all the saplings are oak."[102]

An article in the *Purple Sewanee* states that John Castleberry's house was the first one built in the village. His house was made of logs, and was first located where the post office once stood. Later this house was moved across the railroad and became part of a larger house. The logs were covered with boards.[103] This house is the only one recorded as still standing in the Sewanee Village after the Civil War. Old timers say the Castleberry house and William Tomlinson's house on Kentucky Avenue are the oldest houses in the town of Sewanee. The Castleberry house is located behind the laundry on the right side.

It appears from the 1860 census records that Eli and Elizabeth Bennett were also residents of the mountain. Their children included James W.; Benjamin A; John W; Francis A. and Martha J. Bennett. Eli was born in Tennessee in 1825. His parents were both born in South Carolina. In 1880, Eli was living in the Marion County part of Jump Off, Tennessee, with five more children. They were Jefferson D., William O., Thomas, Robert L., and Munroe B. Bennett. Living near Eli was Nancy Bennett with the following children: James H.; Berry; Mary A. and Rebecca A. Bennett. Living with Nancy was Mary Bennett age twenty-six.[104] Nancy may have been Eli's sister-in-law and Mary his sister.

Abraham Van Vleck and his wife, Emily, with their children Marvin, Trucilla, and Edwin were on the mountain in 1860. The census records give Abraham's occupation as a country lawyer and his place of birth as New York. He came to Franklin County as a surveyor in 1854. He met Emma Jones, and they were married in 1856. The Van Vlecks had a cabin near the railroad, and after the University came to the mountain, they ran a boarding house.

Abraham was a Confederate Lieutenant during the Civil War. Bishop Polk had him take the University's property deeds and other valuable papers to Montgomery, Alabama, for safe keeping during the war. The president of the railroad was entrusted to keep the deeds in his office safe in Montgomery.

The 1860 census records show that A. M. Rutledge was living on the mountain, too. He was a well-to-do farmer. His wife was named Elizabeth. Their children were Lizzie, Emma, Arthur M. and Joseph Rutledge. It is thought that A. M. must have spent his Summers on the mountain. Lanson Rowe had built several cabins by Rowe's Spring where Mr. Rutledge had land, too. Lanson did spent his Summers on the mountain. It is possible that Eli Bennett and Nancy Bennett may have lived in one of Rowe's cabins or maybe at Jump Off, where Eli was found living in the 1880 census.

William H. Tomlinson was the first postmaster at University Place. A box on a tree near the depot served as the first post office. William's wife was named Sarah and they had a son named Willie. Willie married Delila Jones in 1871. Mr. Tomlinson was from North Carolina and his wife Sarah was from South Carolina. They were living in South Carolina when Willie was born in 1847. The Tomlinsons' lived in the first hotel on the University domain, and their store was located in the freight depot. Mr. Tomlinson was described by Sada Elliott as being very large and fat. He became a very successful merchant on the mountain along with his son Willie.

According to "*History of the University of the South*" by George R. Fairbanks, "In 1861, the buildings on the University domain consisted of a hotel, an office for Colonel Barney, three cabins where the bishops lived and the house owned by a local." Hance Roberts was the "local" who was mentioned in the book but not by name.[106] We know that it was Hance, since census records show the people who came to build the University were part of his household.

Deeds show that Hance Roberts was living in a cabin that Lanson Rowe built. John Castleberry lived in the southern end of the settlement. In 1861, the Bennetts, Van Vlecks, and Rutledges were most likely living somewhere on the mountain, since they were listed in the 1860 census records. They are not mentioned in Mr. Fairbanks' book, however, deeds and land grants show there were other cabins scattered throughout the forest before the bishops' arrival.

The bishops observations of the mountain may have only been where the domain area is now located, and places nearby. They may not have known about the area where St. Mary's and Jump Off are located in 1861, since the area was still a dense forest. The Barnes had cabins and plantations on the mountain as early as 1827. This information was ascertained from Dennis Barnes' land grant. The Barnes and Smith property was located in the St. Mary's area. Some of the Barnes eventually moved to Sherwood. but others died on the mountain.[107]

THE STATE OF TENNESSEE. No. [illegible]

To all to whom these presents shall come:

Greeting.

Know Ye, that in consideration of an ENTRY made in the Entry Taker's Office of Marion County, of No. 336 dated the 27th day of September 1824 at the rate of TWELVE AND A HALF CENTS PER ACRE by William Barns

there is GRANTED by the said State of Tennessee unto the said William Barns and his heirs, a certain TRACT OR PARCEL OF LAND containing fifty acres, lying in the County aforesaid, on Cumberland mountain, adjoining what is called Salley's fork, on the waters of cove creek Beginning at a poplar, thence East eighty poles to a white oak, thence North one hundred poles to a black oak thence West eighty poles to a chesnut oak, thence South one hundred poles to the Beginning. Including a spring.

Surveyed the 15th day of October 1824.

with its appurtenances, to have and to hold the said TRACT or PARCEL of LAND with its appurtenances, to the said William Barns and his heirs forever. In witness whereof William Carroll, GOVERNOR OF THE STATE OF TENNESSEE, has hereunto set his hand and caused the Great Seal of the said State to be affixed at MURFREESBOROUGH on the 24th day of August in the YEAR OF OUR LORD, ONE THOUSAND EIGHT HUNDRED AND TWENTY five, and of American Independence the fiftieth.

BY THE GOVERNOR,

Daniel Graham, SECRETARY.

Wm. Carroll

Heiskell & Brown, Pr's.

First known Land Grant found for Sewanee mountain property issued to William Barns September 27, 1824 (Obtained from Tennessee State Archives)

The State of Tennessee,

To all to whom these Presents shall come—Greeting:

Know Ye, that in consideration of Entry No. 1970 Made in the Office of the Entry Taker of Franklin County, and entered on the 13th day of February 1832 Pursuant to the provisions of an act of the General Assembly of said State passed on the 9th day of January 1830

there is granted by the said State of Tennessee, unto Thomas S Logan and Madison Porter

a certain Tract or Parcel of LAND, containing One hundred Acres by survey, bearing date the 14th day of August 1847 lying in said county of Franklin County on Cumberland Mountain. Beginning on a Chestnut Oak tree standing near a drain that runs into Roarks Cove on the west bluff from the coal bed, about two hundred and fifty yards and about One hundred from the place where the wagons drawn the coal on the bluff. Thence running South forty five degrees east One hundred poles crossing a large branch that runs through the coal bed. Thence North forty five degrees east One hundred and sixty poles to a stake. Thence North forty five degrees West One hundred poles to a stake. Thence South forty five degrees West One hundred and sixty poles to the Beginning.

With the hereditaments and appurtenances. To have and to hold the said tract or parcel of LAND, with its appurtenances, to the said Thomas S Logan and Madison Porter and their heirs forever.

In Witness Whereof, A. V. Brown, Governor of the State of Tennessee, hath hereunto set his hand and caused the Great Seal of the State to be affixed, at Nashville, on the 25th day of August in the year of our Lord one thousand eight hundred and forty-seven and of the Independence of the United States the seventy-second year.

A V Brown

By the Governor

W. B. A. Ramsey, Secretary.

Tennessee Land Grant issued to Thomas Logan and Madison Porter where Sewanee coal was found. Entry #1970, 13 February 1832

77 State of Tennessee No 8341. 5000

To all to whom these presents shall come Greeting Know Ye that by virtue of Entry No 1987 made in the office of the Entry Taker of Franklin County and Entered on the 21st day of April 1834 pursuant to the provisions of an act of the General Assembly of said State passed on the 9th day of January 1830 there is Granted by the said State of Tennessee unto Wallis Estill, Thomas S. Logan and Madison Porter a Certain Tract or parcel of Land Containing Five Thousand Acres by survey bearing date the 9th day of October 1838. Said Land is Granted in the following proportions, towit: to Wallis Estill, one third; to Thomas S. Logan and Madison Porter one third each as assignees of said Wallis Estill) Lying in said County principally on the Waters of the Tall Cove of Crow Creek of Tennessee River. Beginning on a post oak standing on the north Bluff of Tallys Cove it being the South East Corner of Thomas S. Logans 5000 acre Entry. and runs South Crossing the Head of Tallys Cove and the Jasper road in all 833⅓ poles to a Stake. Then East 960 poles to the West boundary of Old James Dorris 5000 acres; and with the same north Crossing the Jasper road at 548 poles and passing J. Dorris north west Corner at 588 poles, in all 833⅓ poles to a double poplar and Black oak. Then West Crossing said Road twice in all 960. poles to the Beginning — Including the Tall Bluffs of the Tall Cove.

With the Hereditaments and Appurtenances to have and to hold the said Tract or parcel of Land with its Appurtenances to the said Wallis Estill, Thomas S. Logan and Madison Porter and their Heirs forever. In witness whereof James K Polk Governor of the State of Tennessee has hereunto set his hand and Caused the Great Seal of the State to be affixed at Nashville on the 5th day of July 1841. and 66th Year of our Independence

Jno S. Young Secty. By the Governor James K Polk

Land Grant issued to Wallis Estill, Madison Porter, and Thomas Logan for Sewanee mountian property. Grant signed by Governor James K. Polk, future President of the United States

768

January 14th 1828

THE STATE OF TENNESSEE—No. 71[illegible]

To all to whom these presents shall come—GREETING.

KNOW YE, That, for and in consideration of the sum of One cent per acre, paid into the office of the Entry-Taker of Franklin county, and entered on the 12th day of October 1826 pursuant to the provisions of an Act of the General Assembly of said state, passed on the twentysecond day of November, one thousand eight hundred and twentythree, and the acts supplemental thereto &c. No. 1017.

there is granted by the said state of Tennessee, unto Miles Vasser

a certain Tract or Parcel of LAND, containing One hundred & thirty Acres by survey bearing date the 15th day of October 1826 lying in said county. On the mountain and bounded as follows to wit beginning at a poplar and white Oak standing on the Road leading from Winchester to Jasper on or near a drain of Cross Creek and Runs north One hundred and thirty poles to a white Oak thence east One hundred and sixty poles to a black Gum thence South Crossing the said Road at sixty eight poles in all One hundred and thirty poles to a stake and west to the Beginning including the land on both sides of the Road West of Edward Harris

With the hereditaments and appurtenances. To have and to hold the said Tract or Parcel of LAND, with its appurtenances, to the said Miles Vasser and his heirs forever.

In Witness Whereof, Sam Houston Governor of the State of Tennessee hath hereunto set his hand, and caused the Great Seal of the State to be affixed, at Nashville on the 30th day of October in the year of our Lord one thousand eight hundred and twenty-seven and of the independence of the United States the fiftysecond.

BY THE GOVERNOR:

Sam Houston

Daniel Graham

Secretary.

Miles Vasser's Land Grant for Sewanee Property that is now part of the University of the South Domain. Land Grant signed by Governor Sam Houston.

25

Registered August 8th 1859

For the consideration of five hundred dollars to me paid I Lanson Rowe have bargained and sold and hereby convey to A M Ruthledge a tract of land known as the Rowe Spring tract on the top of the Cumberland Mountain in Franklin County and bounded entirely by the Sewanee Company lands and the Bowers tract being the same tract on which I built some cabins in which I have been in the habit of spending my summers containing two hundred acres more or less. I hereby covenant that I will warrant the titles to said Ruthledge against the lawful claims of all persons. Given under my hand & seal this 5th day of July 1858. The note of A S Colyar shall be delivered up

attest
A S Colyar
Thos S Logan
Hugh Francis

Lanson Rowe (Seal)

State of Tennessee }
Franklin County } Personally appeared before me Thos Short deputy for R F Sims Clk of the county court of said county the within subscribing witnesses A S Colyar & Hu Francis to me well known who being first sworn disposed and said that they are personally acquainted with Lanson Rowe the bargainor and that he acknowledged that he executed the within deed of conveyance in their presence and upon the day it bears date, to be his act & deed for the purposes therein contained. Witness my hand at office this 8th day of August 1859

Thos Short D.C

Received at 2½ Oclock P.M. August 8th 1859

Adam Hancock Regtr
By Thos Short D.C

Lanson Rowe's deed to A.M. Ruthledge for Sewanee property. The deed states that Lanson Rowe built cabins on this property before 1858 and spent summers there.

37

Registered August 20th 1859 Thos. Short D.R.
For the consideration of benefits to be derived by the location of the University of the South in Franklin County State of Tennessee I Arthur M Rutledge have given and granted bargained and sold and do hereby transfer & convey to the University of the South a tract of land in Franklin County known as the Rowe Spring Tract on the top of the Cumberland Mountain in the State of Tennessee on the head waters of the Boiling fork of Elk river & bounded entirely by the land of the Sewanee Mining Company and the Borders Tract, the same tract of land on which Lanson Rowe built some Cabins several years ago and where he has been in the habit of spending his Summers & on which H H Roberts at this time resides. Containing by the survey of C R Barney two hundred Acres be the same more or less. To have and to hold the said Tract of land to the University of the South And I warrant the title against all persons whomsoever. August 20th 1859

A. M. Rutledge [seal]

State of Tennessee
Personally appeared before me Thos. Short deputy for R. F. Sims Clk of the County Court of Franklin in said State A. M. Rutledge the bargainor with whom I am personally acquainted and who acknowledged that he executed the above deed of Conveyance for the purposes therein expressed. Witness my hand at office this 20th day of August 1859.

Thos. Short D.C.

Received at 10½ Oclock A.M. August 20 1859

Adam Hancock Regtr
By Thos. Short D.R.

Deed to the University of the South granted by Arthur M. Rutledge. This is the same property that Lanson Rowe built his cabins and where H.H. Roberts lived. Dated August 20, 1859.

corner of said twenty-five acre and with the West boundary of the same [illegible] hundred and two poles to the South West corner, And East with the South boundary to the Beginning. With the hereditaments and appurtenances. To have and to hold the said tract or parcel of land with [illegible] [illegible] and his heirs forever. In Witness whereof William [illegible] hand and caused the [illegible] [illegible] of May in the year of our Lord [illegible] of the United States the fifty [illegible]

By the Governor [illegible] Wm Carroll

Daniel Graham Secretary

Dennis Barnes Sr.'s land grant from State of Tennessee in 1827, shows Jesse Barnes and George Smith were the former residents and houses, a spring and plantations were on the land that was granted to Dennis. It was located on the mountain now known as Sewanee.

State of Tennessee No 1057

To all to whom these presents shall come Greeting: Know ye that for and in consideration of the sum of twelve and a half cents per acre paid into the office of the Entry Taker of Franklin County and entered on the 10th day of April 1827 pursuant to the provisions of an act of the General Assembly of said State passed on the third day of Decr One thousand eight hundred and twenty five by No 1057 there is granted by the said State of Tennessee unto Dennis Barnes a certain tract or parcel of land containing One Hundred acres by survey bearing date the 31 day of January 1828 lying in said County on the waters of Boiling Fork of Elk River and bounded as follows Beginning at a black oak standing on the top of the Bluff of the Mountain running north through the [illegible] of Barnes field in all One Hundred and twenty six and a half poles to a stake in [illegible]. Thence East One hundred and twenty six and a half poles to a stake. Thence South One hundred and twenty six and a half poles to a chesnut oak, thence West One hundred and twenty six and a half poles to the Beginning including the houses and spring and plantations whereon Jesse Barnes and George Smith formerly lived on the Mountain. With the hereditaments and appurtenances. To have and to hold the said tract or parcel of land with its appurtenances to the said Dennis Barnes and his heirs forever. In Witness whereof William Carroll Governor of the State of Tennessee has hereunto set his hand and caused the Great Seal of the State to be affixed at Nashville on the 7 day of May in the year of our Lord One thousand Eight hundred and thirty, and of the Independence of the United States the fifty fourth.

By the Governor Wm Carroll

Daniel Graham Secretary

CIVIL WAR AT UNIVERSITY PLACE

The first incident to occur at University Place linked to the Civil War was the burning of Bishop Polk and Bishop Elliott's log cabins on the night of April 12, 1861. [108] Bishop Polk's cabin was located where the Rebel's Rest now stands, and Bishop Elliott's house was at the A.T.O. site. [109] Ironically, the burning took place on the same date as Fort Sumter was attacked in Charleston Harbor, South Carolina, to start the Civil War.

Mrs. Frances Devereux Polk and her children just barely escaped with their lives. It is thought that union sympathizers around Monteagle and Tracy City were responsible. They were unhappy with the University and the Southern Episcopal Churches favoring the Confederate's plan to secede from the union. Tennessee had not yet seceded from the union when this incident occurred. Although Bishop Polk was not at home when his house was burned, it is thought that this incident caused him to decide to join the Confederacy in the early stages of the war. [110] He became one of the Confederate's best Generals and was often referred to as "General Bishop Polk" by many of his soldiers.

At first, Tennessee voted not to secede from the union. This action made people in Franklin County so angry they made plans to annex their county to the State of Alabama. Another vote was taken in June 1861, and this time Tennessee joined the other Confederate States of America. [111] People in the eastern part of Tennessee were loyal to the union, and at times soldiers did not know their enemies. Some joined the Union and Confederacy freely while others were forced to join or be sent to prison.

During the Civil War, the Cumberland Plateau was referred to as "University Place," "University Heights," and "Camp University." People living on the mountain and in the coves were often terrorized by gangs of men and were forced to desert their homes during the war. These desperadoes would steal food, horses, and anything they could find. [112] All the homes in the University of the South were burned except one old log cabin shed that is now preserved as part of Arthur and Elizabeth Chitty's home. Elizabeth Chitty said that the cabin was moved to the premises after the war and incorporated into the residence of George Quintard, son of Bishop Charles T. Quintard.

Thousand of soldiers crossed the Cumberland Plateau during the war, since it was the shortest route to Chattanooga. Many great generals such Polk; Rosecrans; Hardee; Johnson; Bragg, Green, Sheridan, and the beloved General Joe Wheeler were all on the mountain. General Wheeler took his army into the mountains and coves to find the men who were terrorizing the people in the area. [113]

People in Franklin County loved General Polk and General Wheeler. Even though both the North and South camped on the Cumberland Plateau, there were no big battles fought there. There was fighting where the Sherwood Road now intersects with the Cowan Road, at St. Mary's and near the old depot. The rear guard of General Polk's Corps had a few skirmishes with the advancing federal troops on the University domain.

Union soldiers of Company G, 27th Illinois Infantry, were camped on the Cumberland. Plateau. Corporal Fleming, a member of this company told the story of the cornerstone of the University of the South being torn down. He said, "My regiment was camped at the University grounds during the month of July (1863). Some vandals broke up the cornerstone and I took one of the pieces and going to a little spring near the foundation of the University with no tools but the spring water, a piece of sandstone and my pocket knife, I made this little book. I would also like to state that the Colonel of our regiment was very angry when he found out that the cornerstone had been broken, and would have severely punished the miscreants could he have found out who they were. Our Colonel was Colonel Miles from Miles Station, near Alton, Illinois, and he was also a Churchman." Information taken from a letter sent to Trustees of the University of the South by Rev. W.S. Slack in May 1904 with the piece of cornerstone that he returned to the University of the South from Corporal Fleming). The Fleming letter can be found in the University of the South Archives. This is the corrected version of the story of the cornerstone that I previously told about in this book. .

A correspondent with General Rosecrans wrote to the New York Observer from "University Heights in the Cumberland Mountains," Franklin County, Tennessee, on August 12, 1863. "The sheds erected for the workmen of the future builders of the great edifice are now filled with commissary stores of the United States. Two brigades of U.S. soldiers are camping on the grounds of the University of the South." [116]

The war took its toll on the Cumberland Plateau and the church university was all in shambles. The worst part was the death of Bishop Leonidas Polk who was killed by cannon fire at Pine Mountain in Marietta, Georgia, on June 14, 1864. [117] University Place was in ashes, but the hopes and dreams of the surviving members did not perish in the smoke. They were determined to start from the ashes and rebuild their beloved University.

BUILDING THE UNIVERSITY OF THE SOUTH

In 1866, members of the diocese met and made a decision to resume the work of building the University. It was agreed that Reverend Dr. Charles Todd Quintard, Dr. David Pise and George Fairbanks initiate the first steps in reviving the University. The diocese of Tennessee was to take measures for establishing on the domain with the concurrence of the surviving members of the executive committee, a training school for candidates for the ministry. Reverend Pise, Francis B. Fogg and George Fairbanks were elected trustees of the University of the South. Reverend Quintard was elected bishop of the diocese.[118]

Since money was now scarce in the southern states, Bishop Quintard went to England and raised money to help build the University.[119] As Bishop Quintard was planning the University, he was also planning the town. This is how the small town or village was first started around the depot station and expanded from there up the hill.

The mountain village that was formerly known as "The Nation" and "University Place" was not officially named until 1867. George Fairbanks is credited with getting the town its Indian name of Sewanee. There was another town in west Tennessee that was named Sewanee, however, it ceased to be a town, and Mr. Fairbanks took steps and obtained the name of Sewanee for our little mountain town.[120]

Mr. Fairbanks was also the first law enforcement officer at Sewanee.[121] His beautiful old log cabin that is called "Rebel's Rest" was built by 1866, and has been preserved in the University. It is the oldest house in the University and stands on the same spot where Bishop Polk's cabin was burned with the start of the Civil War.

Bishop Quintard was elected Vice Chancellor of the University of the South and George Fairbanks, a retired lawyer, was elected commissioner of buildings and lands.[122] Bishop Quintard was quite successful with his solicitation of funds to build the University, both in England and the United States. With funds donated in England, a large boarding house known as Tremlett Hall was build in 1868. Personnel from Oxford and Cambridge Universities donated 4,000 books to start a library.[123] St. Augustine chapel was built the same year from donated funds.

The University officially opened its doors on September 18, 1868.[124] The Sewanee Mining Company's deed to the University was executed with the following provisions. "That active operations shall be commenced for the construction of the buildings of the University on the lands above described within three years from the twenty-seventh day of April 1858. And if the said University shall not be put in operation within ten years, the said lands shall be re-conveyed by said University to the said Sewanee Mining Company." Samuel Tracy, President of the Mining Company, on September 23, 1858, signed the deed. It was filed in the office for registration at Franklin County Court House in Winchester, Tennessee, on December 31, 1858.[125]

General Josiah Gorgas was chosen head master of the junior department but was unable to be in Sewanee until March of 1869. Professor Robert Dabney of Virginia was the acting head master in General Gorgas' absence. Professor Dabney was the English and Metaphysic instructor. Reverend F. L. Knight served as instructor for Greek and Latin and Mr. G. B. Green was instructor for mathematics. [126]

The first students to attend the University of the South were Charles M. Fairbanks from Florida; F.W. Knight from Tennessee; R.W. Sherwood of Alabama; Joseph C. Nash of Tennessee; N. J. Conger of Georgia; C. Barkley Dorr of Florida; C. Hawks Dorr of Florida; J E. Creary of Florida and J.A. Skipwich of Mississippi. The rear of St. Augustine chapel was used as a school room. Most of the boys boarded with Mrs. S. E. Cotten in Otey Hall. The tuition was $100. per annum. [127]

The University committee made up rules that no part of the original land donated or bought by the University of the South would ever be sold to raise funds for the University. The University possessed around 10,000 acres of land. All leases were in a one thousand acre reserve. The annual rental for the leased land was $25. a year. The houses to be constructed on the leased land could not cost less than $800. They did not want flimsy little cabins, but attractive looking homes. A regulation was adopted that no timber could be cut without the permission of the commissioner of buildings and lands on leased land. No lease could extend beyond thirty-three years, but could be renewed for two more equal terms making it a possible ninety-nine year lease. No one leasing University land could sell liquors, permit gambling or conduct any type business. [128]

Two years after the University opened its doors, the litigation began. [129] This will not surprise any long term local resident of Sewanee. There are people who feel that some of the old settlers and land owners lost their land due to their lack of education and being taken advantage of by people securing land for the University of the South.

THE SEWANEE DEPOT VILLAGE

The people of Sewanee were referred to as the "Village Depot People" in 1870. They adored Bishop Quintard and considered him a true friend. He was as concerned with their welfare as the University's population. He served as their minister and doctor. He was a surgeon during the Civil War, and continued his practice after the war. He doctored many people living in the village and surrounding coves. He made it his duty to bring people to the village that would establish businesses to provide jobs for local residents.[130]

Bishop Quintard encouraged Jabez Hayes, a religious man of means, to move to Sewanee from Newark, New Jersey. Jabez leased a tract of land from the University for the purpose of planting fruit orchards and vegetable gardens.[131] He built his home and farm where St. Mary's is now located. This land is thought to be part of William and Dennis Barnes' original land grants from the State of Tennessee. In the 1880's, there was litigation over Mr. Hayes leases.

Charles Hayes was related to Jabez, but the writer does not know their exact relationship. Charles wanted to build a business so he leased a tract of land from the University in the Depot Village. He planned to build a store or some type business. He was charged one dollar per year provided that within one year he would build a substantial store or cement building. His lease was for a ten-year period and he could renew the lease for another twenty-three years after each term. He was not permitted to allow gambling, or have a bowling alley, billiard table or shooting gallery in his establishment. He was not allowed to sell any ale, wine, or liquors whatsoever. However, there was clause in the lease in reference to the sale of liquors. It was not considered as applying to the sale of wine for communion or wine and liquor that was ordered by the physician of the University. The lease was dated July 1, 1870. The writer could find no record of Charles ever building a business.[132]

Jabez Hayes did build a large steam sawmill. According to old timers, the sawmill was located near the Senior Citizen's building. In later years, a man named Lappins had a sawmill at the same location. Mr. Hayes' sawmill was destroyed by fire the year after it was built, but was eventually replaced. He also built the first concrete building near the old depot.[133] At one time the Masonic hall was located in it. The Masonic Lodge was called the Summit Lodge in 1878.[134] The Masonic Hall building is the same building that is now Taylor's Flower Shop and for many years was Preston Brook's General Store.

Mr. Hayes is responsible for financing the first village public school. It was called "Saint-Pauls-on-the-Mountain." Miss Charlotte Elliott, daughter of Bishop Stephen Elliott, and Miss Flora Fairbanks, daughter of George Fairbanks, were the first teachers at the school. The first village church adjoined the first village school.[135] One side was used as a church and the other as a school. In later years, St. Paul's became a church for the black citizens. It was moved to where the playgrounds for the Sewanee Public School are now located.

Life in the village revolved around the depot area and St. Paul's Church. Many of the early depot village people were baptized and attended church there. Church was not only held on Sunday, classes were conducted at night to teach religion. Records of people being baptized at Saint-Paul's-on-the-Mountain can be found in the duPont Library.

The first train to come up the mountain to Sewanee was called "The Sewanee Mountain Goat." Passenger had to sit in the coal car on their way up the mountain. The little engine's reliability was always questionable. When the train finally reached the top of the mountain, the engineer (Charlie Porter in 1870) would blow its steam whistle to let Hance Roberts know that passengers were arriving. Hance ran the hack (carriage for hire) service in the 1870's. He would take passengers anywhere they wanted to go for a small fee.

In the early 1870's, some of the men from the Depot Village decided to run all the blacks off the mountain. One black man was cut badly and left for dead near Otey Parish. The whole mountain was in an uproar over the incident. For many nights afterwards, patrols could be seen everywhere. The marshal located the leader of the group and arrested him. That ended the uprising. [136]

The first store in the village was owned by Pleasant Gilliam, son of Thomas and Elizabeth Gilliam. It was located across from the old Post Office. [137] The first telegraph office was located in Gilliam's store. The first telegraph operator was J. M. Stuart, a boarder at the home of Pleasant and Caroline Lide Gilliam. The 1870 census records show that Allen Gipson also owned a dry goods store at Sewanee. [138]

In 1874, there was a calaboose (jail) built in the University. Their only prisoner was arrested for selling liquor. [139] George Fairbanks was the law enforcement officer at this time. The Sewanee moonshiners must have been causing Mr. Fairbanks a lot of trouble, since he is responsible for getting the "Four Mile Law" passed by the Tennessee State Legislature on March 20, 1877. The law prohibited the selling of any intoxicating liquors within four miles of any incorporated institution of learning. [140]

The moonshiners and their customers were probably pretty mad at Mr. Fairbanks for getting that law passed. The fresh pure water supply from all those mountain springs made Sewanee moonshine the best you could buy anywhere. People were coming from all over the area to buy the moonshine. My father, grandfather, and great-grandfather were all moonshiners. That is how they made a living. The University of the South could only employ so many people and the others had to fend for themselves.

Gangs of moonshiners lived in and around Sewanee. They would often make whiskey together, since it took more than one moonshiner to supply all the customers needs. Ironically, their best customers were the elite of the University of the South and hotel managers from Chattanooga and Nashville. Their product was in great demand, and at one time their customers numbered in the hundreds and possibly more.

Many times wives would sell and deliver the moonshine to keep suspicion away from their husbands. When moonshiners were caught making or selling whiskey, some of their wealthier customers would often supply the money to pay the fines. Sewanee moonshine was noted as being a clear, good tasting whiskey of the highest quality. It was very popular with the ladies, too. Most moonshiners were not making whiskey to get rich, but simply to feed and clothe their families. Jobs were scarce during this time.

At one time there was a fence that separated the Sewanee village from the University of the South. The domain was called the corporation. People from the University of the South would say the fence was built to keep out the animals, but old timers at Sewanee say it was also used to keep out the Depot Village people. According to my sources, the fence was erected just a little north of the Sewanee Public School. One thousand acres of University property was located inside the fence.

There were gates at all roads leading to the outside. One gate was near Otey Parish, another at the Rowarks Cove Road, and a third at the University Cemetery. To get through the gates a person would have to drive their wagon or carriage under a rope attached to a swinging beam and pull it. This would open the gate. Then they would drive under another rope on the other side, and repeat the process to close the gate. People going into the University domain were usually the local hired help. Most people coming out of the domain owned businesses in the village. At times, peddlers were allowed to go inside the University domain, but would have to go to the back door, since they were not allowed to enter from the front door.

Old timers will tell you that the majority of people living in the University did not associate with people living around the Depot Village or in the outskirts of the town. Ely Green in his autobiography titled "Ely" called the people living outside the corporation "sagers." That is a word he used for the poor white trash. [141]

Ely wrote that he was the son of a white man and a so-called Negress. According to Ely, "In Sewanee many of the better class of white people often taken Negro boys and girls into their homes to train them to be efficient help. This is how my mother became a victim of misfortune by producing me when she was seventeen years old. When she discovered she was pregnant her mistress sent her away for me to be born." [142]

Ely spent most of his early years inside the University domain sheltered away from the sagers. He did make friends with Jack Prince who gave him a job and taught him how to shoot guns and hunt. He never thought of Jack as being like the other sagers. Some people living in the University had branded the poor white people as being poor white trash, and that is what Ely had heard all his life. According to Ely's book, during the early 1900's, people living outside the University were considered the rejected, whether they be white or black. [143] The fence segregated the two classes of people.

There were many interesting characters living in the village of Sewanee. Charles Wadams can be described as such a character. He was born in Colinton near Edinburgh,

Scotland. In 1828, he left Scotland and went to London, where he became one of Queen Victoria's light guards. In 1852, Charles brought his bride, Elizabeth Gibson Wadhams, to America. They first lived in New York, where he worked as a steward in a hotel. In 1858, he moved to Nashville where he also worked as a steward. He moved to Sewanee in 1871.[146]

Charles and Elizabeth had a daughter named Elizabeth "Lizzie" who taught music and crafts in the village. Lizzie was also an accomplished painter. Some of her paintings are still hanging in Sewanee homes. She never married and was considered a good friend to many of the villagers.

Mr. Wadhams' owned a bakery on top of the hill in the Village. He sold a variety of goods including cookies, freshly baked bread, pies, cakes, and home made ice cream was his specialty. His bakery was the most popular place in the village. He became affectionately known as "Bishop Wadhams."[147]

Samuel C. Hoge was an early merchant and Justice of Peace in the village of Sewanee. He married Sarah "Temmie" Holland in 1872. Together they ran a little dry good store. Their children were Nellie, Eunice, Nannie and John.[148] Samuel was a veteran of the Confederacy. Many of the early court transactions at Sewanee had Samuel's name as being the notary on the document. After Samuel's death, Temmie ran a boarding house for University students. Samuel and Temmie are buried in the University of the South Cemetery.

The French must have loved the Sewanee Mountain scene, since so many of its citizens moved to the village and started businesses. They were: Julier Burks; Josephen, Frank, and Guest Marquet; Simon and Mary Creset; M. P. Barbot; Leon Pillet and Madame Pillet.[149] They had a daughter named Alice Mariette who died young. Simon Creset, M. P. Barbot and Leon Pillet were all tailors in Sewanee. They probably came to the village to take advantage of business opportunities afforded by the University of the South. Mr. Pillet made uniforms for the students.

Besides the French, the Swiss, English, Irish, Russians, Swedes, Canadians, and Germans seemed to enjoy Sewanee's fresh air, too. Many of them owned businesses in the village. The Swiss and German families consisted of the Schneiches, Arn, Kuntz, Fischers, Steigers, Ruefs, Lutsingers, Gruetters, Lautenkeisers, Bonholtzers, Hooks, Grezinsteins, Biery, and Hunzikers. The Irish were the Rileys, Clays, Duncans and Thomas Hamilton. The Jewish Levovitzs were born in Russia. The Hardys, Joslins, Murrays, Colmores, and Frys were all born in England. There were two residents from Canada. They were Blanche Ellison and Hannah Norton. Carrie Hartis was the lone Swede at Sewanee.[150]

Allen Gibson, a deaf mute since birth, was a shoe cobbler, a merchant, photographer, and house builder in the village of Sewanee. He operated three different businesses at different times. He was the grandson of Allen Gibson who was an early settler in

Rowarks Cove. He married Emma Short, daughter of Reuben and Julia Ann Short. Allen was able to run his businesses with the help of his family who knew sign language, and could interpret for him. Almost everyone called him Dummy Gibson. Some people who still live at Sewanee have photographs taken by Allen. People in the area considered him an outstanding artist. A house that he built is still standing on Bob Stewman Road. [151]

At one time, Spencer Judd had a photography studio in the village of Sewanee. In 1870, Spencer was living with his brother, Harvey in Winchester. Harvey was an early photographer at Winchester. When the Civil War came, Harvey gave up his occupation and went to Alabama, and made gun caps and bullets for the Confederate Soldiers.

After the war, he came back to Franklin County. He and his brother, Charles, went into the photography business in Winchester. Not long afterwards, Harvey entered the ministry and became an Episcopal Priest.

Spencer's father, R. S. Judd, served as a missionary to the Indians. [152] Spencer was born while his family were living in Minnesota. Charles S. Judd, Spencer's brother, had the first Judd's photography studio at Sewanee. [153] It opened in the middle of May in 1876. It is not known when and why Charles left Sewanee. When Spencer came back to Franklin County in 1884, he went into the photography business at Sewanee. He loved nature and it was evident in his photographs.

The University News, Volume 2, Number 17, dated May 3, 1876, printed a copy of advertisements for businesses. "Businesses advertising in this issue include Fairmount School for Girls at Moffat (Monteagle), Tennessee, with Mrs. M. L. Yerger and Mrs. H. B. Kells in charge. W. A. Gibson and C. S. Dwight advertise clothing, hardware, seeds, and groceries. Gibson also advertises a fourteen room house for sale. Mr. R. S. Stuart advertises the Phelan House as an Inn. Dr. L. M. Hall advertises that he will open an office as dental surgeon during the month of May, 1876. Greens advertises fresh and staple groceries, cigars, tobacco, sporting goods, toilet articles, stationery. Joseph F. Bork advertises tin and sheet iron, stoves, kitchen furniture, grates, lamps and chimneys. Charles H. Wadham advertises hot mince pies, fancy groceries, tobacco, cigarette papers. Richard Perry advertises boots and shoes at Moynihan's old stand. Fred Fisher advertises cabinet work, repairing, varnishing, tables, wardrobes, book shelves, etc, and also advertises that he is an undertaker."

Mrs. Mary Statem Hamilton gave me a glance of early Sewanee in 1983. Mrs. Mary was born at Sewanee in 1899. When her memory begins concerning Sewanee she was around five years old. She writes, "there was a large sandstone freight depot as everything was brought up the mountain by train. There were waiting rooms, one for the white people and one for the colored people. Henry Hoskins met the trains and carried passengers to their destinations. Fifty cent was a big price to carry you all over town. Harry Hawkins met the train with a wagon to carry the freight and baggage where it was to go."

"The post office stayed open at night and people waited until the mail was put up. The night train brought the Nashville Banner Newspaper and many came to get the evening paper. Miss Bessie Kirby-Smith was post mistress and her sister, Miss Carrie, was assistant. Eva Thomas in later years. Mrs. Harry Hawkins also helped in the Post Office."

"Going up the street on the right side after you leave the freight depot was a small store owned by Allen Gipson. Mr. Gipson was deaf and dumb, but he had a large family and some of them stayed with him most of the time. Mostly his wife (Emma Short Gipson). He had candy a penny each and you get a lot of candy for a dime, chewing gum and cokes. I remember the pencils made of cedar. He catered mostly to school children with tablets and sold some groceries." Around the highway, no longer active

"Next was the P.S. Brooks' store owned and operated by Mr. Brooks and his two sons, Bert and Preston. He sold dry goods, groceries, and some hardware, feed for the horses, cows and hogs. Everyone owned their own stock. This building is now owned by William J. Hamilton Jr. and is an electric and hardware store." Taylor's

"Next was a dry goods store owned by Benny Levolvitz. He was Jewish. He left Sewanee and many businesses have operated there, Cumberland Electric, John Powell had a grocery store, William Kennedy had a grocery store, the Bank of Sewanee was there several years. Mrs. Baker operated a dress shop. It is now the Headquarters Beauty Shop." Lunch

"Next was the hardware store owned by Joseph Fisher. He also carried toys and bicycles. Next was a building which was used as a residence for many families. J. W. Beakley also ran a grocery store there for a short time. Then came the residence of Mrs. Martha Jane Castleberry who lived there with her daughters. The last one passed away in recent years. The residence was torn down." Pavilion / Angel Park / American Legion formerly 3 residences

"The next residence was occupied by the Sewells who lived there for many years. It was later sold to Robert Winn and used as a residence for sometime. Later he sold it to Arthur Long who had a grocery store, and now Mrs. Lawrence Alvarez has a craft and gift shop, The Lemon Fair, in the same building." Lemon Fair

"One house was destroyed by fire and the Texaco Filling Station is now in business there. Next was a house owned by the Winns. Sam Winn had a soda fountain and sold ice cream. It was a nice place to go on Sunday afternoon. He had tables and many people went there. His residence joined the store." Sewanee Auto

"Next came the residence of Christian Ruef who had a butcher shop. He had a slaughter pen back of the Pierce residence (now the Sholey residence) under a bluff. Every afternoon he would take his animals over to the slaughter pen. Later in the afternoon he would bring the meat to his shop where he kept it cool. People were there waiting for the meat. You could buy nearly a whole liver for a quarter. His steaks were also cheap. No meat was brought into Sewanee while he was in business. The Post Office now occupies this place. Next was the residence of Mrs. Johnson and now its the Cardwell residence."

"Next was the home of Mr. and Mrs. Wadhams and their daughter, Lizzie. After Mr. and Mrs. Wadhams died, Lizzie sold the place and lived in an apartment for years. J. D. Sutherland bought it and had a cafe there, later selling it to Mr. Baker. It was used as a residence for a long time. T.V.A. now has an electric office there."

"On the left side of the street beginning at the lower end was Hoge's store in later years used as a garage by A.F. Jackson. Lewis Reed also ran a garage there. Hoyte Baker had a tin shop and Otto Bailey now owns it for a body shop and car wash."

"Next was the grocery store owned by Tom Gipson. Later William Anderson and George Green had a used furniture store there . Also, it was used by Mrs. Sneed as a skating rink. Henry Sewell and Arthur Long had a tin shop there . Later it was owned by L.C. Winn Sr. and Son as a grocery store. It is now known as Shenanigans."

"On the corner as you go up the street was a grocery store owned by Grant Lappin. This store was later sold to Edward Short who had a grocery store there. After the store burned the post office and telegraph office were built there. After the post office was moved to a new location, these building were used as a dress shop, beauty parlor, and gift shop. The buildings were later destroyed by fire."

"Next is the cafe owned by Lawrence Green. This was the Sewanee Post Office until a new one was built. The building now occupied by Tupper Saussy was the Express Office where all express was brought from the train. The train which arrived at noon always carried gallons of Jack Daniel's whiskey. This was brought up every Saturday as a big square dance was held on Saturday Night. Many men were at the train to pick up their gallon. In later years this building was used as a shoe shop and Hamilton Electric had their first shop here until they moved to the store they now occupy."

"The store building next door was built by Mr. Rosenborough who sold men's clothing. This business did not last too long and the building was then used as a cafe by Mr. John Glover. Ina May Myers operated a dry cleaning shop here and it is now owned by Mr. and Mrs. McPherson who operates the County Squire, a dry cleaning establishment."

"The Jim Thomas residence stood next door and was destroyed by fire. Mr. Mansfield also had a business which was also destroyed. A garage was operated here by Cotton

Terrill, William Hamilton, and Tony Griswold. The Franklin County Bank occupies this place now."

"Next was the blacksmith shop where Mr. Jim Thomas was a blacksmith for many years. He was a busy man as everyone had horses and wagons. He did not go out of business until he got in bad health and retired."

"Next door was the livery stable owned by Joe Riley. He had horses and wagons and did hauling for the people on the mountain. Mr. Riley transported bodies to the cemetery for burial. Lewis Riley was the undertaker. Lewis' daughter, Miss Nellie May Riley, was a teacher at Sewanee Public School for many years. Mr. Riley had a residence next door that still stands and is owned by Otis Haley. Otto Bailey bought the livery stable place which had been changed to a garage and operated by others. Albert Green owned and operated a garage there for many years. The garage is now operated by Otto Bailey and is known as Otto Platz."

"On top of the hill was a residence and one side of the residence was used as a bakery shop and later as a cafe. In the back of the house was the bakery that was owned and operated by John Ruef, son of Christian Ruef. He made delicious bread and you could buy it right after he took it from the oven. He took it to the shop in the residence where he sold it. He later left here and the bakery was torn down. Hoyte Baker bought the house and built the brick buildings, one is used as an apartment and one as a beauty parlor. The beauty parlor has been operated for years by Mrs. A. J. Loftis." [154]

Herman Green, a long time Sewanee resident, made a list of people who had dairies in Sewanee. They were: Rufus Mosley, Sam Biery, Fred Bonholzer, Charles Owens, Matt Terrill, and Bob Tripp. He included an Oak Park Dairy and a University Dairy. He also made another list of bank directors. They were: Telfair Hodgson, Dr. R. M. Kirby-Smith, William Nauts, David Shepherd, Thomas Hamilton, Dr. B. F. Finney, and himself.

Herman's information included the names of various halls where students lived, since there were no dorms in the beginning. They were: Palmetto, Magnolia, McCrady, Selden, Barnwell, Kendall, Van Ness, Powotan, Gahler, Miller, and Wicks Halls. The places of business that he listed that were not included in Mrs. Mary Hamilton's story are: Gipson, Glover, and Gruetter Shoe Shops, Tiger Cafe that was run by J. O. and Laura Sutherland, and the Ice house that was run by Hoskins and Mansfield. The ice house was located near the Sewanee Pharmacy.

My father, Reece Short, wrote a story about his life at Sewanee. It provides a glimpse into a mountaineer's life at Sewanee from the turn of the century through the 1940's. "I was born December 6, 1905, in a railroad section house down the mountain below St. Mary's School. My Daddy worked for the railroad. He bought land on top of the mountain from his mother and Daddy, Reuben and Julia Ann Short. He built a two room log house on the land.

I was baptized at St. Mary's and when I got older I went to Sunday school there. Ed Short was our teacher. In the evenings, we went to Church. I have forgotten the preacher's name. I would trap through the winter. I was just strong enough to set a trap and do hunting throughout the summer.

I worked for Sister Hughetta several times. I worked making barrels of kraut and apple cider. Then she gave me a job painting some of the walls. I started to school at Sewanee on Billy Goat Hill when I was seven years old. Mrs. Willie Denton was my teacher. She taught up to the fourth grade. I went to Miss Johnson's class the last of the fourth grade. Then I had to quit school to help my Daddy cut chestnut wood. Me and my brother, Marvin, had to cut cross ties and wood for people who would make fence post out of them. (Dad got three toes cut off cutting cross ties at age 12.)

My Daddy's brother, Ed Short, bought a team of horses and we worked for him. He had a store in town and we would get our groceries from him. We would get our clothes from the St. Mary's mission room.

When I went to school Mr. Bratton taught the high school. It went through the 10th grade up here then. Mr. Theron Myers taught the high school when I had to quit. He was the one who looked after the rest of the teachers. If some of us done wrong, they would send us to him or Mr. Bratton. Before Mr. Myers took his place, there were several of us who went to school from out there, the place they called Rag Nation at that time. I will name some of the names. Me and Marvin, Dorothy, Lawrence, Walter, and Louise Short. Albert, Beatrice, Alma, and Marine Sutherland, Martha, Raymond and Lily Henley, Bill, Flora, Frank, Raymond, and Jim Short. Gurity McBee; Irene Green; Gladys Rowsey; Ethel Tucker; James Montgomery; Delpha ?, Lyle, Clifford, Roberta, and Neville Hawkins. Bessie and Leonard Crownover.

We had to walk to school no matter how cold or deep the snow got. There was a dirt road out there and plenty of mud and deep wagon ruts where Mr. John Pack hauled cross ties over the road. He had four yoke of steers (oxen) that he pulled the ties with. My Daddy had one yoke of steers.

I used to help Reece Garner cut cross ties. We would cut 15 a day and quit. He said that was a day's work. Sometimes we would get through at three o'clock and sometimes it would take longer. We used a cross cut saw to cut the ties with. We would mark the tie and measure it. Then cut the jugglers out and take a broad ax and removed the bark. Then we smoothed it out. We got thirty cents for each tie we cut.

Me and Marvin helped our Daddy cut cross ties down on the side of the mountain above the railroad about one mile from the section houses. We would pull them (cross ties) down to the railroad with a yoke of steers and then stop the train and load them there.

I worked on the highway (Dixie Highway now 41A/64) coming up the mountain for seventy-five cents a day for ten hours of work. Then George Collins gave me a dollar a day to work for him and I worked for him for quite a while. Then Wallace Pack went to working a crew of men and I went to work for him. He gave me a dollar and a half a day to work for him. I worked for him for quite a while, too.

My Daddy went to working a few men on the mud slide that is down the mountain below where Paul Hawkins lives, where that wall is built on the left. Then my Daddy quit the highway work. That is when I went to work for C. Pearson working on the highway. We would use a mule and dump cart to move the dirt and gravel and rock to fill up the places on the highway. At that time, we used picks and shovels and wheels barrows. We had to roll some of the rock over and fill the holes by hand.

When that job was through, I got a job working with White Campbell working in the rock quarry. He would ship car loads of rock to Nashville. Then we got out a lot of rock for the University. The last rock I got out for them, me and Will Campbell, got one out to make a cross to go on the top of that building where the clock is now. One of them blew off some years ago.

After that job, I went to work for my Uncle Ed Short doing farming work. After farming season, I went to work again for Wallace Pack at Cowan. We would haul slag stone and put it down under where they put the gravel, the same road you still ride over now going from Sewanee to Cowan. (the slag stone came from the Tennessee Coal, Iron and Railroad Company's blast furnace in Cowan.)

I worked for Wallace Pack for several months. I would get two dollars a day helping him with the road work. Then I went down on the train they call the Mountain Goat at that time. It ran from 7 A.M. and came back at 8 O'clock at night. We just lived on top of the mountain above St. Mary's station. Then finally I got a job on the railroad under Harvey Sutherland and worked for him a while, and several of us got laid off. Then we moved to St. Mary's old place that is about a mile around the top of the bluff from where we did live.

I kept up my hunting and trapping. I would squirrel hunt and trap during the Winter months. I would get a lot of meat to eat. I would get me two hogs to kill for the Winter and that is how I helped out my family. When World War I started food was scarce. We just had biscuits on Sundays. The rest of the week was meal bread. I couldn't get any work in the Winter, so I went to see a fellow and he told me I could put up some whiskey with him. I bought the sugar, meal and malt, and we went to making whiskey.

I watched everything he did. I wanted to learn how to make the whiskey myself. I didn't want to be around a place where they were drinking and gambling. That was the way it was. I put up some more whiskey with them, I think about ten or twelve gallons. I told them that was all I wanted to make. I thanked the man for letting me make whiskey with him, and then I quit making it with that group of moonshiners.

I made me a still and went to making by myself. I was never bothered as long as I worked by myself. I saved up some money and started to the oil fields in Oklahoma. I stopped in East St. Louis for a few days. I talked with a man who had just come from Oklahoma, and he said he believed there were a thousand men waiting on work when he left Oklahoma. He said that we should go to Kansas City, Missouri. He told me that he saw where they were wanting men to work on the railroad. The railroad paid our way there and when we got there, they had already hired all the men they needed. We caught a freight train (as hobos)and came back to St. Louis.

I picked up a few jobs at the unemployment office, but nothing permanent. I finally decided that I would go back to Tennessee, and start my old job again of making liquor. When I got back, those who weren't making moonshine was selling it, and stealing it from the others.

I did pick up several small jobs and kept up my trapping and hunting. Then finally, my Grandmother Barnes moved over in Sewanee where her son (Jack Hill) owned a restaurant. She wanted my mother to move over there (Bob Town) in her house. My mother bought her (mother's) place for $250. for one acre with a house on the land. I didn't want to move over to Bob Town since my friends lived at St. Mary's.

Not being able to find a permanent job, I began making whiskey with a group of moonshiners. There were fifteen of us working together. We would make two hundred gallons of whiskey a night. I would bring ten gallons back home with me each night. I ain't mentioning no names, but this whiskey was sold in Nashville and to people at the University of the South.

This was about Christmas time in 1928. You could buy this whiskey for about a dollar and twenty five cents a gallon. You could make it cheap at that time. A lot of people couldn't get any work and making whiskey was the only way they could make a living."

After making whiskey for many years, Dad went to work for Sheriff Bud Jackson at Jump Off in 1942. He cut bug wood, cleared land, worked in the quarry, and was a tenant farmer for many years. He continued to make a little moonshine for his own consumption and for his regular customers. He was also a barber among other professions. He would cut people's hair for whatever they could afford to pay. I remember that our house was usually filled on the week-ends and at night with people getting free hair cuts.[155]

Photograph of Dixie Highway (US 41A) coming from Cowan.
Buildings from left to right: A.F. Jackson's Garage, Sewanee Depot, and the Sewanee Steam Laundry.
(Courtesy of Benton Green, ca. 1930)

Photograph of Highway 41A coming from Cowan.
Buildings from left to right: Post Office, Jip Long's Store, Bill Kennedy's Store, P.S. Brooks Store.
(From an old post card, ca. 1950. Courtesy of Tommy Andrews)

Photograph of Main Street, Sewanee, Tenessee. Building in center is Otey Parish Episcopal Church.
(Courtesy of Annie Armour, duPont Library, University of the South)

Photograph of interior of Jack Hill's General Store, presently Joe David McBee's Antique Shop.
Persons from left to right: Allen McCreary, Rosie Long, Margie Barnes, and owner Jack Hill.
(Courtesy of Dorothy Short Andrews)

Descendants of the first white settlers in Tennessee and on Sewanee mountain. From left to right: (Front row) Emma Short Gipson holding son Clarence, standing in from of Emma is daughter Lora , Zella Gipson behind Julia Ann Austin Short's right shoulder, Marvin Short in front of his grand mother Julia Ann, Nancy McKnight Barnes with Nanny May Beene her grand daughter leaning on her lap, Elizabeth Tatum Beene holding daughter Ella, Litha Barnes Short holding son Reece, child Layton Gipson standing by Reece. Adults standing: Margie Barnes, Joice Gipson, Minerva "Jennie" Beene, Edward Short, and Henry H. Beene. Standing in the wagon: Lois Gipson, Mildred Beene, John Crit Beene, William Burns Beene, Austin Gipson, Sylvester Gipson, Limuel Beene (Taken by Allen "Dummy" Gipson, 1907 a family reunion at Sherwood, Tennessee)

JOHN WILKES BOOTH

John Wilkes Booth was said to be in the Sewanee Depot Village during the latter part of 1871 and early 1872. [156] Many older Sewanee residents have heard the story about John Wilkes Booth pawning his watch at Preston Brooks' store. It was reported and later verified that he married Louisa Price Payne while at Sewanee and fathered a daughter by her. If this was the real John Wilkes Booth, which many people think he was, then he got away with murdering President Abraham Lincoln. If he was not the real one, then he was one of the greatest impostors that ever lived.

GENERAL EDMUND KIRBY-SMITH

In 1875, General Edmund Kirby-Smith came to teach mathematics at the University of the South. [157] My father told me that Sewanee people were very happy that General Kirby-Smith had lived in their town. During my father's childhood, the Civil War was still fresh on people's mind. Many families living around Sewanee had lost all their possessions and some had lost family members during the war. Almost everybody knew about General Kirby-Smith's heroics and how he had won battles while other Confederate generals were losing. They knew about him being shot in the neck at the Battle of Bull Run and still wanting to continue the fight. He was their hero.

Not only was General Kirby-Smith a good friend to the Sewanee villagers, but many other generations of his family have been as well. General Kirby-Smith's granddaughter, Dr. Betty Kirby-Smith, was our family doctor. During her time as a doctor, she probably delivered the majority of babies born at Sewanee. I remember going to see Dr. Betty as a child. She never charged my parents a penny for her service, but being proud people, they would always take her a little gift of sorts. My Dad would also do handy work around her airplane shaped house that I loved to visit. My father was proud to be one of the stone masons who helped build the monument to honor General Kirby-Smith.

General Kirby-Smith Monument at Sewanee, Tennessee
(Courtesy of Steve Makris)

ST MARY'S

Bishop Quintard was responsible for the order of Episcopal nuns coming to Sewanee in 1888. He asked his friend, Sister Harriet Cannon, to send nuns to help people living in the village and nearby coves. Sister Harriet had already established the "Sisters of St. Marys" in New York, the first religious community in the Episcopal Church. [158]

In 1887, Mother Harriet came to Tennessee to find a suitable mountain retreat where the Sisters could get some relief from the hot weather in Memphis. She chose the Jabez Hayes Farm as a suitable place for the Sisters to stay. She described the mountaineers as being "proud, reserved, honest and fiercely independent. They lived in windowless one-room cabins and scratched out a living on the mountain slopes or distilled corn whiskey. Few of them could read." [158]

The Sisters welcomed a chance to live and work among the mountain people, but the mountaineers regarded them as heathens. The Sisters organized an all day picnic to get acquainted with their neighbors, but only three little boys showed up. The little boys told the Sisters that people were saying they worshipped an idol. The idol they were talking about was a brass altar cross, which a local man had unpacked. However, the mountaineers got over being suspicious of the Sisters. Everyone for twenty miles away attended the dedication of St. Mary's-on-the-Mountain on August 6, 1888. [158]

The Hayes farm was purchased for three thousand dollars. It was a three story farm house with enough room for a chapel, living quarters and guest rooms. The one hundred acre farm was leased from the University of the South for ninety-nine years at a cost of twenty-five dollars a year. There were a number of families living near St. Mary's, including the Short family, who helped the Sisters make gardens and with handy work. [158]

. In 1902, Sister Hughetta was the first Mother Superior at St. Mary's. She was from a wealthy Memphis family named Snowden. She came to Sewanee to reopen a training school. The nuns taught a plain English education that included religion and homemaking. At least twenty girls lived at the school for eight months a year. They were from ten to eighteen years of age, and were required to wear a blue dress uniform with a white apron and cap. Tuition was fifty dollars a year. Much of the money to keep the school open was obtained through donations. The nuns published a mission leaflet containing stories about mountaineer families in order to solicit funds for their school. [158]

By 1906, the nuns had more than three hundred godchildren on the mountain. [158] My father, Reece Short, was one of Sister Hughetta's godsons. Since he only lived a short distance away, Sister Hughetta gave him a job working in her garden when he was ten years old. He also helped her make barrels full of sauerkraut and apple cider. When he got older, she gave him a job making wine. She would keep the wine locked away in the cellar. She also provided employment for my grandmother, Litha Barnes Short, washing clothes for the Sisters. Sister Hughetta's friendly ghostly spirit is still alive and well at St. Mary's. [159]

Saint Joseph's Cabin located at Saint Mary's,
built by Joseph "Bud" Long, date unknown.
(Photograph obtained from Bud's wife, Rosie Hill Long.)

J.W. Hayes home. This house was used as the first Saint Mary's.
(Photograph obtained from Sister Kiara at Saint Mary's)

Young girls attending school at Saint Mary's. Names and date unknown.
(Courtesy of Sister Kiara)

CHRISTMAS AT ST. MARY'S

The only Christmas celebration that some people had was at St. Mary's. How well I remember my Christmases there. My Mother, Lou Sullivan Short, would wake me early on Christmas morning to get ready to go to St. Mary's. We lived about two or three miles away and would walk there with a large group of neighbors and family from Bob Town. The road we took through the woods was lined with tall pine trees. That is why the smell of fresh pine is still the fragrance of Christmas for me.

As we walked, the kids would talk about the presents they would choose this year. Many of the fathers came along, however, most would stay in the yard talking, while the mothers and children went inside. The hall was filled with people. It was truly standing room only for most of the time. One nun would start the celebration by playing the piano and another nun would lead the singing of Christmas carols. When Santa entered the room, all the children were excited to see him. He would always ask if we had been good boys and girls this year, and then proceeded to give each child a brown bag that contained an apple, orange, hard candy, and a candy cane.

The Sisters would lead a large group of people into another big room filled with tables covered with unwrapped gifts to choose from. The parents also received a gift. I usually chose a doll and a tea set. These were always my favorite Christmas gifts as a child. My Mom would pick a gift for herself and one for my Dad. I remember one year she chose a box of beautiful embroidered handkerchiefs. Everyone was welcome to come to St. Mary's, as it was for all people, not just for Episcopalians.[160]

RAG NATION

The Sisters of St. Mary's ran a mission room and people from all over went there to buy their clothes. Clothes were very cheap and you could buy a nice dress for a quarter. Some people would bring vegetables to exchange for clothes. My father told me that his mother, Litha Barnes Short, bought all his clothes from the mission room. Granny worked in the St. Mary's laundry, and would pay for his clothes from money earned washing clothes for the nuns. Dad told me that "Rag Nation" got its name from the nuns selling clothes at the mission room. "People around here would laugh and joke about wearing somebody else's rags, and would say they had to go to the mission room to get some more rags. Everybody started calling the area "Rag Nation."

When my Dad was telling me about Rag Nation, he just laughed and said, "nobody was poor out there cause we got all our clothes from St. Mary's and we growed our own vegetables. I was a good hunter and killed a lot of game to eat, and my Daddy had his own house and a team of Oxen to haul logs out from under the bluff. We cut cross ties for a living then. We had plenty. Anybody that can hunt and grow a garden ain't going to starve."[161]

A Christmas party held at Saint Mary's for the Sewanee. Date and names unknown.
(Courtesy of Sister Kiara)

THE MEMORIAL CROSS

The first documented entry in the Sewanee Purple newspaper concerning the building of a cross at Sewanee was on March 30, 1922. The article related that, "A suggestion was made by Mr. Finney (Vice-Chancellor Benjamin Finney) that should claim the attention of the entire mountain, is that of erecting a memorial at Morgan's Steep to the Sewanee men who gave their lives in the world war. [162]" The only world war that was fought up to that date was World War I.

The memorial cross project turned out to be bigger than every-one had anticipated. The site changed from Morgan's Steep to University View. People from all over the area volunteered to assist with its construction. Mr. Ralph Black, a professor of engineering at the University of the South, was the architect who designed the cross. [163]

In an article by the Sewanee Purple dated April 16, 1958, page 1, Mr. Black tells about the cross. "After the selection of the site for the cross, a wooden cross was nailed to a tree to show the location. A Roman Cross design was adopted. The particular design was a duplicate of the cross on the altar of All Saints' Church in Atlanta, which was enlarged to scale by measurements. The cross is built of concrete and reinforced with rods and railroad rails that the N.C. & ST. L. gave. Also, the concrete from the plant at Cowan, the stone, and the first day's labor were all given. From top to bottom of the base, the cross is seventy feet tall." [164]

Mr. Black goes on to say, "The building of the cross was a memorable and gala occasion. On the morning of November 11, 1922, a procession was formed at the University, of Sewanee and county citizenship and was headed by Dr. Finney. Everyone marched to the site for work and a picnic. The hole was dug for the foundation and rocks were thrown in by children and the men who had gathered them. When the hole was filled, the concrete was poured over them. This great day was enjoyed by everyone. "A day of fun that ended with the supreme satisfaction that the work on the foundation was started for the cross to rise toward heaven to become forever Sewanee's trade mark." [165]

"Mrs. George Washington of Nashville, better known as "Miss Queenie" compiled a cook book of favorite mountain recipes. The proceeds from the sale of this cook book pays for the lighting of the cross at night."[166]

Mr. Black ends with, "Now for the centennial celebration, the cross stands right as built thirty-six years previously, forever a glorious monument, for not only to our soldiers, but to the Sewanee people who started its rise from the ground upward. This is the one engineering project that I take the greatest pride in, and value more than all others that I have worked on."

According to the above article by Mr. Black, the cross was to be a memorial to Sewanee men who lost their lives in the service of their country during the World War I and the Spanish American War.[167]

In another article in the Sewanee Purple dated April 28, 1983, William "Bill" Hamilton relates that he was a water boy during the construction of the cross. His father, Thomas Hamilton, was one of the men who worked on the construction of the cross.[168] Mr. Thomas Hamilton was in charge of the construction of the cross.

In the same Sewanee Purple article dated April 28, 1983, it was announced that on Monday, June 18, 1923, at three O'clock, the cross erected on University View to the honor of Sewanee men who served in the Great War was unveiled before a hundred or more people. The cross with its covering of white, is clearly visible now at a distance of twenty or more miles from the valley, and at night it is to be illuminated by indirect lighting from the front base. On November 12, 1927, the light had been installed and funded through sales of the Sewanee cook book. By 1929, after repeated acts of vandalism, the cross went dark for three years, but now the light blaze again on the beacon for all Franklin County.[169]

The Memorial Cross was rededicated on May 8, 1983, to honor all Franklin County veterans not only of World War I, but also World War II, the Korean War, and the Vietnam War. Before the rededication, a renovation took place on the cross under the direction of Retired Reverend, William Mann. Memorial plaques were installed to honor participants of the four wars, refurbishing of the stone pedestal, landscaping the circle in which the cross stands, installing a new system of night lighting, improved the parking and picnic areas, and a perpetual care group was installed. The APTA undertook the restoration of the inspirational beacon under the chairmanship of Rev. Mann. Over $30,000 was raised in private funding to complete the renovation project.[170]

According to the above article, Senator Howard Baker, Senator James Sassar, Congressman Albert Gore, and Congressman Jim Cooper were to be in attendance.[171] Senator Howard Baker, a former student at the University of the South, became the Minority Leader in the United States Senate, and afterwards, President Ronald Reagan's Chief of Staff. Congressman Albert Gore became Vice President of the United States of America.

Many local Sewanee residents gave money and provided the labor so that the Memorial Cross could to be built at University View. There is no list to show all the people's names who contributed to the labor force. We do know there were plenty volunteers from the articles that were written about the cross.

When people drive up the mountain from Cowan for the first time, they are in awe of the magnificent Memorial Cross perched proudly on the mountain over looking Hawkins Cove. It is truly a befitting memorial to those brave soldiers who paid the ultimate price for our country's freedom, and to those who served so proudly.

PRESIDENT TAFT'S VISIT TO SEWANEE

William Howard Taft, 27th President of the United States, paid a visit to Sewanee on November 10, 1911. According to Miss Johnnie Tucker, Matron of Tuckaway Inn, "Major Archie Butt had persuaded his chief to give a few hours of his precious time to visit Sewanee, Major Butt's Alma Mater."

Miss Johnnie described the visit in the following way. "It was a typical fall day; a fine drizzle was falling, and the unpaved street from the railroad station to the University was rough and muddy. A very mixed and motley crowd had gathered to meet the Mountain Goat at eight-fifteen."

"Henry Hoskins had decorated one of his old sea going hacks in red, white, and blue bunting for the President to ride in, but someone had spied the only automobile on the Mountain, belonging to a gentleman from Tracy City, coming down the street. It was immediately commandeered for the President, Bishop Gailor, the vice-chancellor, and two secret servicemen. Henry proudly drove the Major and some more secret service men."

"Chief McBee swore in twelve men to assist him. (Tom Hamilton and White Campbell rode the best steeds.) The chief himself, clad in a costume of Charles the First, with Vandyke beard and buskins, the nether (lower) portion of a billiard cue in one hand and a sack of handcuffs on the pommel of his Pegasus, and four revolvers dispersed about his person, was a living exponent of Tennessee law."

"Just before the arrival of the Presidential train he gathered his underlings behind John Reuf's barn and served out as many guns and as much ammunition as their clothing would hold. Their horses aroused such admiration that the offers which were wired in for them would, if accepted, have brought more money to the Mountain than ever before seen except in the coffers of the Supply Store and the Civic League."

"We note that Mrs. Lovell refused to go to the window to look, though they passed her house, because he was a Republican President!" [172]

Five months after President Taft's visit to Sewanee, Major Butt, his chief of staff, went down with the Titanic. [173] Most of above article was taken from "Purple Sewanee" pages 131-132. It was a reprint of "Sewanee."

UNIVERSITY OF THE SOUTH VERSUS FRANKLIN COUNTY

Evidently, there was a problem between Franklin County and the University of the South over taxes. The case first went to the Chancery Court, and then to the State Supreme Court over the question of taxing the University of the South. In 1887, Vice Chancellor Telfair Hodgson sent answers about the University's properties to the Franklin County Chancery Court. His answers provide a wealth of historical information concerning early Sewanee and the University of the South, which could probably never be found in any other document in full.

Vice Chancellor says that it is true that the University was established in Franklin County on the plateau of the Cumberland Mountains, and on the line of a coal railway with its terminal at Cowan and Tracy City. That it was incorporated. It is not true that the University Corporation acquired any part of its land by gift. A part of them were convey to it in consideration it would agree to establish its University at the place adopted, and part of the lands were purchased by it.

It is true that the University corporation erected several structures for its University purposes up on the part of its land exempted from taxation. The structures already erected cost perhaps as much as $75,000.00. But it will require at least $350,000.00 to erect all the structures for the purposes contemplated by its charter.

It is true that so much of the lands belonging to the University corporation as were exempted by its charter from taxation were set apart by survey. Their boundary established and designed upon the map of its lands and that this was done immediately after the acceptance of said charter, and before any improvements had been made and place thereon.

It is certainly true that the University corporation did not have a dollar of capital stock and that all its property of every kind came to it as a donation in some form or as the usufruct of such donations.

The fact are that while the original purpose was to raise a fund of $3,000,000.00, equip and endow the University, there have been but about $500,000.00 subscriptions when the Civil War began and this sum had been subscribed mainly by the citizens of the state of Louisiana, through the agency of Bishop Polk.

When the subscription was made it was believed by all the incorporators that the whole sum desired would be subscribed without delay or hesitation, and therefore in the Fall of 1860, the educational structures of University were planned upon a scale commensurate with the extensive design contemplated at the time the University was incorporated, but when the war closed, not one stone was left upon another and the whole subscription was lost by the insolvency of the subscribers.

The whole South was completely bankrupt. The University had its lands but nothing else, not until 1867, was an attempt made to realize the hopes of the University promoters. The attempt was then made in the face of difficulties almost insurmountable. With infinite pains and difficulty, two wooden structures were build and the University began its career with nine grammar school scholars. The Bishops of the states of the South united in an earnest effort to place the University upon its feet, but the poverty of the South rendered their effort unavailing. An earnest appeal was made to the Episcopal church of the North and while the response was gratifying, yet the aid from that quarter was inadequate.

As a last resort the Bishops of the Southern States sent one of their number to England to appeal to the Mother Church for aid, and as the result of this appeal sufficient funds were donated to give life here and energy to the enterprise. In this way and from these sources came the money which built the University's educational structures save one built by the present Vice Chancellor of the University.

It is true about thirty years there was some evidence that a town would probably be built on the land now owned by the University. This expectation however speedily proved illusory. It came about in this way. The Sewanee Mining Company then owned a large part of the land now belonging to the University. The said company believing the land had valuable coal on them built a railway to them and began to mine for coal.

The experiment failed as the quantity of coal expected was not found. While this experiment was in progress there was some expectation there would be a town there but before the town was started or even a single house was built, it was found the experiment was a failure. The railway was pushed on to Tracy City. Sewanee was left thirty years ago, a barren waşte without house or inhabitant. And so 28 years ago, there was again anticipation that a town would be built there, but the only ground for it was the prospect that the University would make it there, and so Sewanee remained a wild waste until the University in 1867, began improvements there.

The truth is that a village at Sewanee was an impossibility, until the University made it possible, by establishing the University near there, and using every possible means to keep it in existence. It so happened that while Sewanee is an eminently eligible site for a University, yet the liveliest imagination could not conceive of its eligibility for anything else that could possibility give birth to a town, and therefore, the University denies that it was ever evident that a town of some considerable size and importance would be built at Sewanee as charged.

It is not true that the railway leased a lot from the University and erected a depot on it. The fact being that the depot is on the right of way of the railway, and the Sewanee Mining company, as consideration to induce the University to establish the University there, conveyed to the University all its land in the vicinity reserving its right of way. The Railway Company had no depot there for the reason it was a mere forest without an inhabitant or a single article of commerce to contribute to the traffic of the railway. Since the University has been established and to accommodate the traffic, the railway has built a substantial and valuable depot, and from which Franklin County collects a tax. It would never have had but for the establishment of the University.

It is true that the University had all of the lands carefully surveyed, immediately after it acquired title to them, and to Bishop Hopkins of Vermont, who had a great reputation for judgment and taste in such matters, was committed to the task of laying out the portion of the domain which was expected to be occupied by the educational structures.

To this labor, Bishop Hopkins who had the success of the University much at heart, devoted a great deal of time and in pursuance of his plans, the tract exempted was set apart by meters and bounds, and the boundaries indicated clearly and distinctly. The sites for the various educational structures intended by University were selected by him upon said tract.

Having selected these sites, he had a map made of the whole tract and upon this map streets, avenues, and building sites, were indicated in such manner as his taste suggested. It was a part of his plan to appropriate an area to each intended educational building, and after indicating broad streets and avenues, the area was sub-divided into lots of four acres each. It was after 1867, that the attempt was made to improve these lots so as to make them valuable.

The taxable value of the whole tract was not then as much as $1,000. The University did not receive a tax upon any lands in its borders of like value and character at that time, valued at so much as $1.00 per acre. It is probable that this tract of land ever paid as much as $50, 000 taxes altogether to Franklin County for all the years it had the right to tax it. It is true that as a part of its scheme to create, establish, and sustain for which it could find suitable tenants upon suitable terms. It is true that various tenants used said lots for residences and business purposes as stated, but the extent of the business and the population of the town are much exaggerated in the bill.

Commencing with nine students nineteen years ago, the University has now between three and four hundred. But its present attendance has been recently acquired. During the years of its bitter struggle, seventy-five to one hundred and fifty students were all that it had. The business of the town is limited almost exclusively to the supply of the wants of the students, professors, and others connected with the University, and the presence of the relations of some of the students and many friends of the University during the Summer months. Hence the business of the town is necessarily limited, and so limited that from all sources the amount of rent it receives does not exceed $1,500.00.

The annual rent paid by the professors and others connected with the University is merely nominal, for the reason that the small rent charged them is compensated by the moderate amount of their salaries. In other instances, leases have been made at nominal rates either to reward sacrifices made on behalf of the University or with the hope of promoting the interest of the University.

It is true that said leases have been made from time to time. Some for a longer some for a shorter period of time. Some of said leases as made from time to time were for one year, some for ten years, some for thirty-three years. It is true that by the terms of many of the leases, the tenants are required to place particular improvement upon the property leased, but it is not true that at the end of such leases the improvements placed on the lots so leased then revert to the University. The facts of course are, that the whole property, both lots and the improvements thereon are owned by the University, and the right of the tenant is of course limited to the use and enjoyment of the lot and improvement thereon, upon his rendering the payments required of him by his contract, whether that payment be in improvements, in money or partly in both.

It is perhaps true that the University's village is second in size in Franklin County, which is not saying much, but the averts, suggest an erroneous conclusion for the reason Franklin County has but one town in its borders, and that town has probably less than 1,500 inhabitants. It has several small villages, but none of them of any size.

The University believes it to be true that the Legislature when it granted the exemption to the University, it did not consider how the University would pay for the improvements placed upon the land exempted. For the plain reason it was a matter wholly immaterial to the State how they were to pay for it.

It is probable that none of said leases are registered. It is true that said leases provided for the payment of rent at stated periods and stipulated that the tenant should pay the taxes assessed thereon, but the latter stipulation has a fix and certain meaning understood quite well by Franklin County, and while this statement is made in the bill suggestive simply. Yet, the University desires to better explain it, so as to avoid the possible difficulty of misinterpretation.

It will be seen from the Charter and Amendments thereto, granted the University by the Legislature that it is clothed with certain municipal powers. When the University came to lease its lots, grade and improve the streets, and side walks, it was found that by reason of the character of the soil, the repairs of its streets and sidewalks would be a constant and considerable expense. In addition, it was necessary to have municipal officers to preserve order and enforce the laws.

To accomplish these objects and out of abundant caution, the Charter of the University was so amended by the Chancery Court, as to confer the power upon it, to lay a tax upon its property to meet these necessary demands for these municipal purposes. Before this was done, by a formal request made by the University's commissioners, the attention of the Board of the University Trustees was called to the fact, that the lessees had no taxes to pay upon the property they occupied belonging to the University, and that it was just that the lessees should contribute to the municipal tax, as they had the benefit of the improvements made upon the streets and side walks, and the benefit of the protection the municipal government gave.

After this had been done and to compel the prompt payment of such tax as in many instances its payment could not be otherwise compelled, a stipulation for its payment was inserted in each lease. This was not only well understood by the University and its lessees, but by Franklin County and the State as well, since it was known to all and recognized by all that the University property was exempt from taxation, and all parties so treated for nearly thirty years.

The statement that many handsome and substantial residences, store houses, shops, offices and other buildings, usually erected in large town and cities have been built on the lots so laid off, is an exaggeration. Aside from the residences of those connected with the University, there are comparatively few residences in the town. The business houses and stores are comparatively few in number, and altogether yield the University about $1,500 per years rent.

It is not true that any part of said property has ever been used for any purpose other than contemplated by its charter. The University has done all in its power to make said property as profitable as possible, and every dollar it has been made to yield, has been applied to the objects contemplated in the University's Charter, and after such exclusive dedication, it has not been able to do more than approximate the purpose of its Charter and to accomplish what it has done, to accomplish these ends. It has been compelled to incur a large debt, and although the rents it gets are all applied to said debt, yet they are not sufficient to pay the interest thereon.

The inference that the renting to its property by the University to attain means to sustain the University, renders it subject to taxation, is a misconception. This can be said with no more reason than it may be said, its bonds and other evidence of debt are taxable, since the interest thereon is applied in the same way.

The University answers that no part of its property has been used for any purpose whatever other than for the design of its creation. The University repeats that the whole income of said property is devoted exclusively to the objects authorized and contemplated by its Charter, and not otherwise. The University has never engaged in the real estate business, nor in the building a town. It has done nothing with respect to its property save to exert itself to the uttermost to build up its University.[174]

CUMBERLAND PRESBYTERIAN CHURCH

The Cumberland Presbyterian Church graces the hillside in the section of Sewanee known as Bob Town. Its simple white frame structure with a double tiered belfry steeple makes it one of the most beautiful buildings in Sewanee. It gives the appearance of being uncomplicated and inviting.

The church is located on land that was part of the original land granted to Wallis Estill, Thomas Logan and Madison Porter by the State of Tennessee. All three men were well-to-do businessmen living in Winchester, Tennessee. They probably secured the land grants for investment purposes.

The church founders obtained the land from the Tennessee Coal, Iron, and Railroad Company, which was previously known as the Sewanee Mining Company. The Sewanee Mining Company purchased the same land from Thomas Logan and Madison Porter. The western section of land where the church is located was part of the Estill grant. G. M. and Jennie W. Ray owned this section of the land. Jennie Ray was the former Jennie Wright Estill, daughter of Wallis Estill Sr. She probably inherited the land. There is no record of these Rays ever living at Sewanee.

The Cumberland Presbyterian Church at Sewanee was founded by William L. Myers, Albert S. Johnson, and James Collins around 1891 The church was probably built in 1891 or 1892. The first record of services in the church was on September 16, 1892. The first pastor of record was Reverend Simpson. [175]

Almost all the children in Bob Town went to Sunday School at the Cumberland Presbyterian Church when I was a child living there. We always participated in plays on Christmas Eve based on the birth of Jesus. Our Sunday School teacher was Evelyn Jean Hawkins, who is now married to Paul Mooney. She directed the plays and played the piano. She was always involved in activities for the children, even though, she was a young girl herself. She could sure make those Bible stories come alive.

I remember Mr. Theron Myers leading the prayers at the church and how his strong voice seemed to make the rafters shake. Everyone seemed to listen to every word he had to say including the children. You could tell that his prayers came straight from his heart. He was a wonderful man and gifted teacher.

Santa Claus always came to visit the children at the Cumberland Presbyterian Church. All the children received nice gifts from Santa Claus on Christmas Eve night. The gifts were nicely wrapped and placed under a beautifully decorated tree. There was a lot of caring and sharing going on in that church. It was a small church with a big heart, and the children loved to go there during my childhood.

BOB TOWN

The section of Sewanee known as Bob Town was part of the original land grant that Porter, Estill, and Logan received from the State of Tennessee in 1834. It was named Bob Town in honor of Robert "Bob" Stewman. At one time, Bob and his family lived in front of the Cumberland Presbyterian Church.

During my childhood, there were two ways to get to Bob Town from Sewanee. From the depot you could go past the laundry where there was a path going through the woods to the left. Many of the women living at Bob Town worked at the laundry and would take this path to work each day. The other road ran to the left side of the Sewanee Market, and then went right. It was a graveled road during my childhood.

There is a beautiful view of the mountain looking into Lost Cove from Bob Town. You can also see the mountain ridge that comes up from Sherwood to Jump off. I remember seeing mountain goats roaming on top of the ridges.

The mountain is filled with numerous caves where stills were hidden and moonshine whiskey was made. My Dad made whiskey in the caves below the mountain where the deBarys once lived. In the 1920's, my Dad lived in one of the caves and made whiskey in the other. He was hiding from Sheriff Jackson who had spotted him making whiskey in another section of the mountain. Dad was seventeen years old at the time. He liked living in a cave better than being locked up in jail.

There were other things in the mountain besides moonshine stills. I remember a creek called "The Minniehaha." This is the only place in Sewanee known to have kept its original Indian name. Not many people knew about the Minniehaha except for people living in Bob Town. It was located just a little below a hill in back of the old Christian Ruef house, which was the Silas and Mary Guyear's house during my childhood. Most of the children at Bob Town would go there on hot summer afternoons to take a dip in its cool water. There was a vine growing over its bank, and some of the older kids would swing on the vine and act like Tarzan, then jump into the water.

There was a path in back of the deBary's house that went down into Lost Cove. On some Sunday afternoons, my Dad would take Mom and us kids down the steep mountain path into the cove. He would show us the caves and other things he had discovered on his many ventures into the cove. One of the caves he discovered was called "Grape Vine Cave." In one of the caves he saw some Indian drawings.

Farmers would let their hogs run wild in the mountain. On one of our trips into the cove, we heard a roaring noise just as we went down into the cove. Dad told us to hurry up and get behind the rocks because there was a herd of wild pigs coming our way. I can still remember seeing the cloud of dust and pigs running so fast that it was hard to see them. There seemed to be hundreds of pigs in the herd. We just barely found refuge before the pigs were running in the same path where we had just been walking.

In the middle of Lost Cove was the house of the Garners. We never went inside their house, but Dad showed us where they lived. He referred to them as Mose, Sol, and Mu Garner. There were many people living in Lost Cove when my Dad was a child, but most of them died and the others moved away. The only people who stayed were Moses, Solomon, and Musidore, who were sister and brothers and children of Isaac Calvin and Lucinda Rose Garner. My Dad was their most frequent visitor. He kept the Garners updated on news from Sewanee. At times, Mr. Sol and Mr. Mose would ride their horses up the mountain to Bob Town to see my Dad. According to my Dad, Miss Mu never cared anything about leaving Lost Cove. Some people called her Mood, but my Dad always called her Mu.

At one time there was a Church of Christ located just above the Slaughter Pen Rock. Most people referred to it as a "Camelite Church." There were two roads leading to the church. One went by the Robert Stewman's house and the other by Allen McCreary's house. Many people went to the church in a horse and wagon. Mr. J. L. Long who owned the Sewanee Hardware Store was the minister at the church. This was the first known Pentecostal Church to be located on the Sewanee Mountain.

There is a rock a short distance below the mountain behind the deBary house. This rock is called the Annie Rock in honor of Annie Ross. (***Photo on left***) Annie Ross was an early woman minister at Sewanee. She was not a minister in a church, since women were not usually allowed to be preachers during this time in our history. She would preach to the people getting off the trains. My father told me people made fun of her in Sewanee for preaching.

Annie was a good friend of my paternal great-grandmother, Nancy Barnes. They would often go to the rock below a hill on the side of the mountain and pray for hours. People around began to believe in her as a religious leader. When anyone was sick, they would summons Annie to come to their house and pray for them to be healed.

After a while, Annie's reputation as a religious leader was known throughout the area. She had many followers, mostly women. They would go to the rock with her to pray. People from as far as Tracy City would join the caravan to the praying rock.

I have heard that a vision was seen at the Annie Rock. That is the extent of my knowledge about the vision. My father knew the story about the forest being on fire while women were at the praying rock. Some men from Sewanee went to the rock and warned the women to get out of the woods before they got burned up, but they wouldn't leave. They simply told the men to go back to town because the fire would go out before reaching them, and it did. This may be the story that became a vision in later years.

Another place that we would often visit was the Slaughter Pen Rock. It was on our way through the woods to Jump Off. The slaughter pen was a big rock with another top rock that looked like a cap bill or a stove's hood over the lower rock. It was the coolest place on the mountain. There was water running over the rocks that made the surface very slick. Christian Ruef slaughtered animals there to be sold in his Sewanee Village Meat Market.

In Bob Town "The Point of Disappointment," is one of most beautiful views on the mountain looking into Lost Cove. According to my father, the Point of Disappointment got its name from a boy who lived in Bob Town. He had bragged about getting married to a local girl. He took her to the point to pop the question and to his surprised, she turned him down. When people asked about his marriage plans, he replied, "that point turned out to be the point of disappointment for me." From then on people in Bob Town called it "The Point of Disappointment." It was a favorite place for young couples to go on dates during the 1920's 30's and 40's. It was like a modern day parking place. Many people went to the Point in horse drawn wagons or carriages.

The Hat Rock Road is off Bob Stewman Road to the left coming from Sewanee. During my childhood, there was only one house on Hat Rock Road. It was Harrison Gudger's house, and my Uncle Jack Hill and Aunt Margie Barnes lived there. Many people went there to have their pictures taken sitting on the big rock that resembles a hat. People also went there for picnics and other family outings. [176]

Some of the people who lived at Bob Town were: the Kennedys, Collins, Guyears, Levans, Shorts, Barnes, Barnetts, Gipsons, McBees, Barnes, Tatums, Princes, Sholeys, Longs, Hills, Hunzikers, Pierce, Yates, Sutherlands, Andrews, Blacks, Kings, Stewmans, Sullivans, Parsons, deBarys, and Terrills. There could be others that I have missed.

JUMP OFF

Jump Off is located about seven miles from Sewanee. It is actually another section of Sewanee on the southeast side. Part of Jump Off is located in Franklin County and the other part in Marion County. It is a rural area with farms and lakes. Many people who lived at Jump Off were farmers, sawmill workers or in the timber business.

In the early years, farmers from Rowarks Cove would herd their cattle to Jump Off for summer grazing in its fertile green fields. After the University of the South was built, the cattle caused such a commotion going through the University, that a fence was built around the domain.

A story in the Purple Sewanee tells about John A. Murrel and a companion robbing a trader on Brakefield Road and throwing him over a high cliff while still alive. A big rock on the edge of the mountain became known as the "Jump Off." This supposedly happened at Jump Off in Franklin County, Tennessee.

John A. Murrel was a well-known highwayman or road agent on the Natchez Trace. The Natchez Trace was a migration and trade route that ran between Nashville and Natchez, Mississippi. Before the white man, it was an Indian trail through the Chickasaw and Choctaw Nations. Later the Indian trail was widened and became known as the Natchez Trace. There were many incidents of bandits robbing travelers on the Natchez Trace. The incident at Jump Off was one of the crimes committed by Murrel that led to his hanging.[177]

The Jump Off School is off to the east side of the Jump Off Road. The building consisted of one classroom with a kitchen off to the left, and a coat closet to the right. There was a three-hole wooden out-house behind the schoolhouse and a little pump well for water in the side yard. The date the schoolhouse was built is unknown to the writer. Mr. Charles Grimes' father donated the land and building. The building is still standing, but is no longer used as a school. It is now used for storage.

On Sundays the Baptist Church members used the school until the Jump Off Baptist Church was built around 1956. A minister from the Highland Park Missionary Baptist Church in Chattanooga would conduct services there on Sunday morning and night. This was the first church where I heard the old traditional hymns being sung. Many of the church members had beautiful sounding voices.

When I attended Jump Off School from 1954 to 1956, Mrs. Minnie Dykes Hindman from Tracy City, Tennessee, was the teacher. She was an extraordinary person and gifted teacher. Her students were able to compete academically with students from larger schools throughout the county. During the winter months, she made fires in a coal stove that stood in the middle of the little schoolhouse. Every school day, she prepared and cooked food for the school children's lunches. Her husband drove a pickup truck from Tracy City with a camper on top with benches for transporting students to and from school. She was so organized that everything seemed to fall into place. She gave her time and attention to all her students, and she would also spend time with a retarded boy that would often come to school to be with the other children.

She wasn't shy about using the switch. If her students misbehaved or failed to do their homework, then they had a choice of writing off a whole bunch of homework or taking a switching. She was very good to her students. Many times she would invite students to her house to spend the week-end with her children.

To raise funds for the school, Mrs. Hindman would sponsor box supper nights. She would have cake walks and auction off box suppers. The students would be excited for days about going to the box suppers. Most families had to work hard and it was good to get away from home and animals to attend the box suppers. All the families who had children attending school would usually show up to support the box supper functions.

Telephone service came to Jump Off for the first time in the 1950's. I remember our first telephone there. We were on a party line with eight other families. Oh, my was that a great time in my life. I was warned not to listen in to other people's conversation, but I was a curious kid, and I listened in every time I had a chance. Somebody was always talking on the telephone, and I knew everybody's business. It didn't bother me that my closest neighbor was two miles away or that I didn't have any friends living nearby. I had that trusty ole soap opera telephone. The worst part, I couldn't tell anybody what I heard on the telephone because I didn't want to get a whipping. Each family had a different ring and I knew them all. Ours was two short rings.

My father worked from dawn to dust, six days a week. My mother had to do all the milking of the cows, getting in the fire wood, cooking all the meals, and herding the animals to the barns or wherever they needed to go. Life was hard for my parents on the farm at Jump Off. But, the little things seemed to mean a lot to our family. It was a treat to go to the store and get an ice cream cone or an orange drink to half with my brother or sister. When we were without transportation to go to the store, we would buy our groceries from Culpepper's Rolling Store that stopped by our mail box every Monday morning.

There is a section of Jump Off known as Gudger Town. Gudger Town was named for William Gudger, an early resident of Jump Off. William and his wife. Jane, were the parents of Harrison, Carrie Belle, Gailton, Lillie, Lawton, John, and Pressie Gudger. All the Gudgers were well known in Sewanee.

A few miles further out Jump Off Road on the left side was the Jump Off Baptist Church. I remember when it was built, but I can't remember the exact date or the name of the minister who was responsible for having it built. It was around 1956.

There is a Civilian Conservation Corps (C.C.C.) Camp and recreation center located at Jump Off. It has been there for many years. Most people refer to it as the C.C.C. camp. The boys based at the camp were often seen around Sewanee doing various types jobs to help the community.[178]

Some of the people who lived at Jump Off are: the Greens, Shorts, Princes, Hughes, Champions, Yokleys, Gasses, Gudgers, McBees, Copelands, Tates, Owensbys, Statums, Bennetts, Packs, Morrises, Taylors, Hunts, Smiths, and Williams. There could be others that I missed in my research.

INHABITANTS OF LOST COVE

It was once thought that no census taker had ever made a trip to Lost Cove to get a record of the inhabitants living there. However, not only did a census taker go to Lost Cove, but the Episcopal Priest went there as well, and held services. Records of known Lost Cove inhabitants have been found in the 1870 Franklin County census records. Baptismal records have been found in the duPont Library Archives of the University of the South.

The 1870 census records list the following people who were all known to have lived in Lost Cove: Isaac C. Garner age 38; Lucinda Rose Garner age 38; Sarah A. Garner age 15; Martha A Garner age 10; John H. Garner age 6, Musidore Garner age 4; Moses C. Garner age 3. (2) Louisa Rose age 34, Sarah Garner age 30, John Wells age 13, and Thomas Rose age 11. (3) Henry G. Garner age 37, Mary Garner age 35, Andrew Garner age 19, Marshall Garner age 17, William Garner age 15, John M. Garner age 13, Nancy J. Garner age 11, Sarah Garner age 10, James W. Garner age 7, George P. Garner age 5, Elizabeth Garner age 3, and Mary E. Garner age 1.[179]

The baptismal records at duPont Archives list the following as being baptized at Lost Cove. They were: Mary and Ellen Pentergrass. Martha, Musidora, John Henry, and John Garner. Nancy and William Bean Stephens. Loula and William Yancy Rose, and Tennessee Beauguard Pearson.[180]

MIDWAY AND TICK BUSH COMMUNITIES

The small communities of Midway and Tick Bush are located on Sewanee's eastern side by just a few miles. Tick Bush is adjacent to Midway. They have been known as Tick Bush and Midway since at lease the early 1900's, but the writer was unable to find anyone who knew how they got their names.

To get to Midway and Tick Bush from Sewanee, you can take the airport exit road off highway 41A/64, going toward Monteagle. You will pass the Jackson-Myers Airfield on the way. The small airport was built in the late forties or early fifties. It was named for two Sewanee military men who gave their lives for our country. They are Marion Francis "M.. F." Jackson Jr. and George Clifton Myers.[181] Ensign Jackson was a Navy pilot during World War II. He was killed on April 23, 1942, while flying missions off the Wasp, in Scapa Flow, Scotland.[182] Lieutenant George Clifton Myers was a member of the Army Air Corps. He was killed in action over Hanau, Germany, on December 11, 1944.[183] M. F. was the son of Sheriff M. F. Sr., better known as Sheriff Bud Jackson, and his wife, Eva. George Clifton was the son of Reverend George B. Myers and his wife, Margaret.

After you pass the airport, keep on the same road. When you see St. James Episcopal Church you will be in Midway. There are no signs to tell you that you are in Midway or Tick Bush. Across the road from the church was Manuel Knott's store. Manuel always had candy, ice cream, and cold drinks, which sure made a kid happy. It was always a treat to go to Knott's store, not only for the goodies, but also for the kindness shown by the proprietors. Manuel and Savannah always had time to talk to their customers and were kind to everyone.

In the 1930's, there was a public school at Midway. It was called Summit School. Besides teaching school children, classes were also held at night for adults. I never learned where the school was located.

There were two other stores located at Midway. Raymond Knott had a store and so did a Mr. Jacobs. Raymond once ran a rolling store, and people around Sewanee would buy their groceries from him. Later, he became a Baptist minister. Raymond is Manuel Knott's uncle. There is a Church of Christ at Midway and Harrison Cemetery is located behind it.[184]

Some of the people who lived at Midway and Tick Bush besides the Knotts were: the Hobacks, Kings, Barrys, Jacksons, Rollins, Greens, Fosters, Jacobs, Gilliams, Marlows, Bohannons, Reids, Mooneys, Stephens, Simmons, Ricketts, Gipsons, and Caldwells families. Mrs. Lackey lived in the house where St. Andrews' Post Office was located. She was the postmistress. In the early days, St. Andrews Post Office was known as Gipson Switch. This is where Allen Gipson ran a trading post in the early days of Sewanee. The trains stopped at Gipson Switch to pick up coal and timber for delivery.

SHERWOOD ROAD COMMUNITY

Sherwood Road is the first road on the right (south on highway 56)after coming up route 41A/64 from Cowan. There are many wonderful natural attractions on Sherwood Road, since it skirts the mountain on the western edge. Natural Bridge is one of nature's many wonders and we are privileged to have it in our midst. It is located off Sherwood Road to the left going toward the town of Sherwood. People have been fascinated with its multi-story high rock bridge structure for many years.

The grove below the bridge was sacred territory during the Indian days. From the bridge, there is a beautiful view looking into Lost Cove. Below the bridge is a mountain spring, where people would go for picnics and family outings when I was a child. There's a cave below the bluff at bridge. Some people say that Indians once lived in the cave.

There is a Pollard Rock sun dial near natural bridge. Mr. Pollard built the sun dial and a stone house near Natural Bridge. Many people would go there just to view the sun dial since it was so unusual to this area.

Natural Bridge, East of Sherwood Road
(From an old post card. Courtesy of Tommy Andrews)

Sewanee has its own castle. It is located near Natural Bridge. The first occupants were the Warner family. The Warners raised peonies and would ship them to florist all over the country. Besides bringing the peonies to the mountain, the Warners also brought the first automobile to the mountain. It was delivered on a railroad car.

After the Warners left Sewanee, the Pattons lived in the castle. Mr. Patton owned a pants' factory at Decherd. The Advents and a man who was associated with the Coors Brewery and his family also lived in the castle at different times. Clara Shoemate ran a club in the castle. Private parties and wedding receptions were held there during Clara's tenure. After many years, the once beautiful castle became old and was in disrepair. It was sold at an auction. People still remember the good ole days at the castle, and the lake near the castle, where they would go for a dip in its cool refreshing waters.

A family named McDowell built a camp off Sherwood Road. Their camp was called "Camp Robin Hood". One year it would be used as a girl's camp and the next year as a boy's camp. I have been told that school was held at the camp. Besides Natural Bridge, Camp Robin Hood, and the castle, Sherwood Road Community also had Ascension Rock and Grace's Shack below St. Mary's.

On the bluff a short distance from Natural Bridge was an area known as Pack Town. It was named for Mr. John Pack. Mr. Pack was an early blacksmith in the area. He would also cut cross ties from Lost Cove and haul them to the railroad station for delivery. He had a team of oxen and was often seen driving the oxen between his cabin and the depot.

There is a story about the Packs in the Franklin County Historical Review, Volume XXVI, 1996. It is titled, "A Log Cabin Welcome." It describes the Pack cabin as being near Gordon's Spring. The Packs were a musical family. Mr. Pack played the fiddle. One of the daughters played a banjo and another member of the family played the accordion. They sang folk songs and hymns. A minister would come to Pack's house to conduct church. At one time, an Indian family lived in a Wigwam near their house.

A small community off Sherwood Road is known as Garner Town. It was named for Samuel Garner. The Garners that live at Garner Town descend from the Garners of Lost Cove. Mose, Sol, and Musidore Garner, the last residents of Lost Cove, were related to the same Garner family. Garners in this area are also related to John Nance Garner, Vice-President of the United States, during President Franklin D. Roosevelt's first two terms. John Nance's family left Tennessee before his birth, settling in Red River County, Texas.

Another attraction off Sherwood Road was man made. It was called the Green Lantern Beer Garden. Uncle Ed Short was the proprietor of the Green Lantern. Besides beer, he served the best food in town. People could also go there to play the pin ball machine and other tavern type games. Since, no intoxicants were sold in the town of Sewanee, the Green Lantern became a popular place to go to for a relaxing evening. Besides the Green Lantern, Uncle Ed owned a store in the village of Sewanee, and was a stone mason who built the front entrance of the Emerald Hodgson Hospital. His rock work can also be seen at O'Dear/St.Mary's Cemetery, where he made a cross to mark the graves of his first wife and baby.

The O'Dear-St.Mary's Cemetery is off Sherwood Road on the right. The original Cemetery was called the Hayes Farm Cemetery. Burial Records in the duPont Library Archives show that two children were buried at Hayes Farm Cemetery. They were Mary Ellen Prince age six years old who died from a fall on January 6, 1877. She was the daughter of Henry and Elizabeth Prince. Mary Jane Van Doran died at age nine on May 18, 1875, from Pneumonia. There are no markers to show their graves sites. The cemetery became know as St. Mary's Cemetery after the Sisters arrived in 1888.

The O'Dear Cemetery was a separate cemetery adjacent to the Hayes Cemetery. James O'Dear was the first to be buried in the cemetery, therefore, the cemetery was named for him. He died in 1883. There was a fence that separated St. Mary's Cemetery from O'Dear Cemetery. The fence was located by Robert Sutherland's grave site. When my great-grandmother, Julia Ann Austin Short, was buried there in 1925, the record of her death at the duPont Library Archives list her as being buried at Sister's Cemetery. All the family know that she was buried in the St. Mary's section of O'Dear Cemetery. The cemetery may have been called Sisters Cemetery, too. The cemetery is now one cemetery called O'Dear/St.Mary's Cemetery. There are many unmarked graves in the cemetery. People with relatives buried there donate money for its up keep.

Some of the people who lived off Sherwood Road were the Castleberrys, Roddys, Janeys, Garners, Minors, Pollards, Warners, Crownovers, Hawkins, Montgomerys, Gipsons, Greens, Smiths, Sells, Sutherlands, Yokleys, Peytons, Mitchells, Terrills, Garners, Shorts, Packs, Hughes, Wises, Kings, O'Dears, Rowseys, Andrews, and Elliotts. There could be others that were missed in my research. [185]

BALL PARK ROAD

Billy Goat Hill stood on Ball Park Road. There are people living at Sewanee who attended Billy Goat Hill School as a child. It stood high on a hill near the Campbell house. The school consisted of four classrooms, two on each side with a hall in the middle. Old timers at Sewanee spoke fondly of Billy Goat Hill School.

Another attraction on Ball Park Road is the ballpark. It has been there for many years. In the 1920's and 30's, there was a baseball team at Sewanee called the Cumberland Mountaineers. Their home games were played at this field. They were the team to beat in Franklin County. Their team was made up of boys who cut cross ties and did manual labor for a living. Many of the other teams in Franklin County didn't have a chance playing against them. They had the muscle power to knock the cover off the ball, and hardly ever lost a game.

The steam laundry was located on Ball Park Road. I remember hearing the whistle blowing at the laundry to let workers know that it was noon, and time for their dinner break. Most of the employees were women. The first laundry in Sewanee was a two-story building. The one I remember is still standing and is now a coin-operated laundry.

John Castleberry's house is located right off Ball Park Road. The Castleberry house is thought to be the oldest house in Sewanee. John Castleberry was a resident of Sewanee when the cornerstone was laid to start the University of the South in 1860. Some information found says that John Castleberry's house was moved from across the highway to its present location. The house was enlarged and the logs were covered with boards.[186] This house may be the one mentioned in books as being the only house still standing in the village of Sewanee after the Civil War.[187] Some older residents say that William Tomlinson's house on Kentucky Avenue was standing after the Civil War, too. These two houses may just be the oldest houses in Sewanee and would date back to the 1860's.

Jabez Hayes' sawmill was located near Ball Park Road. He was a religious man of means who paid for the first Sewanee Village School and Church. They were both called St. Paul's-on-the Mountain. He did much to help the village depot people by providing their first church and school. He also provided jobs for the local residents on his farm and in his businesses near the depot.

The people who lived on Ball Park Road were: the Castleberrys, Campbells, Yates, Reids, Norvells, and Smiths. Luther Smith delivered mail on horseback. His house is still standing on the hill above John Castleberry's house. There were probably other people who lived on Ball Park Road. These were the ones that have been identified as living there.

Billy Goat Hill School, the second public school in Sewanee. Names unknown, ca. 1900.
(Courtesy of Una McBee)

Billy Goat Hill School, the second public school in Sewanee. Names unknown, ca. 1910.
(Courtesy of Una McBee)

SEWANEE PUBLIC SCHOOL

John Henry Castleberry supervised the construction of the Sewanee Public School. The site for the school was in front of St. Paul's Negro Church and School. The Sewanee Public School was built by the Sewanee Civilian Club and operated by Franklin County. The lease for the land on which the school was located was secured from the University of the South on May 12, 1927. The lease was for 33 years and could be renewed for two more equal terms, thus, making it a 99 year lease at $1.00 per annum. The furnishings in the school were provided by the Franklin County School Board.

The school was dedicated on October 4, 1926, which was the beginning of the school year. According to people that attended school there, Mr. Ralph Black was the first principal. At this time, school normally ran from August through March. The total cost of the school was $16, 804. 95.

Mr. Theron Myers became principal of the Sewanee Public School in June of 1927. Some of the teachers who taught at the school at various times were: Bessie Anderson, 1st grade; Felicia Thurgood, 1st grade; Mary Norton Hicks, 1st grade; Lorraine Kennedy 3rd grade; Nellie May Riley, 3rd grade; Elsie Johnson, 4th grade; Mignonne Myers Winn, 4th grade; Mary Kinningham, 5th grade; Sarah Moore 5th grade, 7th grade, and was a librarian. Mr. Hershel Riley was a principal at one time, and he and also taught school. Mr. Bratton was a principal and also taught school there. Lillian Gore was thought to be a principal at Sewanee Public School or Billy Goat Hill. Mr. Myers taught the 9th, 10th, and 11th grades at Sewanee Public School. School went through the 12th grade during the early years. Some teachers taught two grades of school at the same time.[188]

The teachers that I remember from 1949 through 1953 were Mrs. George Harris, 1st grade; Miss Nelly Mae Riley, 2nd and 3rd grades; Mrs. Mignonne Winn, 4th grade; Miss Esther Brasher, 5th grade; Mrs. Pickle Long 6th grade; and Mrs. Fanta Kennedy, Principal. Mrs. Majors and Mr. Fred Langford were teacher and principal when my sister and brother attended school there.

I remember the teachers at Sewanee Public School were very dedicated to their profession. They didn't mind sending you to the principal for a paddling if you misbehaved. Miss Esther Brasher didn't bother sending you to the principal, she could handle a paddle just fine. The teachers seemed to take their jobs seriously, and wanted their students to do well in life. I also remember those loud gobbling turkeys in Mr. Hunt's yard, which was next to the school house. I never ate turkey until I became an adult because of those gobbling turkeys.[189]

Sewanee Public School 1957-58

First Row front to back. Douglas Cameron, Robbie Craig, Arthur Long, Herbert Johnson. 2nd Row, Linda Varnell, Randa Terrill, Clayton McBee, Betty Lou Wilkerson, Mike Reid, Tommy Andrews, 3rd Row, Larry Dykes with eyes closed,Judy Nunley, Chip Keepler, Unknown, Vernon Sutherland, Jerry Jacobs, William Short, Larry Short, 4th Row, Ethel King, Pearl Weaver, Sylvia Fraley, Ann YatesMartha Taylor, Jackie Hawkins, Unknown ? Sumter, Doolie Knott, 5th Row LindaMcBee, David McBee, Mary Frances Rollins, Jane Eire or Eyre, O.L. Knott, EmmettKing, Joe Green, Jimmy Williams standing by Mrs. Mignonne Myers [illegible] and Shirley Jean King. Students of class who are not pictured are Ben Chitty, Jimmy Yates, Mike Winn. Students identified by William Louis Short

THE LAW OFFICERS AT SEWANEE

The first law officer at Sewanee was George Fairbanks. Next was a Colonel Sevier who did the honors when there was a disturbance. In the beginning, the only trouble was from people getting drunk and causing a commotion. Colonel Sevier was a drillmaster and proctor at the University. The proctor also served as town Marshal. [190]

In July of 1882, Vice Chancellor Telfair Hodgson complained about the police powers. He said, "The peace of the University Place was disturbed by a drunken desperado. He (Vice-Chancellor Hodgson) applied to the magistrate for a warrant for his arrest. The magistrate seemed to place every obstacle in the way of issuing the warrant. First, the drunkenness, cursing, and swearing were not indictable. Second, if the warrant was issued, there was no constable to make the arrest. The constable had moved to Cowan. Third, if the arrest was made that he (the desperado) would be released since there was no place of confinement, and no money to pay for sending him to Winchester."

Not to be out maneuvered by the magistrate, Vice Chancellor Hodgson made the arrest himself. The Vice Chancellor then offered to pay to have the desperado kept in jail at Winchester if he was convicted. The desperado was fined $45.00 plus court cost, and was suppose to secure a $250.00 security bond to keep the peace. Being unable to pay the fine or make the bond, the desperado was sent to jail. But was afterwards released upon the payment of $15.00 and didn't have to make the bond. [191]

The McBees have been providing law enforcement for three generations at Sewanee. First was Chief John Wesley McBee. He was the chief in 1911, when President William Howard Taft visited Sewanee. He was tasked with providing protection for President Taft while he was visiting Sewanee. [192]

Later, John Wesley's son, Hayden McBee, became Chief of Police. Hayden organized the first police department. Hayden's dad was referred to as the big chief and he was the little chief. [193] The third generation McBee to be Sewanee's chief of police was Wayne McBee, son of son of Buford "Guinnie" McBee. Wayne is the grandson of John Wesley and nephew of Hayden.

Marion Francis Jackson, a native of Sinking Cove, was sheriff at the University of the South. He was better known as Sheriff Bud Jackson. He became sheriff in 1920. He was hired by Vice-Chancellor Knight to clean up the town.[194] The University was probably experiencing problems with the moonshiners and drunken desperadoes. There was also trouble with armed men coming into the town from the coalmines during the weekends.

Sheriff Jackson had his own problems with the lawbreakers. He survived a hired gun's bullets, a stabbing in the kidney, and was threatened by a man who had just killed the Sheriff of Grundy County. [195] He also gave chase to moonshiners whenever necessary. [196] His son, Harold, said that he never let the lawbreakers get the best of him. He served a long and successful career as the sheriff of Sewanee.

Paul Waggoner from Winchester was Chief of Police for a time, and so was James Barry from the Midway Community. There may have been other law enforcement officers at Sewanee, but these were the only ones known to the writer.

THE GHOST OF SEWANEE

The latest ghost known to have visited Sewanee was the ghostly image of Sister Hughetta in a window at St. Mary's. [197] Sister Hughetta was a beloved nun that helped many people around Sewanee. She was known as a very caring person. Her ghostly image has to be of the friendly kind.

For many years my father tried to figure out the reason for the ghosts that he and his grandmothers encountered. My Dad and his grandmothers, Julia Ann Short and Nancy Barnes, went ginseng digging in Talley's Cove. When they finished getting the ginseng roots, they walked up the mountain and came out at Darnell Field. As they were walking near the old stagecoach road, they saw two stagecoaches coming up the road. They had never seen a stagecoach on that road before, and knew it was almost impossible for a wagon to get up the mountain at that time. They couldn't believe what they were seeing.

As the stagecoaches went by, my Dad could see people inside playing cards. They were laughing and having a good time. He saw the drivers with the reins in their hands, and could hear a whistling sound and saw a cloud of dust as they went by. It all seemed so real as Dad recalled. He was around twelve years old at the time.

When they returned home, my Dad's father, Dave Short, asked my Dad to take him to the place where they saw the stagecoaches. When they arrived at the stagecoach road, there were no signs of tracks or anything visible to show that stagecoaches had just traveled the road. My Dad's father told him that other people have also seen strange things on the same road.

The place where the stagecoaches appeared was near where Barnes Inn once stood. Travelers spent the night there during the 1830's and 40's. Great-Grandpa George Barnes' family ran the Stage Coach Inn, and Grandma Barnes knew the stagecoaches had stopped running many years earlier. The sudden appearance of the stagecoaches puzzled everyone in the family.

Several years later, my Dad had a second encounter with a ghost near the same area. He was coming out of the mountain from where he had been making moonshine. It was late at night and he was alone. He had to cross a barbed wire fence near Darnell Field to get to his house. He had a couple gallons of moonshine in his hands. As he started crossing the fence, a pack of dogs came out of nowhere, and started barking like they were going to eat him up.

He put down his moonshine and got a stick to knock the dogs away, but they kept coming after him. He was hitting at them with his stick and they continued to bark as loud as ever. He felt them come up next to his leg and he kicked at them, but there was nothing there. That is when he started running as fast as he could for his house, leaving the moonshine on the ground for anybody that wanted it.

He never actually saw the dogs, but heard them bark and felt their presence. Dad never went back to that same area again. He assured me that he had not been drinking moonshine before his encounter with the dogs. Those who knew my Dad, knows he wasn't the scary type or a person who would make up such a story.

Grandpa Dave Short encountered a ghost near the old stage coach road, too. Grandpa heard a baby crying and went over to see about it. He saw a red headed baby wrapped in a blanket laying in the under brush. He stooped over to pick it up, but it suddenly disappeared. Grandpa brothers, Reuben and Ed Short, were afraid to go out with him at night, since strange things seemed to happen in his presence. [198] These stories I have heard since my childhood, and everyone who knows about them swear they are all true. Other mountain residents have said that strange things have happened near the old stage coach road, too.

I had a personal experience with an unexplained strange happening at Bob Town as a child. I still remember it clearly. A bunch of us kids from Bob Town went to the Otey Parish for some type activity. This was in the late forties or early fifties. We always went places in a group. That is the only way our parents would allow us to go out at night. As we were coming back home, and going down a big hill near Joe Long's house. We heard foot steps and a tapping that was coming up from behind us. We didn't see anything, but each time we would take a step, the person or thing would also take a step with us. It was very dark night, and we couldn't see anything. After a while, we got scared and started running. We then heard foot steps that seemed like they were coming from the woods on our left side and then behind us. We could hear sounds like someone was running after us. When we stopped, the sound would stop. It was sure scary.

My cousin, Tommy Andrews, had just recovered from a long hospitalization where he had an operation on his leg and back. Two of the older children were holding his hands and trying to help him get down the hill. But, he kept falling and we just left him. Some other kids fell from us running so fast. We didn't know what to do, but run. At first, we thought it was my uncle playing a joke on us. Then we thought it was a crippled man that we all knew. But, my uncle was home all the time, and so was the crippled man. My Dad went looking in the woods near the hill, but he didn't see anything. The children that I remember being in the group with us were Longs, Shorts, and Andrews from Bob Town. There may have been others with us, but those are the ones I remember. The people who were with us still remember the incident, too.

There have been a number of stories printed in the *Purple Sewanee* about ghosts at Sewanee. There was a crying baby, headless dogs, ghostly gownsman, headless gownsman, footsteps following people, a professor walking, and a foaming black horse running by people at night. [199] Some people in Bob Town told about a headless horseman riding around Sewanee at night. There have been so many ghostly sightings on the Sewanee mountain that it seems to be a ghost haven.

AMERICAN LEGION HALL

No story about Sewanee would be complete without telling about the American Legion Hall, since it has been the community's recreation center since 1949.

John Henry Castleberry supervised the construction of the American Legion Hall. Its complete name is the Bonholzer-Campbell Post Number 51 of the American Legion. It was built at Sewanee to provide a place for club meetings, dances, and various other community events. The Community leaders' main concern was to provide wholesome entertainment and recreation for the community as a whole. They were particularly concerned with the young people, who had no place for dances and parties except for the Otey Parish. With the growing population at Sewanee, the Otey Parish became too small to accommodate all the people who wanted to use their building for a function. Therefore, the focus was placed on building an American Legion Hall to accommodate the recreational needs of the community, and as a memorial to the Sewanee people who had served in the armed forces.[200]

The community leaders who were instrumental in making the American Legion Hall become a reality were: H. J. Cardwell, Chairman of the Building Committee, Hayden McBee, acting commander of the Sewanee American Legion post, James F. Merritt, Jr., Adjutant, Gordon Hamilton and Dr. Robert R. Gatling were members of the American Legion.

The World War II Memorial Rock in front of the American Legion Hall was a project carried out by the Woman's Club to provide a suitable memorial to residents of Sewanee, who had served in the armed forces. Sheriff M. F. Jackson donated the rock, and he along with other Sewanee residents donated their time and services to set the rock in place. The plaque on the rock with the inscribed names of people who served in the armed forces and the American Red Cross, was a gift from Vice Chancellor Alexander Guerry's estate.[201]

The Bonholzer-Campbell for which the American Legion Hall took its name were the only two soldiers from Sewanee known to be killed during World War I. Albert Bonholzer was the son of John and Armia Bonholzer. Ernest Campbell was the son of White and Ellen Riley Campbell. Ironically both boys were killed one day apart on the same battlefield, and a few days before Armistice was signed on November 11, 1918, that ended the war.

I have a personal story about Albert Bonholzer and Ernest Campbell. In 1988, my father came to visit me in Belgium. Plans had already been made to take him on sightseeing trips throughout Europe. When we were getting ready to go on these trips, Dad told me the only place he cared about visiting was the cemetery where his friends were buried. He was talking about Albert and Ernest. He went on to tell the story about being some place with them the night before they left for the war. My Dad was eighty-three years old when he came to visit us in Belgium. This was his first trip to Europe.

I had no idea where Ernest and Albert were buried. All the information that Dad had to offer was that his friends were killed in France. A Belgium friend told us to look in Flanders Field Cemetery in Belgium. Ernest and Albert were not buried there, but personnel at the cemetery found a list with their names on it, which also gave the name and location of the cemetery where they were buried. Dad was thrilled that we finally found them, however, the cemetery turned out to be in the Argonne Forest of France, which was quite a distance from our home in Belgium.

We learned that the area where Ernest and Albert were buried was near Verdun Battlefield where they probably died. Memorial Crosses like the one on the Sewanee Mountain can be seen throughout this area of France. Their graves are marked with white crosses running in perfect rows in the immaculate American Memorial Cemetery of Meuse Argonne. The cemetery is in a huge peaceful looking park where fourteen thousand Americans soldiers are now resting.[202]

It meant more for Dad to visit the graves of those fallen soldiers than it did to see the Eiffel Tower or Notre Dame. The highlight of his trip to Europe was visiting the graves of his friends from Sewanee who had paid the ultimate price for our freedom. When he returned to Sewanee he took pictures of their graves to some of their family members.

I am sure there are many people at Sewanee who have their own stories about the American Legion Hall. I remember that my older sister, Josephine, would look forward to the Saturday night square dances there One time Mama and Daddy made her take me along, and that's when I found out that she had a boy friend. He came from Alto, and she would meet him at the square dance every Saturday night. Mama and Daddy didn't know she was seeing a boy at the dances, since she wasn't allowed to date. Her other friends were seeing boys there, too. It was a meeting place for the young.

I enjoyed watching the people out on the floor square dancing and having fun. I remember that Mr. Tomes was the best square dancer around. There was a band that played square dance music there. Some of the music they were playing, we now call "Blue Grass." I think there was a fiddle player and two guitar players, plus a square dance caller. My sister and her friends were always out on the floor dancing, and never seemed to want the music to stop playing.

I looked forward to the Easter egg hunts and Halloween parties at the American Legion Hall. They gave the best gifts. I always tried to find a prize egg. One year, I did find the golden egg after many years of hunting for it. I remember that it was on top of the memorial rock. Then, one year, my brother, William, won first prize for his Halloween costume. His prize was a cowboy suit with guns and all. He was only around six or seven years old at the time, and he really loved that cowboy suit. The people who were in charge of the American Legion Hall went out of their way to make sure the activities for the children were the best they could offer, and the prizes were always great.[203]

UNIQUE PLACES IN AND AROUND SEWANEE

The beauty of the mountain was meant to be preserved in the design and construction of both the University of the South and the town of Sewanee. Many of these sites were named for early residents, land owners, to honor donors, and to identify terrain features. Locations not already mentioned in other stories are as follows: Bridal Veil Falls; Morgan's Steep; Proctor's Hall; Otey View; Elliot Point; Rutledge Point; Dotson Point; Thumping Dick Hollow; The Elbow; Breakefield Road; High Top View; Armfield Bluff Horror Hole; Polk Lookout; Five Points; Cherry Point; Point of Disappointment; Annie Rock; Slaughter Pen Rock; Hat Rock; High Top View; Natural Bridge; Green's View; Hawkins Cove; Rowarks Cove; Tally's Cove; Love Cove; Dry Cave; Wet Cave; Grape Vine Cave; Sewanee Military Academy; St. Andrews; Abbo's Alley; Fiery Gizzard, Two Mile Branch; Ricketts Springs; Bill Rose Branch; and Running Knob Hollow. Even though Sewanee is a small town, it is filled with interesting places to visit, and numerous mountain trails, water falls, and caves to explore. The Sewanee Mountain is one of God's masterpieces. It is nature at it very best.

Point of Disappointment, located in Bob Town
(From an old post card. Courtesy of Tommy Andrews)

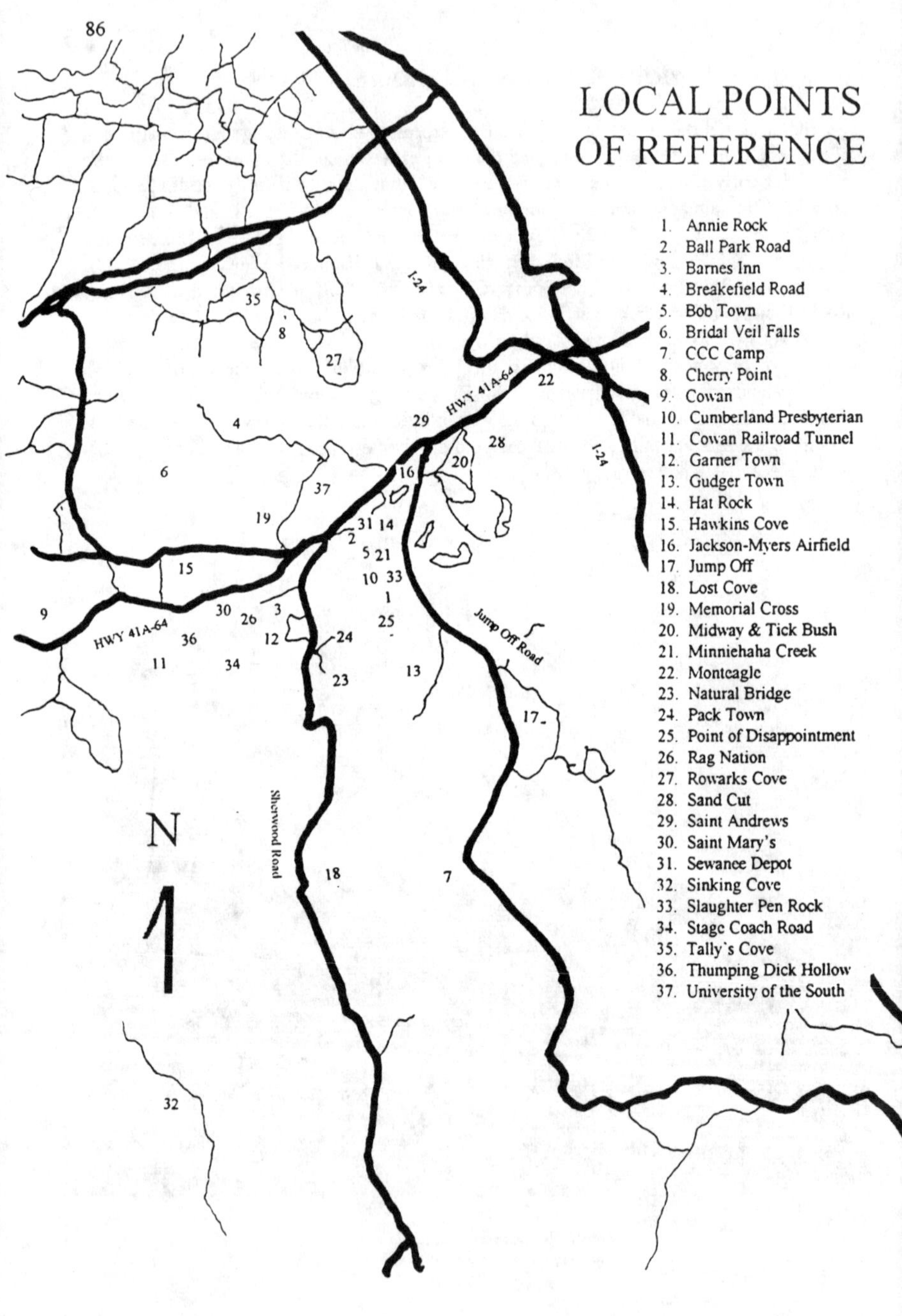

LOCAL POINTS OF REFERENCE
1. Annie Rock
2. Ball Park Road
3. Barnes Inn
4. Breakefield Road
5. Bob Town
6. Bridal Veil Falls
7. CCC Camp
8. Cherry Point
9. Cowan
10. Cumberland Presbyterian
11. Cowan Railroad Tunnel
12. Garner Town
13. Gudger Town
14. Hat Rock
15. Hawkins Cove
16. Jackson-Myers Airfield
17. Jump Off
18. Lost Cove
19. Memorial Cross
20. Midway & Tick Bush
21. Minniehaha Creek
22. Monteagle
23. Natural Bridge
24. Pack Town
25. Point of Disappointment
26. Rag Nation
27. Rowarks Cove
28. Sand Cut
29. Saint Andrews
30. Saint Mary's
31. Sewanee Depot
32. Sinking Cove
33. Slaughter Pen Rock
34. Stage Coach Road
35. Tally's Cove
36. Thumping Dick Hollow
37. University of the South
86
I-24
HWY 41A-64
Jump Off Road
Sherwood Road
N

STONE MASONS, CARPENTERS, AND MANUAL LABORERS

People who have driven up University Avenue and see all those magnificent gothic style buildings gracing the whole mountain top campus are in awe of its beauty. It's like looking at a picture of Cambridge or Oxford University in England.

Those beautiful buildings were created out of Sewanee Mountain sandstone by masterpiece stone masons, carpenters, and manual laborers. The first known stone masons at Sewanee were listed in the 1880 census records. They were: Frank and Reuben Short, their brother-in-law, William "Buck" Thomas, P. Tate Statem, and R. J. Gillespie. Frank Short was the master stone mason in charge of the others. One of his first projects was constructing the first freight sandstone depot.

Besides the stone masons, the carpenters and manual labors had a lot to do with building the town of Sewanee and the University of the South. The earliest carpenters listed in the 1870 census records were: W. McCoy, Frank Marquet, Frank and John Pratt. Elick Johnson, Peter Foster, and Claiborne Rose were the manual laborers, and R. J. Gillespie was listed as a plasterer.

The carpenters at Sewanee during 1880 were: J. B. and Robert Jackson, Andrew Short, J. W. Bennett, J. G. McAllister, Joseph Amstutz, William and Virgil Guthrie, and E. J. Todd. General laborers were: John Gipson, Alex Tripp, Samuel Sutherland, Clay Buchanan, Jacob Foster, F. Nipper, Jack Arnett, Samuel Garner, William Ladd, and John Statem.

This is just a sprinkling of the early builders of Sewanee. There are many, many more unknown to the writer. My father, Reece Short, told me that Mr. James "White" Campbell was one of the master stone masons while he was working at the University of the South quarry. Later on Will Campbell, son of White, was the master stone mason at the University of the South. Mr. White Campbell and his masons would get out railroad cars full of Sewanee sandstone to be sent to other areas of the state.

I do know that Berry Gipson, Tommy Pack, J. C. Wise, Ed Yates, John Hawkersmith, Edward and Reece Short, Wallace Pack, Fred and Carl Reid, White and Will Campbell, Buck King, Thomas Hamilton, and Felix Long were all stone masons at Sewanee and helped construct buildings throughout the University of the South. Carl Reid was the master stone mason for the construction of All Saints Chapel.

There are many more stone masons, carpenters, and manual laborers unknown to the public, but their work is well documented in the stones. There is no other place quite like Sewanee, and most everyone credits its magnificent stone structures as being the main ingredient in its splendor. Everyone should be proud of what happened at Sewanee. Bishop Polk and Bishop Quintard are probably smiling down from heaven at all those people who made their dream of a church university, and a town come to life in a dense rugged forest. They probably never dreamed it would be such a magnificant creation.

Stone masons working at University of the South stone quarry. Left to right, (Standing): Doug Vaughn (University Treasurer), Will Campbell (Master Stone Mason), Ed Yates, and Mr. Nimitz (from University), (Sitting): Tommy Pack, J.C. Wise, Berry Gipson, and John Hawkersmith. Date unknown. (Courtesy of Louise Terrill, step-daughter of Will Campbell)

ALL SAINTS CHAPEL

According to Men who made Sewanee by Guerry and Chittys. "Beginning in 1903, when the Chaplain (William Alexander Guerry) first conceived of the possibility that the time had come to build the new stone chapel, he traveled from North Carolina to Texas seeking funds for building All Saints. The first plans of which had been drawn by his wife's brother, Silas McBee. McBee was an editor with a vocation in architecture."

"It was left to a successor, Bishop of South Carolina, Thomas N. Carruthers, to hold the first service in the completed building 55 years after ground was broken in 1904."

The stained glass in All Saints chapel depicts the history of the University of the South and Sewanee. There is a set of four stained glass windows with twenty-four panels dedicated to its history. They are located in the narthex of the chapel. One of the window panels depict Bishop Polk and his fellow bishops making plans for their church university. It shows the blowing up of the cornerstone by the union soldiers during the Civil War. It also shows Will Campbell, a Sewanee stone mason, working on the chapel. He worked there in 1904, and was still there for the final product fifty-five years later. The stained glass also depicts Thomas Hamilton working on the Memorial Cross. It depicts a donor, and Woodrow Wilson's doctor, who was a student at the University of the South.

The stain glass windows, like the building, are a masterpiece. The windows were designed by Arthur Erridge of Exeter, England and George L. Payne of Patterson, New Jersey. The glass was installed by Geza Zelinka who came from New Jersey. The photographs that depict the events and people were obtained from the University Archives and from descendants of people who are depicted in the stain glass panels.

From the beginning, the University of the South had to rely upon donations. There have been many generous donors throughout the years. One such donor was Tennessee Williams who left the bulk of his estate to the University of the South. His grandfather, Reverend Walter E. Dakin, attended the divinity school at Sewanee in 1895. There was an heiress from New York that left the University five million dollars, and had only visited the school on one occasion. Donations have played an important part in the University being able to keeps its doors open since 1868.

Ironically, Winchester Female Academy, Mary Sharp College, and Carrick Academy were all established schools in Winchester before the University of the South was created. They are no longer in existence. But, the church university built in the midst of a wilderness is still alive, and is one of the best in the nation.

The above information was taken from: MEN WHO MADE SEWANEE by Moultrie Guerry, Arthur Ben and Elizabeth N. Chitty, The University Press, Sewanee, Tennessee, 1981, page 107; THE LIVING CHURCH, History in Stain Glass, March 12, 1961 issue, page 15-17; SEWANEE, HOW I LOVE YOU, Time Magazine, April 4, 1983, page 67.

All Saints' Chapel. Construction began 1904 and was completed in 1955. The original design was by Silas McBee.
(Courtesy of Steve Makris, 1970)

PEOPLE LIVING AT SEWANEE IN 1870

The following census records give the names, sex, color, age, occupation, and place of birth for each person at Sewanee. Starting with 1880 census, I also list the relationship to head of household. M/is male, F/is female, W/is white, B/is black, MU/is mulatto.

1. MORRIS, T.A., M/W, age 49, Minister born on Ohio. (Thomas Morris)
   Ellen, F/W, age 37, born North Carolina.
   Saley, F/W, age 11, born Alabama
   Ida, F/W, age 9, born Tenn. .
   Thomas, M/W, age 6, born Ohio.
   Armie, F/W, age 3. born Ohio.
   Emma, F/W, born Sept. 1869 in Tenn.
   Walker, E., M/MU, age 26, laborer, born Tenn.
   Morgan, Edmon, M/B, age 48, laborer, born in Alabama.
   Hamton, Carline, F/W, age 35, domestic servant, born Alabama.
   Higgs, Lousind, F/W, age 16, servant, born in Alabama.
2. FAREBANKS, G., M/W, age 50, Retired Lawyer, born Tenn.
   Susan , F/W, age 43, born N.C.
   Florid, F/W, (Flora) age 21 born N.Y.
   Write (Wright), Ann, F/W, age 17, born Florida.
   Charles, F/W, age 20, laborer, born Florida.
   Sarah, F/W, age 12 born Florida.
   Susan, F/W, age 17, born Tenn.
   Eva Lee, F/W, age 5 born Georgia.
   Rulell, Louis, M/B, age 70, servant, born Virginia.
   Susanner, F/B, age 60, born Virginia.
   Hawkins, H., M/B, 40, laborer, born Tenn.
   Marior, F/B, age (30?)born Tenn.
   Margret, F/B, age 14, born Tenn.
   James, M/B, age 5, born Tenn.
   Moley, F/B, age 3, born Tenn.
   William, M/B, age 1, born Tenn.
   Agness, F/B, age 15, born Tenn.
3. JOHNSON, ELICK, M/B, age 40, laborer, born Tenn.
   Katey, F/B, age 30, born Tenn.
   Hariet, F/B, age 17, born Tenn.
   Jane, F/B, age 12, born Tenn.
   Mary, F/B, age 10, born Tenn.
4. COTTON, SARAH, F/W, age 49, house keeper, born N.C. (ran Otey Hall)
   Thomas W., M/B, age 45, laborer, born Tenn.
   Prince, Abet (Albert?), M/B, age 30, laborer, born Tenn.
   Stewart, M/B, age 30, cook in restaurant, born Tenn.
   Gennet, F/B, age 12, born Tenn.
   Fred, M/B, age 10, born Tenn.
5. PHELAN, JOHN, M/W, age 61, Retired Lawyer, born N.J.
   Presilia, F/W, age 22, born Alabama.
   Mary, F/W, age 20, born Alabama.
   Aer, F/W, age 17, born Alabama.
   Sidney, M/W, age 16, Civil Engineer, born Alabama.
   James, M/W, age 10, born Alabama.
   Lacey, F/B, age 35, cook, born Alabama.
   Sofey, F/MU, age 13, born Alabama.
   Dorey, F/MU, age 10, born Alabama.
   Fred, M/MU, age 4, born Alabama.
   William, M/MU, born October 1869.
6. GREEN, WILLIAM, M/W, age 72, Minister, born N. C.(Bishop of Mississippi.)
   Berkley, M/W, age 29, Teacher, born N.C.
   George, M/B, age 28, born N.C.
   Elizabeth (Lily), F/W, age 32, born N.C. (established Kendall Hall)
   Wells, Elick, M/B, age 50, Laborer, born N.C.
   Rachel, F/B, age 40, Cook, born Virginia.
   Henry, F/B, age 16, born Virginia.
   Ann, F/B, age 14, born Virginia.
   Richard, M/B, age 6, born Virginia.
   Ruthlege, William, M/B, Laborer, born Tenn.
   Estill, Faney, F/B, age 27, cook, born TN.
   Emmer, F/B, age 20, born Tenn.
   Comfort, F/B, age 67, born Tenn.
   George, M/B, age 4, born Tenn.
   Robins, Charley, M/B, age 35, Carpenter, born Tenn.
   Johnson, Loyd, M/B, age 50, Shoemaker, born Tenn.
   Hill, Sarah, F/W, age 46, born Alabama.
7. POKE, ELIZABETH, F/W, age 40, born N.C. (actually Polk)
   Irene, F/W, age 14, born Louisiana.
   Lucey, F/M, age 12, born Tenn.
   Eliza, F/M, age 7, born Tenn.
   Thomas, M/W, age 4, born Tenn.
   Maze, Sarah, F/B, age 30, Cook, born Tenn.
   Laura F/B, age 13, born Tenn.

Andrew, M/B, age 11, born Tenn.
George, M/B, age 9, born Tenn.
Guinn, John, M/B, age 30, laborer, born Tenn.
Colyer, Bell, F/B, age 25, born Tenn.

8 PRATT, FRANK, M/W, age 37, Carpenter, born Tenn.
Sarah, F/W, age 35, born Tenn.
Arther, M/W, age 6, born Georgia.
Philip, M/W, age 4, born Tenn.
Cornelius M/W, age 1, born Tenn.
John M/W, born May 1870, in Tenn.

9 PRATT, JOHN, M/W, age 34, Carpenter, born Tenn.
Jane, F/W, age 33, born Tenn.

10. THOMAS, LOUISA, F/B, age 35. Washer, born Tenn.
William, M/B, age 4, born Tenn.

11. FOSTER, PETER, M/W, age 57, Laborer, born Ireland.
Catherine, F/W, age 57, born Ireland.

12. NOAKS, GEORGE, M/W, age 38, born Tenn. (could be Noah)
Evaline, F/W, age 60, born Tenn.

13. BURKS, J. H. M/W, age 25, a tinner, born N.Y.
Julier, F/W, age 25, born France.
Frank, M/W, age 3, born N.Y.
Joseph, M/W, age 2, born N.Y.
William, M/W, born 1870, in Tenn.
Crussan, Mary, F/W, age 18, born Pennsylvania.

14. COTTON, J.M. , M/W, age 27, Post Master, born Tenn.
Sarah, F/W, age 24, born Mississippi.

15. ARNELL, JAMES, M/W, age 55, Farmer, born Tenn.
Mornin, F/W, age 55, born Tenn.
Tricia, F/W, age 21, born Tenn.
Mary, F/W, age 18, born Tenn.
William, M/W, age 17, born Tenn.
John, M/W, age 12, born Tenn.
Sherill, Sarah, F/W, age 3, born Tenn.

16. BERRY, JOHN, M/W, age 29, Railroad Boss, born Tenn.
Rachel, F/W, age 24, born Tenn. (Rachel Garner Berry)
Nancy, F/W, age 11, born Tenn.
William, M/W, age 7, born Tenn.
Pauline, F/W, age 2, born Tenn.

17. THOMAS, GEORGE, M/W, age 24, Laborer on railroad, born Tenn.
Rachel, F/W, age 24, born Tenn.
William, M/W, age 4, born Tenn.
Mary, F/W, age 1, born Tenn.

18. WILEY, JOHN, M/W, age 19, born Tenn.
Sarah, F/W, age 21, born Tenn.

19. SHORT, DAVID, M/W, age 41, Farmer, born Georgia.
Mary, F/W, age 35, born Tenn.
Rufus, M/W, age 16, born Alabama.
Mary F/W, age 12, born Tenn.
Jessie, M/W, age 10, born Tenn.
William, M/W, age 6, born Tenn.

20. SMITH, ANDREW, M/W, age 52, Farmer, born Tenn.
Sarah, F/W, age 37, born Georgia.
Margaret, F/W, age 16, born Tenn.
William, M/W, age 13, born Tenn.
Mary, F/W, age 10, born Tenn.
Sarah, F/W, age 6, born Tenn.
Pauline, F/W, age 2, born Tenn.

21. ANDERSON, BIRD, M/W, age 55, Farmer, born Tenn.(Albert Anderson)
Rebecca, F/W, age 54, born Tenn. (Mary Rebecca Anderson)
David, M/W, age 19, Laborer on farm, born Tenn.
Sarah, F/W, age 18, born Tenn.
Rachel, F/W, age 17, born Tenn.
Martha, F/W, age 14, born Tenn.
John, M/W, age 12, born Tenn.
James, M/W, age 11, born Tenn.

22. ANDERSON, JOHN, M/W, age 21, born Tenn.
Elizabeth, F/W, age 20, born Tenn. (nee: Elizabeth Winford)

23. GARNER, WILLIAM, M/W, age 80, Farmer, born Georgia.
Delitha, F/W, age 60, born N.C.
Andrew, M/W, age 17, laborer on farm, born Tenn.

24. GARNER, JOHN, M/W, age 21, Laborer on railroad, born Tenn.
Margaret, F/W, age 21, born Tenn.(nee: Kelly ?)
Philadelphia, F/W, age 3, born Tenn.
William, M/W, age 1, born Tenn.

25. PARTON, JANE, F/W, age 50, born S.C. (May be Partin instead of Parton)
Simpson, M/W, age 17, Laborer on railroad, born Georgia.
Wells, Sarah, F/W, age 57, born S.C.
Greeter, Betsey, F/W, age 40, born Tenn.

26. HILL, WILLIAM, M/W, age 26, Laborer on railroad, born Tenn.
Martha, F/W, age 25, born Georgia.
John, M/W, age 4, born Tenn.

27. FARRIS, FLETCHER, M/W, age 57, Laborer on farm, born Tenn.
Martha, F/W, age 52, born Tenn. (Martha Henley Farris)
Catherine, F/W, age 20, born Tenn.
John, M/W, age 16, born Tenn.
Tenn., F/W, age 15, born Tenn.
Rathimore, F/W, age 12, born Tenn.
28. KELLY, ABRAM, M/W, age 58, Butcher, born Tenn.
Martha, F/W, age 48, born Tenn.
Ruth, F/W, age 12, born Tenn.
William, M/W, age 6, born Tenn.
Crusan, John, M/W, age 17, laborer on farm, born Pennsylvania.
Pack, Penesia, M/W, age 39, laborer on railroad, born Alabama.
Mary, F/W, age 17, born Alabama,.
Pack or Pace, Sarah, F/W, age 21, born Georgia.
James, M/W, age 5, born Tenn.
Murphy, W., M/W, age 32, born Georgia.
William, M/W, born October 1869.
Smith, W., M/W, age 18, born Tenn.
Barnet, T. M. , M/W, age 16, born Alabama.
29. GILLIAM, T.S., M/W, age 16, born Alabama.
McCoy, W, M/W, age 16, Carpenter, born Louisiana.
Greenhew, W. M/W, age 18, born Tenn.
Gray, C. M., M/W, age 20, born Tenn..
J. R., M/W, age 17, born Tenn.
Hawkins, James, M/W, age 16, born Alabama.
Rucker, R.W., M/W, age 20, born Texas.
Sherwood, R.W., M/W, age 20, born Pennsylvania.
Briars, F.M., M/W, age 16, laborer, born Alabama.
Roberts, L., M/W, age 32, laborer on farm, born Alabama.
Gillespie, R. J. M/W, age 21, Plasterer, born Tenn.
Phillips, Ezekial, M/W, age 29, Plasterer, born Tenn.
30. JONES, ELIZABETH, F/W, age 40, born Alabama.
Martha, F/W, age 20, born Alabama.
Frances, F/W, age 20, born Alabama.
Joseph, M/W, age 4, born Tenn.
Patsy, F/W, age 2, born Tenn.
Mase, David, M/B, age 30, Laborer, born Tenn.
Hawkins, J., M/W, age 19, born Alabama.
31. HILL, MARION, M/W, age 27, born Tenn.
Sarah, F/W, age 30, born Tenn.
Allen, M/W, age 6, born Tenn.
William, M/W, age 2, born Tenn.
Coker, Martha, F/W, age 18, born Tenn.
32. GIBSON, ALLEN, M/W, age 19, laborer on farm, born Tenn.
Lucinda, F/W, age 24, born Tenn.
33. SEVIER, T.S., M/W, age 38, School Teacher, born Kentucky. (Theodore Sevier)
Mary, F/W, age 28, born Texas.
Frank, M/W, age 8, born Georgia.
Louisa, F/W, age 2, born Alabama.
Charley, M/W, born 1869 or 70, in Tenn.
Douglas, Mines, M/W, age 53, born Tenn.
Benton, Mary, F/W, age 74, born Tenn.
Gorden, Mike, M/B, age 51, laborer, born Georgia.
Taylor, Edward, M/B, age 30, laborer, born Tenn.
Hoge, S.C., M/W, age 31, clerk in store, born Alabama. (Samuel Hoge).
34. THOMLINSON, W., M/W, age 52, farmer, born N.C.(William Thomlinson)
Sarah, F/W, age 50, born S.C.
William, M/W, age 23, merchant, born S.C.
Farebanks, G., M/W, age 37, laborer, born is S.C.
Hariet F/W, age 37, born N.C.
Crenshaw, H. F/B, age 15, born S.C.
Louisa, F/B, age 5, born Georgia.
Sarah, F/B, age 2, born Tenn.
35. GILLIAM, MARY, F/W, age 43, housekeeper, born Tenn.
Castleberry, A., F/W, age 33, housekeeper, born Georgia.
James, M/W, age 31, Carpenter, born Georgia.
36. ROSE, CLABORN, M/W, age 52, laborer, born Tenn.
Amanda, F/W, age 53, born Kentucky.
37. CASTLEBERRY, R., F/W, age 30, born Tenn.
Sarah, F/W, age 10, born Tenn.
Virginia, F/W, age 4, born Tenn.
Jane, F/W, age 1, born Tenn.
38. GIBSON, ALLEN, M/W, age 65, Merchant, born S.C.
Minerva, F/W, age 33, born Tenn. (Minerva Garner Gibson)
Mary, F/W, age 17, born Tenn.
Delitha, F/W, age 13, born Tenn.
Thomas, M/W, age 11, born Tenn.
Jane , F/W, age 7, born Tenn.
Dolly, F/W, age 3, born Tenn.

39. GIBSON, ANDREW, M/W, age 45, Farmer, born Tenn.
Betsy, F/W, age 34, born Tenn. (nee: Elizabeth Hill)
John, M/W, age 25, farm laborer, born Tenn.
Johnson M/W, age 19, farm laborer, born Tenn.
Ann, F/W, age 17, born Tenn.
Manervie, F/W, age 15, born Tenn.
Andrew, M/W, age 13, born Tenn.
George, M/W, age 11, born Tenn.
Nancy, F/W, age 8, born Tenn.
James, F/W, age 5, born Tenn.
40. ANDERSON, W., M/W, age 32, painter, born N.Y.
Jane, F/W, age 28, born Georgia.
Sarah, F/W, age 7, born Tenn.
41. CRESET, SIMON, M/W, age 51, Tailor, born France.
Mary, F/W, age 51, born France.
Louis, M/W, age 24, laborer, born N.Y.
Henry, M/W, age 22, laborer on farm, born N.Y.
George, M/W, age 17, born N.Y.
Edward, M/W, age 14, born N.Y.
42. MARQUET, JOSEPHEN, F/W, age 50, born France.
Frank, M/W, age 23, Carpenter, born France.
Guest, M/W, age 20, laborer on farm, born France.
43. HELTON, JAMES, M/W, age 36, Carpenter, born Tenn.
Jane, F/W, age 75, born South Carolina.
Arnell, James, M/W, age 29, laborer on farm, born Tenn.
Lucinda, F/W, age 29, born Tenn.
Nancy, F/W, age 4, born Tenn.
Robert, M/W, born January 1870, in Tenn.
44. ROBERTS, HANCE, M/W, age 50, farmer, born Tenn.
Mary, F/W, age 44, born Tenn. (Mary Lynch Roberts)
Ross (Roberts?), John, M/W, age 27, Carpenter, born Tenn.
Swiney, Thomas, M/W, age 28, laborer on farm, born N.Y.
Roberts, Juley, F/W, age 76, born Tenn. (Hance's mother).
45. O'DEAR, JAMES, M/W, age 76, Blacksmith, born Tenn.
Malinda, F/W, age 50, born Tenn.
Sarah, F/W, age 26, born Tenn.
Betty, F/W, age 24, born Tenn.
Susan, F/W, age 20, born Tenn.
Susan, F/W, age 7, born Tenn.
Dick, M/W, age 6, born Tenn.
John, M/W, age 4, born Tenn.
46. COX, WILLIAM, M/W, age 26, Laborer on railroad, born Georgia.
Cansady, F/W, age 23, born Alabama.
Mary, F/W, age 1, born Tenn.
George, M/W, born January 1870 in Tenn.
Walraven, W., M/W, age 17, Laborer on railroad, born Tenn.
47. MALONE, THOMAS, M/W, age 22, Laborer on railroad, born Tenn.
Margaret, F/W, age 27, born Alabama.
48. SHORT, RUBEN, M/W, age 22, born Tenn.
Ann, F/W, age 2, born Tenn.
Reuben, M/W, age 1, born Tenn.
Martha, F/W, age 1, born N.C.
49. WEAVER, PATTON, M/W, age 39, Laborer on railroad, born Tenn.
Mary, F/W, age 39, born Tenn. (Mary Gibson, Austin Mcknight)
50. BOHANNON, W., M/W, age 20, laborer on railroad., born Tenn. (Wm. E.)
Nancy, F/W, age 20, born Tenn.(nee: Nancy Ann Smith)
Thomas, M/W, age 2, born Tenn.
51. BASS, M., M/W, age 17, Laborer on railroad, born Tenn.
Eliser, F/W, age 17, born Tenn.
McNite (McKnight), Nancy, F/W, age 17, born Tenn.
Peggy, F/W, age 1, born Tenn. (Hill is her surname).
52. SHORT, ANDREW, M/W, age 19, Laborer on railroad, born Tenn.
Lizey, F/W, age 21, born Tenn. (Elizabeth Linsey)
David, M/W, born 1870, in Tenn.
Short, J., M/W, age 21, Laborer on railroad, born Georgia.
53. SHORT, FRANKLIN M., M/W, age 36, Laborer on railroad, born Georgia.
Alis, F/W, age 28, born Georgia.
Columbus, M/W, age 12, born Tenn.
54. BRUCE, ROBERT, M/W, age 23, Laborer, born Georgia.
Emaline, F/W, age 19, born Georgia.
55. MARTIN, SPENCER, M/B, age 43, laborer on farm, born Alabama.
Margaret, F/B, age 40, born Alabama,.
Albert, M/B, age 4, born Alabama.
John, M/B, age 3, born Tenn.
Aaron, M/B, born 1870, Tenn.
Mulagan, R., F/B, age 70, born Maryland.

56 GILLIAM, PLEASANT, M/W, age 51, merchant, born Tenn.
Caroline, F/W, age 43, born Tenn. (Caroline Lide Gilliam)
Martha, F/W, age 14, born Tenn.
Thomas, M/W, age 13, born Tenn.
Mary, F/W, age 11, born Tenn.
James, M/W, age 8, born Tenn.
Ida, F/W, age 7, born Tenn.
Sergeant, F/W, age 30, cook, born TN.
Lide, Mary, F/W, age 67, born Tenn. (Caroline's mother).
Stuart, J.M., M/W, age 22, telegraph operator, born Tenn.

57 JORDAN, T. M/W, age 42, Grocer, born Tenn.
Mary, F/W, age 19, born Tenn.

58 HAWKINS, JOHN, M/W, age 40, Farmer, born Tenn.
Mary, age 35, F/W, born Tenn.
John, M/W, age 33, Laborer, born TN.
Janey, F/W, age 35, born Tenn.
Betty, F/W, age 18, born Tenn.
Laura, F/W, age 12, born Tenn.
Clara, F/W, age 11, born Tenn.
Sarah, F/W, age 9, born Tenn.

59. PORTER, CHARLIE, M/W, age 51, Engineer on railroad, born Tenn.
Eliser, F/W, age 22, born Virginia.
John, M/W, age 1, born Alabama.
Whitesides, Fanny, F/W, age 24, Domestic Servant, born Alabama.

60. HAWKINS, S.M., M/W, age 41, Farmer, born Alabama. (Samuel M. Hawkins)
Jane, F/W, age 18, born Tenn.
John, M/W, age 17, born Tenn.
Mary, F/W, age 30, born Tenn.
Fanny, F/W, age 11, born Tenn.
Nancy, F/W, age 6, born Tenn.
Brasier, Linda, F/W, 41, housekeeper, born Tenn.
Dick, M/W, born March 1870 in Tenn.

61. SARGANT, JAMES, M/W, age 37, Farmer, born Tenn.
Sarenia, F/W, age 41, born Tenn.
Margaret, F/W, age 28, born Tenn.
Sarah, F/W, age 27, born Tenn.
John, M/W, age 24, born Tenn.
James, M/W, age 18, born Tenn.
Mattie, F/W, age 17, born Tenn.
George, M/W, age 14, born Tenn.
Virginia, F/W, age 12, born Tenn.
Fanny, F/W, age 9, born Tenn.

62. WILLIAMS, LENT M/W, age 61, Farmer, born Tenn. (son of Sherrod)
Violet, F/W, age 48, born Tenn. (Violet McIllheran Williams)
John, M/W, age 48, farmer, born TN.
Peggy, F/W, age 19, born Tenn.
Susan, F/W, age 17, born Tenn.
Phillip, M/W, age 15, born Tenn.
Sarah, F/W, age 13, born Tenn.
Terry, F/W, age 7, born Tenn.

STUDENTS ATTENDING SCHOOL AT SEWANEE IN 1870

1. HARRIS, DREW, age 16, born Florida.
2. BEARD, GEORGE, age 18, born Florida.
3. RANDOLPH, C., age 17, born Florida.
4. MUDD, W., age 20, born N.J.
5. FARMER, age 15, born Kentucky.
6. HAWK, J. age 15, born Pennsylvania.
7. RECU, E., age 17, born Georgia.
8. DOW, C.D., age 17, born Georgia.
9. STOUT, W., age 16, born Alabama.
10.STOUT, J, age 14, born Alabama.
11. HILL, A.C., age 17, born Louisiana.
12. LIGHT, W., age 15, born Louisiana.
13. ROPTER, W., age 16, born Alabama.
14. HAMEN, D.B., age 18, born Georgia.
15. SPYKER, D, age 15, born Indiana.
16. BRINKLEY, M., age 15, born MS.
17. CAMTIN, E. age 14, born Alabama.
18. GREEN, W. age 18, born Georgia.
19. ROBERTSON, J., age 18, born TN.
20. DULANEY, M., age 16, born Alabama.
21. HOLCOMB, J., age 18, born Tenn.
22. KING, H. , age 16, born Virginia.
23. STONE, B. age 19, born Tenn.
24. COUFFER, T.B., age 16, born PA.
25. TURNEY, TOM, age 11, born Virginia.
26. HOLCOMB, Y., age 18, born N.J.
27. HERLAND, W. age 16, born Texas.
28. HILL, W., age 15, born Tenn.
29. CADE, O. age 17, born Louisiana.
30. PIERS, W.H., age 18, born Florida.
31. TURNBUL, D.E., age 13, born Florida.
32. PHILLIPS, W. age 19, born Florida.
33. WEATHERBY, H. age 16, born AL.
34. TROUPER, H.G. age 14, born Alabama.
35. COOK, B. D., age 16, born Mississippi.
36. MIX, H.A., age 16, born N.Y.
37. TURNBULL, W., age 12, born Alabama.
38. TURNBULL, D., age 16, born Alabama.
39. WHITSON, J., age 14, born Alabama.
40. NAPIER, J. age 16, born Texas.
41. SHOUP, G., age 17, born Mississippi.
42. SMITH, M. age 18, born Mississippi.
43. SMITH, O.E. age 15, born Mississippi.
44. WEATHERBY, C., age 17, born AL.
45. CHILTERY, S. age 19, born Mississippi.
46. CADE, E. age 19, born Mississippi.
47 WHITESIDES, S., age 15, born MS.
48. TUCKER, J., age 18, born Alabama.
49. WILLIAMS, S. age 15, born Florida.
50. PHILLIPS, E., age 16, born Mississippi.
51. BROOKS, B. age 13, born Tenn.
52. PEARS, W., age 16, born Texas.
53. MURPHY, J., age 15, born Mississippi.
54. OLDHAM, R. age 14, born Tenn.
55. HOOD, B., age 13, born Louisiana.
56. HOOD, A. age 13, born Louisiana.
57. FINLEYSON, K., age 11, born Alabama.
58. FINLEYSON, E., age 15, born Texas.
59. DAVIS, R.H., age 12, born Mississippi.
60. DBORDHAM, P., age 16, born Louisiana.
61. BARNETT, D.R. age 18, born Texas.
62. BARTLEY, S. age 17, born Alabama.
63. CLAYTON, A., age 16, born Georgia.
64. POPE, J. G., age 16, born N.C.
65. HODGTON, H. age 19, born Georgia.
66. HUTCHINS, E. age 14, born Tenn.
67. MILES, C., age 18, born Alabama.
68. MILES, B. age 17, born Georgia.
69. WHITE, B., age 14, born N.C.

In 1870, there were sixty-two households and sixty nine students living at Sewanee. Bishop Quintard was living there, however, his name did not appear on the census. Perhaps, he was out of the state trying to solicit funds for the University when the census was taken. Informaiton on census records may not be completely correct, but in many cases, it is the only remaining record for many people. By using the census records, the majority of people who lived at Sewanee from 1860 to 1920, have now been identified. All the above students were listed as white males.

PEOPLE LIVING AT SEWANEE IN 1880

1. HOGE, S.C., M/W age 41, Retail Merchant, born Alabama.
   Sarah T., F/W, age 37, wife, ran a boarding house, born Tenn.
   Nelly M. F/W, age 6, daughter, attending school, born Tenn.
   Eunice H., F/W, age 4, daughter, born Tenn.
   KENDALL, W. M., M/W, age 26, clerk in store, born Virginia.
2. PRESTON, F.M., F/W, age 43, ran a boarding house, born Kentucky
   T. C.., M/W, son, age 17, attending school, born Texas.
   EUSIGY, W. P., M/W, age 44, retail merchant, born New York.
3. WADHAMS, C. H., M/W, Baker, age 52, born Scotland.
   E., F/W, age 53, born Scotland.
   L. W. F/W, age 24, daughter, book keeper, born New York.
4. LOWRY, JOHN, W/M age 45, teacher, born Ireland.
5. TALLICHOST, C. R. L., M/W, age 36, teacher, born France.
   V. C., F/W, age 27, wife, born North Carolina.
   J. H., M/W, age 3, son, born Tenn.
   J. M., F/W, age 1, daughter, born Tenn.
   SNAVLEY, W. C., M/W, age 23, teacher, born Alabama.
6. BRAZELTON, K. W., M/W, age 33, telegraph operator, born Tenn.
   D. M. , F/W, age 21, wife, born Iowa.
   H. W. M/W, age 1, son, born Tenn.
7. HARRISON, C., M/W, age 31, Teacher, born Virginia.
   M. C. , F/W, age 30 wife, born Virginia.
   M. C., F/W, age 6, daughter, born Tenn.
   A. P. F/W, age 3, daughter, born Tenn.
   L. N. , F/W, age 2, daughter, born Tenn.
   W. S., M/W, son, born 1880, Tenn.
   LEIGH, R. F/B, age 13, servant, born Virginia.
8. TUCKER, S. L. M/W, age 22, Gardener, born Tenn.
   Ophra, F/W, age 21, wife, born Tenn.
   H. L., M/W, age 3, son, born Tenn.
   I. A., F/W, age 1, daughter, born Tenn.
9. GIPSON, JOHN, M/W, age 25, general work, born Tenn.
   V. E., F/W, age 22, wife, born Tenn.
   I. E., M/W, age 6, son, born Tenn.
   S. F., F/W, age 4, daughter, born Tenn.
   W. T., M/W, age 3, son, born Tenn.
   B. A., F/W, age 1, daughter, born Tenn.
10. ESTILL, W. D., M/W, age 33, farmer, born Tenn.
   S.A., F/W, age 20, wife, born Alabama.
   N. J., F/W, age 2, daughter, born Tenn.
   L. A. F/W, daughter, born 1880, Tenn.
   ROSE, FANNY, F/W, age 15, daughter, born Tenn.
11. IVES, WILLIAM, M/W, age 70? illegible, Gardener, born North Dakota.
   S. J., F/W, wife, age 49? illegible, born Virginia.
   M. E., F/W, age 14, daughter, attending school, born Tenn.
   C. W., M/W, age 13, son, attending school, born Tenn.
   I. E., F/W, age 12, daughter, attending school, born Tenn.
   A.P., F/W, age 8, daughter, attending school, born Tenn.
   G. G., M/W, age 7, son, attending school, born Tenn.
12. HARRISON, J. H. M/W, age 35, blacksmith, born Tenn.
   S.A., F/W, age 30, wife, born Tenn.
   T.A., M/W, age 12, son, attending school, born Tenn.
   John, M/W, age 8, son, attending school, born Tenn.
   Jerry, M/W, age 4, son, born Tenn.
   G.W., M/W, age 2, son, born Tenn.
13. SHORT, F. H., M/W, age 36, stone mason, born Georgia.
   Alice, F/W, age 39, wife, born North Carolina.
   C.C., M/W, age 10, step-son, born Tenn.
14. CASTLEBERRY, J. M., M/W, age 41, born Georgia.
   Patty, F/W, age 24, wife, born Tenn.
   John, M/W, age 6, son, born Tenn.
   Tom, M/W, age 4, son, born Tenn.
   James, M/W, age 2, son, born Tenn.
   Ellen, F/W, born 1880, daughter, born Tenn.
15. COKER, MANSEL, M/W, age 65, wagon maker, born South Carolina.
   Mary, F/W, age 64, wife, born Tenn.
   QUINN, MARGARET, F/W, age 35, daughter, born Tenn.
   WALL, MARTHA, F/W, age 30, daughter, born Tenn.

COKER, A., M/W, age 20, son, born Tenn.
QUINN, MARGARET, F/W, age 7, granddaughter, born Tenn.
Bettie, F/W, age 5, granddaughter, born Tenn.
WALL, WILLIAM, M/W, age 5, born Tenn.
Thomas, M/W, age 3, grandson, born Tenn.
COKER, CATHERINE, F/W, age 26, daughter, born Tenn.

16. ARNOLD, J. L., M/W, age 28, born Tenn.
S. E., F/W, age 21, born Tenn.
?, W., M/W, age 1, son, born Tenn.

17. GIBSON, W. A., M/W, age 51. retail merchant, born Georgia.
S. M., M/W, age 19, son, clerk in store, born Texas.
Annie, F/W, age 18, daughter, born Mississippi.
A. E., F/W, age 55, sister, born Georgia.
CONWAY, MARY T. F/W, age 52, sister, born Georgia.

18. MYERS, W. L., M/W, age 23, huckster (peddler) born Tenn.
E. J., F/W, age 20, wife, born Tenn.
L. O. M/W, age 1, son, born Tenn.

19. THOMAS, J. illegible, M/W, age 23, painter, born Tenn.
Name illegible, M/W, age 26, brother, born Tenn.
Mary, F/W, age 30, sister, born Tenn.
Thomas, M/W, age 3, nephew, born Tenn.

20. JACKSON, J. B., M/W, age 62, carpenter, born Tenn.
S.M., F/W, age 44, wife, born Alabama.
Lily, F/W, age 16, daughter, attending school, born Tenn.
Annie, F/W, age 14, daughter, attending school, born Tenn.
Jessie, F/W, age 12, daughter, attending school, born Tenn.
Charles, M/W, age 9, son, attending school, born Tenn.
Daisy M., F/W, age 7, daughter, attending school, born Tenn.
James, M/W, age 18, nephew, born Tenn.

21. JOHNSON, W. H., M/W, age 32, shoe and boot maker, born Alabama.
S.E., F/W, age 27, wife, born Tenn.
A. L. M/W, age 7, son, attending school, born Tenn.
Name illegible, F/W, age 6, daughter, attending school, born Tenn.
M. M., F/W, age 4, daughter, born Tenn.
W. A., M/W, age 2, son, born Tenn.
H. R., M/W, son, born December 1879, in Tenn.

22. OLIVER, J. H., M/W, age 21, shoe and boot maker, born Tenn.

23. MOONEY, R., M/W, age 32, gardener, born Mississippi.
Catherine, F/W, age 24, wife, born North Carolina.
John, M/W, age 6, son, attending school, born Tenn.
Willie, M/W, age 4, son, born Tenn.
Mary C., F/W, age 1, daughter, born Tenn.

24. BROWN, P. H., F/W, age 40, mid-wife, born Prussia. (former German state)
R. T. or K. T., F/W, age 17, daughter, seamstress, born Missouri.
Annie, F/W, age illegible, daughter, born Illinois.

25. DARDIS, J. C., M/W, age 25, retail merchant, born Tenn.
Name illegible, M/W, age 25, brother, retail merchant, born Tenn.
R.W, M/W, age 22, brother, farming, born Tenn.
Susie, F/W, age 21, wife, born Tenn.

26. FISCHER, FRED, M/W, age 50, cabinet maker, born Bavaria, Germany.
Rosa, F/W, age 48, wife, born Baden, Germany.
Carrie, F/W, age 24, daughter, seamstress, born Ohio.
William, M/W, age 22, son, tinner, born Ohio.
Otto, M/W, age 20, son, attending school, born Ohio.
Rosa, F/W, age 15, daughter, house work, born Ohio.
Joseph, M/W, age 14, son, attending school, born Ohio.
Maggie M., F/W, age 8, granddaughter, at school, born Tenn.

27. SHORT, A., M/W, age 28, carpenter, born Tenn.
E. M., F/W, age 29, wife, born Alabama.
D. S., M/W, age 10, son, attending school, born Tenn.
R. J., M/W, age 8, son, attending school, born Tenn.
Geo., M/W, age 5, son, born Tenn.
JOS. A. J., M/W, age 3, son, born Tenn.
HILL, JANE P., F/W, age 48, boarder and a dress maker, born New York.

28. ANDERSON, name illegible, M/W, age 21, painter, born Canada.
Jane E., F/W, age 37, wife, born Georgia.

Sarah E., F/W, age 7, daughter, born Tenn.
J.W., M/W, age 9, adopted son, born Tenn.

29. MCKINNEY, G. W., M/W, age 25, clerk in store, born Mississippi.
S. C., F/W, age 31, wife, born Tenn.
Christine, F/W, age 19, sister, seamstress, born Mississippi.
Julia A., F/W, age 32, sister, born Alabama.
CARTER, S. E, M/W, age 7, nephew, attending school, born Mississippi.

30. LUCUS, JOHN, M/W, age illegible, barber, born Sicily.
Mary, F/W, age 23, wife, born Tenn.
Rose, F/W, age 6, daughter, born Tenn.
Joseph, M/W, age 5, son, born Tenn.
Julia, F/W, age 2, daughter, born Tenn.
HEATH, D. S., M/W, age 32, boarder and a Jeweler, born Iowa.

31. RUEF, C., M/W, age 31, butcher, born Switzerland.
Agnes, F/W, age 27, wife, born Switzerland.
John, M/W, age 3, son, born Tenn.
F. N., M/W, son born Feb. 1879, in Tenn.
SYIN, ALFRED, M/W, age 6, adopted child, born Tenn.
BOLLINGER, B., F/W, age 20, sister-in-law servant, born Switzerland.

32. CASTLEBERRY, SALLY, F/W, age 74, born Tenn.
A., F/W, age 41, daughter, cook, born Georgia.
Agnes, F/W, age 36, wash woman, born Georgia.

33. JACKSON, ROBERT, M/W, age 50, carpenter, born Tenn.
M. C., F/W, age 25, wife, born Tenn.

34. BENNETT, J. W., M/W, age 27, carpenter, born Tenn.
E. C., F/W, age 20, wife, born Tenn.
M. E., F/W, daughter born October 1879, Tenn.

35. WILLIAMSON, M. J., F/W, age 40, wash woman, born Tenn.
S. H., M/W, age 15, working on farm, born Tenn.
A.J., M/W, age 8, son, attending school, born Tenn.
N.C., F/W, age 4, daughter, born Tennessee.
GAMBLE, DINAH, F/W, age 9, boarder, attending school, born Tenn.

36. WITT, G. R., M/W, age 28, carpenter, born Tenn.
L. W., F/W, age 25, wife, born England.
L. D., F/W, age 2, daughter, born Tenn.
George, M/W, son, born January 1880, in Tenn.
MAYHEW, THOMAS, M/W, age 63, boarder stone mason, born Tenn.

37. MILLER, M. A., F/W, age 35, born Tenn.
Annie D., F/W, age 13, daughter, attending school, born Tenn.
James H., M/W, age 12, son, attending school, born Tenn.
Ella F. F/W, daughter born September 1879, in Tenn.

38. DENSON, L. H, F/W, age 35, seamstress. born Tenn.
Jourdan, M/W, age 14, son, working on farm, born Tenn.
Annie Belle, F/W, age 13, daughter, attending school, born Tenn.

39. ARMSTRONG, J. H, M/W, age 37, book keeper, born Georgia.
S. J., M/W, age 9, son, attending school, born Alabama.
M. W., F/W, age 7, daughter, attending school, born Alabama.
M. C., F/W, age 5, daughter, born Alabama.
A. E., F/W, age 2, daughter, born Tenn.

40. PILLET, L, M/W, age 36, tailor, born France.
H.C., F/W, age 33, wife, born France.
GALLET, J., M/W, age 42, boarder, tailor, born France.
C., F/W, age 31, wife, born France.
LUCHSINGER, M., F/W, age 19, servant cook , born Switzerland.

41. GILLIAM, C. W., F/W, age 53, born Tenn.
T. D., M/W, age 22, son, born Tenn.
M. E., F/W, age 21, daughter, born Tenn.
J. P., M/W, age 19, son, clerk in store, born Tenn.

42. SOUTHERLAND, B., M/W, age 36, farming, born Alabama.
Mary, F/W, age 32, wife, wash woman, born Tenn.
J. C., M/W, age 20, son, working on farm, born N. C.
William G., M/W, age 18, son, working on farm, born N.C.
John, M/W, age 5, son, attending school, born Tenn.
Arthur, M/W, age 4, son, born Tenn.
J.R., M/W, age 2, son, born Tenn.
WEST, SALLY, F/W, age 10, step-daughter, born Tenn.
Ida, F/W, age 9, step-daughter, born Tenn.

43. RICE, MARTHA, F/W, age 63, wash woman, born Tenn.
Zac, M/W, age 27, adopted son, waggoner, born Tenn.
Nancy, F/W, age 27, wife, seamstress, born Tenn.
Mitty, F/W, age 7, daughter, attending school, born Tenn.
M. M.,, F/W, age 4, daughter, born Tenn.
Charley, M/W, age 2, son, born Tenn.
S. Gail, F/W, daughter, born June 1879, in Tenn.
GILLIAM, illegible ?Fanny, F/W, age 14, servant, born Tenn.
44. MONTGOMERY, NANCY, F/W, age 64, general work, born Alabama.
Lizzie, F/W, age 20, daughter, seamstress, born Tenn.
John, M/W, age 17, son, attending school, born Tenn.
Luther, M/W, age 24, son, laborer, born Tenn.
L. A., F/W, age 18, wife of Luther, born Tenn.
45. MCALLLISTER, J. G., M/W, age 44, carpenter, born Alabama.
Mattie, F/W, age 36, wife, born Ala.
James, M/W, age 15, son, attending school, born Georgia.
Walter, M/W, age 6, son, attending school, born Tenn.
Gracy, F/W, age 4, daughter, born Tenn.
46. THOMAS, WILLIAM, M/W, age 36, stone mason, born Tenn.
Mary, F/W, age 34, wife, born Georgia.
John, M/W, age 13, son, attending school, born Tenn.
Josephine, F/W, age 12, daughter, attending school, born Tenn.
William, M/W, age 10, son, attending school, born Alabama.
J. F., M/W, age 8, son, attending school, born Tenn.
Mollie, F/W, age 6, daughter, born Tenn.
R. O., F/W, age 4, daughter, born Tenn.
Eddie, M/W, age 1, son, born Tenn.
47. MESSICK, K. M., F/W, age 38, wash woman, born Virginia.
Julia A., F/W, age 18, daughter, wash woman, Tenn.
R. J., F/W, age 12, son, attending school, born Tenn.
J.W., M/W, age 12, son, attending school, born Tenn.
J. A., M/W, age 10, son, attending school, born Tenn.
48. STATEM, P. T., M/W, age 52, stone mason, born Virginia.
E. J., F/W, age 48, wife, born Tenn.
49. PRINCE, M. A., F/W, age 55, nurse, born Tenn.
Robert, M/W, age 18, farm hand, born Tenn.
James, M/W, age 12, attending school, born Tenn.
50. BAKER, name illegible, M/W, age 37, gardener, born Tenn.
? E, F/W, age 29, wife, born Tenn.
Name illegible, F/W, age 8, daughter, born Tenn.
Madeline, F/W, age 4, daughter, born Tenn.
51. DUGGAR, SARAH, F/W, age 64, wash woman, born North Carolina.
Delia, F/W, age 19, daughter, teacher, born Tenn.
M. J., F/W, age 15, daughter, attending school, born Tenn.
52. SUGGS, MARGARET, F/W, age 64, born Tenn.
? A., F/W, age 23, daughter, wash woman, born Alabama.
Jeff, M/W, age 18, son, farm hand, born Tenn.
53. GADDIS, J. W., M/W, age 26, farm hand, born Alabama.
Sophia, F/W, age 23, wife, born Alabama.
S. F, F/W, age 6, daughter, born Alabama.
Daisy, F/W, age 1, daughter, born Alabama.
HENDEN, FUCNCIA, F/W, age 48, mother-in-law, nurse, born Tenn.
54. REEF, A.J, M/W, age 28, miner, born Georgia.
E. J., F/W, age 25, wife, born Alabama.
R. M. L., F/W, age 3, daughter, born Tenn.
J. R., M/W, age 1, son, born Tenn.
55. WALKER, J. T., M/W, age 33, wood chopper, born Tenn.
E., F/W, age 29, wife, born Tenn.
Della, F/W, age 7, twin daughter, born Tenn.
Addeline, F/W, age 7, twin daughter, born Tenn.
Jas. H., M/W, age 3, son, born Tenn.
S.C., F/W, age 1, daughter, born Tenn.
56. OWENS, E., F/W, age 35, wash woman, born Tenn.
J.E., F/W, age 14, daughter, attending school, born Tenn.

Seborn, M/W, age 12, son, working on farm, born Tenn.
James, M/W, age 10, son, working on farm, born Tenn.
Martha, F/W, age 8, daughter, attending school, born Alabama.

57. LACK, S.?, M/W, age 63, pauper, born Virginia.
M. M.,, F/W, age 34, wife, wash woman, born Tenn.
F., F/W, age 15, daughter, wash woman, born Tenn.
M. A. B., F/W, age 9, daughter, attending school, born Tenn.
M. E., F/W, age 6, daughter, attending school, born Tenn.
F. A. , F/W, age 66, sister, pauper, born Virginia.
M. E., F/W, age 44, sister, wash woman, born Tenn.

58. AMSTUTZ, JOSEPH, M/W, age 52, carpenter, born Switzerland.
Anna, F/W, age 30, wife, wash woman, born Switzerland.
Anna, F/W, age 18, daughter, attending school, born Ohio.
Lena, , F/W, age 15, daughter, attending school, born Ohio.
Emma, F/W, age 12, daughter, attending school, born Ohio.
Joseph, M/W, age 11, son, attending school, born Tenn.

59. PEA, MARIA, F/B, age 22, cook, born Tenn.
ACKLIN, JAS., M/B, age 50, servant, born Tenn.

60. TRIPP, ALEX, M/W, age 26, laborer, born North Carolina.
S.C., F/W, age 26, wife, wash woman, born Tenn.
A.M., F/W, age 4, daughter, born Tenn.
J.A., F/W, son, born March 1880, in Tenn.

61. SOUTHERLAND, SAMUEL, M/W, age 33, laborer, born North Carolina.
Roxanna, F/W, age 44, wife, born Tenn.
J. O., M/W, age 12, son, at school, born Tenn.
R. McDaniel, M/W, age 8, son, at school, born Tenn.
K. A., F/W, age 4, daughter, born Tenn.
Lonzo, M/W, age 3, son, born Tenn.
Jennie Belle, F/W, age 1, daughter, born Tenn.
HALL, JOHN, M/W, age 30, boarder, born England.
QUINN, CAMPBELL, M/W, age 2, son, born Tenn.
COKER, D. F/W, age 1, daughter, born Tenn.

62. CASTLEBERRY, A., F/W, age 43, seamstress, born Tenn.
Sarah, F/W, age 19, daughter, seamstress, born Tenn.
V., F/W, age 14, daughter, attending school, born Tenn.
Lily, F/W, age 10, daughter, attending school, born Tenn.

63. GREEN, J. R., M/W, age 42, butcher, born Tenn.
Bettie, F/W, age 39, wife, born Tenn.
Beulah, F/W, age 13, daughter, attending school, born Tenn.
J. E., M/W, age 10, son, attending school, born Tenn.
T. W., F/W, age 7, daughter, attending school, born Tenn.
M. E.., F/W, age 6, daughter, born Tenn.
Willie, F/W, age 3, daughter, born Tenn.
GREEN, A. S., M/W, age 1, son, born Tenn.

64. GRAUTHAUS, H.A., M/W, age 28, lay reader, born England.
M. D., F/W, age 19, wife, born Tenn.
T. DuBose, F/W, daughter born June 1879, born Tenn.

65. COLBY, NELLIE, F/W, age 75, born England.
EASTIN, MARY, F/W, age 40, boarding, born Maryland.
H., M/W, age 21, grandson, retail merchant, born Georgia.
Nellie, F/W, age 15, granddaughter, at school, born Georgia.

66. HOLDER, MILLY, F/B, age 43, servant, born Tenn.
Robert, M/B, age 11, servant, born Tenn.
Molly, F/B, age 7, attending school, born Tenn.

67. TOLLIVER, WILLIAM, M/W, age 30, wood chopper, born Tenn.
Ellen, F/W, age 30, wash and irons, born Tenn.
N. I., M/W, age 1, son, born Tenn.
I. W., M/W, age 9, son, born Tenn.

68. HARLOW, T .J., F/W, age 56, born New York.
W., M/W, age 27, son, journalist, born Maine.
J.B., F/W, age 25, daughter, born Illinois.
LACK, S.C., F/W, age 18, niece, attending school, born Illinois.

TOWNSEND, MARY, B/W, age 20, servant, born Alabama.

69. MAYHEW, E. S., F/W, age 71, book keeper, born New York.
C. G., F/W, age 35, daughter, born New York.
C. S., M/W, age 19, son, drug clerk, born New Jersey.
A. W., F/W, age 17, daughter at school, born New Jersey.
? P., F/W, age 12, daughter, attending school, born New Jersey.

70. JONES, E. W., M/W, age 52, physician, born Maryland.
S.A. P., F/W, age 51, wife, born Washington , D.C.
S.L., F/W, age 18, daughter, attending school, born Virginia.
E., F/W, age 16, son, attending school, born Virginia.
CHEATHAM, SALLY, F/B, age 23, servant, born Tenn.

71. COPERING, W. A., F/W, age 35, born Tenn.
R.V., M/W, age 18, son, student, born North Carolina.
C.M., M/W, age 15, son, attending school, born N.C.
J.M., M/W, age 13, son, attending school, born N.C.
S. P., F/W, age 7, daughter, born N.C.
U. V., F/W, age 5, daughter, born N.C.

72. LIPCOMB, CHARLES, M/B, age 19, servant, born Tenn.

73. RAMSEY, MARY, F/B, age 26, servant, born Tenn.
Ella, F/B, age 6, daughter, attending school, born Tenn.
Willie, M/B, age 3, son, attending school, born Tenn.

74. SIMS, BELLE, F/B, age 22, servant, born Mississippi.

75. SESSANS, M. F/W, age 44, born Miss.
Davis, M/W, age 22, son, teacher, born Texas.
TUCKER, E. B. F/W, age 32, sister-in-law, born Mississippi.
C.D., F/W, age 12, niece, attending school, born Texas.
S. B., F/W, age 9, niece, attending school, born Texas.
J.B., F/W, age 5, niece, attending school, born Texas.
LASATER, LIZZIE, F/MU, age 29, servant born Tenn.

76. ROBERTS, M. E., F/W, age 55, born Tenn.
LYNCH, EMILY, F/W, age 12, niece, born Tenn.

77. JEWELL, J. B., M/W, age 27, blacksmith, born Tenn.
Bridget, F/W, age 24, wife, born Tenn.
Benton, M/W, age 6, son, attending school, born Tenn.
Ada Lee, F/W, age 4, daughter, born Tenn.

78. FARRIS, P., M/B, age 46, servant, born Tenn.
Matilda, F/B, age 44, born Tenn.

79. NORWOOD, S. H., M/W, age 38, farmer, born Tenn.
Peggy, F/W, age 36, wife, born Tenn.
Robert, M/W, age 12, son, attending school, born Tenn.
S. H., M/W, age 6, born England.
C. P., M/W, age 2, born Tenn.

80. LAWRENCE, EMMA, F/W, age 54, seamstress, born Georgia.

81. PHILPOT, W. W. , M/W, age 29, carpenter, born England.
Amanda, F/W, age 36, wife, born Tenn.
COWLIER, THOMAS, M/W, age 13, step-son, at school, born Tenn.

82. CARTER, ARCH, M/B, age not given, servant, born Tenn.
Nancy, F/B, age 17, wife, washes and irons, born Alabama.

83. PAINE, WILLIAM, M/MU, age 40, waiter, born Mississippi.
Julia, F/MU, age 30, wife, cook, born Tenn.

84. DORCEE, JANE, F/B, age 23, wash and irons, born Tenn.
Alex, M/B, age 3, son, born Tenn.
Walter, M/B, age 1, son, born Tenn.
David, M/B, age 6, son, born Tenn.
Bettie, F/B, age 9, daughter, born Tenn.

85. PATTON, LOU, F/MU, age 29, washes, born Tenn.

86. LEE, HARRIET, F/MU, age 55, wash woman, born Tenn.
P., M/B, age 12, son, attending school, born Tenn.

87. WILLIAMS, JERRY, M/B, age 40, waggoner, born Tenn.
Annie, F/B, age 30, wife, washing, born Georgia.
Josey, F/B, age 1, daughter, born Tenn.
Sam, M/B, age 8, born Tenn.

88. JUNY, C.V., F/W, age 48, born Alabama.
W., F/W, age 6, attending school, born Mississippi.

TAYLOR, W. J., M/W, age 20, clerk in store, born Texas.

89. POLK, BETTIE, F/W, age 52, keeps boarding house, born North Carolina.
W.A., M/W, age 19, step-son, at school, born Louisiana.
M. E., F/W, age, 17, daughter, born Louisiana.
J.R., M/W, age 14, son, attending school, born Louisiana.
SIMMONS, HESTER, F/B, age 62, servant, born Tenn.
JOURDAN, ANN, F/B, age 36, Hester's daughter, born Tenn.
RUSSELL, M., F/B, age 22, servant, born Alabama.
Rose, F/B, age 4, daughter, born Tenn.

90. DUBOSE, W. P., M/W, age 44, minister, born South Carolina.
M. L, F/W, age 44, born Tenn.
Susie, W/F, age 14, attending school, born South Carolina.
May, W/F, age 12, attending school, born South Carolina.
W.H, M/W, age 10, attending school, born Tenn.
PERONNEAU, S. H., F/W, age 49, teacher, born South Carolina.
COPFY, BARBARA, F/W, age 18, servant, born Switzerland.
Lizzie, F/W, age 16, servant, born Switzerland.

91. ELLIOTT, C. B., M/W, age 70, born S.C.
S. B., F/W, age 31, daughter, born GA.
C. B., F/W, age 29, daughter, born GA.
DUNBAR, VIRGINIA, F/W, age 28, boarder, teacher, born Mississippi.
BROWN, S. G., M/B, age 10, servant, born Georgia.

92. PHILLIPS, JOHN, M/B, age 24, servant, born Tenn.
Mandy, F/B, age 18, wife, servant, born Tenn.
Oscar, M/B, son, born 1879, in Tenn.

93. KNICCASION, CLARA, F/B, age 24, servant, born Tenn.
Josy, F/B, age 10, daughter, attending school, born Tenn.
Gatzy, F/B, age 26, wash woman, born Tenn.
Ada, F/B, age 10, daughter, born Tenn.
Clara, F/B, age 8, daughter, born Tenn.
Hugh, M/B, age 5, son, born Tenn.
Mattie, F/B, age 4, daughter, born Tenn.

94. SCOTT, NANCY N., F/W, age 50, hotel keeper, born Tenn.

95. FARRIS, PETER, M/B, age 29, servant, born Tenn.
Heneritta, F/B, age 30, wife, cook, born Georgia.

96. BRANNON, HARRIET, F/MU, age 46, cook , born North Carolina.
Tom, M/B, age 12, son, working on farm, born Tenn.
Sally, F/B, age 10, daughter, born Tenn.
Sauld, M/B, age 8, son, born Tenn.
MCFARLAND, LOU, F/B, age 14, daughter, washer and irons, born Georgia.
CRUSHAN, H. C., M/B, age 22, son, janitor and miner, born South Carolina.
WALLACE, JOSEPH, M/B, age 16, ?, laborer, born South Carolina.

97. ELLIOTT, J.B., M/W, age 38, physician, born South Carolina.
P. H., F/W, age 31, wife, born Georgia.
John, M/W, age 9, son, attending school, born Georgia.
Esther, M/W, age 8, daughter, attending school, born Tenn.
Joseph, M/W, age 6, son, attending school, born Tenn.
Charlotte, F/W, age 4, daughter, attending school, born Tenn.
R. H., M/W, age 2, son, born Tenn.

98. HUGER, M. E., F/W, age 59, teacher, born South Carolina.
K. M., F/W, age 25, daughter, artist, born South Carolina.
M. E., F/W, age 18, daughter, teacher, born South Carolina.
L. H., F/W, age 18, daughter, attending school, born Georgia.
VANDERNE, MATTIE, F/W, 21, servant, born Georgia.
WILSON, ELISA, F/B, age 18, servant, born Tenn.
ARNET, TOM, M/B, age 19, servant, born Tenn.

99. BUCHANAN, CLAY, M/MU, age 30, laborer, born Tenn.
Francis, F/MU, age 25, wife, wash woman, born Tenn.
Maria, F/MU, age 5, daughter, born Tenn.
Virgil, F/MU, age 1, daughter, born Tenn.
Geo., M/MU, age 4, son, born Tenn.

100. SMITH, M., F/W, age 33, born Alabama.
Emma, F/W, age 12, attending school, born Alabama.

James, M/W, age 10, son, attending school, born Alabama.
TAYLOR, ELLEN, F/B, age 18, servant, born Tenn.
Joseph, M/MU, age 1, born Tenn.

101. GREEN, ALLEN, M/B, age 40, cook, born South Carolina.
Elsie, F/B, age 33, wash woman, born South Carolina.
Freddy, M/B, age 4, son, born Tenn.
Catherine, F/B, daughter, born Dec. 1879, in Tenn.

102. MURPHY, EMMA, F/MU, age 33, wash woman, born Tenn.
S.B., F/B, age 16, daughter, cook, born Tenn.
G. A., F/MU, age 7, daughter, attending school, born Tenn.
Willie, M/B, age 6, born Tenn.
John, M/MU, age 3, son, born Tenn.

103. PRINTESS, A. M/W, age 23, theological student, born South Carolina.

104. GRABAUS, H. P. L, M/W, age 20, theological student, born Virginia.

105. BARRY, JOHN, M/W, age 39, railroad foreman, born Tenn.
Rachel, F/W, age 38, wife, born Georgia.
Nancy, F/W, age 18, daughter, born Tenn.
W.B, M/W, age 16, son, farming, born Tenn.
John, M/W, age 14, son, works on railroad, born Tenn.
Sarah, F/W, age 12, attending school, born Tenn.
Auston, M/W, age 9, attending school, born Tenn.
Joseph, M/W, age 8, son, attending school, born Tenn.

106. GREEN, J., M/W, age 55, physician, born North Carolina.
E., F/W, age 38, wife, born Georgia.
M. W., F/W, age 21, daughter, born Miss.
Cora, F/W, age 16, daughter, attending school, born Mississippi.
Oh Polk, M/W, age 14, son, born Miss.

107. YARWORTH, JOHN, M/W, age 59, miner of coal, born England.
Martha, F/W, age 41, wife, born Tenn.
William, M/W, age 17, son, gardening, born Alabama.
Geo. W, M/W, age 15, son, coal miner, born Tenn.
Mary E., F/W, age 13, daughter, attending school, born Tenn.
M. J., F/W, age 11, daughter, attending school, born Tenn.
A. T., M/W, age 9, son, attending school, born Tenn.
ANN, F/W, age 7, daughter, attending school, born Tenn.
Edward, M/W, age 5, son, born Tenn.
Sarah, F/W, age 2, daughter, born Tenn.
Orvil, M/W, son born February 1880, in Tenn.

108. PERRY, THOMAS, M/W, age 31, wood chopper, born Tenn.
Sarah, F/W, age 28, wife, born Tenn.
John, M/W, age 14, son, work on farm, born Tenn.
M. J., F/W, age 11, daughter, attending school, born Tenn.
Roland, M/W, age 7, son, born Tenn.

109. TOMLINSON, W. H., M/W, age 32, commercial tourist, born South Carolina.
Delia, F/W, age 30, wife, ran boarding house, born Mississippi.
Mammie O., F/W, age 6, daughter, born Tenn.
Sada C., F/W, age 3, daughter, born Tenn.

110. AVERY, CLARA, F/B, age 40, wash woman, born North Carolina.

111. ANDERSON, H. M., M/W, age 56, physician, born Maryland.
J. I., F/W, age 48, wife, born Georgia.
J.M., F/W, age 21, daughter, born Georgia.
Rosalie, F/W, age 19, daughter, born Georgia.

112. HANNA, NATHAN, M/B, age 29, cook, born Tenn.
Sally, F/B, age 28, wife, nurse, born Tenn.

113. ROSE, W. M.,., M/W, age 40, farmer, born Tenn.
E. C., F/W, age 36, wife, born Tenn.
Alice J., F/W, age 18, daughter, born Tenn.
N.C., F/W, age 16, daughter, born Tenn.
Nora B., F/W, age 14, daughter, born Tenn.
Victoria L., F/W, age 11, daughter, born Tenn.
James P., M/W, age 9, son, attending school, born Tenn.
David L., M/W, age 7, son, attending school, born Tenn.
W. H., M/W, age 3, son, born Tenn.
Emma C., F/W, daughter, born December 1879, in Tenn.

114. CHEATHAM, WILLIAM, M/B, age 23, cook, born Tenn.
Hannah, F/W, age 24, wife, servant, born Tenn.

115. LOVELL, L. Q., M/W, age 50, born Mississippi.
Eva, F/W, age 23, daughter, born Mississippi.
Alice Q., age 16, daughter, attending school, born Tenn.
FOSTER, SARAH, F/MU, age 65, servant nurse, born Mississippi.

116. DUBOSE, M.A., F/W, age 44, keeping a boarding house, born S.C.
T. M., M/W, age 21, medical student, born South Carolina.
McNeely, M/W, age 20, son, student, born South Carolina.
CARTER, M. J., F/MU, age 45, dining room servant, born Tenn.
Georgia, F/Mu, age 8, daughter, attending school, born Alabama.
BLANTON, Lorina, F/Mu, age 36, wash woman, born Tenn.
Joseph, M/MU, age 10, waiter, born Tenn.
SCHNAIDER, C.H.A.E., M/W, age 24, gardener, born Switzerland.
MERCER, LAUREN, F/MU, age 22, wash woman, born Tenn.
BAUK, ADELINE, F/MU, age 53, cook born Tenn.

117. ELMORE, FANNY A., F/W, age 37, boarding house keeper, born Alabama.
THOMAS, M/W, age 13, son, attending school, born Alabama.
Charles, M/W, age 8, son, attending school, born Alabama.
C. E., M/W, age 52, son-in-law, teacher, born South Carolina.
MORRIS, MATTIE, F/W, age 21, cook, born Georgia.
JOHNSON, LUTHER, M/B, age 29, waiter, born Tenn.

118. MCCRADY, JOHN, M/W, age 48, Zoologist, born South Carolina.
Sarah, F/W, age 40, wife, born Tenn.
E. L. B, F/W, age 19, attending school, born South Carolina.
L. R.. L., F/W, age 17, daughter, attending school, born S.C.
Sabinn L. F/W, age 15, daughter, attending school, born S.C.
Edward, M/W, age 12, son, attending school born S. C.
GARNER, JOSEPH, M/B, age 15, servant, waiter, born Tenn.
SEWELL, MARY, M/W, age 21, cook, born Tenn.

119. KIRBY-SMITH, E., M/W, age 55, teacher, born Florida.
Cassie S., F/W, age 42, wife, born Virginia.
Carrie S., F/W, age 17, daughter, at school, born Virginia.
Francis K., F/W, age 15, daughter, at school, born Texas,
Edmund Kirby, MW, age 13, son, at school, born Kentucky.
Lydia, F/W, age 11, daughter, at school, born Kentucky.
S. Rowena S. F/W, age 9, at school, born Kentucky.

119. KIRBY-SMITH E. Chaplain, F/W, age 7, at school, born Tenn.
Reynold Morris, M/W, age 5, son, at school, born Tenn.
Wm. Selden, M/W, age 3, son, born Tenn.
Josephine B., F/W, age 1, daughter, born Tenn.
MCKINNY, SAMANTHA, F/B, age 14, nurse, born Georgia.
HANNAH, JOHN, M/B, age 21, gardener, born Tenn.
BRADY, LIZZIE, F/MU, age 19, house servant, born Tenn.
McDANIEL, E., F/W, age 59, visitor, born Virginia.
Oreianna, F/W, age 25, visitor, born Virginia.
AIKEN, C.A., M/W, age 18, visitor, born South Carolina.

120. JAEGRER, A., M/W, age 41, minister, born Austria.
Annie F., F/W, age 32, born Virginia.
THOMI, KATE, F/W, age 16, servant, born Switzerland.

121. FAIRBANKS, G. R., M/W, age 59, lawyer, born New York.
S. B., .F/W, age 53, wife, born North Carolina.
Flora, F/W, age 31, daughter, born New York.
C. M., M/W, age 29, son, physician, born Florida.
G. C., F/W, age 21, daughter, born Florida.
S. Rainy, F/W, age 18, daughter, at school, born Tenn.
E. L., F/W, age 15, daughter, at school, born Georgia.
COTTEN, R. W, M/W, age 4, grandson, born Texas.
A. W., F/W, age 3, granddaughter, born Tenn.
G. R. F., M/W, age 1, grandson, born Tenn.

COTTEN, C. B., M/W, grandson born Dec. 1879, in Tenn.

122. KING, SAMUEL J., M/W, age 20, born Tenn.

123. VAN DAMM, W.S., M/W, age 65, farmer, born New Jersey.
Maria, F/W, age 36, wife, born Ireland.
Julie, F/W, age 1, daughter, born Tenn.
SCANLIN, BRIDGET, F/W, age 18, sister-in-law, born Ireland.

124. TALLERIN, R. K., M/W, age 64, laborer, born Tenn.
P.A., F/W, age 35, wife, wash woman, born Tenn.

125. ANDERSON, A. H., M/W, age 48, laborer, born Tenn.
Margaret, F/W, age 48, wife, born Tenn.
S.E., F/W, age 22, daughter, born Tenn.
M. J., F/W, age 19, daughter, born Tenn.
N. E., F/W, age 16, daughter, born Tenn.
F. C., F/W, age 14, daughter, born Tenn.
Ivey A., F/W, age 12, daughter, born Tenn.
M. B., F/W, age 10, daughter, born Tenn.
J. H. F., M/W, age 9, son, born Tenn.
Geo. G., M/W, age 6, son, born Tenn.

126. HAYNER, MATTIE, F/B, age 25, wash woman, born Alabama.

127. HAFLER, F.M., F/W, age 31, seamstress, born Alabama.

128. GUTHRIE, WM. F., M/W, age 38, carpenter, born Tenn.
Ida L., F/W, age 20, wife, wash woman, born Tenn.
Geo. E., M/W, age 4, son, born Tenn.
Mary E., F/W, born May 1879, in Tenn.
WILLIAMS, J., F/W, age 17, servant, born Tenn.

129. GUTHRIE, VIRGIL, M/W, age 28, carpenter, born Tenn.
S. T., F/W, age 26, wife, born Tenn.
MCPONDY, J. E., F/W, age 7, step-daughter, born Tenn.
John, M/W, age 5, step-son, born Tenn.
GUTHRIE, SARAH, F/W, age 72, mother, born Alabama.

130. DARWIN, ELLEN, F/B, age 45, cook , born Tenn.
James, M/B, age 23, cook, born Tenn.
Ben, M/B, age 17, farm hand, born Tenn.
CLARK, CLARK, M/B, age 17, dining room servant, born Tenn.

131. ROSE, SOLOMON, M/W, age 36, teamster, born Tenn.
Lucinda, F/W, age 36, wife, born Tenn.
J., M/W, age 15, son, attending school, born Tenn.
W. C., F/W, age 9, daughter, attending school, born Tenn.
Alice, F/W, age 8, daughter, attending school, born Tenn.
Elizabeth, F/W, age 7, daughter, attending school, born Tenn.
Peggy Jane, F/W, age 4, daughter, attending school, born Tenn.
Dolly, F/W, age 3, daughter, attending school, born Tenn.
Rebecca, F/W, daughter, born May, 1879, in Tenn.

132. HUNZIKER, MARY, F/W, age 44, farming, born Switzerland
Jacob, M/W, age 20, son, working on farm, born Switzerland
Lizzie, F/W, age 18, daughter, born Switzerland.
Mary, F/W, age 17, daughter, works on farm, born Switzerland.
Fred, M/W, age 16, son, works on farm, born Switzerland.
Paul, M/W, age 15, son, works on farm, born Switzerland.
Emil, M/W, age 14, son, works on farm, born Switzerland.
Adolph, M/W, age 13, son, works on farm, born Switzerland.
Bettie, F/W, age 7, daughter, at school, born Switzerland.
John, M/W, age 5, son, born Switzerland.
Emma, F/W, age 4, daughter, born Switzerland.

133. JONES, SAMUEL G., M/W, age 64, civil engineer, born Virginia.
A.S., F/W, age 49, wife, keeps boarding house, born South Carolina.
Samuel G., M/W, age 14, son, at school, born Alabama.
J. B., M/W, age 12, son, at school, born Alabama.
J. Scott, M/W, age 10, son, at school, born Alabama.
G. M., M/W, age 9, son, at school, born Alabama.
T. E., M/W, age 8, son, at school, born Alabama.

134. RICHARDSON, CHARLES, M/W, age 51, born South Carolina.
S.E., F/W, age 54, wife, born S.C.
WOODSON, CHARLES, M/B, age 32, gardener, born Virginia.

135. DUBOSE, name illegible, M/B, age 56, servant, born South Carolina.
Rachel, F/B, age 45, wife, cook, born Tenn.

136. PORCHER, M. L., W/F, age 51, keeps a boarding house, born S.C.
EGGLESTON, M. E., W/F, age 28, half-sister, born South Carolina.
FAILY, W. P., M/W, age 13, at school, born South Carolina.
U. L., M/W, age 8, at school, born South Carolina.

137. MCLEOD, U. L, M/W, age 35, planter, born Scotland.
Daredarelle, F/W, age 19, daughter, born Louisiana.
W.B., M/W, age 14, son, at school, born Louisiana.

138. DUBOSE, R. M., M/W, age 38, teacher, born South Carolina.
E., F/W, age 35, wife, born S.C.
R. M., M/W, age 5, son, at school, born Tenn.
M. P. M/W, son born November 1879, Tenn.
ERSEY, MARY, F/W, age 33, cook, born Tenn.
Nancy, F/W, age 16, nurse, born Tenn.
Henry, M/W, age 5, Mary's son, born Tenn.
MILLER, JENNIE, F/B, age 19, servant, born South Carolina.
HAWKINS, SAMUEL, M/B, age 20, servant, born Tenn.

139. GARNER, TOM, M/B, age 24, house servant, born Tenn.
Lou, F/B, age 16, sister, servant, born Tenn.

140. STORY, ALENE, F/MU, age 28, wash woman, born Tenn.

141. KLEISS, WILLIAM, M/W, age 31, minister, born England.
HALL, F. S., M/W, age 39, visitor, work minister, born England.
THOMPSON, W. G. G. , M/W, age 24, theological student, born England.
WEBBER, P. W., M/W, age 23, minister, born Mississippi.
HARRIS, N.B., M/W, age 21, theological student, born Mississippi.
HARRIS, J. A., M/W, age 17, brother, born Mississippi.
TAYLOR, A. R., M/W, age 21, theological student, born England.

142. THOMI, M., M/W, age 31, janitor at U. of South., born Switzerland.
E., F/W, age 31, wife, born Switzerland.
Rosa, F/W, age 7, daughter, at school, born Tenn.
Lenah, F/W, age 3, daughter, born TN.
Mary, F/W, age 1, daughter, born TN.
John, M/W, son, born March, 1880, in Tenn.
RYCHEW, MARGARET, F/W, age 60, mother-in-law, born Switzerland.

143. FASLER, JACOB, M/W, age 36, laborer, born Switzerland.
ANNIE, F/W, age 26, wife, born Switzerland.
Jacob, M/W, age 8, son, born Tenn.
ROSE, S., F/W, age 65, born Tenn.

144. QUINTARD, C. T., M/W, age 55, Bishop, born Connecticut.
E. C., F/W, age 53, wife, born Georgia.
C. E., F/W, age 27, daughter, born Georgia.
G. W., M/W, age 24, son, at school, born England
E. A., M/W, age 20, son, at school, born North Carolina.
BAYARD, E. B., F/W, age 72, mother-in-law, born Georgia.
WRIGHT, C. G., M/W, age 16, ward, at school, born Alabama.
STAMPTON, Maria, F/MU, age 63, servant, cook, born Tenn.
COLYAR, Maggie, F/MU, age 10, at school, born Georgia.
DAMOND, Charity, F/MU, age 23, servant, house maid, born Tenn.
HORN, JULIUS, M/B, age 17, servant, waiter, born Tenn.

145. RUSSELL, LEWIS, M/B, age 69, laborer, born Georgia.
Charlotte, F/B, age 50, wife, wash woman, born Missouri.

146. STAMPS, CASSIA, F/B, age 60, cook, born Tenn.
Becky, F/B, age 19, daughter, servant, born Tenn.

147. SARTIN, MARY, F/B, age 40, wash woman, born Missouri.
Lige, M/B, age 11, house servant, born Tenn.
Emma, F/B, age 13, born Tenn.
McKinn, R., M/B, age 7, adopted child, born Mississippi.
COWAN, J., F/B, age 22, nurse, born Tenn.
MATHEWS, LOUSA, F/B, age 20, nurse, born Tenn.

RUTLEDGE, THOS., M/MU, age 19, born Mississippi.
EMBRY, HENRY, M/B, age 16, waiter, born Georgia.
BROWN, BEN, M/B, age 51, laborer, born Georgia.

148. COTTON, J.M., M/W, age 38, born Tenn.
S., F/W, age 35, born North Carolina.
M., F/W, age 3, daughter, born Mississippi.

149. GRAY, FRANK, M/MU, age 20, dining room servant, born Tenn.

150. WILMER, GEORGE, M/W, age 61, clergyman, born Virginia.
Mary H., F/W, age 30, daughter, born Virginia.
G. G., M/W, age 23, son, civil engineer, born Virginia.
C. B., M/W, age 21, son, teacher, born Virginia.
L. P., F/W, age 19, daughter, born Virginia.
W. P., M/W, age 11, son , born Virginia.
J. R., M/W, age 9, son, born Virginia.
C. K., F/W, age 12, daughter, born Virginia.
DODSON, ALIA, F/W, age 73, born England.

151. HARRIS, MARY, F/B, age 51, wash woman, born Virginia.
Willis M., M/B, age 15, waiter, born Tenn.
Wallace, Joseph, M/B, age 15, laborer, born South Carolina.

152. GILLESPIE. R. J., M/W, age 39, brick mason, born Tenn.
Litha, F/W, age 25, wife, born Tenn.
Minnie Lee, F/W, age 7, born Tenn.
Tho. M., M/W, age 6, son, born Tenn.
Joseph A., M/W, age 4, son, born Tenn.
R. J., M/W, son born 1880, in Tenn.

153. GARNER, CATHERINE, F/B, age 40, wash woman, born Tenn.
Mary, F/B, age 17, daughter, nurse, born Tenn.
Hugh, M/B, age 10, son, born Tenn.
Lizzie, F/B, age 7, daughter, born Tenn.

154. GREEN, WILL, M/W, age 82, Bishop of Mississippi, born North Carolina.
L. W., F/W, age 34, daughter, born North Carolina.
Paul, M/W, age 10, grandson, at school, born Mississippi.
ASKINSON, VENIE, F/W, age 65, servant, cook, born Tenn.
PERKINS, MARY. F/B, age 14, servant, born Tenn.

155. WRIGHT, SALYTA, F/B, age 55, cook, born North Carolina.
Garnett, F/B, age 26, daughter, nurse, born Tenn.
Lenah, F/B, age 3, granddaughter, born Tenn.
ANDERSON, MARY, F/MU, age 12, granddaughter, nurse, born Tenn.

156. GIPSON, A, M/W, age 27, farmer, born Tenn.
Lucinda, F/W, age 39, wife, works on farm, born Tenn.
William, F/W, age 8, son, born Tenn.
Ida, F/W, age 2, daughter, born Tenn.

157. NORTHCUT, A. J., M/W, age 44, coal miner, born Tenn.
M. E., F/W, age 34, wife, born Tenn.
M. E., F/W, age 18, daughter, born Tenn.
R. F., F/W, age 16, daughter, born Tenn.
L. A., F/W, age 13, daughter, born Tenn.
Fanny, F/W, age 10, daughter, born Tenn.
J. R., M/W, age 8, son, born Tenn.
M. L., F/W, age 5, daughter, born Tenn.
J.A., M/W, son born 1879, in Tenn.

158. MCCLELLAN, V., F/W, age 52, wash woman, born Tenn.
Josie, F/W, age 22, daughter, seamstress, born Kentucky.
Morris, M/W, age 17, son, working on farm, born Kentucky.
Lawrence, M/W, age 13, son, working on farm, born Ky.
William, M/W, age 10, son, born Ky.

159. SHORT, R., M/W, age 46, stone mason, born Alabama.
J. A., F/W, age 33, working on farm, born Tenn.
Frank, M/W, age 13, son, born Tenn.
Emma Lee, F/W, age 10, daughter, born Tenn.
John, M/W, age 8, son, born Tenn.
David, M/W, age 5, son, born Tenn.

160. ROBERTSON, WM., M/B, age 45, born Tenn.

161. WYLEY, T. A., M/W, age 48, farmer, born Tenn.
E. C., F/W, age 46, wife, born Tenn.
J. D., M/W, age 19, son, at school, born Tenn.
A. J., F/W, age 17, daughter, at school, born Tenn.
Alla, F/W, age 9, daughter, at school, born Tenn.
Elizabeth, F/W, age 13, daughter, at school, born Tenn.
M. B., F/W, age 7, daughter, born Tenn.

162. BOWMAN, T., M/W, age 27, working on farm, born Alabama.
name illegible, F/W, age 24, wife, born Alabama.
R., M/W, age 9, son, born Alabama.
Addie, F/W, age 5, daughter, born Alabama.

163. O'DEAR, JAMES, W/M, age 84, pensioner in 1812 War, farmer, born Tenn.
S.M., F/W, age 47, wife, works on farm, born Alabama.
S. J., F/W, age 38, daughter, farming, born Tenn.
Virginia, F/W, age 28, daughter, farming, born Tenn.
Jack, M/W, age 40, son, farming, born Tenn.
M. C., F/W, age 33, daughter, farming, born Tenn.
Ben., M/W, age 26, son, farming, born Tenn.
Catherine, F/W, age 40, daughter-in-law, born Tenn.
Bailey, M/W, age 16, grandson, works on farm, born Tenn.
Parily, F/W, age 12, granddaughter, works on farm, born Tenn.
Jas. W., M/W, age 10, grandson, works on farm, born Tenn.
Susie, F/W, age 16, granddaughter, works on farm, born Tenn.
W. J., F/W, age 6, granddaughter, works on farm, born Tenn.
Rosella, F/W, age 4, granddaughter, born Tenn.
Taylor, M/W, age 6, grandson, born Tenn.
Franny, F/W, granddaughter, born Dec. 1879, in Tenn.
T. W., F/W, granddaughter, born 1879, in Tenn.
A. J., M/W, age 16, grandson, working on farm, born Tenn.
J. D., M/W, age 11, grandson, working on farm, born Tenn.
Thomas, M/W, age 7, grandson, born Tenn.
Benf., M/W, age 5, grandson, born Tenn.
Walter, M/W, age 2, grandson, born Tenn.

164. GREEN, J.M., M/W, age 43, farming, born Tenn.
M. A, F/W, age 42, wife, born Tenn.
R. C., M/W, age 21, son, born Tenn.
J. B., M/W, age 19, son, working on farm, born Alabama.
M. J. , F/W, age 14, daughter, working on farm, born Alabama.
J. T., F/W, age 12, son, working on farm, born Alabama.
W.A., M/W, age 6, son, born Alabama.
S. E., F/W, age 3, daughter, born Alabama.
G. W., M/W, son born April 1880, in Tenn.

165. GREEN, W. R., M/W, age 56, farming, born Tenn.
Rebecca, F/W, age 56, wife, born Tenn.
B.J., F/W, age 23, daughter, working on farm, born Tenn.
J. K., M/W, age 20, son, working on farm, born Alabama.
M. S, F/W, age 18, daughter, working on farm, born Alabama.
Maria, F/W, age 11, daughter, working on farm, born Tenn.

166. NIPPER, F. M/W, age 63, laborer, born Tenn.

167. HALL, EMILY, F/W, age 63, seamstress, born Tenn.

168. SEWELL, HENRY, M/W, age 65, farmer, born Kentucky.
C., F/W, age 60, wife, born Kentucky.
Mariah, F/W, age 21, daughter, cooking, born Tenn.
Rhoda, F/W, age 13, daughter, working on farm, born Tenn.
Henry, M/W, age 16, son, working on farm, born Tenn.
Josie, F/W, age 12, daughter, born Tenn.

169. HOWARD, HADEY, F/W, age 35, wash woman, born Tenn.
Peggy, F/W, age 11, daughter, at school, born Tenn.
Lizzie, F/W, age 8, daughter, at school, born Tenn.
Joe, M/W, age 6, son, born Tenn.

170. STEVENS, WM., M/W, age 27, railroading, born Tenn.
Sarah, F/W, age 27, wife, born Tenn.
Margaret, F/W, age 10, daughter, born Tenn.
Lucy, F/W, age 8, daughter, born Tenn.
Jennie, F/W, age 4, daughter, born Tenn.

171. GARNER, ? first name left out, M/W, age 31, railroading, born Tenn.
Nancy, F/W, age 28, wife, born Tenn.
Ellen, F/W, age 8, daughter, born Tenn.
Rebecca, F/W, age 5, daughter, born Tenn.

172. ELLIOTT, FRANCIS, F/W, age 35, wash woman, born Tenn.
Jack, M/W, age 8, son, working on farm, born Tenn.
Jim, M/W, age, 10, son, working on farm, born Tenn.

Sheppard, M/W, age 3, son, born Tenn.
MCQUEEN, name illegible, M/W, age 22, theological student, born Florida.

173. BRUCE, JACK, M/W, age 65, farmer, born Tenn.
Mary, F/W, age 62, wife, works on farm, born Tenn.
Ellen, F/W, age 21, daughter, works on farm, born Tenn.
Jim, M/W, age 19, son, works on farm, born Tenn.
King, M/W, age 11, step-son, works on farm, born Tenn.

174. GARNER, JACK, M/W, age 30, railroading, born Tenn.
Nancy, F/W, age 30, wife, wash woman, born Tenn.
Kate, F/W, age 8, daughter, born Tenn.
J. Henry, M/W, age 6, son, born Tenn.
Mammie, F/W, age 5, born Tenn.
Carry, F/W, age 16, daughter, born Tenn.

175. ALLEN, F. M., M/W, age 28, farmer, born Tenn.
M. A., F/W, age 34, wife, born Tenn.
J. H., M/W, age 6, son, born Tenn.
M. B., F/W, age 3, daughter, born Tenn.
E. M., F/W, age 2, son, born Tenn.

176. STEVENS, TAYLOR, M/W, age 24, farmer, born Tenn.
Martha, F/W, age 23, working on farm, born Tenn.
Nora, F/W, age 10, daughter, works on farm, born Tenn.
Elizabeth, F/W, age 7, daughter, born Tenn.
L. E., M/W, age 5, son, born Tenn.
Wm., M/W, age 2, son, born Tenn.
Nancy, F/W, age 22, sister, born Tenn.

177. HOLT, J., M/W, age 22, waggoner, born Tenn.
Maggie, F/W, age 22, wife, born Tenn.
C. A., M/W, age 3, son, born Tenn.

178. WEBER, J. W., M/W, age 27, teacher, born Tenn.
M. J., F/W, age 18, wife, born Tenn.
H. C., M/W, age 19, brother, at school, born Tenn.
GREEN, P.A., F/W, age 22, sister-in-law, born Tenn.

179. HUTCHEY, GEO., M/B, age 51, gardener, born Tenn.
Wandy, F/B, age 35, wife, wash woman, born Tenn.
Hannah, F/B, age 20, daughter, nurse, born Tenn.
Sarah, F/B, age 18, daughter, wash woman, born Tenn.
Lizzie, F/B, age 15, daughter, nurse, born Tenn.
Charlotte, F/B, age 13, daughter, nurse, born Tenn.
Geo., M/B, age 12, son, born Tenn.
Rosa, F/B, age 10, daughter, born Tenn.
Orland, M/B, age 9, son, born Tenn.
James, M/B, age 6, son, born Tenn.
C. A., M/B, age 4, daughter, born Tenn.

180. ARNET, JACK, M/B, age 20, laborer, born Tenn.
Letha, F/B, age 20, wife, born Tenn.
John, M/B, age 1, son, born Tenn.

181. ARNET, A. S., M/B, age 62, farmer, born Tenn.
Rebecca, F/B, age 61, wife, born Tenn.
Davis, M/B, age 21, farming, born Tenn.
John, M/B, age 20, farming, born Tenn.
James, M/B, age 18, son, working on farm, born Tenn.
J. D., M/B, age 5, grandson, born Tenn.

182. ANDERSON, I. W., M/W, age 31, farming, born Tenn.
Elizabeth, F/W, age 26, wife, born Tenn.
S. A., F/W, age 8, daughter, born Tenn.
M. A., F/W, age 6, daughter, born Tenn.
S. J., F/W, age 4, daughter, born Tenn.
J. D., M/W, age 4, son, born Tenn.
Rebecca, F/W, age 1, daughter, born Tenn.

183. FARRIS, MARTHA, F/W, age 58, born Tenn.
Joe, M/W, age 26, son, laborer, born Tenn.
B., M/W, age 22, son, laborer, born Tenn.
JACKSON, Jennie, F/W, age 26, daughter, born Tenn.
Martha, F/W, age 10, granddaughter, at school, born Tenn.
Catherine, F/W, age 8, granddaughter, at school, born Tenn.
Minnie Lee, F/W, age 4, granddaughter, born Tenn.
Luler, F/W, age 9, granddaughter, at school, born Tenn.
Ora, F/W, age 1, granddaughter, at school, born Tenn.

184. WALKER, TOM, M/W, age 34, farming, born Tenn.
Nancy, F/W, age 33, wife, born Ala.
Elizabeth, F/W, age 13, daughter, born Tenn.
Madison, M/W, age 11, son, born Tenn.
Virginia W., F/W, age 11, daughter, born Tenn.

Lilly, F/W, age 8, daughter, born Tenn.
A., F/W, age 6, daughter, born Tenn.
W., M/W, age 4, son, born Tenn.

185. READ, THOS., M/W, age 19, servant, born Tenn.

186. GARNER, SAML., M/B, age 52, laborer, born Tenn.

187. PRESCOTT, no first name given, M/W, age 51, born Tenn.
Jane, F/W, age 30, daughter, born Tenn.
Rachel, F/W, age 20, daughter, born Tenn.

188. ROLLINS, HALL, M/MU, age 61, hack driver, born Virginia.
Rose, F/B, age 40, wife, born South Carolina.

189. MCBEE, V., M/W, age 20, music teacher, born North Carolina.

190. TODD, E. J., M/W, age 29, carpenter, born Tenn.
R. A., F/W, age 36, wife, seamstress, born Tenn.

191. HODGSON, TELFAIR, M/W, age 40, minister, born Virginia.
Fanny, F/W, age illegible, born Pennsylvania.
J. H., M/W, age 14, son, at school, born New Jersey.
Telfair, M/W, age 3, son, born New Jersey.
Sarah, F/W, daughter, born 1880, born New York.
Duncan, Lizzie, F/W, age 35, nurse, born Ireland.
McGrady, Mary, F/W, age 35, nurse, born Ireland.

192. COLEMAN, HENRY, M/B, age 35, coal miner, born Georgia.
Jennie, F/B, age 30, wife, born Alabama.
Geo., M/B, son, born April 1879, in Georgia.
GYN, Adalin, F/B, age 50, mother, born Georgia.
Sis, F/B, age 8, niece, born Georgia.
Kitty, F/B, age 1, niece, born Tenn.

193. GREEN, J. S., M/W, age 26, magistrate, born Mississippi.
L. G, F/W, age 23, wife, born Louisiana.
J. S., M/W, age 2, , born Tenn.

194. GRAHAM, W. F., M/W, age 53, music teacher, born Germany.
A. A., F/W, age 50, wife, born Maryland.
SEAY, M. L., F/W, age 25, daughter, born Maryland.
C. W., F/W, age 6, granddaughter, born Tenn.
A. K., F/W, age 5, granddaughter, born Tenn.

195. LADD, WM. M., M/W, age 34, laborer, born Tenn.
Ellen, F/W, age 25, wife, born Tenn.

196. BURKS, J.H., M/W, age 35, retail merchant, born New York.
Julia, F/W, age 35, wife, born France.
Frank J., M/W, age 13, son, at school, born New York.
Jos. J., M/W, age 11, son, at school, born New York.
W. D., M/W, age 9, son, at school, born Tenn.
Eddie, M/W, age 7, son, at school, born Tenn.
RILEY, ELLEN, F/W, age 20, boarding, born Texas.

SEWANEE, MARION COUNTY, TENN., RESIDENTS IN 1880 CENSUS

197. BENNETT, ELY, M/W, age 47, farmer, born Tenn.
Martha J., F/W, age 21, daughter, born Tenn.
Jefferson D., M/W age 18, son, born Tenn.
William O., M/W, age 14, son, born Tenn.
Thomas, M/W, age 12, son, born Tenn.
Robert L., M/W, age 10, son, born Tenn.
Munroe B., M/W, age 8, son, born Tenn.
198. TATE, ELISHA D., M/W, age 47, farmer, born Tenn.
Mary J., F/W, age 31, wife, born Tenn.
Edward R., M/W, age 8, son, born Tenn.
Susan A., F/W, age 6, daughter, born Tenn.
Rachel T., F/W, age 4, daughter, born Tenn.
Elijah D., M/W, age 2, son, born Tenn.
Austin A., M/W, son born August 1879, in Tenn.
199. GARNER, JOHN, M/W, age 24, working on farm, born Tenn.
Jennie, F/W, age 19, wife, born Minnesota.
Griffith, M/W, son born August 1879, in Tenn.
200. HENLEY, ISAAC, M/W, age 22, farmer, born Tenn.
Caroline, F/W, age 21, wife, born Tenn.
201. STATUM, JOHN, M/W, age 32, laborer, born Tenn.
Nancy A., F/W, age 35, wife, born Georgia.
Leonidas T., M/W, age 3, son, born Tenn.
William M., M/W, age 1, son, born Tenn.

STUDENTS AT SEWANEE DURING 1880 CENSUS

1. SMITH, S. W, age 20, born S. Carolina.
2. BRUSSON, R. age 16, born Arkansas.
3. RARNELL, M. P. age 19, born S.C..
4. McGLAHAN, S.B, age 21, born Tenn.
5. CONYERS, W. C., age 21, born S.C.
6. LIONELL, W.S., age 19, born Mississippi.
7. REID, J.A., age 19, born Tenn.
8. DUNCAN, W. P., age 17, born Miss.
9. CORNISH, J. J., age 22, born S.C.
10. SHIPPARD, L. F., age 16, born Texas.
11. PRICE, I. F., age 19, born Louisiana.
12. DON, C. H., age 19, born Georgia.
13. GORWOOD, H. W., age 18, born Texas.
14. BUTTS, J. J., age 18, born Louisiana.
15. CHRITTEN, H. W., age 16, born Tenn.
16. CODY, W. C., age 19, born Connecticut.
17. MANSFIELD, C. F., age 16, born Ill.
18. WHITE, F. H., age 16, born Louisiana.
19. WILSON, S., age 17, born Louisiana.
20. GIBBS, J., age 19, born New York.
21. GAINES, first name illegible, age 19, born Arkansas.
22. THOMPSON, J., age 20, born Tenn.
23. SLASS OR GLASS, J.W., age 16, born Alabama.
24. BASSIN, WM. R, age 15, born Texas.
25. BRAMONT, R. R., age 15, born Texas.
26. BRAMONT, Walter, age 15, born Texas
27. ROBINSON, E, age 18, born Texas.
28. ROBINSON, JOHN, age 18, born Miss.
29. PULER, W. A., age 16, born Mississippi.
30. HARRISON, G. E., age 15, born VA.
31. BOLLING, J., age 19, born Texas.
32. THOMPSON, J. B., age 14, born Miss.
33. NOBLE, R. S., age 17, born Louisiana.
34. STARR, E. A., age 17, born Texas.
35. DOUGLASS, W. T., age 21, Theological Student, born Mississippi.
36. STICKEN, S. P., age 17, born Alabama.
37. COBB, J. H., age 17, born Alabama.
38. POINDEXTER, S. L., age 16, born Mississippi.
39. SCHARFFER, T.A., age 15, born Louisiana.
40. COX. illegible name, age 15, born N.C.
41. MCBEE, THOMAS, age 15, born N.C.
42. MCBEE, W. B., age 17, born S.C.
43. COPENS, F. F., age 18, born S.C.
44. FUILAY, J. F. , age 17, born S.C.
45. POVAM, J. F., age 17, born Florida.
46. LUCHT, W. R, age 14. born Mississippi.
47. HORTIGO, A., age 14, born Mississippi.
48. FORTNER, G. D., age 16, born Georgia.
49. POOSEY, W. J., age 15, born Miss.
50. POOSEY, W. A., age 17, born Miss.
51. PEDUR, H. H., age 13, born Illinois.
52. CLARK, J. C., age 15, born Alabama.
53. NATHANIEL, H. S., age 13, born Tenn.
54. DREADEL, A., age 17, born Florida.
55. WOODRUFF, A, age 15, born Tenn.
56. PEARSON, G. W., age 26, born Tenn.
57. JOHNSON, BURR, age 14, born Miss.
58. JOHNSON, H. R., age 17, born Miss.
59. RAUDOLPH, P. R., age 15, born Tenn.
60. STILES, J. C., age 16, born Georgia.
61. TABER, A. R., age 19, born S.C.
62. KELLY, R., age 15, born Louisiana.
63. LUSK, G., age 16, born Louisiana.
64. GLASS, J. G. age 19, born S.C.
65. MARKBAUM, F. D, age 17, born Miss.
66. PALFREY, T.B., age 17, born Louisiana.
67. PALFREY, F. R., age 17, born Louisiana.
68. ELLIOT, H., age 17, born Georgia.
69. MARKS, N. M., age 17, born Alabama.
70. WILBURN, E. L., age 17, born Tenn.
71. HOLLAND, C., age 14, born Louisiana.
72. GARNET, H., age 19, born Arkansas.
73. COACHMINER, J. R., age 20, born FL.
74. ELLIOT, S., age 15, born Texas.
75. SEAY, S., age 18, born Tenn.
76. McALLEN, J., age 17, born Texas.
77. GARRETT, H., age 19, born Texas.
78. MORRISON, J. C., age 17, born N.C.
79. LIPPINT, F. B., age 17, born N.C.
80. MYERS, B. S., age 19, born N.C.
81. HUGHES, E. W., age 16, born S.C.
82. Name illegible, age 19, born S.C.
83. SWAN, D. D., age 15, born Florida.
84. HOSKINS, W. S., age 16, born Tenn.
85. FROST, F. R., age 17, born S.C.
86. COOPER, J. H., age 18, born Georgia.
87. JUDSON, L. F., age 17, born Florida.
88. DYER, W. R., age 19, born Georgia.
89. FRASSAN, C.C., age 21, born Georgia.
90. STUDMAYD, L. R. age 15, born S.C.
91. BOUCHER, A., age 15, born Louisiana.
92. BLACK, E. M., age 14, born N.C.
93. ALTRY, W. B., age 18, born Mississippi.
94. STILES, H. C. age 17, born Georgia.
95. ROBERTSON, E. T., age 18, born LA.
96. MORGAN, W. M., age 17, born Tenn.
97. BRATTON, W. D., age 19, born S.C.
98. BALLINEN, W.B., age 19, born GA.
99. BOYKIN, L., age 19, born S.C.
100. HOLTBRAHAM, E., age 17, born GA.
101. GALDIN, E. H., age 18, born S.C.
102. REMMICK, ED, age 16, born Texas.

103. HODGINS, C. B., age 26, theological student, born Virginia.
104. GREAT, M. E., age 22, born Kentucky.
105. ELLIOTT A.B., age 18, , born Georgia.
106. WIGGINS. B. L., age 19, born S.C.
107. MORELAND, W. H., age 19, born S.C.
108. KING, S.W., age 21, born Kentucky.
109. NAUTS, W. B., age 20, born Kentucky.
110. DAVIS, F., age 18, born S.C.
111. BARNWELL, R. W., age 19, born S.C.
112. KELLO, J., age 15, born Tenn.
113. KERR, J. B., age 18, born Tenn.
114. C name illegible, age 17, born Tenn.
115. CORNISH, C. C., age 18, born S.C.
116. BECKETT, J., age 19, born Texas.
117. LYMAN, A., age 25, born N.C.
118. MILES, W. M., age 18, born S.C.
119. BLANE, H. W., age 19, born Louisiana.
120. CROWNOVER, M., age 23, born Tenn.
121. NOBEL, W. W. age 25, born Georgia.

In the 1880 census records, there were 201 households listed in Sewanee, and 121 out of town students.

PEOPLE LIVING AT SEWANEE IN 1900

The following data was taken from the 1900 census records for the 18th District of Franklin County, Tennessee.. The most important genealogy information has been printed. It includes: name, sex, color, month, year and place of birth, years married, and relationship to head of family. F for female, M for male, W for white, B for black.

1. COLLINS, JAMES, M/W, July 1853, Tenn., married 26 yrs.
   Sarah, F/W, Nov. 1855, born in Tenn., wife.
   Arrus W, M/W, Oct. 1878, Tenn., son
   Phillip B., M/W, Feb. 1877, Tenn., son
   Edna M., F/W, Oct. 1883, Tenn., daughter
   Catherine V., F/W, Jan. 1887, Tenn., daughter
   James F. M/W, July 1889, Tenn., son
   Jay D., M/W, Feb. 1892, Tenn.,
   George H. M/W, born Sept. 1894, Tenn., son
   Anna A., F/W, Sept. 1898, Tenn.,
   Terrill, Matt, M/W, Mar. 1880, Tenn., boarder in Collins household.
2. BLACK, SAMUEL H, M/W, born Nov. 1865, married 15 years, born in Tenn.,
   Josephine, F/W, Feb. 1868, Tenn., wife
   Frank B., M/W, Mar. 1886, Tenn., son
   Scott, M/W, Feb. 1889, Tenn., son
   Bessie, F/W, Jul., 1891, Tenn., daughter
   Charlie, M/W, Feb. 1894, Tenn., son
   Beulah, F/W, Dec. 1896, Tenn., daughter
   Estell, F/W, Mar. 1899, Tenn., daughter
3. CAMPBELL, WHITE, M/W, born Dec., 1861, Tenn., married 15 yrs.
   Ellen, F/W, born Apr. 1861, Tenn., wife
   Sallie, F/W, Oct. 1885, Tenn., daughter
   William, M/W, July 1887, Tenn., son
   Nannie, F/W, June 1889, Tenn., daughter
   Petry, M/W, July 1891, Tenn., son.
   Earnest, M/W, Dec. 1894, Tenn., son.
   Dessie, F/W, Feb. 1896, Tenn., son
   Elsie, F/W, Feb. 1898, Tenn., son.
4. MURRELL, ALFRED, M/W, born Jun. 1844, married 24 yrs., born in Tenn.,
   Saisa, F/W, born Oct. 1854, Tenn., wife
   Ridgely, F/W, Aug. 1879, Tenn., daughter.
   Alfred H., M/W, Sept. 1886, Tenn., son.
5. O'DEAR, ANDREW J., M/W, born Aug. 1838, Tenn., married 33 yrs.
   Catherine. F/W, born Sept. 1846, Tenn., wife
   Rachel, F/W, July 1885, Tenn., daughter.
   Jeff. M/W, M/W, Apr., 1886, Tenn., son
6. SHORT, JULEY, F/W, born Nov. 1848, born in Tenn., widow
   Ruben, M/W, born Apr. 1881, Tenn., son.
   Edd, M/W, born Apr. 1889, Tenn., son.
7. HARRIS, MILES, M/W, born Nov. 1853, married 18 yrs., born in Tenn.,
   Nannie, F/W, born Aug. 1860, Tenn., wife
   Etta, F/W, Sept. 1882, Tenn., daughter.
   Mattie, F/W, Apr. 1885, Tenn., daughter.
   David, M/W, Sept. 1889, Tenn., son.
   Jimmie, M/W, Oct. 1893, Tenn., son.
   Charles, M/W, Sept 1899, Tenn., son.
8. MONTGOMERY, STEWART, M/W, born Oct 1843, Tenn., widower
   William, M/W, born Feb. 1856, Tenn., brother.
   Lizzie, F/W, born Jun. 1860, Tenn., sister.
   Annie E., F/W, Jun. 1875, Tenn., daughter.
9. SCHNEICHE, HENRY, M/W, born Feb., 1857, Switzerland, married 20 yrs.
   Carrie, F/W, born 1856, Ohio, parents from Germany, wife
10. MCDOWELL, MALCOLM, M/W, born 1857, Iowa, married 11 yrs.
    MAUD, F/W, born Dec. 1862, Vermont, wife.
    Adair, F/W, born May 1890, Tenn., daughter.
    Geraldine, F/W, Sept. 1892, Tenn., daughter.
    STOWE, CLARANCE, M/W, Feb. 1873, Vermont. brother-in-law.
    HUNT OR HURST, ABE, M/B, Mar. 1839 Alabama, Servant.
    SPRYER, LILLIE, F/W, Sept. 1879, Tenn., Servant.
11. GREEN, WILLIAM, M/W, born Mar. 1873, Tenn., married 2 yrs.
    Sina, F/W, Aug. 1879, Tenn., wife.
    Roy, M/W, Dec., 1898, Tenn., son.
12. O'DEAR, WILLIAM, M/W, born Sept. 1870, Tenn., single.
13. DYER, THOMAS J. M/W, born Sept. 1875, Tenn., married 4 yrs.
    Bettie, F/W, born May 1875, Tenn., wife.
    Margrett, F/W, born Oct. 1896, Tenn., daughter.

Emma, F/W, born Sept. 1898, Tenn., daughter.

14. McCOY, WILLIAM A., M/W, born 1845, Tenn., married 21 yrs.
Lou, F/W, born Feb. 1856, Tenn., wife.
Clara, F/W, born June 1882, Tenn., daughter.
William, M/W, Mar. 1884, Tenn., son.
Dessie, F/W, Aug. 1887, Tenn., daughter.
Laura, F/W, Mar. 1891, Tenn., daughter.
John, M/W, Apr.. 1892, Tenn., son.
Ollie F/W, May 1894, Tenn., daughter.
Mildred, F/W, Feb. 1900, Tenn., daughter.

15. ARMISTEAD, ROBERT P., M/W, born Jan. 1846, Kentucky, married 19 yrs.
Jannie, F/W, born Apr. 1863, Kentucky, wife. (no children)
Dora or Nora M, F/W, born May 1896, Tenn., adopted child.

16. GIPSON, ALLEN, M/W, born Mar. 1859, Tenn., married 10 yrs.
Emma, F/W, born Aug 1871, Tenn., wife.
Joice, F/W, born Aug. 1892, Tenn., daughter.
Lois, F/W, born July 1895, Tenn., daughter.
Sylvester, M/W, born May, 1896, Tenn., son.
Austin, M/W, born June 1897, Tenn., son.

17. BARNES, NANCY F/W, born Jan. 1854, Tenn., widow.
Joe, M/W, born May 1876, Tenn., son.
Litha F/W, born Jun. 1883, Tenn., daughter.
David, M/W, born Apr. 1885, Tenn., son.
Alice, F/W, born Dec. 1886, Tenn., daughter.
Margilee, F/W, born Nov. 1889, Tenn., daughter.

18. REED, JOHN, M/W, born Feb. 1870, Tenn., married 16 yrs.
Hattie, F/W, born Apr. 1867, Tenn., wife.
Louis F., M/W, born Aug. 1886, Tenn., son.
Auther L., M/W, born Feb. 1889, Tenn., son.
Jessie, F/W, born July 1893, Tenn., daughter.
Willie, F/W, born Dec. 1894, Tenn., daughter.
Hattie, F/W, born Oct. 1896, Tenn., daughter.
John, M/W, born Dec. 1900, Tenn., son.

19. HENLEY, JNO, M/W, born Apr. 1872, Tenn., married 6 yrs.
Mary, F/W, born Dec. 1872, Tenn., wife.
Hattie, F/W, born Mar. 1895, Tenn., daughter.
Hazzard, M/W, born July 1896, Tenn., son.

20. MITCHELL, ROBERT, M/W, born Aug. 1870, Tenn., married 11 yrs.
Jeane, F/W, born May 1873, Tenn., wife.
William L., M/W, born July 1890, Tenn., son.
Robert R., M/W, born Mar. 1892, Tenn., son.
Lawrence, M/W, born June 1895, Tenn., son.
Irene J., F/W, born Oct. 1897, Tenn., daughter.
Herbert, M/W, born Mar. 1900, Tenn., son.

21. STATEM, JOHN, W/M, born Jan. 1861, Tenn., married 8 yrs.
Saidie, F/W, born June 1863, Tenn., wife.
Katie F/W, born July, 1888, Tenn., daughter.
Blanche, F/W, born Apr. 1895, Tenn., daughter
Mary, F/W, born Nov. 1899, Tenn., daughter.
BIDDLE, TOM, M/W, born Nov. 1859, Tenn., brother-in-law, single.

22. FOSTER, WILLIAM, M/W, born Mar. 1877, Tenn., married 6 yrs.
Tennie, F/W, born Dec. 1876, Tenn., wife.
Carl, M/W, born Nov. 1895, Tenn., son.
Columbus C., M/W, born Mar. 1896, Tenn., son.
Sylvia A., F/W, born June 1899, Tenn., daughter.
WILLIAMSON, Mary, F/W, born Nov. 1839, Tenn., mother-in-law, widow.

23. FISCHER, OTTO, M/W, born June 1861, Germany, married 18 yrs.
Cordelia, F/W, born Nov. 1861, Tenn., wife.
Delia, F/W, born Nov. 1883, Tenn., daughter.
Eawarda, F/W, born June 1885, Tenn., daughter.
Carl, M/W, born Dec. 1886, Tenn., son.
Sarah, F/W, born Nov. 1888, Tenn., daughter.
William, M/W, born June 1891, Tenn., son.
Jane, F/W, born Jun. 1893, Tennessee, daughter.

24. WALKER, TAYLOR, M/W, born June 1848, Tenn., married 26 yrs.
Elizabeth, F/W, born Jan. 1850, Tenn., wife.
True, F/W, born June 1873, Tenn.,

daughter.
James, M/W, born May 1876, Tenn., son.
Delia, (Hattie) F/W, born Apr. 1881, Tenn., daughter
Wayne H., M/W, born Nov. 1886, Tenn., son.

25. STEWMAN, ELIZABETH, F/W, born Jan. 1865, Tenn., widow.
Mamie, F/W, born Aug. 1886, Tenn., daughter.
Ollie, M/W, born Sept. 1888, Tenn., son.
Albert, M/W, born Apr. 1892, Tenn., son.
David, M/W, born Nov. 1896, Tenn., son.
Mai, F/W, born Apr., 1900, Tenn., daughter.

26. TERRILL, CUROD, M/W, born Oct. 1875, Tenn., married 5 yrs.
Mahala, F/W, born Sept, 1878, Tenn., wife.

27. MYERS, BETTIE, F/W, born Feb. 1850, Tenn., married 21 yrs.
William, M/W, born Sept. 1854, Tenn., husband.
Osco, M/W, born Nov. 1879, Tenn., son.
Beulah, F/W, born Jan, 1882, Tenn., daughter.
Evert, M/W, born May 1884, Tenn., son.
Cecil, M/W, born Jan. 1888, Tenn., son.
Beatrice, F/W, born Aug. 1890, Tenn., daughter.
Theron, M/W, born Aug. 1893, Tenn., son.

28. GREEN, BENTON J., M/W, born Feb. 1861, Tenn., married 18 yrs.
Mary, F/W, born June 1861, Tenn., wife.
Martha, F/W, born Apr. 1882, Tenn., daughter.
Jimmie F/W, born Oct. 1884, Tenn., daughter. (may be a son)
Phannas, M/W, born Oct. 1889, Tenn., son. (Thomas)
Rebecca, F/W, born Feb. 1892, Tenn., daughter.
Lou, F/W, born June 1895, Tenn., son.

29. O'DEAR, SARAH, F/W, born Sept. 1844, Tenn., widow.
Alice F/W, born Sept. 1891, Tenn., granddaughter.
Robert, M/W, born Feb. 1895, Tenn., grandson.

30. PACK, JOHN, M/W, born Feb. 1869, Tenn., married 10 yrs.
Ellen, F/W, born Feb. 1875, Tenn., wife.
Susana, F/W, born July 1893, Tenn., daughter.
Bruce A., M/W, born Dec. 1895, Tenn., son.
William W., M/W, born Feb. 1898, Tenn., son.

31. GUDGER, ROBERT P. M/W, born Sept. 1849, Georgia, married 20 yrs.
Nancy, F/W, born July 1859, Tenn., wife.
Mary A., F/W, born Sept. 1855, Tenn., daughter.
James F., M/W, born Dec. 1888, Tenn., son.

32. GARNER, SAMUEL, M/W, born Dec. 1872, Tenn., married 8 yrs.
Mary J., F/W, born June 1876, Tenn., wife.
Bert, M/W, born Dec. 1892, Tenn., son.
Thomas A., M/W, born Oct. 1894, Tenn., son.
Gracy C., F/W, born July 1896, Tenn., daughter.
Samuel R., M/W, born Aug. 1898, Tenn., son.
Flora E., F/W, born May 1900, Tenn., daughter.

33. GUDGER, WILLIAM, M/W, born Sept. 1849, Georgia, married 13 yrs.
Jane, F/W, born Jan. 1870, Illinois, wife.
Harrison, M/W, born Oct. 1888, Tenn., son.
Carrie, F/W, born Jan. 1891, Tenn., daughter.
James G., M/W, born Apr. 1893, Tenn., son.
William, M/W, born July 1895, Tenn., son.
Lillie E., F/W, born Feb. 1899, Tenn., daughter.

34. ?FARMER, FARRIS , WILLIAM, M/W born Feb. 1852, Tenn., married 18 yrs.
Bell, F/W, born Feb. 1865, Tenn., wife.
Samuel, M/W, born June 1888, Tenn., son.
Sallie, F/W, born Sept 1885, Tenn., daughter.
Minnie, F/W, born Jan. 1886, Tenn., daughter.
Noah, M/W, born Jan. 1891, Tenn., son.
Andrew, M/W, born Aug. 1892, Tenn., son.
Pollie, F/W, born July 1895, Tenn., daughter.
WILBANKS, CHILLATA, F/W, Apr. 1840, Tenn., mother-in-law, widow.

35. FOSTER, BOYD, M/W, born Apr. 1843, Tenn., married 36 yrs.
Susan A., F/W, born Nov. 1846, Tenn., wife.
Caswell, M/W, born July 1880, Tenn., son.
Ida C., F/W, born Sept 1889, Tenn., daughter.

36. BARNES, GEORGE, M/W, born Apr. 1850, Tenn.,
Washington, M/W, born Mar. 1896, Tenn., son.
GILLIAM, BILL, M/W, born Mar. 1853, Tenn.,.
37. HARRISON, THOMAS, M/W, born, June 1876, Tenn., married 3 yrs.
Annie, F/W, born 1875, Tenn., wife.
Hays, M/W, born Oct. 1897, Tenn., son.
Ollie, F/W, born 1900, Tenn., daughter.
FARRIS, LIZZIE, F/W, born Jan. 1883, Tenn., sister-in-law, single.
38. IVES, GRANT, M/W, born Sept. 1872, Tenn., widower.
Garnett, F/W, born May, 1896, Tenn., daughter.
FRANCES, F/W, born June 1897, Tenn., daughter.
Robert, M/W, born Jan. 1899, Tenn., son.
Susie J., F/W, born June 1829, Virginia, mother.
39. PERRY, GEORGE, M/W, born July 1850, Tenn., married 30 yrs.
Sarah, F/W, born July 1850, Tenn., wife.
John T., M/W, born July 1882, Tenn., son.
Dolly, F/W, born Feb. 1885, Tenn., daughter
Lee, M/W, born Feb. 1891, Tenn., son.
40. ANDERSON, IKE, M/W, born Nov. 1848, Tenn., married 31 yrs.
Elizabeth, F/W, born Mar. 1850, Tenn., wife.
Thelopius, M/W, born Aug. 1877, Tenn., son.
Sopha, F/W, born Aug. 1879, Tenn., daughter.
William, M/W born Apr. 1882, Tenn., son.
Lucy, F/W, born May 1884, Tenn., daughter.
Albert, M/W, born Oct. 1886, Tenn., son.
Mahala J., F/W, born Aug. 1888, Tenn., daughter.
41. AUSTIN, MARTIN G., M/W, born Dec. 1854, Tenn., married 19 yrs.
Julia A., F/W, born Feb. 1861, Tenn., wife.
John W., M/W, born Sept. 1882, Tenn., son.
Isaac O., M/W, born July 1891, Tenn., son.
42. HARRISON, SALLIE, F/W, born Feb. 1850, Tenn., widow.
George, M/W, Feb. 1879, Tenn., son.
Bettie, F/W, Jan., 1883, Tenn., daughter.
Addie F/W, born Jun. 1885, Tenn., daughter.
Nannie A., F/W, born Mar. 1887, Tenn., daughter.
Harvey, M/W, born Jan. 1889, Tenn., son.
Fredrick, M/W, born Jan. 1891, Tenn., son.
43. ROLLINS, JOHN, M/W, born Dec. 1854, Tenn., married 19 yrs.
Margret, F/W, born Mar. 1856, Tenn., wife.
Edmon, M/W, born Oct. 1880, Tenn., son.
Willie, M/W, Aug. 1884, Tenn., son.
Georgie M/W, Aug. 1886, Tenn., son.
James, M/W, born Aug 1889, Tenn., son.
44. GREEN, JAMES, M/W, born Feb. 1835, Tenn., married 43 yrs.
Martha, F/W, born Jan. 1836, Tenn., wife.
George, M/W, born Apr. 1880, Tenn., son.
John, M/W, born May 1883, Tenn., son.
45. DYER, JOSLIN S., M/W, born Aug. 1838, Tenn., married 32 yrs.
Margaret, F/W, born Apr. 1834, Tenn., wife.
William, M/W, born Jan. 1876, Tenn., son.
Jacob L., M/W, born Jan. 1879, Tenn., son.
Johnnie R., M/W, born Nov. 1882, Tenn., son.
46. HARRISON, THOMAS, M/W, born Feb. 1853, Tenn., married 18 yrs.
Louisa, F/W, born July 1863, Tenn., wife.
Frank, M/W, born Nov. 1889, Tenn., son.
47. HARRISON, JERRY, M/W, born Mar. 1825, Missouri, married 22 yrs.
Eliza, F/W, born May 1840, Tenn., wife
48. ROLLINS, FRANK, M/W, born Apr. 1871, Tenn., married 7 yrs.
Zilphia, F/W, born Oct. 1875, Tenn., wife.
Jackson M., M/W, born Aug. 1883, Tenn., son.
James B., M/W, b. Dec. 1895, Tenn., son.
Jennie, F/W, born May 1898, Tenn., daughter.
49. LEWIS, JOE, M/W, born Jun. 1877, Tenn., married 5 yrs.
Mary, F/W, born Aug. 1875, Tenn., wife.
Tom, M/W, Aug. 1896, Tenn., son.
Cora, F/W, Apr. 1898, Tenn., daughter.
Stella M., F/W, born May 1899, Tenn., daughter.
50. PARTON, DICK, M/W, born Jan. 1853, Tenn., married 23 yrs.
Jane, F/W, born Apr. 1857, Tenn., wife.
Jannie, F/W, born Feb. 1880, Tenn., daughter.
Huston, M/W, born Jun. 1883, Tenn., son.
Louisa, F/W, born May 1885, Tenn., daughter.
Sallie, F/W, born Dec. 1889, Tenn.,

daughter.
Ben, M/W, born Feb. 1893, Tenn., son.
John, M/W, born June 1895, Tenn., son.

51. GODBEY, THOMAS, M/W, born Feb. 1840, Kentucky, married 29 yrs.
Sallie, F/W, born, Jan. 1850, Tenn., wife.
Francis M., M/W, born Dec. 1871, Tenn., son.
Mary M., F/W, born Dec. 1875, Tenn., daughter.
Lizzie S., F/W, born Sept. 1879, Tenn., daughter.
John M., M/W, born June 1883, Tenn., son.
Gussie M., F/W, born Aug. 1889, Tenn., daughter.
Clarence M/W, born July 1892, Tenn., son.

52. ANDERSON, JEANNIE, F/W born Mar. 1866, Tenn., widow.
Alfred, M/W, born July 1889, Tenn., son.
Petway, M/W, born Feb. 1891, Tenn., son.
Andrew J., M/W, born Feb. 1893, Tenn., son.
Beulah, F/W, born Mar. 1895, Tenn., daughter.
SUTHERLAND, POLLY, F/W, born Dec. 1834, Alabama, aunt.

53. HUNZIKER, EMILE, M/W, born Apr. 1865, Switzerland.
Virginia, F/W, born May 1880, Tenn., wife.
KLIENWACHTER, CHALLEY, M/W, born Aug. 1884, Tenn., boarder.

54. DISHROOM, GABRIEL, M/W, born Mar. 1836, Georgia, married 33 yrs.
Maudy A., F/W, born Jan. 1846, Tenn., wife.
GIPSON, MARTHA, F/W, born July 1873, Tenn., daughter.
Dewitt, M/W, born June 1897, Tenn., grandson.
Ruhama, F/W, born Oct. 1898, Tenn., granddaughter.

55. NORWOOD, PEGGY, F/W, born Mar. 1848, Tenn., widow.
Rosa, F/W, born Oct. 1885, Tenn., daughter.
Maud, F/W, born Aug. 1880, Tenn., daughter.

56. TRUSSELL, MARTHA, F/W, born July 1848, Tenn., widow.
Sadie, F/W, born Aug. 1872, Tenn., daughter.
Jackson, M/W, born Sept. 1877, Tenn., son.
Nancy, F/W, born June 1880, Tenn., daughter.
Paul, M/W, born Aug. 1890, Tenn., son.

57. ANDERSON, DAVID, M/W, born Mar. 1858, Tenn., married 17 yrs.
Annie, F/W, born June 1866, Tenn., wife.
Dora, F/W, born Jan. 1885, Tenn., daughter.
Otsie, F/W, born Jan. 1889, Tenn., daughter.
Rebecca E., F/W, born May 1890, Tenn., daughter.
Roy, M/W, born July 1893, Tenn., son.
Edna M., F/W, born June 1895, Tenn., daughter.
Ike, M/W, born Jan. 1897, Tenn., son.
Flora, F/W, born Apr. 1898, Tenn., daughter.

58. GILLIAM, MACK, M/W, born Jan. 1871, Tenn., married 8 yrs.
Bettie A., F/W, born Sept. 1872, Tenn., wife.
Mary, F/W, born 1892, Tenn., daughter.
Andrew, M/W, born Mar. 1894, Tenn., son.
Edd, M/W, born Nov. 1895, Tenn., son.
Cora, F/W, born July 1899, Tenn., twin-daughter.
Flora, F/W, born July 1899 Tenn., twin-daughter.

59. CHURCH, JOE, M/W, born Aug. 1871, Tenn., married 5 yrs.
Susie, F/W, born July 1877, Tenn., wife.
William, M/W, born Sept. 1896, Tenn., son.
Walter, M/W, born Sept. 1898, Tenn., son.

60. ELLIS, JAMES, M/W, born Mar. 1865, Tenn., married 12 yrs.
Maggie, F/W, born May 1855, Tenn., wife.

61. HUNZIKER, FLOYD, M/W, born Nov. 1862, Switzerland, married 11 yrs.
Ida, F/W, born Mar. 1872, Tenn., wife.
Eddie, M/W, born Mar. 1890, Tenn., son.
Bessie, F/W, born Aug. 1891, Tenn., daughter.
Beulah, F/W, born Oct. 1892, Tenn., daughter.
Charlie, M/W, born Aug. 1894, Tenn., son.
Frank, M/W, born Jan. 1896, Tenn., son.
Annie, F/W, born Sept. 1899, daughter.

62. HUNZIKER, MAUD, F/W, born July 1855, Switzerland, widow.
Adolph, M/W, born Sept. 1871, Switzerland, son.
Emma, F/W, born Sept. 1880, Tenn., daughter.
YOGI, JOHN, M/W, born July 1822, Switzerland, boarder or brother.

KLEINWACHTER, WILLIAM, M/W, born Mar. 1880, Tenn., grandson.

63. ARN, JOHN, M/W, born Nov. 1860, Switzerland, married 8 yrs.
Mary Ann, F/W, born Nov. 1854, Switzerland, wife.
Lenah, F/W, born May 1881, Switzerland, daughter.
Bertie, F/W, born Nov. 1892, Tenn., daughter.
BLUER, MARY, F/W, born Feb. 1849, Switzerland, sister-in-law, single.

64. KNOTT, MARION, M/W, born Aug. 1880, Tenn., married 8 yrs.
Alice, F/W, born Oct. 1875, Tenn., wife.
Willie, M/W, born Aug. 1893, Tenn., son.
Robert M/W, born Sept. 1895, Tenn., son.
Oscar, M/W, born Mar. 1899, Tenn., son.
BASS, MARY, F/W, born Feb. 1886, Tenn., sister

65. STPEHENS, NANCY, F/W, born Jan. 1853, Tenn., widow.

66. STEPHENS, WILLIAM, M/W, born Mar. 1878, Tenn., married 3 yrs.
Adella, F/W, born June 1874, Tenn., wife.
James H., M/W, born Oct. 1897, Tenn., son.
Raney, M/W, born Nov. 1899, Tenn., son.

67. COOKE, MARTHA, F/W, born May 1827, Tenn., widow.
Joe, M/W, born Dec. 1879, Tenn., son.
Mary C., F/W, born Feb. 1881, Tenn., daughter.

68. MOONEY, JOHN, M/W, born Apr. 1874, Tenn., married 6 yrs.
Sarah, F/W, born June 1877, Tenn., wife.
Bessie, F/W, born Oct. 1895, Tenn., daughter.
George, M/W, born Feb. 1898, Tenn., son.
Frank, M/W, born Oct. 1899, Tenn., son.

69. MYERS, DAVID, M/W, born Apr. 1864, Ohio, married 12 yrs.
Susan, F/W, born Feb. 1869, Tenn., wife.
William, M/W, born Sept. 1885, Tenn., son.
Mattie, F/W, born Dec. 1889, Tenn., daughter.
Cleveland, M/W, born June 1892, Tenn., son.
PAINTER, WILLIAM, M/W, born Aug. 1841, Tenn., step-father.

70. ASHLEY, JACK, M/W, born Sept. 1877, Tenn., married 6 yrs.
Nora, F/W, born Feb. 1878, Tenn., wife.
Mary, F/W, born Feb. 1898, Tenn., daughter.

71. KING, GEORGE, M/W, born Feb. 1868, Tenn., married 16 yrs.
Emaline, F/W, born Dec. 1869, Tenn., wife.
Robby, M/W, born Apr. 1889, Tenn., son.
George, M/W, born June 1890, Tenn., son.
Eddie L., M/W, born May 1895, Tenn., son.
Freddie, M/W, born Mar. 1898, Tenn., son.

72. JONES, TEAD OR TOAD, M/W, born July 1872, Tenn., married 4 yrs.
Caroline, F/W, born Sept. 1880, Tenn., wife.
Claude, M/W, born Dec. 1895, Tenn., son.
Joe, M/W, born May 1899, Tenn., son.
GIPSON, WILLIE, M/W, born Sept. 1890, Tenn., nephew.

73. BERRY, JOE, M/W, born Oct. 1871, Tenn., married 11 yrs.
Mattie, F/W, born Feb. 1871, Tenn., wife.
Annie, F/W, born June 1890, Tenn., daughter.
Lizzie, F/W, b. Jan. 1894, Tenn., daughter
Esther, F/W, born. July 1896, Tenn., daughter.
Ethel, F/W, born Mar. 1898, Tenn., daughter.

74. HARRIS, ELLIS, M/W, born Oct. 1859, Tenn., married 25 yrs.
Lou, F/W, born Nov., 1860, North Carolina, wife.
George, M/W, born Oct. 1884, N. Carolina, son.
James, M/W, born Feb. 1887, N. Carolina, son.
Henry W., M/W, born Jan. 1889, N. Carolina, son.
Susie, F/W, born May 1891, N. Carolina, daughter.
Jessie, M/W, b. Apr. 1893, N. Carolina., son.
Lulah M., F/W, born Aug. 1895, N. Carolina, daughter.

75. MOONEY, RICHARD, M/W, born Sept 1848, Mississippi, married 27 yrs.
Catherine, F/W, born Feb. 1857, N. Carolina, wife.
James, M/W, born July 1883, Tenn., son.
Charles, M/W, born Apr. 1885, Tenn., son.
Lizzie, F/W, born Feb. 1889, Tenn., daughter.
Martha, F/W, born Apr. 1896, Tenn., daughter.
Flora E., F/W, born June 1898, Tenn., daughter.

76. MOONEY, WILLIAM, M/W, born May 1876, Tenn., married 4 yrs.
Martha, F/W, born Aug. 1876, Tenn., wife.
Lillie, F/W, born Mar. 1895, Tenn., daughter.
Joseph, M/W, born June 1898, Tenn., son.

77. COLLINS, WILLIAM, M/W, born Dec. 1848, Tenn., married 6 yrs.
Sarah, F/W, born May 1854, Tenn., wife.
James, M/W, born Jan. 1881, Tenn., son.
Isaac, M/W, born Sept. 1878, Tenn., son.
John, M/W, born Sept. 1880, Tenn., son.
Jennie, F/W, born Feb., 1885, Tenn., daughter.
Bettie, F/W, born Apr. 1889, Tenn., daughter.

78. ARNOLD, WILLIAM , M/W, born Dec. 1853, Tenn., married 21 yrs.
Mattie, F/W, born Apr. 1861, Tenn., wife.
Arther, M/W, born Dec. 1881, Tenn., son.

79. WESTLAND, CHARLIE, M/W, born Sept. 1869, Tenn.,
George, M/W, born Apr. 1892, Tenn., son.
Mable A., F/W, born Aug. 1893, Tenn., daughter.
Harry W., M/W, born Aug. 1896, Tenn., son.

80. RILEY, PATSY, M/W, born Apr. 1840, Ireland, married 33 yrs.
Sophia, F/W, born June 1847, Tenn., wife.
Joseph, M/W, born Mar. 1874, Tenn., son.
Louis, M/W, born Nov. 1879, Tenn., son.
Edward, M/W, born Mar. 1887, Tenn., son.
Thomas, M/W, born Jan. 1888, Tenn., son.

81. JACKSON, ROBERT, M/W, born Aug. 1828, North Carolina, married 27 yrs.
Mary, F/W, born Apr. 1851, Tenn., wife.

82. FINNEY, LEE, M/W, born Mar. 1867, Tenn., married 8 yrs.
Minnie, F/W, born May 1870, Tenn., wife.

83. FINNEY, MATT, M/W, born Feb. 1878, Tenn.,
Julia, F/W, born Jan. 1882, Tenn., wife.

84. CASTLEBERRY, MARION, M/W, born Aug. 1841, Georgia, married 29 yrs.
Frances, F/W, born July 1855, Tenn., wife.
James, M/W, born Nov. 1877, Tenn., son.
Ellen, F/W, born Feb. 1880, Tenn., daughter.
Fannie, F/W, born July 1884, Tenn., daughter.
Marion, M/W, born Dec. 1886, Tenn., son.
Grover, M/W, born Oct, 1889, Tenn., son.
Therador, M/W, b. Mar. 1893, Tenn., son.
Catherine, F/W, born July 1895, Tenn., daughter.
Frank, M/W, born Aug. 1896, Tenn., son.
Laura, F/W, b. Oct. 1898, Tenn., daughter.

85. GIPSON, WILLIAM, M/W, born Feb. 1871, Tenn., married 4 yrs.
Kate, F/W, born Sept 1870, Tenn., wife.

86. PRINCE, SAMUEL, M/W, born Feb. 1868, Tenn., married 8 yrs.
Edna, F/W, born June 1876, Tenn., wife.
Ulah, F/W, born Dec. 1892, Tenn., daughter.
HARTIS, CARRIE, F/W, born July 1855, Sweden, servant and widow.

87. CASTLEBERRY, JAMES, M/W, born June 1868, Georgia, married 10 yrs.
Lillie, F/W, born Dec. 1869, Tenn., wife.
Carl F., M/W, born June 1894, Tenn., son.
Annie M., F/W, born Dec. 1895, Tenn., daughter.
Lillian L., F/W, born Sept. 1898, Tenn., daughter.
Rebecca, F/W, born Sept. 1835, Tenn., mother-in-law.

88. PRINCE, ROBERT, M/W, born Apr. 1861, Tenn., married 18 yrs.
Jennie, F/W, born May 1866, Tenn., wife.
Author, M/W, born Sept. 1886, Tenn., son.
William, M/W, born July 1888, Tenn., son.
Lillie, F/W, born Mar. 1891, Tenn., daughter.
Harry, M/W, born Mar 1893, Tenn., son.
Mary, F/W, born Nov. 1894, Tenn., son.
Renau, M/W, born Nov. 1895, Tenn., son.
Earnest, M/W, born July 1899, Tenn., son.

89. SUTHERLAND, JAMES, M/W, born Mar. 1868, Tenn., married 10 yrs.
Mary, F/W, born Feb., 1870, Tenn., wife.
William, F/W, born June 1894, Tenn., son.
Ervin, M/W, born Sept. 1896, Tenn., son.
Annie, F/W, born June 1898, Tenn., daughter.

90. FISCHER, JOSEPH, M/W, born Sept. 1866, Ohio, married 13 yrs.
Lena, F/W, born Mar. 1867, Ohio, wife.
Clara, F/W, born July 1886, Tenn., daughter.
Lillie, F/W, born Nov. 1887, Tenn., daughter.
Eupherosina, F/W, born Oct. 1889, Tenn., daughter.
Joseph, M/W, born Jan. 1892, Tenn., son.

91. SHORT, FRANK, M/W, born Dec. 1845, Alabama, married 30 yrs.
Alice, F/W, born June 1842, South Carolina, wife.

92. HAWKINS, WALLACE, M/W, born Oct. 1859, Tenn., married 19 yrs.
Margrett, F/W, born Oct. 1860, Switzerland, wife.
Harry, M/W, born Oct. 1882, Tenn., son.
Charles, M/W, born July 1885, Tenn., son.
Hilarius, M/W, born May 1889, Tenn., son.
Flora, F/W, born Mar. 1891, Tenn., daughter.
Margrett, F/W, born June 1883, Tenn., daughter.
Bualbuia, M/W, born June 1893, Tenn., son.
Jack, M/W, born Oct. 1895, Tenn., son.
Thomas, M/W, born Mar. 1899, Tenn., son.
LUCHSINGER, BARBARA, F/W, born Nov. 1835, Switzerland, mother-in-law.

93. HARRISON, J.M., M/W, born July 1873, Tenn., married 2 yrs.
Minnie, F/W, born Jan. 1876, Tenn., wife.
William, M/W, born Sept. 1878, Tenn., brother.

94. RICKETTS, WILLIAM, M/W, born Aug. 1857, Tenn., married 16 yrs.
Louzana, F/W, born Aug. 1854, Tenn., wife.
MADEWELL, JOHN E., M/W, born Feb. 1897, grandson.
TURNER, MARY, F/W, born Sept. 1875, Tenn., servant, single.

95. GILLESPIE, DORA, F/W, born Jan. 1869, Tenn., widow.
Mary, F/W, born Apr. 1888, Tenn., daughter.
Nellie, F/W, born Apr. 1890, Tenn., daughter.
Nathan, M/W, born Feb. 1892, Tenn., son.
Emett, M/W, born July 1898, Tenn., son.

96. KENNEDY, PETE, M/W, born May 1870, Tenn., married 4 yrs.
Martha, F/W, born Sept. 1876, Tenn., wife.
Ola, F/W, born Aug. 1896, Tenn., daughter.
Bessie, F/W, born Sept. 1897, Tenn., daughter.
TURNER, ELIZABETH, F/W, born Oct. 1859, Missouri, servant, widow.

97. POWELL, JOHN, M/W, born Aug. 1822, Tenn., married 56 yrs.
Nancy, F/W, born Feb. 1826, Tenn., wife.
(name not given in census)
BEST, BEULAH, F/W, born Feb. 1882, Tenn., granddaughter.

98. CROWNOVER, ROBERT, M/W, born Aug. 1878, Texas, single.
BLANTON, THOMAS, M/W, born Aug. 1879, Tenn., partner.
Ling, M/W, born Jan. 1878, Tenn., partner.

99. SUTHERLAND, ROSANA, F/W, born Dec. 1847, North Carolina, widow.
Jannie, F/W, born Apr. 1880, Tenn., daughter.

100. GARNER, WILLIAM, M/W, born Feb. 1854, Tenn., married 26 yrs.
Nancy, F/W, born July 1859, Tenn., wife.
Frank, M/W, born Mar. 1872, Tenn., son.
?Howard, M/W, born May 1883, Tenn., son.
Ida, F/W, born Aug. 1885, Tenn., daughter.
Annie, F/W, born July 1888, Tenn., daughter.
Otza, F/W, born May 1890, Tenn., daughter.
Dollia, F/W, born Dec. 1893, Tenn., daughter.
Robert, M/W, born Dec. 1894, Tenn., son.
Georgie, M/W, born Feb. 1897, Tenn., son.
HENLEY, MARGIE, F/W, born Aug. 1882, Tenn., servant, single.

101. RICE, ZACK, M/W, born Dec. 1852, Tenn., married 21 yrs.
Nancy, F/W, born Mar. 1852, Tenn., wife.
Tennie, F/W, born Mar. 1882, Tenn., daughter.
Henry, M/W, born Feb. 1886, Tenn., son.
Edward, M/W, born July 1893, Tenn., son.
Lillie, F/W, born Apr. 1896, Tenn., daughter.

102. THOMAS, WILLIAM, M/B, born June 1826, Georgia., widower.

103. THOMAS, LEE, M/B, born July 1873, Tenn., married 10 yrs.
Stella, F/B, born Jan. 1871, Tenn., wife.
Oscar, M/B, born May 1890, Tenn., son.
Louise, F/B, born Apr. 1893, Tenn., daughter.
Mary, F/B, born May 1895, Tenn., daughter.
Elizabeth, F/B, born Feb. 1897, Tenn., daughter.
Santiago, F/B, born Oct. 1898, Tenn., daughter.
Lenord R., M/B, born Apr. 1900, Tenn., son.

104. CHILDRESS, ALFRED, M/B, born Apr. 1870, Tenn., married 4 yrs.
Helen, F/B, born Mar. 1877, Georgia, wife.
Moss, M/B, born Sept. 1894, Tenn., son.

105. RILEY, ROBERT, M/W, born Mar. 1866, Tenn., married 8 yrs.
Viola, F/W, born Feb. 1871, Tenn., wife.
Aylene, F/W, born May 1893, Tenn., daughter.
Christine, F/W, born Aug. 1895, Tenn., daughter.

106. O'DEAR, TAYLOR, M/W, born Mar. 1875, Tenn., married 3 yrs.
Malinda, F/W, born Oct. 1869, Tenn., wife.
Carl, M/W, born Nov. 1897, Tenn., son.
Albert, M/W, born Apr. 1900, Tenn., son.
HENDLEY, EDD, M/W, born Sept. 1887, Tenn., step-son.
LONG, LEM OR LEE, born Jan. 1881, Tenn., brother-in-law.

107. GIPSON, MANERVA, F/W, born Sept. 1835, Tenn., widow.
CLARK, JOHN, M/W, born Apr. 1864, England, son-in-law, widower.
John, M/W, born Sept. 1885, Tenn., grandson.
Tom, M/W, born Aug. 1887, Tenn., grandson.
Flora, F/W, born June 1889, Tenn., granddaughter.
Edward, M/W born Dec. 1894, Tenn., grandson.
William, M/W, born Dec. 1896, Tenn., grandson.

108. LONG, HENRY, M/W, born Mar. 1870, Tenn., married 5 yrs.
Bettie, F/W, born Mar. 1880, Tenn., wife.
Noble, M/W, born Sept. 1896, Tenn., son.
Roda, F/W, born Sept. 1898, Tenn., daughter.

109. GIPSON, IDA, F/W, born Mar. 1862, Alabama, widow.
George, M/W, born Dec. 1884, Tenn., son.
Hattie, F/W, born Mar. 1886, Tenn., daughter.
Rebecca, F/W, born Oct. 1889, Tenn., daughter.
Noble, M/W, born Aug. 1891, Tenn., son.
Homer, M/W, born Feb. 1895, Tenn., son.

110. KUNTZ, EMILE, M/W, born July 1858, Germany, married 8 yrs.
Della, F/W, born Dec. 1874, Tenn., wife.
Hattie, F/W, born Nov. 1892, Tenn., daughter.
Ray, F/W, born July 1894, Tenn., daughter.
Flora, F/W, born Dec. 1895, Tenn., daughter.
Pearl, F/W, born Nov. 1898, Tenn., daughter.
Alene, F/W, born May 1900, Tenn., daughter.
HUNTING, MARY, F/W, born Aug. 1867, Kentucky, boarder, married 11 yrs.
Daisy, F/W, born Jan. 1891, Kentucky, boarder.
Harry, M/W, born Sept. 1893, Tenn., boarder.
Ivey, F/W, born Dec. 1899, Tenn., boarder.

111. VANVLECK, (VAN VLECK) EMMA, F/W born Aug. 1826, Tenn., widow.

112. WESTLAND, EMMA, F/W, born Aug. 1865, Tenn., married 12 yrs.
Jennett, F/W, born Dec. 1888, Tenn., daughter.
May, F/W, born May 1892, Tenn., daughter.

113. HOLLAND, SAMUEL, M/W, born Feb. 1848, Tenn., married 13 yrs.
Celestie, F/W, born June 1870, Tenn., wife.
Mollie, F/W, born Sept. 1890, Tenn., daughter.
Layton, M/W, b. Aug. 1893, Tenn., son.
Zula, F/W, born Apr. 1897, Tenn., daughter.
GOSSAGE, THOMAS, M/W, born Mar. 1840, Tenn., father-in-law, widower.

114. BRAZELTON, WITTY, M/W, born June 1847, Tenn., married 22 yrs.
Charlotte, W/F, born Sept. 1847, Iowa, wife.
Abbie, F/W, born Feb. 1883, Tenn., daughter.
Lorraine, F/W, born May 1885, Tenn., daughter.
Nannie, F/W, born May 1890, Tenn., daughter.
Grace, F/W, born May 1893, Tenn., daughter.
Mabel, F/W, born Dec. 1895, Tenn., daughter.
Auther, M/W, born Aug. 1899, Tenn., son.
Samyna, F/W, born Oct 1824, Tenn., mother-in-law. widow.
JOHNSON, ESTELL, F/W, born Nov. 1880, Tenn., daughter, married 2 yrs.
CLAY, PATSY, M/W, born Nov. 1867, Ireland, boarder, single.

115. PRINCE, JAMES, M/W, born July 1868, Tenn., married 10 yrs.
Emma, F/W, born Nov. 1869, Ohio, wife.
Edith E., F/W, born Apr. 1880, Tenn., daughter.
Preston, M/W, born June 1892, Tenn., son.
Rena, F/W, born Apr. 1896, Tenn., daughter.
Baby son, (Milton)M/W, June 1899, Tenn., son.

116. THOMAS, JAMES, M/W, born Nov. 1861, Tenn., married 16 yrs.
Fannie E., F/W, born June 1866, Tenn., wife.
Flora, F/W, born June 1884, Tenn., daughter.
Martha, F/W, born Dec. 1886, Tenn., daughter.
Dean, M/W, born Sept 1891, Tenn., son.
Ester, F/W, born Jan. 1894, Tenn., daughter.
Eva, F/W, born July 1896, Tenn., daughter.
Katie, F/W, born Oct. 1881, Tenn., sister.
STATEM, DEAN, M/W, born Jan. 1827, Virginia, father-in-law, widower.

117. GRUETTER, GODFREY, M/W, born Jan. 1862, Switzerland, married 13 yrs.
Risty, M/W, born June 1869, Tenn., wife.
Myrtle, F/W, born Apr. 1889, Tenn., daughter.
Pearl, F/W, born Mar. 1892, Tenn., daughter.
William, M/W, born Sept. 1899, Tenn., son.
PLUMONS, WILLIAM, M/W, born Jan. 1856, Tenn., boarder, single.

118. CASTLEBERRY, MARTHA, F/W, born Dec. 1851, Tenn., widow.
John H., M/W, born May 1880, Tenn., son.
Mariah, F/W, born June 1882, Tenn., daughter.
Minzie, F/W, born May 1885, Tenn., daughter.
Hattie, F/W, born May 1898, Tenn., daughter.

119. TUCKER, GEORGE, M/W, born Apr. 1891, Tenn., married 10 yrs.
Jennie, F/W, born Dec. 1871, Tenn., wife.
Sam, M/W, born May 1888, Tenn., son.
Sharpe, M/W, born May 1890, Tenn., son.
Nora, F/W, born June 1892, Tenn., daughter.

120. DARDIS, JAMES C., M/W, born Apr. 1849, Tenn., married 16 yrs.
Sallie, F/W, born June 1863, Alabama, wife.
Zulier, F/W, born Dec. 1886, Tenn., daughter.
Charles, M/W, born Jan. 1890, Tenn., son.
Lawrence, M/W, b. Jan. 1895, Tenn., son.

121. HOFFOR, HENRY, M/W, born Apr. 1849, Tenn., married 5 yrs.
Martha, F/W, born, Mar. 1865, Tenn., wife.
FISCHER, CARRIE, F/W, born Nov. 1886, Tenn., step-daughter.

122. POWELL, JOHN, M/W, born Dec. 1859, Tenn., married 6 yrs.
Mattie, F/W, born Oct. 1862, Tenn., wife. (name not given in census).

123. FISCHER, EFRENNA ?, F/W, born Oct. 1831, Germany, widow.
Maggie, F/W, born June 1879, Tenn., daughter.

124. RUEF, CHRISTIAN, M/W, born Sept. 1849, Switzerland, married 25 yrs.
Agnes, F/W, born Aug. 1851, Switzerland, wife.
Agnes, F/W, born June 1881, Tenn., daughter.
Lizzie, F/W, born Mar. 1884, Tenn., daughter.

124. RUEF, Fannie, F/W, born Nov. 1887, Tenn., daughter.
Louise, F/W, born Dec. 1890, Tenn., daughter.
Helen, F/W, born Aug. 1894, Tenn., daughter.
Martha, F/W, born June 1897, Tenn., daughter.

125. RUEF, JOHN, M/W, born Oct. 1879, Tenn., married 2 yrs.
Winnie, F/W, born Apr. 1879, Tenn., wife.
RICHI, JOSEPH, M/W, born Sept. 1861, Italy, boarder, widower.

126. JOHNSON, BETTIE, F/W, born Nov. 1848, Tenn., widow.
Sallie, F/W, born Jan. 1889, Tenn., daughter.
Albert, M/W, born Aug. 1872, Tenn., son.
BOYD, Delia, F/W, born Oct. 1882, Tenn., daughter, married 1 yr.
Charlie, M/W, born Aug. 1875, Tenn., son-in-law.
Albert, M/W, born June 1900, Tenn., grandson.

HOFER, LOUISE, F/W, born Nov. 1881, Tenn., servant, single.

127. LEVOVITZ, ABRAHAM, M/W, born Mar. 1868, Russia, married 15 yrs.
Annie, F/W, born June 1868, Russia, wife.
Benjamin, M/W, born June 1880, Tenn., son.
Haynian, M/W, b. Apr. 1886, Tenn., son.

128. WHITLOCK, ANDREW, M/W, born Nov. 1871, Tenn., married 2 yrs.
Frances, F/W, b. Feb. 1872, Tenn., wife.

129. HOGE, SAMUEL, M/W, born Apr. 1839, Alabama, married 29 yrs.
Sarah, M/W, born Apr. 1849, Tenn., wife.
Nellie, F/W, born Aug. 1874, Tenn., daughter.
Eunice, F/W, born July 1876, Tenn., daughter.
Nancy, F/W, born . Sept. 1878, Tenn., daughter.
Edward, M/W, born Oct. 1891, Tenn., son.
Lyman, M/W, born Sept. 1899, Tenn., son.

130. LOONEY, WILLIAM, M/W, born Sept. 1858, Alabama, married 15 yrs.
Ettie, F/W, born Mar. 1863, Alabama, wife.
Rosie, F/W, born Sept. 1886, Tenn., daughter.
Leona, F/W, born Jan. 1888, Tenn., daughter.
Bessie M/W, born Oct. 1891, Tenn., (says son, could be daughter)
Lillian, F/W, born Nov. 1893, Tenn., daughter.
Irene, F/W, b. Feb. 1897, Tenn., daughter.

131. MAYHEW, CECIL A., M/W, born Mar. 1845, New York, single.

132. OWENS, ELIZABETH, F/W, born Oct. 1842, Tenn., widow.
Julia, F/W, born Mar. 1866, Tenn., daughter.
Martha, F/W, born Feb. 1872, Tenn., daughter.
Myrtle, F/W, born Oct. 1898, Tenn., daughter.

133. HARRISON, VIRGINIA, F/W, born May 1852, Louisiana, single.
JORDAN, FRANCES, F/W, born May 1882, Louisiana, cousin.

134. MOSLEY, RUFUS, M/B, born Apr. 1850, Tenn., married 10 yrs.
Mollie, F/B, born Mar. 1868, Tenn., wife.
?Cres, M/B, born July 1890, Tenn., son.
Francis, F/B, born Oct. 1893, Tenn., daughter.
Willfed, F/B, born Nov. 1897, Tenn., daughter.
Katie, F/B, b. Feb. 1900, Tenn., daughter.
Lucy, F/B, born Apr. 1883, Tenn., niece.

135. HANDLY, ?MARCUS, M/B, born Apr. 1853, Tenn., married 27 yrs.
Percilla, F/B, born Nov. 1852, Tenn., wife.
HUNT, LENAH, F/B, born Nov. 1872, Tenn., daughter.
Henry, M/B, Nov. 1872, Tenn., son-in-law, married 6 yrs.
Irine, F/B, born Mar. 1896, Tenn., granddaughter.
Percilla M., F/B, born Aug. 1898, Tenn., granddaughter.
SIMS, RUFUS, M/B, born Apr. 1878, Tenn., nephew.
BRAZELTON, ZAKE OR JAKE, M/B, born Apr. 1881, Tenn., nephew.

136. ?KIX, HIX, MIX, ?HERMAN, M/W, born Sept. 1872, Kentucky, married 5 yrs.
Elinora, F/W, b. Jul 1874, Kentucky, wife.
Mary, F/W, born Feb. 1875, Kentucky, daughter.
Chester, M/W, b. Oct. 1899, Kentucky, son.

137. HAWKINS, SALLIE, F/W, born Apr. 1849, Tenn., married 29 yrs.
Ruth, F/W, born July 1872, Tenn., daughter.
Luke, M/W, born June 1877, Tenn., son.
?Fannie, F/W, born June 1880, Tenn., daughter.
Sallie, F/W, born Aug. 1884, Tenn., daughter.
Addie, F/W, born Oct 1886, Tenn., daughter.
Jenette, F/W, born July 1891, Tenn., daughter.
MONTGOMERY, ?JOHN A., M/W, born Sept. 1896, Tenn., grandson.

138. HOWARD/HANNAH, ?SAIDY/SARAY, F/B, born Mar. 1875, TN. single.
COLYAR, ?NOAH, M/B, born Sept. 1897, Tenn., son.

139. ?BRANNON, THOMAS, M/B, born Apr. 1872, Tenn., married 7 yrs.
Lucy, F/W, born Mar. 1876, Tenn., wife.
Robert, F/B, born Apr. 1894, Tenn., son.
Marion, M/B, born Mar. 1896, Tenn., son.
Mary, F/B, born Aug. 1897, Tenn., daughter.

140. CLARK, JOHN, M/W, born Aug. 1871,

Tenn., married 5 yrs.
Minnie, F/W, born Aug. 1871, Tenn., wife.
Grace, F/W, born May 1898, Tenn., daughter.
JACKSON, JOHN, M/W, born Jan. 1879, Georgia, boarder, single.

141. POWELL, JOSEPH, M/W, born Feb. 1850, Tenn., married 25 yrs.
Emma, F/W, born May 1853, Pennsylvania, wife.
Homer, M/W, born Apr. 1881, Tenn., son.
Elmer, M/W, born Aug. 1875, Tenn., son, married 2 yrs.
Mannie, F/W, born July 1881, Tenn., daughter-in-law.

142. SUTTON, EMMA, F/W, born Mar. 1832, Tenn., widow.
CARTER, EMMA, F/W, born Aug. 1890, Tenn., granddaughter.
HENLEY, EMMA, F/W, born, Jan 1884, Tenn., servant, single.
Minnie, F/W, born Oct. 1880, Tenn., servant, single.

143. GULHAIR, WILLIAM, M/W, born Feb. 1845, South Carolina, married 4 yrs.
Isabel, F/W, born May 1857, Tenn., wife.
Thomas, M/W, b. May 1891, Tenn., son.
John, M/W, born Apr. 1880, Tenn., son, married 1 yr.
Etta, F/W, born Dec. 1884, Tenn., daughter-in-law.
Horace, M/W, born Dec. 1887, Tenn., son.
RIGHT, (WRIGHT) CLARANCE, M/W, born June 1896, TN. stepson.

144. WEBER, ?, F/W, born Dec. 1824, North Carolina, widow.
John, M/W, born Dec. 1890, Tenn., grandson.

145. OAKLY, JANE, F/W or B, born Apr. 1844, Tenn., widow.

146. SHEPHARD, REBECCA, F/W, born June 1837, Pennsylvania, widow.
David, M/W, born Mar. 1879, Tenn., son.
TATE. EDDIE, M/B, born Dec. 1871, Alabama, servant, widower.

147. RAMAGE, BURR, M/W, born July 1859, South Carolina, married 3 yrs.
Bird, F/W, born Aug. 1875, Texas, wife.
JONES, ANNIE, F/W, born Jan. 1861, Tenn., servant, single.
Delia, F/W, born June 1889, Tenn., servant.

148. HARRIS, WALTER, M/W, born Dec. 1869, Illinois, married ? years.
Elizabeth, F/W, b. Oct 1879, Tenn., wife.

149. BENNETT, JOHN, M/W, born Aug. 1852, Tenn., married 22 yrs.
Emily, F/W, born May 1860, Tenn., wife.
Jessie, M/W, born June 1881, Tenn., son.
William, M/W, b. Mar. 1883, Tenn., son.
Harlon, M/W, born Jan. 1885, Tenn., son.
Ethel, F/W, born July 1886, Tenn., daughter.
Lulah, F/W, born May 1888, Tenn., daughter.
Nellie, F/W, born Oct. 1889, Tenn., daughter.
?Ada, F/W, born Mar. 1891, Tenn., daughter.
Cora, F/W, born July 1892, Tenn., daughter.
Eva, F/W, born Dec. 1895, Tenn., daughter.
Charlotte, F/W, born May 1897, Tenn., daughter.

150. PRICE, GEORGE, M/B, born Apr. 1875, Tenn., married 1 yr.
Anna, F/B, born Oct. 1875, Tenn., wife.
Mable, F/B, born Nov. 1899, Tenn., daughter.

151. SANDERS, WILLIAM, M/B, born Mar. 1877, Tenn., married 5 yrs.
Birtie, F/B, born Mar. 1877, Tenn., wife.
?Lizzie, F/B, born Apr. 1898, Tenn., daughter.

152. SIMS, PINK, M/B, born Apr. 1860, Tenn., married 7 yrs.
Maggie, F/B, Jan. 1872, Tenn., wife.
Charlie, M/B, born Oct. 1895, Tenn., son.
Clara, F/B, b. Oct. 1898, Tenn., daughter.

153. FOSTER, FRANK, M/W, born Aug. 1872, Tenn., married 2 yrs.
Sallie, F/W, born Jan. 1876, Tenn., wife.
William, M/W, b. Mar. 1897, Tenn., son.
Florence, F/W, born Sept. 1899, Tenn., daughter.
CLARK, LUCY, F/W, born Sept. 1854, Tenn., mother-in-law.
James W., M/W, born Feb. 1888, Tenn., brother-in-law.
Dora, F/W, born Mar. 1892, Tenn., sister-in-law.

154. MESICK, JAMES, M/W, born Feb. 1864, Tenn., married 11 yrs.
Minnie, F/W, born Feb. 1879, Tenn., wife.
Johnnie, M/W, Dec. 1890, Tenn., son.
James, M/W, born Aug. 1894, Tenn., son.
Katie, F/W, b. Mar. 1895, Tenn., daughter.

Jeff, M/W, born Sept. 1896, Tenn., son.
William, M/W, born May 1898, Tenn., daughter.
Mattie, F/W, born Mar. 1900, Tenn., daughter.

155. GREEN, JAMES S., M/W, born Mar. 1825, North Carolina, married 42 yrs.
Ella P., F/W, b. July 1846, Georgia, wife.
MARTIN, JANIE, F/B, born July 1865, Virginia, servant.

156. FINCH, ADAM, M/B, born Apr. 1869, Tenn., married 4 yrs.
Jessie, F/B, born Mar. 1879, Tenn., wife.
Thelma, F/B, born Jan. 1899, Tenn., daughter.
BUCKNER, IZRA, F/B, born Nov. 1882, Tenn., boarder, single.
Ada, F/B, born Feb. 1874, Tenn., sister, married 3 yrs.
Henry, M/B, born Feb. 1898, Tenn., son.
Anna, F/B, b. Sept, 1899, Tenn., daughter.

157. PHILLIPS, FRANK, M/B, born Sept. 1875, Tenn., married 2 yrs.
Tina, F/B, born June 1888, Tenn., wife.

158. QUINTARD, CLARA, F/B, born Apr. 1822, N. Carolina, single.
SIMMONS, GEORGE, M/B, born Apr. 1872, Tenn., boarder, married 5 yrs.
Doris, F/B, born Dec. 1875, Tenn., boarder's wife.
Willie, M/B, born May 1896, Tenn., boarder's son. .
Georgia, F/W, born Nov. 1899, Tenn., boarder's daughter.
TRIGG, JULIA, F/B, born Sept. 1883, Tenn., sister-in-law.
FINCH, HARRY, M/B, born Dec. 1884, Tenn., boarder.
JONES, CARRIE, F/W, born Dec. 1883, Tenn., boarder.
TRIGG, ELICK, M/B, born Apr. 1879, Tenn., boarder.

159. BERRY, ALICE, F/B, born Jan. 1863, Mississippi, single.

160. ?CRETON, CLABORNE, M/B, born Jan 1850, Alabama, married 15 yrs.
Harlon, M/B, born Apr. 1889, Tenn., son.

161. MORRIS, ELIZABETH, F/W, Nov. 1846, Alabama, widow.
Lou Ellen, F/W, born July 1881, Tenn., daughter.
Pearl, F/W, b. June 1882, Tenn., daughter.

162. JUDD, SPENCER, M/W, born Nov. 1855, Minnesota, married 18 yrs.
Hallie, F/W, born Dec. 1862, Alabama, wife.
Carl, M/W, born Jan. 1887, Illinois, son.

163. GUTHRIE, CALLIE, F/W, born May 1885, Tenn., single.

164. ARNOLD, LILLIE, F/W, born Mar. 1848, Tenn., widow.
Charles, M/W, born Jan 1884, Tenn., son.
Meadie, F/W, born Sept. 1886, Tenn., daughter.
Edd, M/W, born Aug. 1894, Tenn., son.
CROWNOVER, LULAH, F/W, born Dec. 1885, Tenn., granddaughter.

165. RANKINS, DOUGLAS, M/B, born Apr. 1840, Tenn., married 22 yrs.
Ellen, F/B, born Feb. 1850, Tenn., wife.
Alice, F/B, b. July 1880, Tenn., daughter.
Arbis, M/B, born 1883, Tenn., son.
?Guinn, F/B, born Jan. 1887, Tenn., daughter.
?Oalandus, M/B, born Jan,. 1890, Tenn., son.
Carl, M/B, born Sept. 1892, Tenn., son.
William, M/B, born Feb. 1897, Tenn., son.

166. MARSH, DAVID, M/B, born Apr. 1852, ?, married 23 yrs.
Lizzie, F/B, born Feb. 1860, Tenn., wife.
Allin, M/B, born Dec. 1887, Tenn., son.
Lauran, F/B, born Feb. 1893, Tenn., daughter.

167. HENLEY, GEORGE, M/W, born Apr. 1849, Tenn., widower.
Jannie, F/W, born Feb. 1887, Tenn., daughter.
Annie, F/W, born July 1888, Tenn., daughter.
Berry, M/W, born Nov. 1890, Tenn., son.

168. LUCHSINGER, RUDOLF, M/W, born Mar. 1846, Switzerland, married 16 yrs.
Maggie, F/W, born Mar. 1867, Tenn., wife.
John, M/W, born May 1889, Tenn., son.
Mary, F/W, born Sept. 1893, Illinois, daughter.

169. BROWN, MARY, F/B, born 1850, Missouri, widow.
Emma, F/B, born Mar. 1874, Tenn., daughter.
KENNLEY, MARY, F/B, born Apr. 1890, Tenn., granddaughter.
COLYAD, CAREY K, F/B, born Mar. 1897, Tenn., granddaughter.

170. GARNER, JOE, M/W, born Apr. 1850, Tenn., married 16 yrs.
Edna, F/W, born Feb. 1859, Tenn., wife.

Beulah, F/W, born Sept. 1885, Tenn., daughter.
Walter, M/W, born Dec. 1888, Tenn., son.
Ervin, M/W, born July 1893, Tenn., son.
MCMILLIN, JAMES, M/W, born Dec. 1856, Kentucky, student, married 5 yrs.

171. FARRIS, PETER, M/B, born Aug. 1848, Tenn., married 33 yrs.
Henrietter, F/B, b. Sept. 1850, Fla., wife.
Daisy, F/B, b. Apr. 1884, Tenn., daughter.
FREEMAN, MINNIE, F/B, born Apr. 1882, Tenn., boarder.
OTTO, JACOB, M/B, born Mar. 1900, Tenn., grandson.

172. JOHNSON, SARAH, F/B, born Feb. 1862, Tenn., widow.
Prince, F/B, b. Mar. 1882, Tenn., daughter.
?Leonard, M/B, b. Feb. 1887, Tenn., son.
Simon, M/B, born Feb. 1888, Tenn., son.
Ezekiel, M/B, born Feb. 1895, Tenn., son.
HAVEN, JULIA, F/B, born Mar. 1820, Tenn., mother, widow.

173. CLARK, CALVIN, M/B, born Apr. 1866, Tenn., married 11 yrs.
Surin, F/B, born May 1871, Tenn., wife.
Willie, F/B, b. June 1881, TN., daughter.
Marcus, M/B, born Nov. 1890, Tenn., son.
Ethel L., F/B, born Jan. 1893, Tenn., daughter.
Calvin, M/B, born Sept. 1896, Tenn., son.

174. CHILDRESS, WILLIAM, M/B, born Apr. 1879, married but years not given.
Grace, F/B, born July 1881, Tenn., wife.
Elexander, M/B, b. Apr. 1900, Tenn., son.

175. CHILDRESS, CALVIN, M/B, born Mar. 1844, Tenn., married years not given.
Hattie, F/B, born Aug. 1875, Tenn., wife.
Lillie, F/B, b. Apr. 1886, Tenn., daughter.
Anna, F/B, born Mar. 1888, Tenn., daughter.

176. WINTON, CROCKET, M/B, born Apr. 1840, married 19 yrs.
Harret, F/B, born Mar. 1840, Tenn., wife.
AUSTILL, GEORGE, M/B, born Apr. 1889, nephew.

177. ?RUCEL, ABRAHAM, M/B, Apr. 1854, Tenn., married 18 yrs.
Sallie, F/B, Jan. 1866, Tenn., wife.
Eva, F/B, Mar. 1886, Tenn., daughter.
Willie, M/B, Mar. 1892, Tenn., son.
David M/B, born Aug. 1896, Tenn., son.
Mary L., F/B, born Oct. 1895, Tenn., daughter.

178. BRYANT, BETTIE, F/B, born June 1829, Tenn., widow.
MCDONALD, LEATHER, F/B, born Feb. 1870, Tenn., granddaughter, married.
Henry, M/B, born Dec. 1889, Tenn., gr-grandson.
Elijah, M/B, born Oct. 1898, Tenn., gr-grandson.
BRYANT, TAYLOR, M/B, born Aug. 1849, Tenn., son.
Oscar, M/B, born Jan. 1878, Tenn., son. of Taylor.
Fred, M/B, born Feb. 1880, Tenn., son. of Taylor
Benn, M/B, born Aug. 1881, Tenn., son of Taylor.

179. GARNER, GEORGE, M/B, born Feb. 1855, Tenn., married 1 yr.
Rachel, F/B, born Mar. 1876, Tenn., wife.
RUTHLAGE, LENAH, M/B, born Feb. 1863, Tenn., servant.
DUBOSE, RACHEL, F/B, Mar. 1830, Tenn., grandmother, widow.

180. SHARP, ELLA, F/B, born Mar. 1874, Tenn., married 13 yrs.
William, M/B, born July 1897, Tenn., son.
Carnett, M/B, born Apr. 1900, Tenn., son.

181. WISEMAN, JACK, M/B, born Feb. 1877, Tenn., married 3 yrs.
Zori, F/B, born June 1877, Tenn., wife.
Egelsion, M/B, born Apr. 1899, Tenn., son.

182. LOSSING, ALLEN, M/W, born Jan. 1869, Illinois, married 6 yrs.
Hattie, F/W, born Nov. 1875, South Dakota, wife.
Franklin, M/W, born July 1894, South Dakota, son.
Mary L. F/W, born Jan. 1896, Missouri, daughter.
Arthur D., M/W, born May 1898, Missouri.

183. FARRIS, DOCK, M/W, born Nov. 1860, Tenn., married 7 yrs.
Annie, F/W, b. May 1880, Indiana, wife.
Eva, F/W, born Apr. 1895, Tenn., daughter.
Pascal, M/W, born June 1898, Tenn., son.

184. SMITH, BILL, M/B, born Feb. 1850, Tenn., married 12 yrs.
Sallie, F/B, born Mar. 1852, Tenn., wife.
Huston, M/B, born Jan. 1889, Tenn., son.
Simon, M/B, born Feb. 1891, Tenn., son.

185. CHINN, JULIE, F/B, born 1840, Tenn., widow.
ROWE, JENNIE, F/B, born Apr. 1880,

Tenn., daughter, married 3 yrs.
Anderson, M/B, born Mar. 1879, Tenn., son-in-law.
Bessie, F/B, born Jan. 1896, Tenn., granddaughter.
ROWE, Carrie, F/B, born Apr. 1898, Tenn., granddaughter.
James E. M/B, born May 1900, Tenn., grandson.
GILLESPIE, Grant, M/B, born Aug. 1885, Tenn., son.
BRYAN, Hester, F/B, born Jan. 1861, Tenn., servant. married 24 yrs.
Addie, F/B, born June 1888, Tenn., daughter of servant.

186. ANDREWS, WILLIAM, M/W, born Oct. 1864, Tenn., married 3 yrs.
Eva, F/W, born Oct. 1878, Tenn., wife.
Edward, M/W, b. Mar. 1898, Tenn., son.

187. MORRIS, EMITT, M/W, born May 1879, Alabama, married but years not given.
Arian, F/W, born July 1883, Alabama, wife.

188. HARD?, WILLIAM, M/W, born Oct. 1823, England, widower.
Annie M., F/W, born Dec. 1852, England, daughter.

189. ERVIN, CHARLIE, M/B, born Mar. 1876, Tenn., married 1 yr.
Lulah, F/B, born Apr. 1881, Tenn., wife.

190. WILLIS, RHODA, F/B, born Oct. 1839, Tenn., widow.
WOOTEN, JANNIE, F/B, born Nov. 1869, Tenn., niece.

191. ROE, CATHERINE, F/B, born Apr. 1853, Tenn., single. (may be a widow)
William, M/B, born Feb. 1876, Tenn., son.
Aucen, M/B, born Sept. 1875, Tenn., son.
Charlie, M/B, born Dec. 1881, Tenn., son.
Annie, F/B, born Jun. 1890, Tenn., daughter.
RUTLEDGE, LETTIE, F/B, born Sept 1869, Tenn., niece.

192. FRY, JESS, M/W, born Dec. 1857, England, married 14 yrs.
Anna B., F/W, born Mar. 1869, Tenn., wife.
ROBINSON, LIZA, F/W, born Jan. 1881, Tenn., servant.

193. MESSICK, JEFFERSON, M/W, born Oct. 1863, Tenn., married 7 yrs.
Mattie, F/W, b. Apr. 1863, Georgia, wife.
PACK, PERNEGY, F/W, born June 1833, servant, widow.
PIPPINS, DUBLÌN?, M/W, born Jan. 1864, Tenn., lodger, single.

194. PRINCE, JACK, M/W, born Jan. 1864, Tenn., married 10 yrs.
Alice, F/W, born Mar. 1872, Tenn., wife.
James B., M/W, b. Jan. 1891, Tenn., son.
Henry, M/W, born Jan. 1893, Tenn., son.
PACK, MARTHA, F/W, born Aug. 1851, Tenn., mother-in-law.

195. FOSTER ?, CHARLIE, M/W, born July 1875, Tenn., married 3 yrs.
Myrtle, F/W, born July 1859, Tenn., wife.
James, M/W, born Apr. 1900, Tenn., son.

196. LAUTZENHEIGER, ,?LUCY, F/W, born Aug. 1834, Ohio, widow.

197. ADAMS, JOSEPH, M/W, born Sept. 1849, Louisiana, married 25 yrs.
Marie, F/W, born Apr. 1880, Louisiana, daughter.
Vira, F/W, born July 1881, Louisiana, daughter.

198. ROBERSON, JAKE, M/W, born Apr. 1838, S. Carolina, married 42 yrs.
Mary F/W, born Jan. 1832, Illinois, wife.
John, M/W, born June 1878, Tenn., son.
Nannie, F/W, born Aug. 1890, Tenn. (may be granddaughter)

199. GUTHERIE, GEORGE, M/W, born Mar. 1876, Tenn., married 2 yrs.
Stella, F/W, born Apr. 1882, Tenn., wife.
Victoria, F/W, born Sept. 1898, Tenn.,

200. JONES, JAMES, M/B, born Apr. 1863, Tenn., married 10 yrs.
Barbra, F/B, born Mar. 1876, Tenn., wife
Jessie, F/B, b. Dec. 1881, Tenn., daughter.
Barbra E., F/B, born May 1897, Tenn., daughter.
Charlie, M/B, born Apr. 1900, Tenn., son.
GRAY, MARIAN, F/B, born Apr. 1840, Tenn., mother.

201. MILLER, MARY, F/W, born Mar. 1845, England, single.
ALEXANDER, LIZZIE, F/B, born Aug. 1873, Tenn., servant.

202. DUBOSE, WILLIAM, M/W, born May 1870, South Carolina, married 3 yrs.
Deane S., F/W, born Oct. 1871, Missouri, wife.
MOSS, IDA, F/B, born Feb. 1872, Tenn., servant.

203. BIERY, SAMUEL, M/W, born Apr. 1859, Switzerland, married 19 yrs.
Mary, F/W, born July 1864, Switzerland, wife
Charlie, M/W, born May 1885, Tenn., son.

Fritz, M/W, born 1890, Tenn., son.
Samuel, M/W, born 1895, Tenn., son.

204. EWING, FANNIE, F/W, born Aug. 1849, Louisiana, widow.
Thomas, M/W, born Mar. 1887, Louisiana, grandson.
CHILDRESS, WILLIE, M/B, born Apr. 1880, Tenn., servant. married 1 yr.

205. JOHNSON, SOPHIA, M/W, born Dec. 1849, Georgia, widow.
Flourine, F/W, born Dec. 1877, Georgia, daughter.

206. VAN NESS, MARY, F/W, born Aug 1841, Kentucky, widow.
Carita, F/W, born May 1874, Florida, daughter.

207. DUBOSE, ROBERT M. M/W, born Sept. 1841, South Carolina, married 26 yrs.
Elizabeth, F/W, born Nov. 1849, South Carolina, wife.
Marion, M/W, b. Nov. 1879, Tenn., son.
Elizabeth, F/W, born Aug. 1881, Tenn., daughter.
Beverly, F/W, born Jan. 1876, Tenn., daughter.
Annie, F/W, born Nov. 1889, Tenn., daughter.
PORCHER, MARIAH, F/W, born Nov. 1828, South Carolina, sister-in-law, single.
BURBANK, KYLE, M/W, born Apr. 1865, Ohio, married 13 yrs., boarder.
Lyle, F/W, born May 1861, Kentucky, boarder.
Samuel M., M/W born Oct. 1887, Ohio, boarder.
Dorothy, F/W, born Aug. 1899, Georgia, boarder.
FINLEY, MARIAH, F/W, born Nov. 1871, South Carolina, boarder.

208. MCCRADY, JOHN, M/W, born May 1840, Tenn., widower.
Catherine, F/W, born June 1876, Tenn., daughter.

209. SELDEN, MARY, F/W, born Feb. 1854, Georgia, widow.
Joe, M/W, born Dec. 1876, Georgia, son.
Robert F., M/W, born Sept. 1883, South Carolina, son.
ALREDGE, MARIKA., F/B, Apr. 1840, Tenn., servant, widow.
Joe, M/B, born Feb. 1872, Tenn., servant.

209. ALREDGE, Anderson, M/B, born Feb. 1879, Tenn., servant.
Arby, M/B, born Feb. 1866, Tenn., servant.

210. CALHOUN, WILLIAM R., M/W, born Dec. 1876, Georgia, married 3 yrs.
Nettie, F/W, born Oct, 1879, Georgia, wife.

211. BARNWELL, FLORENCE, F/W, born May 1844, Florida, widow.
Sarah, F/W, born 1870, South Carolina, daughter.
Bower, M/W, born Nov. 1880, South Carolina.
JOSALINE, LOUISA, F/W, born Mar. 1845, England, boarder.
William F., M/W, born Mar. 1842, England, boarder.
STEWMAN, RUDOLPH, M/W, born Mar. 1872, Louisiana, boarder.
Grace, F/W, born Oct. 1874, S.D. boarder.
Rudolph, M/W born Apr. 1900, Tenn., boarder.
HOLLAND, FRANK, M/B, born Feb. 1871, Tenn., servant.
Hattie, F/B, born Oct. 1873, Tenn., servant.
ARLEDGE, ASIA, F/B, born Sept. 1879, Tenn., servant.
Georgia F/B, born Oct. 1888, Tenn., servant.

212. AIKENS, WILLIAM D., M/W, born July 1846, South Carolina, married 25 yrs.
Alice, F/W, born Aug. 1845, Louisiana, wife.
Leila, F/W, born Dec. 1879, Louisiana, daughter.
Budd L., M/W, born Dec. 1881, South Carolina, son.
William, M/W, born July 1882, South Carolina, son.
James, M/W, born Jan. 1894, South Carolina, son.
John M., M/W, born Sept. 1891, New Jersey, son.

213. WILMERDING, MARY, F/W, born Dec. 1876, Texas, single.
Mary, F/W, born Apr. 1851, South Carolina, widowed-mother.

214. WILEY, LIZZIE, F/W, born Mar. 1871, Tenn., single.
CURLE, ALICE, F/W, born May 1872, Tenn., widowed-sister.
Eva, F/W, born Jan. 1892, Tenn., niece.
Hazel, F/W, born Oct. 1896, Tenn., niece.

215. GREEN, LILLIE, F/W, born Jan 1848, North Carolina, single.

COTTON, SALLIE, F/W, born Dec. 1846, North Carolina, sister.
Arthur L., M/W, born Aug. 1884, Tenn., nephew.

216. ALLISON?, MATILDA C. F/W, born May 1835, Tenn., widow.
GRAY, ELIZABETH, F/W, born Mar. 1869, New York, daughter.
Vernon S., M/W, born Mar. 1890, Pennsylvania, grandson.
Elizabeth A., F/W, born Feb., 1893, Pennsylvania, granddaughter.

217. PRINCE, WILLIAM, M/W, born Aug. 1855, Alabama, married 9 yrs.
Mariah, F/W, born Nov. 1858, Tenn., wife.
Jessie, F/W, born Feb. 1892, Tenn., daughter.
Mildred, F/W, born Aug, 1895, Tenn., daughter.
Opal, F/W, born Jan. 1899, Tenn., daughter.
SEWELL, PAMELA, F/W, born Nov. 1820, Kentucky, widowed, mother-in-law.
VERDILL, WILLIAM A., M/W, born June 1871, South Carolina, boarder.
Ella, F/W, born Sept. 1873, Georgia, wife of boarder.
James E, M/W, born Nov. 1896, Georgia, son of boarder.

218. REESE, WALLIS, F/W, born June 1862, Alabama, married 20 yrs.
John A., M/W, born June 1885, Alabama, son.
POWELL, NELLIE, F/W, born June 1882, Alabama, niece.

219. BROOKS, PRESTON, M/W, born, July 1854, South Carolina, married 22 yrs.
Mariah, F/W, born Nov. 1855, South Carolina, wife.
Preston B. M/W, born Apr. 1879, South Carolina, son.
Berten R. M/W, b. Apr. 1883, Tenn., son.
Lewis, M/W born May 1884, Tenn., son.
Catherine, F/W, born Mar. 1886, Tenn., daughter.
Mary, F/W, born Apr. 1887, Tenn., daughter.
Mariah, F/W, born May 1889, Tenn., daughter.
Amy, F/W, born May 1893, Tenn., daughter.
HAMILTON, THOMAS, M/W, born Mar. 1869, Ireland, boarder.

220. ?COOPER, ?Cliff, M/W, born Nov. 1862, Tenn., married 7 yrs.
Willie, F/W, b. July 1867, Miss., wife.
Pollie B., F/W, born Nov. 1894, Tenn., daughter.
WAKEFIELD, EMMA, F/B, born Jan. 1875, Tenn., servant.

221. MURRAY, LIZZIE, F/W, born Dec. 1869, England, widow.
Gerald, M/W, b. Aug. 1891, England, son.

222. HOPKINS, HENRY, M/W, born Mar. 1868, Tenn., married 7 yrs.
Ada, F/W, born June 1870, Tenn., wife.
Gladys F/W, born 1889, Tenn., daughter.
Charlie, M/W, b. Apr. 1894, Tenn., son.
Ruby, F/W, born July 1896, Tenn., daughter.

223. MANSFIELD, ANDREW, M/W, born Dec. 1851, Tenn., married 31 yrs.
Mary, F/W, born Oct. 1852, Tenn., wife.
Tallis, M/W, born Oct. 1879, Tenn., son.
Maud, F/W, born Dec. 1884, Tenn., daughter.
Halley, F/W, born Jan. 1891, Tenn., daughter.
Grace, F/W, born May 1895, Tenn., daughter.
TURNER, JOHN, M/W, born Oct. 1877, Tenn., boarder.
FAYETT, WILLIAM, OR WILLIAM, M/B, born Oct. 1877, Tenn. , servant.

224. MOORE, ANDREW M., M/W, born Dec. 1845, Tenn., married 20 yrs.
Jannie F., F/W, born June 1859, Tenn., wife.
Mary, F/W, born Sept. 1881, Virginia, daughter.
DREAK, MAGGIE, F/B, born Apr. 1865, Tenn., servant, single.
Nora, F/B, born Mar. 1886, Tenn., servant.

225. PUCKETTE, CHARLOTTE, F/W, born Nov. 1859, Georgia.
Stephen E., M/W, born Sept. 1884, Tenn., son.
Charles M., M/W, born July 1887, Tenn., son.
John K., M/W, born Aug. 1890, Tenn., son.
ELYATT, MARGRETT, F/B, born Apr. 1872, Texas, boarder.

226. BARTON, SAMUEL M., M/W, born May 1861, Virginia, married 2 yrs.
Mary M, F/W, born Mar. 1867, Virginia, wife.
Mary K., F/W, born Mar. 1899, Virginia,

daughter.
DAVIS, MATTIE, F/B, born Apr. 1850, Tenn., servant, widow.
Annie, F/B, born Feb. 1884, Tenn., servant, single.

227. GUERRY, WILLIAM, M/W, born July 1861, South Carolina, married 11 yrs.
Annie, F/W, born Aug. 1864, North Carolina, wife.
Elexander, M/W, born Oct. 1890, South Carolina, son.
Summer, M/W, born Oct. 1892, South Carolina, son.
Annie, F/W, born Dec. 1894, South Carolina, daughter.
Moultrie, M/W, born Feb. 1899, South Carolina, son.
MCBEE, SILAS, M/W, born June 1887, Tenn., boarder.
WILLIAMS, JAMES T. JR., M/W, born Aug. 1881, South Carolina, boarder.
MOSS, ELLEN, F/B, born Dec. 1879, Tenn., servant.
WALKER, MAGGIE, F/B, born Mar. 1882, Tenn., servant.

228. ELMORE, FRANKLIN, M/W, born Apr. 1840, Alabama, widower.
Caroline, F/W, born June 1827, South Carolina, widowed-sister.

229. LAUTZENHEISER, FRANK, M/W, born, Feb. 1867, Ohio, married 5 yrs.
May, F/W, born June 1870, Ohio, wife.
?Rene, F/W, born Dec. 1895, Tenn., daughter.

230. TRENT, WILLIAM, M/W, born Nov. 1862, Virginia, married 4 yrs.
Alice, F/W, born June 1871, New Jersey, wife.
Lucia, F/W, born Dec. 1898, Virginia, daughter.

231. COLMORE, ROBERT L., M/W, born Oct. 1840, England, married 25 yrs.
Priscilla D, F/W, born June 1852, England, wife.
Charlie, M/W, born Nov., 1879, Tenn., son.
Dora, F/W, born Oct. 1880, Tenn., daughter.
Robert, M/W, born 1883, Tenn., son.
?Lily, F/W, born ?, Tenn., daughter.

232. HODGTON, FRANCES, F/W, born Jan. 1845, Pennsylvania, widow.
Telfair, M/W, born Sept. 1876, New Jersey, son.
Sarah, F/W, born Apr. 1880, New York, daughter.
DUNCAN, ELIZABETH, F/W, born Feb. 1860, Ireland, servant.
CASTLEBERRY, LAURA, F/W, born Nov. 1875, Tenn., servant.
KING, MOLLIE, F/W, born Apr. 1850, Tenn., servant.

233. ARNOLD, SARAH, F/W, born July 1854, Tenn., widow.
Kate, F/W, born Oct. 1881, Tenn., daughter.
DAVIS, EMMA, F/W, born June 1881, Tenn., niece.

234. MANSFIELD, JAMES, M/W, born May 1875, Tenn., married 2 yrs.
Mary, F/W, born May 1877, Tenn., wife.
Mary L. F/W, born Feb. 1899, Tenn., daughter.

235. BONHOLZER, JOHN, M/W, born Aug. 1855, Switzerland, married 20 yrs.
Anna, F/W, born Sept. 1857, Switzerland, wife.
Maggie, F/W, born Mar. 1881, Tenn., daughter.
Kate, F/W, born Jan. 1882, Tenn., son.
Fred, M/W, born Jun. 1884, Tenn., son.
Anna, F/W, born Dec. 1885, Tenn., son.
John, M/W, born June 1888, Tenn., son.
Albert, M/W, born Dec. 1890, Tenn., son.
Andrew, M/W, b. July 1893, Tenn., son.

236. ELLISON, WILLIAM T., M/W, born Mar. 1878, Kentucky, married 3 yrs.
Blanche, F/W, born Dec. 1878, Canada, wife.

237. PIGGOT, CAMERON, M/W, born Sept. 1855, Maryland, married 10 yrs.
Annie, F/W, born Jan. 1866, Maryland, wife.
Charles S., M/W, born June 1892, Tenn., son.
ROBERTSON, WILL, M/B, born Mar. 1882, Tenn., servant.
NORTON, HANNAH, F/B, born Sept. 1871, Canada, servant.
DABNEY, EDWARD H., M/W, born Mississippi, boarder.
WARD, MARY, F/W, born Dec. 1842, Mississippi, boarder, widow.

238. THERWARD, SOPHIA, W/F, born Feb. 1842, Mississippi, widow.
SMEDES, SUSAN, W/F, born Aug. 1840, Mississippi, sister.
DABNEY, LELIA, W/F, born Apr. 1852, Mississippi, sister.

239. GALLEHER, CHARLOTTE, F/W, born Apr. 1896, Kentucky, widow.
Charlotte, F/W, born June 1875, New York daughter.
Elizabeth, F/W, born May 1837, Kentucky, sister-in-law.
RUTLEDGE, illegible, F/B, born Apr. 1872, Tenn., servant.
RAWKINS, JOICE, F/?, illegible, Tenn., servant.
SHARP, ?ADDIE, F/B, born Mar. 1884, Tenn., servant.
SCOTT, ROSE, F/B, born 1855, Tenn., servant.

240. WIGGINS, BENJAMIN, M/W, born Sept. 1861, South Carolina, married 14 yrs.
Clara, F/W, b. Oct. 1852, England, wife.
Katherine, F/W, born Feb. 1887, England, daughter.
Charles, M/W, born Jan. 1890, Tenn., son.
Elizabeth, F/W, born June 1891, Tenn., daughter
QUINTARD, KATE, F/W, born Feb. 1827, England, widow.

241. SEWELL, HENRY, M/W, born Aug. 1865, Tenn., married 10 yrs.
Rosa, F/W, born Apr. 1862, Ohio, daughter.
Marie, F/W, born Nov. 1891, Tenn., daughter.
Ross, M/W, born Mar. 1895, Tenn., son.

242. MALADHO, SALLIE, F/W, Apr. 1840, Virginia, single.
SMITH, F., F/W, born Mar. 1850, Virginia, partner.

243. DANIEL, ARION, M/B, born Nov. 1847, Tenn., married 18 yrs.
Lizzie, F/B, born Sept. 1860, Tenn., wife.
Willie, F/B, born June 1883, Tenn., daughter.
Henry, M/B, born July 1885, Tenn., son.
Jesse, M/B, born Nov. 1887, Tenn., son.
Annie, F/B, born Oct. 1889, Tenn., daughter.
Selden, M/B, born Apr. 1891, Tenn., son.
NUCKLES, JESSIE, M/B, born Apr. 1880, Tenn., boarder.
KENNLY, illegible, M/B, born Aug. 1880, Tenn., servant.

244. KIRBY SMITH, CASEY, F/W, born Sept. 1838, Virginia, widow.
Caroline, F/W, born Oct. 1866, Virginia, daughter.
Frances, F/W, born July 1868, Texas, daughter.
Edmond, M/W, born, August, 1869, Kentucky, son.
Lydia, F/W, born Apr. 1871, Kentucky, daughter.
Rowena, F/W, born Oct, 1872, Kentucky, daughter.
Elizabeth, F/W, born Jan. 1876, Tenn., daughter.
Josephine, F/W, born Oct. 1880, Tenn., daughter.
Joseph L., M/W, b. Apr. 1883, Tenn., son.
Ephraim, M/W, b. Aug. 1885, Tenn., son.

245. HALL, WILLIAM B., M/W, born Jan. 1866, Alabama, married 3 yrs.
Irene, F/W, born Apr. 1876, Alabama, wife.

PEOPLE LIVING IN MARION COUNTY SECTION OF SEWANEE IN 1900

246. TATE, ELISHA, M/W, born July 1832, Tenn., married 37 yrs.
Mary J., F/W, born January 1848, Tenn., wife.
Milton G., M/W, born September 1886, Tenn., son.
Franky A., F/W, born July 1889, Tenn., daughter.
David W., M/W, born February 1894, Tenn., son.

247. MCBEE, GEORGE, M/W, born March 1853, Tenn., married 27 yrs.
Mary, F/W, born July 1854, Tenn., wife.
Albert, M/W, born February 1881, Tenn., son.
Vinie, F/W, born January 1884, Tenn., daughter.
Sallie A., F/W, born May 1886, Tenn., daughter.
Robert, M/W, born September 1888, Tenn., son.
Lawrence, M/W, born January 1890, Tenn., son.
Clarence, M/W, born January 1890, Tenn., son.
Raulie, M/W, born November 1893, Tenn., son.

248. MCBEE, SAMUEL, M/W, born February , Tenn., married 2 yrs.
L. Elizabeth, F/W, b. in 1845, Tenn., wife.
John, M/W, born May 1892, Tenn., son.
William H., M/W, born December 1845, Tenn., son.

249. MCBEE, GEORGE W., M/W, born January 1865, married 17 yrs.
Nancy, F/W, born in 1870, Tenn., wife.
Willie, M/W, born April 1884, Tenn., son.
Samuel, M/W, born March 1886, Tenn., son.
Joe, M/W, b. February 1888, Tenn., son.
Jesse, M/W, born November 1899, Tenn..

250. YOKLEY, DALLAS, M/W, born May 1874, Tenn., married 7 yrs.
Luella A., F/W, born March 1876, Tenn., wife.
William, M/W, born September 1893, Tenn., son.
James, M/W, born December 1896, Tenn., son.
Sallie, F/W, born September 1898, Tenn., daughter.
MEEKS, SARAH J., F/W, born November 1844, Tenn., mother-in-law.

251. MCBEE, ROBERT, M/W, born December 1860, Tenn., married 14 yrs.
Lizzie S., F/W, born September 1870, Tenn., wife.
Margaret, F/W, born December 1890, Tenn., daughter.
Obediah, M/W, born February 1892, Tenn., son.
Church, M/W, born August 1896, Tenn., son.
Della M., F/W, born May 1900, Tenn., daughter.

252. MCBEE, ROBERT W., M/W, born 1855, Tenn., married 12 yrs.
Lena., F/W, born September 1868, Tenn., wife.
Jesse, M/W, b. October 1889, Tenn., son.
Lee, M/W, born October 1892, Tenn., son.

253. MCBEE, SILAS F., M/W, born March 1867, Tenn..
Lou, F/W, born Jan. 1881, Tenn., wife.
Susan, F/W, born December 1826, Tenn., mother.

254. LAPPIN, GRANT H., M/W, born June 1865, Ohio, married 3 yrs.
Lizzie S., F/W, born November 1865, Tenn., wife.
Annie, F/W, born December 1887, Tenn., daughter.
Carrie, F/W, born April 1889, Tenn., daughter.
Fred S., M/W, born September 1890, Tenn., son.
Albert A., M/W, born January 1892, Tenn., son.
Lizzie M., F/W, born February 1896, Tenn., daughter.
Hobert, M/W, born Jan. 1898, Tenn., son.
Emma, F/W, born August 1899, Tenn., daughter.
SULLIVAN, WILLIAM, M/W, born June 1868, Tenn., brother-in-law.
BOUNDS, ANNIE, F/W, born March 1889, Tenn., step-daughter.

255. LAPPIN, JESSE M., M/W, born January 1853, Ohio, married 24 yrs.
Martha E., F/W, born October 1852, Alabama, wife.
Olive, F/W, born July 1887, Tenn., daughter.
Ada, F/W, born July 1887, Tenn., daughter.

Jesse W., M/W, born September 1889, Tenn., son.
Mattie, F/W, born March 1892, Tenn., daughter.
Bertha, F/W, born April 1894, Tenn., daughter.
William M., M/W, born September 1897, Tenn., son.
SULLIVAN, SARAH E., F/W, born November 1897, Tenn., daughter.
Samuel, M/W, born March 1870, Tenn., son-in-law.
Estelle, F/W, born February 1896. Tenn., granddaughter.
Ethel, F/W, born September 1897, Tenn. granddaughter.
Madie, F/W, born May 1900, Tenn., granddaughter.
SARGENT, SAMUEL, M/W, born September 1881, boarder.

256. GARNER, ALBERT, M/W, born June 1881, Tenn., married 1 yr.
Sarah, F/W, born May 1883, Tenn., wife.
James B., M/W, born April 1900, Tenn., son.

257. YOUNG, JACOB A., M/W, born March 1834 New Jersey, married 29 yrs.
Elizabeth, F/W, born November 1828, Alabama, wife. .
MCADAMS, FANNIE, F/W, born July 1850, Alabama, daughter.
Nora, F/W, born July 1886, Tenn., granddaughter.
GIPSON, ARTHUR, M/W, born January 1887, Tenn., gr-gr-grandson.
Ora, F/W, born June 1888, Tenn., gr-gr-granddaughter.
William T., M/W, born February 1890, Tenn., gr-gr-grandson.
George A., M/W, born April 1892, Tenn., gr-gr-grandson.

258. HEAD, JOHN N., M/W, born August 1877, Tenn., married 1 yr.
Jane S., F/W, born October 1871, Tenn., wife.
Samuel M., M/W, born December 1899, Tenn., son.

259. GARNER, JOHN, M/W, born November 1856, Tenn., married 21 yrs.
Jennie M., F/W, born December 1860, Minnesota, wife.
Arthur, M/W, born May 1884, Tenn., son.
Clarence H., M/W, born February 1889, Tenn., son.
Catherine, F/W, born November 1890, Tenn., daughter.
Name illegible, born October 1892, Tenn., daughter.
Lizzie, F/W, born February 1895, Tenn., daughter.
Henry, M/W, born October 1897, Tenn., son.

260. GARNER, L. D., M/W, born August 1870, Tenn..
Elizabeth, F/W, born December 1880, Tenn., wife.
CARTER, WILLIE, M/W, born March 1877, Tenn., brother-in-law.

261. SMITH, PETER, M/W, born 1878, Tenn., married 4 yrs.
Frankie S., F/W, born 1878, Tenn., wife.
Charles, M/W, born 1896, Tenn., son.

262. SMITH, WEST (WESLEY), M/W, born May 1882, Tenn., married 2 yrs.
Annie, F/W, born November 1883, Tenn., wife.
Sarah A., F/W, born March 1899, Tenn., daughter.

263. STATOM, JOHN, M/W, born March 1849, Tenn., married 21 yrs.
Nancy A., F/W, born January 1848, Georgia, wife.
Martha, F/W, born April 1883, Tenn., daughter.
Henry M., M/W, born August 1888, Tenn., son.

SEWANEE STUDENTS

1. LEIGH, J.E., born June 1847, Virginia, HEAD MASTER.
2. PLARA, HUGH, M. T., born Jan. 1872, New York, command.
3. NILES, SWANSON, born Jan. 1887, Mississippi, student.
4. JASON, born Jan. 1887, Mississippi, student.
5. WOODWARD, CHARLES, born Dec. 1885, Georgia, student.
6. REMY, THOMAS, born Apr. 1879, Missouri, student.
7. SCARBROUGH, JOHN, born Oct. 1885, Texas, student.
8. MAXEY, DAGGETT, born Feb. 1887, Arkansas, student.
9. ??GRAHAM, JAMES, born June 1884, Florida, student.
10. ROBINSON, ?, born Nov. 1885, Mississippi, student.
11. MASTIEN, WILLIAM, born June 1886, Louisiana, student.
12. GILLASPIE, SAMUEL D., born Mar. 1884, Louisiana, student.
13. BLOUNT, GUY, born Aug. 1884, Texas, student.
14. ROBERTS, CHARLES, born May 1882, Alabama, student.
15. FUDERCKAR, SAMUEL, born Jan. 1888, Alabama, student.
16. CROOK, GEORGE A., born Mar. 1884, Tenn., student.
17. ROBERTSON, DEROSET, born May 1885, Georgia, student.
18. GATES, GEORGE, born July 1885, Florida, student.
19. SCHIFF, WILLIAM, born Oct. 1883, Ohio, student.
20. SCHOUP, STEPHEN, born Jan. 1885, Tenn., student.
21. THOMPSON, JACOB, born Feb. 1885, Mississippi, student.
22. RAND, FREDRICK, born May 1889, Florida, student.
23. PFAFFER, FRANK L., born June 1882, Texas, student.
24. PRESTON, ALEXANDER, born Feb. 1884, Texas, student.
25. TRIPPE, RICHARD E, born Jan. 1885, Texas, student.
26. THOMPSON, LIVINGSTON, born June 1885, Georgia, student.
27. WHELER, WESLEY E, born Oct, 1883, Arkansas, student.
28. MacMILLIAN,, ALEXANDER, born Feb. 1884,
Tenn., student.
29. HAMPTON, EDWIN, born Aug. 1884, Georgia, student.
30. HAMPTON, WADE, born Jan. 1889, Florida, student.
31. WILKINS, GEORGE W., born Oct. 1882, Massachusetts, student.
32. VAN TORIN, HARRY, born May 1883, Louisiana, student.
33. FRANZ, JOHN F., born Mar. 1882, Ohio, student.
34. MILLER, WILLIAM, born July 1884, Georgia, student.
35. GAITHER, ROWAN, born July 1885, Mississippi, student.
36. GARDELLE, LOUIS, born Oct. 1885, Georgia, student.
37. COWTHERS, JAMES, born Aug. 1887, Kentucky, student.
38. McCLERKY, LOUIS D. M., born Aug. 1884, Georgia, student.
39. COMEGYS, EDWARD T., born Apr. 1884, Indiana territory, student.
40. WETTLIN, DAVID, born May 1886, Mississippi, student.
41. WETTLIN, Charlie, born Mar. 1882, Mississippi, student.
42. REDWOOD, MELVIN, born May 1883, Texas, student.
43. ?BLUM, HERMAN, born Feb. 1884, Louisiana, student.
44. ALSTON, JAMES L., born May 1884, Alabama, student.
45. WEATHERS, BENJAMIN, born May 1884, Alabama, student.
46. YANCY, ALICK, born Mar. 1880, Tenn., student.
47. CONNELL, WILLIAM, born Dec. 1888, Louisiana, student.
48. SINGLETON, WALTER T., born Sept. 1882, Louisiana, student.
49. SKINNER, NATHANIEL, born Apr. 1884, Mississippi, student.
50. JOHNSON, CLAUDE, born Sept. 1882, Mississippi, student.
51. BIDDLE, DRAKE, born Sept. 1888, Tenn., student.

52. JONES, CADWELLANDER, born July 1882, South Carolina, student.
53. SHELLBY, GEORGE B., born Oct. 1881, Mississippi, student.
54. ADAMS, HARRY, born June 1882, Mississippi, student.
55. HAMMUM, JOSEPH, born Jan. 1884, New York, student.
56. BASS, JOHN C., born May 1882, Louisiana, student.
57. SMITH, ALEXANDER A., born Oct 1881, Louisiana, student.
58. GILBERT, CALLIUS D., born June 1884, Florida, student.
59. GOLDSTIEN, MORTIOSE, born Sept. 1883, Mississippi, student.
60. SCOLLARD, THOMAS W., born Oct. 1881, Texas, student.
61. WILLIAMS, JOSEPH B., born Jan. 1882, Texas, student.
62. LINDSEY, COURTIANRY, born July 1882, South Carolina, student.
63. DAGGILL, CHARLES, born Apr. 1885, Arkansas, student.
64. HUBBELL, OCTON. E., born June 1883, Mississippi, student.
65. COPELAND, JEFFERSON D., born Apr. 1882, South Carolina, student.
66. BARNETT, HARLOW, born Dec. 1879, Florida, student.
67. SIMPSON, WILLIAM H., born Nov. 1879, Mississippi, student.
68. GERALD, FLOYD A., born Aug. 1880, Mississippi, student.
69. HALL, THURMAN, born Sept. 1881, Texas, student.
70. LEAU, OVERTON, born Aug. 1877, Tenn., student.
71. CLEVELAND, ÉCAL, born July 1881, Texas, student.
72. MARTYSON, HARRY, born June 1881, Texas, student.
73. HILL, ROBERT, born Mar. 1879, Indiana, student.
74. CAMIN, ALBERT A., born Jan. 1880, Pennsylvania, student.
75. BROWN, JOHN, born Nov. 1880, Tenn., student.
76. LEIGE, RICHARD L., born Sept. 1889, Tenn., student.
77. BARNWELL, ROBERT W., born Aug. 1880, Alabama, student.
78. HUGER, ?, born Mar. 1881, Georgia, student.
79. PHILLIPS, HENRY, born Jan. 1882, Georgia, student.
80. LEA, LUKE, born Apr. 1879, Tenn., student.
81. GRAY, CHARLES QUINTARD, born May 1878, Tenn., student.
82. BROOLIS, JAMES, born Oct. 1879, North Carolina, student.
83. MILES, J.E,, born July 1869, Maryland, student.
84. JAMES OR JONES, JOHN C, born Feb. 1880, Tenn., student.
85. Illegible name, born May 1879, Texas, student
86. WELLS, FRED, born Apr. 1884, Massachusetts, student.
87. CROFI, GEORGE J., July 1881, South Carolina, student.
88. BULL, HENRY, born May 1880, Pennsylvania, student.
89. WILLIAMS, JAMES R., born 1888, South Carolina, student.
90. HALL, RICHARD C., born 1880, Tenn., student.
91. SUTER, HERMAN, born 1873, Pennsylvania, student.
92. Illegible name, JOHN W., born 1877, South Carolina, student.
93. RYLAN?, Joseph B., born 1884, New York, student.
94. MCNEAL, AUSTIN M., born Dec. 1880, Tenn., student.
95. RANDOLPH, VALLEN, born June 1879, Florida, student.
96. EASTIN, HENRY F., born Oct. 1881, Tenn., students.

There were 263 households and 96 out of town students listed at Sewanee in 1900 census.

PEOPLE LIVING AT SEWANEE IN 1910

The following data was taken from the 1910 census records for the 18th District of Franklin County, Tennessee.

1. GIPSON, JOHN, M/W, age 56, married 8 years, born Tenn.
   Sarah, F/W, age 53, wife, born Tenn.
   Charley, M/W, age 15, son, born Tenn.
   Rhoda, F/W, age 11, daughter, b. in Tenn.
   George, M/W, age 9, son, born Tenn.
   Jennie, F/W, age 5, daughter, born Tenn.
   Ernest, M/W, age 3, son, born Tenn.
2. HOLLIER, DARLEY, M/W, age 48, married 22 years, born Iowa.
   Agnes M., F/W, age 37, wife, born Michigan.
   William, M/W, age 19, son, born Iowa.
3. LEROY, LOUIS, M/W, age 49, his parents were born German.
   STERCHE, VIRGIL, M/W, age 12, companion, born Tenn.
   LANE, FRANK, M/W, age 11, companion, born Tenn.
4. REID, TOM, M/W, age 48, married 5 years, born Tenn.
   Lulu, F/W, age 35, wife, born Alabama.
   Sallie, F/W, age 77, widowed mother, born in Georgia.
5. HUNZIKER, MARY, F/W, age 74, widow, born Switzerland.
   Adolph, M/W, age 43, son, born Switzerland.
   BOGT, JOHN, M/W, age 86, companion, born Switzerland.
   KLEINWACHTER, WILLIAM L., M/W, age 30, born Tenn.
6. COLLINS, WILLIAM, M/W, age 60, married 16 years, born Tenn.
   Fanny, F/W, age 56, wife, born Tenn.
   Isaac, M/W, age 31, son, married 2 years, born Tenn.
   Etta, F/W, age 31, daughter-in-law, born Tenn.
   Virginia, F/W, born 1910, granddaughter, born Tenn.
7. ANDERSON, ISAAC, M/W, age 61, married 40 years, born Tenn.
   Lizzie L., F/W, age 60, wife, born Tenn.
   Lily, F/W, age 26, daughter, born Tenn.
   TIDEWELL, MINNIE, F/W, age 8, companion, born Tenn.
8. HARRISON, THOMAS, M/W, age 38, married 18 years, born Tenn.
   Annie, F/W, age 35, wife, born Tenn.
   Hays, M/W, age 12, son, born Tenn.
   James, M/W, age 11, son, born Tenn.
   Floyd, M/W, age 7, son, born Tenn.
   Bennie, M/W, age 4, son, born Tenn.
9. BIDDLE, RICHARD, M/W, age 60, born Pennsylvania.
10. KIRBY SMITH, REYNOLDS M., M/W, age 35, married 7 yrs., born Tenn.
    Maude, F/W, age 35, wife, born Tenn.
    Reynolds M., M/W, age 5, son, born Philippines Islands.
    Henry, M/W, age 3, son, born Tenn.
    Kirby Smith, Elizabeth, F/W, born 1910, daughter, born Tenn.
11. ?KEMICKLEK, JESSE, M/B, age 24, married 8 yrs., born Tenn.
    Willie, F/MU, age 24, wife, born Tenn.
    Mary, F/MU, age 8, daughter, b. in Tenn.
    Ned, M/MU, age 4, son, born Tenn.
    DOUGLAS, Maggie, F/MU, age 18, boarder, born Tenn.
    THOMPSON, Maggie, F/MU, age 24, boarder, born Alabama.
12. COULSON, BENJAMIN, M/W, age 39, married 17 yrs., born Ohio.
    Mary E., F/W, age 37, wife, born Ohio.
    Henry, M/W, age 15, son, born Ohio.
    James, M/W, age 12, son, born Ohio.
13. STEVENS, WILLIAM, M/W, age 35, married 15 yrs., born Tenn.
    Della, F/W, age 35, wife, born Tenn.
    James, M/W, age 15, son, born Tenn.
    Raney, M/W, age 10, son, born Tenn.
    Cora, F/W, age 8, daughter, born Tenn.
    Eva, F/W, age 6, daughter, born Tenn.
    Howard, M/W, age 4, son, born Tenn.
    Ira, M/W, age 2, son, born Tenn.
    Roy, M/W, son born 1909, in Tenn.
14. MOONEY, RICHARD, M/W, age 61, married 37 yrs., born Mississippi.
    Catherine, F/W, age 53, wife, born North Carolina.
    Martha, F/W, age 15, daughter, b. in Tenn.
    Flora, F/W, age 12, daughter, b. in Tenn.
15. BARRY, JOSEPH, M/W, age 39, married 21 yrs., born Tenn.
    Martha, F/W, age 39, wife, born Tenn.
    Esther, F/W, age 14, daughter, born Tenn.

Ethel, F/W, age 12, daughter, born Tenn.
Johnnie, M/W, age 9, son, born Tenn.
William, M/W, age 7, son, born Tenn.
Ida, F/W, age 6, daughter, born Tenn.
Claiborne, M/W, age 4, son, born Tenn.
Ulous, M/W, age 2, son, born Tenn.

16. MARLOW, MEREDITH, M/W, age 29, married 3 yrs., born Tenn.
Lizzie, F/W, age 19, wife, born Tenn.
John, M/W, age 2, son, born Tenn.
Joe, M/W, son born 1909, in Tenn.

17. RICKETTS, JOE, M/W, age 25, married 4 yrs., born Tenn.
Jenny, F/W, age 25, wife, born Tenn.
Elbert, M/W, age 4, son, born Tenn.
J. Nancy, F/W, age 1, daughter, born Tenn.

18. PACK, THOMAS, M/W, age 19, married 2 yrs., born Tenn.
Maggie, F/W, age 17, wife, born Tenn.
Liter, F/W, age 1, daughter, born Tenn.

19. GIPSON, ANDREW, M/W, age 29, married 3 yrs., born Tenn.
Wife's name illegible, age 40, wife, b Tenn.

20. HUNZIKER, EMIL, M/W, age 45, married 11 yrs., born Switzerland.
Virgin, F/W, age 28, wife, born Tenn.
John, M/W, age 10, son, born Tenn.
Lottie, F/W, age 9, daughter, born Tenn.
Veda, F/W, age 7, daughter, born Tenn.
Grace, F/W, age 5, daughter, born Tenn.
Elise, F/W, age 3, daughter, born Tenn.

21. FOSTER, FRANK, M/W, age 37, married 15 yrs., born Tenn.
Sallie, F/W, age 33, wife, born Tenn.
Raney, M/W, age 13, son, born Tenn.
Flora, F/W, age 10, daughter, born Tenn.
Andrew, M/W, age 7, son, born Tenn.
Mary, F/W, age 4, daughter, born Tenn.
CLARK, LUCINDA, F/W, age 55, widowed mother, born Tenn.

22. ANDERSON, JENNIE, F/W, age 42, widow, born Tenn.
Petway, M/W, age 18, son, born Tenn.
Andrew, M/W, age 16, son, born Tenn.
Beulah, F/W, age 15, daughter, born Tenn.
Clara, F/W, age 5, companion, born Tenn.

23. GIPSON, JOHNSON, M/W, age 53, married 37 yrs., born Tenn.
Bettie, F/W, age 55, wife, born Tenn.
Julia, F/W, age 21, daughter, married 6 yrs., born Tenn.
Anna, F/W, age 18, daughter, born Tenn.
Elmer, M/W, age 4, grandson, born Tenn.
Virgie M., M/W, age 5, son, born Tenn.

24. PACK, MONROE, M/W, age 54, married 30 yrs., born Tenn.
Elizabeth, F/W, age 58, wife, born Ala.
Cecil, M/W, age 15, son, born Tenn.
Robert, M/W, age 6, grandson, born Tenn.

25. HOBACK, CHARLES E., M/W, age 26, married 9 yrs., born Texas.
Dollie, F/W, age 28, wife, born Tenn.
Edward, M/W, age 6, son, born Tenn.

26. BARRY, JOHN, M/W, age 69, married 52 yrs., born Tenn.
Rachel, F/W, age 68, wife, born Georgia.

27. PARTIN, ISRAEL S., M/W, age 57, married 31, yrs., born Georgia.
Parlee, F/W, age 53, wife, born Tenn.
Jennie, F/W, age 28, daughter, born Tenn.
Huston, M/W, age 26, son, born Tenn.
Louise, F/W, age 24, daughter, born Tenn.
Sallie, F/W, age 20, daughter, born Tenn.
Bennie, M/W, age 17, son, born Tenn.
John, M/W, age 15, son, born Tenn.

28. LADD, WILLIAM, M/W, age 19, married 2 yrs., born Tenn.
Elllie, F/W, age 20, wife, born Tenn.
WHITE, LUCY, F/W, age 7, companion, born Tenn.

29. JENNINGS, GEORGE W., M/W, age 65, married 16 yrs., born S.C.
Sallie, F/W, age 39, wife, born Tenn.
Nannie, F/W, age 14, daughter, born Tenn.
Elbert, M/W, age 12, son, born Tenn.

30. CLARK, JAMES W., M/W, age 22, widower, born Tenn.
WHITE, RUTH, F/W, age 3, companion, born Tenn.

31. REED, LEWIS, M/W, age 23, married 2 years, born Tenn.
Daisy, F/W, age 22, wife, born Tenn.
Roberta, F/W, age 1, daughter, born Tenn.
HARRISON, JEREMIAH, M/W, age 85, grand-father, born Missouri.

32. ANDERSON, DAVID, M/W, age 54, married 28 yrs., born Tenn.
Annie, F/W, age 42, wife, born Tenn.
Roy, M/W, age 17, son, born Tenn.
Edna, F/W, age 15, daughter, born Tenn.
Isaac, M/W, age 15 or 13, son, born Tenn.
Flora, F/W, age 11, daughter, born Tenn.
Naoma, F/W, age 9, daughter, born Tenn.
Donald, M/W, age 6, son, born Tenn.

32. ANDERSON, Anna, F/W, b 1910, in Tenn.

33. HOPKINS, HARVEY, M/W, age 24, married 5 yrs., born Tenn.
Otsie, F/W, age 21, wife, born Tenn.
Edward, M/W, age 4, son, born Tenn.
Roena, F/W, born 1910, in Tenn.

Hampton, M/W, age 13, brother, born Tenn.

34. ROLLINS, JOHN, M/W, age 56, married 28 yrs., born Tenn.
Martha, F/W, age 53, wife, born Tenn.
Ethel, F/W, age 9, companion, born Tenn.
35. ROLLINS, J. WILLIAM, M/W, age 25, married 3 yrs., born Tenn.
Eva, F/W, age 24, wife, born Tenn.
WHITE, Fannie, F/W, age 13, companion, born Tenn.
36. GREEN, THOMAS, M/W, age 39, married 19 yrs., born Tenn.
Sarah, F/W, age 36, wife, born Tenn.
Rhoda, F/W, age 18, dau. born Tenn.
James, M/W, age 16, son, born Tenn.
Joseph, M/W, age 14, son, born Tenn.
Wesley, M/W, age 11, son, born Tenn.
Margaret, F/W, age 9, daughter, born Tenn.
Robert, M/W, age 8, son, born Tenn.
Benton, M/W, age 6, son, born Tenn.
Thomas, M/W, age 5, son, born Tenn.
Irene, F/W, age 4, daughter, born Tenn.
Bertha, F/W, age 2, daughter, born Tenn.
37. MOTLEY, JAMES, M/W, age 65, widower, born Tenn.
38. ANDERSON, ALFRED, M/W, age 20, married 1 yr., born Tenn.
Hannah, F/W, age 16, wife, born Tenn.
39. FOSTER, CASWELL JAMES, M/W, age 30, married 9 yrs., born Tenn.
Dora, F/W, age 28, wife, born Tenn.
Martha, F/W, age 8, daughter, born Tenn.
Dortha, F/W, age 4, daughter, born Tenn.
James W., M/W, age 2, son, born Tenn.
40. JOHNSON, SARAH E., F/W, age 57, widow, born Tenn.
Sallie, F/W, age 21, daughter, born Tenn.
41. BOWMAN, ROBERT, M/MU, age 16, born Tenn.
Simpson, M/MU, age 14, brother, b. Tenn.
Tode, M/MU, age 12, brother, born Tenn.
42. NORWOOD, MARGARET, F/W, age 64, widow, born Tenn.
BERRYHILL, JOE, M/W, age 25, son-in-law, married 4 yrs., born Tenn.
Rosa, F/W, age 24, daughter, born Tenn.
Elizabeth, F/W, age 2, granddaughter, born Tenn.
43. DISHROOM, ANNIE, F/W, age 62, widow, born Tenn.
FARRIS, JOHN F., M/W, age 54, brother, born Tenn.
44. ROGERS, OSCAR, M/W, age 26, married 9 yrs., born Tenn.
Emma, F/W, age 27, wife, born Tenn.
Nora, F/W, age 8, daughter, born Tenn.
Hurbert, M/W, age 5, son, born Tenn.
Willie, F/W, age 3, daughter, born Tenn.
Lou Mary, F/W, age 1, daughter, b. Tenn.
45. HARRISON, LOUISE, F/W, age 44, widow, born Tenn.
Eliza M., F/W, age 55, mother, born Tenn.
Jerry, F/W, age 84, father, born Tenn.
46. STATEM, JOHN, M/W, age 50, married 18 yrs., born Tenn.
Saidee, F/W, age 47, wife, born Tenn.
Blanche, F/W, age 12, daughter, born Tenn.
Mary, F/W, age 10, daughter, born Tenn.
47. BIDDLE, THOMAS, M/W, age 51, born Tenn.
48. O'DEAR, JEFFERSON, M/W, age 23, married 2 yrs., born Tenn.
Beatrice, F/W, age 20, wife, born Tenn.
Herbert, M/W, born 1910, in Tenn.
49. GRUETTER, GODFREY, M/W, age 44, married 8 yrs., born Switzerland.
Myrtle, F/W, age 26, wife, born Tenn.
Jone, F/W, age 4, daughter, born Tenn.
Ernest, M/W, age 2, son, born Tenn.
Idella, F/W, born 1909, in Tenn.
50. RUSSELL, JAMES, M/W, age 50, married 20 yrs., born Tenn.
Maggie, F/W, age 61, wife, born Penn.
51. KENNEDY, GEORGE, M/W, age 40, married 2 yrs., born Tenn.
Tennie, F/W, age 29, wife, born Tenn.
Ola, F/W, age 13, daughter, born Tenn.
Bessie, F/W, age 12, daughter, born Tenn.
Lucile, F/W, age 8, daughter, born Tenn.
52. GARNER, WILLIAM, M/W, age 62, married 36 yrs., born Tenn.
Nancy, F/W, age 47, wife, born Tenn.
Otsie, F/W, age 19, daughter, born Tenn.
William R., M/W, age 14, son, born Tenn.
George, M/W, age 12, son, born Tenn.
BRATTON, ROSA, F/W, age 24, boarder, born Tenn.
MAGONIRK, OTIS, M/W, age 24, boarder, born Tenn.
NEELEY, WARRIEX, M/W, age 40, boarder, born Indiana.
53. SOUTHERLAND, WARREN M/W, age 60, born North Carolina.
GILLESPIE, NELLIE, F/W, age 19, boarder, born Tenn.
54. CAMP, EDWARD, M/W, age 26, married 1 yr., born Tenn.
Dollie, F/W, age 18, wife, born Tenn.

55. SULLIVAN, WILLIAM, M/W, age 44, married 8 yrs., born Tenn.
Sophia, F/W, age 33, wife, born Tenn.
LADD, GLADYS M., F/W, age 10, niece, born Tenn.
56. TERRILL, MATTHEW, M/W, age 30 married 9 yrs., born Tenn.
Rachel, F/W, age 24, wife, born Tenn.
Claude, M/W, age 8, son, born Tenn.
Walter, M/W, age 6, son, born Tenn.
Arthur, M/W, age 4, son, born Tenn.
James E., M/W, age 2, son, born Tenn.
57. O'DEAR, CATHERINE, F/W, age 66, widow, born Tenn.
58. TERRILL, THOMAS, M/W, age 58, born in Alabama.
Alice, F/W, age 17, daughter, born Tenn.
Willie, F/W, age 16, daughter, b. in Tenn.
Early, M/W, age 13, son, born Tenn.
59. TERRILL, CURGE, M/W, age 58, married 15 yrs., born Alabama.
Mahala, F/W, age 31, wife, born Tenn.
Albert, M/W, age 9, son, born Tenn.
Velma, F/W, age 7, daughter, born Tenn.
Thomas, M/W, age 4, son, born Tenn.
Pearl, F/W, age 2, daughter, born Tenn.
Ernest, M/W, son born 1910, in Tenn.
60. TRIPP, SARAH, F/W, age 53, widow, born Tenn.
Robert, M/W, age 20, son, born Tenn.
John, M/W, age 10, son, born Tenn.
61. MITCHELL, ROBERT, M/W, age 40, married 21 yrs., born Tenn.
Jean, F/W, age 38, wife, born Tenn.
Leroy, M/W, age 19, son, born Tenn.
Robert K., M/W, age 17, son, born Tenn.
Lawrence, M/W, age 14,
son, born Tenn.
Irene, F/W, age 12, daughter, born Tenn.
Otto H., M/W, age 10, son, born Tenn.
Oliver B., M/W, age 4, son, born Tenn.
IVES, GRANT, M/W, bro.in-law, born Tn.
62. HAWKINS, WALLACE, M/W, age 49, widower, born Switzerland.
Halairois, F/W, age 21, daughter, b. Tenn.
Flora, F/W, age 19, daughter, born Tenn.
Margaret, F/W, age 16, twin daughter, born Tenn.
Barbara, F/W, age 16, twin daughter, born Tenn.
Jack, M/W, age 14, son, born Tenn.
Thomas, M/W, age 11, son, born Tenn.
LUCHSINGER, BARBARA, F/W, age 74, mother-in-law, born Switzerland.
63. SHORT, FRANK, M/W, age 53, married 45 yrs. born Georgia.
Alice, F/W, age 64, wife, born S.C.
64. MYERS, WILLIAM L., M/W, age 55, married 31 yrs., born Tenn.
Elizabeth, F/W, age 60, wife, born Tenn.
Cecil, M/W, age 21, son, born Tenn.
Beatrice, F/W, age 19, daughter, b. in Tenn.
Theron, M/W, age 17, son, born Tenn.
65. STEWMAN, ROBERT, M/W, age 45, widower, born Tenn.
Allie or Ollie, M/W, age 21, son, b. Tenn.
Albert, M/W, age 18, son, born Tenn.
Armon, M/W, age 13, son, born Tenn.
Mary, F/W, age 10, daughter, born Tenn.
GARNER, MARY, F/W, age 6, companion, born Tenn.
BRINKLEY, HENRY, M/W, age 48, brother-in-law, born Tenn.
66. PRINCE, JAMES, M/W, age 40, married 21 yrs., born Tenn.
Emma, F/W, age 40, wife, born Ohio.
Emma, F/W, age 19, daughter, b. in Tenn.
James, M/W, age 18, son, born Tenn.
Rina, F/W, age 14, daughter, born Tenn.
Milton, M/W, age 10, son, born Tenn.
Parenthia, F/W, age 7, daughter, b in Tenn.
Hayden, M/W, age 7, son, born Tenn.
Susie, F/W, age 5, daughter, born Tenn.
67. TIRTH, ALFRED, M/W, age 37, married 3 yrs., born England.
Lula, F/W, age 24, wife, born Tenn.
Robert, M/W, age 2, son, born Tenn.
68. PIERCE, JAMES C. M/W, age 54, married 31 yrs., born Tenn.
Mary E., F/W, age 54, wife, born Tenn.
Hilday A., F/W, age 25, daughter, b. Tenn.
John L., M/W, age 20, son, born Tenn.
James H., M/W, age 4, grandson, b. Tenn.
69. MCBEE, JOHN WESLEY, M/W, age 53, married 9 yrs., born Tenn.
Mary, F/W, age 52, wife, born Tenn.
Haskell, M/W, age 7, son, born Tenn.
Buford, M/W, age 5, son, born Tenn.
Irene, F/W, age 3, daughter, born Tenn.
69. McBee, Hayden, M/W, age 1, son, born Tenn.
70. BARNES, NANCY , F/W, age 56, widow, born Tenn.
Margie, F/W, age 20, daughter, b. in Tenn.
HILL, JACK, M/W, age 28, son, married 5 yrs., born Tenn.
Adelle, F/W, age 20, wife, born Tenn.
Otsie, F/W, age 4, daughter, born Tenn.
Rosey, F/W, age 1, daughter, born Tenn.

71. LONG, BUD, M/W, age 35, married 11 yrs., born Tenn.
Nora, F/W, age 31, wife, born Tenn.
Mary, F/W, age 10, daughter, born Tenn.
Rosey, F/W, age 8, daughter, born Tenn.
John, M/W, age 6, son, born Tenn.
Joe, M/W, age 2, son, born Tenn.

72. OWENS, CHARLEY, M/W, age 26, married 1 yr., born Tenn.
Lizzie, F/W, age 28, wife, born Tenn.
Rannie, F/W, age 5, daughter, b. in Tenn.

73. GIPSON, ALLEN, M/W, age 51, married 20 yrs., born Tenn.
Emma, F/W, age 39, wife, born Tenn.
Joice, F/W, age 17, daughter, born Tenn.
Lois, F/W, age 15, daughter, born Tenn.
Sylvester, M/W, age 13, son, born Tenn.
Austin, M/W, age 12, son, born Tenn.
Zella, F/W, age 9, daughter, born Tenn.
Lora, F/W, age 6, daughter, born Tenn.
Layton, M/W, age 4, son, born Tenn.
Clarence, M/W, age 3, son, born Tenn.
Hayden, M/W, age born 1909, in Tenn.
BARNETT, ROBERT L., M/W, age 26, married 1 yr., son-in-law, born Tenn.

74. FISCHER, JOSEPH H., M/W, age 43, married 23 yrs., born Ohio.
Lena, F/W, age 43, wife, born Ohio.
Clara, F/W, age 22, daughter, born Tenn.
Lilly, F/W, age 20, daughter, born Tenn.
Effie, F/W, age 18, daughter, born Tenn.
Joseph, M/W, age 16, son, born Tenn.
AMSTRUTZ, JOSEPH, M/W, age 86, father-in-law, born Switzerland.

75. PRINCE, JENNIE L., F/W, age 43, widow, born Tenn.
Willie, M/W, age 21, son, born Tenn.
Lillie, F/W, age 20, daughter, born Tenn.
Harry, M/W, age 18, son, born Tenn.
Mary, F/W, age 16, daughter, born Tenn.
Reneau, M/W, age 14, son, born Tenn.
Ernest, M/W, age 12, son, born Tenn.
Robert, M/W, age 9, son, born Tenn.

76. CASTLEBERRY, ALMEDA, F/W, age 67, widow, born Tenn.
James, M/W, age 42, son, married 20 yrs., born Georgia.
Lillie, F/W, age 40, daughter-in-law, born Tenn.
Carl, M/W, age 16, grandson, born Tenn.
Annie, F/W, age 14, granddaughter, born Tenn.
William, M/W, age 11, grandson, born Tenn.
Herschel, M/W, age 5, grandson, born Tenn.
Velma, F/W, age 3, granddaughter, b. Tenn.

77. JOHNSON, FREELAND, M/W, age 25, married 1 yr., born Tenn.
Lena, F/W, age 17, wife, born Tenn.

78. HARRISON, JERRY, M/W, age 37, married 12 yrs., born Tenn.
Minnie, F/W, age 34, wife, born Tenn.

79. SUTHERLAND, JAMES, M/W, age 41, married 20 yrs., born Tenn.
Mary E., F/W, age 40, wife, born Tenn.
Willie, M/W, M/W, age 15, son, born Tenn.
Erwin S., M/W, age 13, son, born Tenn.
Annie, F/W, age 11, daughter, born Tenn.
Alvin, M/W, age 9, son, born Tenn.
Earl, M/W, age 8, son, born Tenn.

80. WHEAT, H. WILLIAM, M/W, age 44, married 6 yrs., born Kentucky.
Lulu, F/W, age 39, wife, born Tenn.
GARNER, LOUISA, F/W, age 34, sister-in-law, born Tenn.
WHEAT, DANIEL, M/W, age 15, companion, born Tenn.

81. GREENE, WILLIAM, M/W, age 36, married 12 yrs., born Tenn.
Sina, F/W, age 30, wife, born Tenn.
Roy, M/W, age 11, son, born Tenn.
Sallie, F/W, age 7, daughter, born Tenn.

82. CAMPBELL, WHITE, M/W, age 48, married 25 yrs., born Tenn.
Ellen, F/W, age 49, wife, born Tenn.
Nannie, F/W, age 20, daughter, born Tenn.
Ernest, M/W, age 16, son, born Tenn.
Dessie, F/W, age 14, daughter, born Tenn.
Elsie, F/W, age 12, daughter, born Tenn.
Gertrude, F/W, age 5, daughter, born Tenn.

83. CASTLEBERRY, JOHN H., M/W, age 29, married 13 yrs., born Tenn.
Bertha, F/W, age 27, wife, born Tenn.
John P., M/W, age 1, son, born Tenn.
Lizzie, F/W, born 1910, in Tenn.

84. FINCHUM, MATTHEW, M/W, age 25, married 6 yrs., born Tenn.
Lena, F/W, age 20, wife, born Tenn.
Clarence, M/W, age 6, son, born Tenn.
Ernest, M/W, age 3, son, born Tenn.
Wesley, M/W, age 1, son, born Tenn.

85. ESLICK, JOHN, M/W, age 23, married 1 yr., born Tenn.
Myrtle, F/W, age 18, wife, born Tenn.

86. GOFF, ANDREW, M/W, age 23, married 3 yrs., born Tenn.
Flossie, F/W, age 18, wife, born Tenn.
Fay, F/W, age 1, daughter, born Tenn.

87. WOODARD, ALBERT, M/W, age 20, married 2 yrs., born Tenn.
Rosey, F/W, age 17, wife, born Tenn.
SIMMONS, GEORGE, M/W, age 20, brother-in-law, born Tenn.
James, M/W, age 18, brother-in-law, born in Tenn.
88. SUMMERS, FRANK, M/W, age 25, married 1 yr., born Tenn.
Becky, F/W, age 27, wife, born Tenn.
Edith, F/W, age 1, daughter, born Tenn.
SMOTHERSON, ELSIE, F/W, age 17, sister-in-law, born Tenn.
89. ROACH, ISOM, M/W, age 29, married 6 yrs., born Tenn.
Chrissie, F/W, age 22, wife, born Tenn.
Robert, M/W, age 5, son, born Tenn.
Andrew, M/W, age 4, son, born Tenn.
Nannie, F/W, age 2, daughter, born Tenn.
90. PACK, JAMES L., M/W, age 42, married 12 yrs., born Tenn.
Florence, F/W, age 29, wife, born Tenn.
Marie, F/W, age 11, daughter, born Tenn.
Hugh, M/W, age 9, son, born Tenn.
James L. Jr., M/W, age 5, son, b. in Tenn.
Walter F., M/W, age 2, son, born Tenn.
91. HOLLAND, JAMES, M/MU, age 45, married 3 yrs., born Tenn.
Luella, F/MU, age 39, wife, born Tenn.
WILLIS, CULLY, M/MU, age 3, son, born Tenn.
RUTLEDGE, HENRY, M/B, age 45, boarder, widower, born Tenn.
92. PRINCE, JACK F., M/W, age 46, married 20 years,, born Tenn.
Alice, F/W, age 38, wife, born Tenn.
Jim, M/W, age 19, son, born Tenn.
Henry, M/W, age 17, son, born Tenn.
Grace, F/W, age 9, daughter, born Tenn.
93. O'DEAR, SUSANNA, F/W, age 55, widow, born Tenn.
94. VAN VLECK, EMMA, F/W, age 81, widow, born Tenn.
95. FRY, JESSE, M/W, age 53, married 4 yrs. born Tenn.
J. Mattie, F/W, age 51, wife, born Tenn.
MESSICK, DOVEY, F/W, age 11, companion, born Tenn.
96. KNOTT, MARION, M/W, age 40, married 17 yrs., born Tenn.
Alice, F/W, age 34, wife, born Tenn.
Willie, M/W, age 16, son, born Tenn.
Robert, M/W, age 14, son, born Tenn.
Oscar, M/W, age 11, son, born Tenn.
Sterling, M/W, age 7, son, born Tenn.
Jim M/W, age 6, son, born Tenn.
Averil, F/W, age 3, daughter, born Tenn.
Bessie, F/W, daughter, born 1910, Tenn.
97. STAPLES, AARON, M/MU, age 36, married 3 yrs., born Tenn.
Della, F/MU, age 26, wife, born Tenn.
Mary, F/MU, age 2, daughter, born Tenn.
Abagail, F/MU, daughter, born 1910, Tenn.
98. MAKAY, WILLIAM, M/W, age 44, married 16 yrs., born Mississippi.
Mary, F/W, age 40, wife, born Mississippi.
John, M/W, age 18, son, born Tenn.
William, M/W, age 10, son, born Tenn.
Charles, M/W, age 7, son, born Tenn.
Ernest, M/W, age 5, son, born Illinois.
LEFFINGWELL, ANNA M., F/W, age 62, companion, born Mississippi.
RUSSELL, EMMA, F/MU, age 27, servant, born Tenn.
99. SUTHERLAND, JAMES, M/W, age 51, married 29 yrs., born N. C.
Mary, F/W, age 45, wife, born Tenn.
Cora, F/W, age 20, daughter, born Tenn.
Georgia, F/W, age 18, daughter, born Tenn.
Lillie, F/W, age 12, daughter, born Tenn.
John, M/W, age 9, son, born Tenn.
Katie, F/W, age 7, daughter, born Tenn.
100. GIPSON, NEVA, F/W, age 73, widow, born Tenn.
CLARK, FLORA, F/W, age 20, granddaughter, born Tenn.
101. THAXTON, NEWSON, M/W, age 46, married 5 yrs., born Tenn.
Emma, F/W, age 39, wife, born Tenn.
Hervey, M/W, age 22, son, born Tenn.
Ethel, F/W, age 20, daughter, born Tenn.
Edith, F/W, age 18, daughter, born Tenn.
Porter, M/W, age 18, son, born Tenn.
Joe, M/W, age 12, son, born Tenn.
Lora, F/W, age ge 9, daughter, born Tenn.
102. FINNEY, MATTHEW, M/W, age 32, married 10 yrs., born Tenn.
Julia, F/W, age 28, wife, born Tenn.
Walter, M/W, age 9, son, born Tenn.
Hazel, F/W, age, 6, daughter, born Tenn.
Lorene, F/W, age 2, daughter, born Tenn.
103. CHILDRESS, WILLIAMSON, M/B, age 28, married 10 yrs., born Tenn.
Grace, F/MU, age 28, wife, born Tenn.
Alexander, M/MU, age 9, son, born Tenn.
Williamson, M/MU, age 7, son, b. Tenn.
Alfred, M/B, age 35, brother, widowed, born Tenn.

104. BROWN, MARY, F/B, age 65, widow, born Missouri.
COLLIER, KATHY, F/MU, age 12, granddaughter, born Tenn.
WILLIAMS, CLINTON, M/MU, age 1, grandson, born Tenn.
KINLEY, MARY, W/MU, age 17, boarder, born Tenn.
105. HALL, BELL, F/W, age 38, widow, born in Illinois.
Willie, F/W, age 14, daughter, b. Florida.
Claudie, M/W, age 11, son, born Ala.
106. SLOAN, JOHN D., M/W, age 45, born 16 yrs., born Illinois.
Rowena, F/W, age 33, wife, born Illinois.
Abraham, M/W, age 13, son, born Illinois.
Elmer, M/W, age 11, son, born Illinois.
Zola, F/W, age 9, daughter, born Illinois.
Ulysses, M/W, age 6, son, born Illinois.
107. RANKINS, DOUGLAS, M/MU, age 45, married 25 yrs., born Tenn.
Ellen, F/MU, age 45, wife, born Tenn.
Alexander, M/MU, age 17, son, b. Tenn.
Carl, M/MU, age 14, son, born Tenn.
Willie, M/MU, age 11, son, born Tenn.
Herbert, M/MU, age 10, grandson, born Tenn.
108. RUTLEDGE, MARY, F/MU, age 36, married 20 yrs., born Tenn.
Luther, M/MU, age 12, son, born Tenn.
Ross, M/MU, age 8, son, born Tenn.
J. C., M/MU, age 5, son, born Tenn.
A. B., M/MU, age 4, son, born Tenn.
?AMATA, HARRIETT, M/MU, age 60, mother, born Tenn.
109. SIMS, WILLIE, M/B, age 24, married 2 yrs., born Tenn.
Mollie, F/MU, age 20, wife, born Tenn.
BONNER, MARY, F/B, age 12, companion, born Tenn.
BELL, LULA, F/MU, age 3, companion, born Tenn.
NULEY, FRANCIS, M/MU, companion, born 1910, born Tenn.
110. TAYLOR, GREEN, M/MU, age 53, widower, born Tenn.
Lillie, F/MU, age 17, daughter, born Tenn.
Bettie, F/MU, age 16, daughter, born Tenn.
Catherine, F/MU, age 14, daughter, born in Tenn.
Roosevelt, M/MU, age 7, son, born Tenn.
111. ARLEDGE, ANDERSON, M/MU, age 30, born Tenn.
Amelis, F/MU, age 65, widowed mother, born Tenn.
112. WINTON, HARRIETT, F/MU, age 54, widow, born Tenn.
113. RUTLEDGE, LILLIE, F/B, age 40. widow, born Tenn.
ROWE, ANNIE, F/B, age 19, companion, born Tenn.
Fannie, F/B, age 12, companion, born Tenn.
114. GARNER, GEORGE, M/MU, age 50, married 20 yrs., born Tenn.
Rachel, F/MU, age 38, wife, born Tenn.
115. BRYAN, TAYLOR, M/MU, age 60, widower, born Tenn.
Oscar, M/MU, age 32, son, born Tenn.
Bettie, F/MU, age 80, widowed mother, born Tenn.
STEVENS, HARVEY, M/MU, age 20, companion, born Tenn.
116. ROWE, WILLIAM, M/MU, age, 35, married 8 yrs., born Tenn.
Asie, F/MU, age 29, wife, born Tenn.
117. CHEATHAM, WILLIAM, M/MU, age 34, married 2 yrs., born Tenn.
Carrie, F/MU, age 33, wife, born Tenn.
118. DAVIS, TOMMY, M/MU, age 27, married 2 yrs., born Tenn.
Ora, F/MU, age 28, wife, born Tenn.
Christina, F/MU, age 3, daughter, born Tenn.
119. ARLEDGE, ALFRED, M/B, age 25, married 6 yrs., born Tenn.
Berta, F/B, age 24, wife, born Tenn.
120. MILLER, LEE, M/B, age 33, married 2 yrs., born Tenn.
Sarah, F/B, age 35, wife, born Tenn.
Joe, M/B, age 13, son, born Tenn.
Eddie, M/B, age 12, son, born Tenn.
121. DAVIS, MATTIE, F/MU, age 50, widow, born Tenn.
Scott, M/MU, age 30, son, born Tenn.
GREEN, ELY, M/MU, age 16, nephew, born Tenn.
122. KINLEY, JOHN, M/MU, age 27, married 12 yrs., born Tenn.
Sarah, F/MU, age 29, wife, born Tenn.
Otsie, F/MU, age 12, daughter, born Tenn.
123. SMITH, WILL R., M/MU, age 50, married 24 yrs., born Tenn.
Sallie, F/MU, age 46, wife, born Tenn.
Huston, M/MU, age 19, son, born Tenn.
Simon, M/Mu, age 17, son, born Tenn.

124. CHILDRESS, CALVIN, M/B, age 45, married 11 yrs., born Tenn.
Hattie, F/MU, age 31, wife, born Tenn.
Maggie, F/MU, age 9, daughter, b. Tenn.
Ellen, F/MU, age 6, daughter, born Tenn.
Ethel, F/MU, age 2, daughter, born Tenn.
Son, no name given, M/MU, born 1910, Tenn.
Annie, F/B, age 22, sister, born Tenn.

125. GREEN, NED, M/B, age 45, widower, born Tenn.
Silverine, F/B, age 7, daughter, b. Tenn.

126. BOYCE, BENJ., M/W, age 32, married 9 yrs., born Tenn.
Minnie, F/W, age 28, wife, born Tenn.
Ruby, F/W, age 8, daughter, born Tenn.
Alice, F/W, age 6, daughter, born Tenn.

127. SNEED, ALBERT C., M/W, age 42, married 23 yrs., born Texas.
Mary E., F/W, age 38, wife, born Ark.
Jack, M/W, age 19, son, born Arkansas.
Lorine, F/W, age 17, daughter, born Ark.
Virginia, F/W, age 8, daughter, b. Tenn.
BATES, BAGGAN, M/W, age 20, son-in-law, married 2 yrs., born Ga.
Rolin, M/W, born 1910, grandson, born, Tenn.

128. PRINCE, WILL, M/W, age 54, married 18 yrs., born Georgia.
Maria, F/W, age 51, wife, born Tenn.
PRINCE, JESSIE, F/W, age 18, son , born Tenn.
Mildred, F/W, age 14, daughter, born Tenn.
Opal, F/W, age 11, daughter, born Tenn.

129. SELDEN, MARY J., F/W, age 55, widow, born Georgia.
Jose M., M/W, age 33, son, born Georgia.
Jennie L. F/W, age 28, daughter-in-law, born Georgia.
Eugenia, F/W, age 2, daughter, b. Tenn.
VAUGHN, DOUGLAS, M/W, age 28, boarder, born Tenn.
CHEEK, SAM, M/W, age 35, boarder, born Tenn.
FORD, JORDAN, M/B, age 29, servant, born Tenn.
JOYNER, ADA, F/MU, age 30, servant, born Tenn.
Adaline, F/MU, age 17, servant, b. Tenn.
BONNER, LUCY, F/MU, age 30, servant, born Tenn.

130. MCCRADY, JOHN M., M/W, age 60, widower, born South Carolina.
Kathleen, F/W, age 33, daughter, born South Carolina.

131. LAUTZENHEISER, FRANK, M/W, age 43, married 15 yrs., born Ohio.
May, F/W, age 40, wife, born Ohio.
Renee, F/W, age 14, daughter, born Tenn.
PENNY, IDA, F/W, age 29, sister-in-law, born Tenn.
Alvie, F/W, age 13, niece, born Tenn.
Lawrence, M/W, age 9, nephew, b. Tenn.
Tom, M/W, age 6, nephew, born Tenn.

132. WICKS, MARY C., M/W, age 69, widow, born Arkansas.
Louis, M/W, age 30, son, born Tenn.
Celeste, F/W, age 39, daughter, born Tenn.

133. TIDWELL, TOM M., M/W, age 47, married 10 yrs., born Alabama.
Mary, F/W, age 30, wife, born Tenn.
William, M/W, age 7, son, born Tenn.
Joseph, M/W, age 3, son, born Tenn.

134. GUINN, LOUIS, M/MU, age 24, married 2 yrs., born Tenn.
Cora, F/MU, age 19, wife, born Tenn.
William, M/MU, age 1, son, born Tenn.
WICKS, WILLIE, M/MU, age 15, companion, born Tenn.

135. ARN, MARY, F/W, age 62, widow, born Germany.
GREEN, GEORGE, M/W, age 30, son-in-law, born Tenn.
Lena., F/W, age 28, daughter, born Germany.
W. Herman, M/W, age 2, grandson, born Tenn.
Johnnie, M/W, age 1, grandson, b. Tenn.
Maxy, M/W, age 6, companion, b. Tenn.

136. HUNZIKER, THOMAS, M/W, age 23, married 1 yr., born Tenn.
Stella, F/W, age 18, wife, born Tenn.

137. BIERY, SAM, M/W, age 55, married 27 yrs., born Switzerland.
Mary, F/W, age 45, wife, born Switzerland.
Fred, M/W, age 20, son, born Tenn.
Sam, M/W, age 15, son, born Tenn.
CRAWFORD, PAUL, M/W, age 10, companion, born Illinois.
RODGERS, VIDA, F/W, age 10, companion, born Tenn.

138. ALDERSON, ALBERT, M/W, age 24, married 1 yr., born Tenn.
Bessie, F/W, age 20, wife, born Tenn.
Irene, F/W, daughter, born 1910, Tenn.
DONEY, ROY, M/W, age 16, brother-in-law, born Tenn.

139. WALKER, ISAAC, M/W, age 64, married 30 yrs., born Tenn.
Lizzie, F/W, age 62, wife, born Tenn.
140. BEAN, WILLIAM, M/W, age 30, married 7 yrs., born Tenn.
Lizzie, F/W, age 28, wife, born Tenn.
Willie, M/W, age 6, son, born Tenn.
Ernest, M/W, age 2, son, born Tenn.
141. CLARK, JOHN, M/W, age 44, married 2 yrs., born England.
Alice, F/W, age 41, wife, born Tenn.
George, M/W, son, born 1910, in Tenn.
William, M/W, age 13, son, born Tenn.
142. WALKER, TAYLOR, M/W, age 24, married 1 yr., born Tenn.
Etta, F/W, age 24, wife, born Tenn.
143. MONTGOMERY, FRED, M/W, age 29, married 4 yrs., born Tenn.
Sallie, F/W, age 24, wife, born Tenn.
James, M/W, age 3, son, born Tenn.
Zelphia, M/W, age 1, son, born Tenn.
144. RILEY, ROBERT, M/W, age 44, married 18 yrs., born Tenn.
Viola, F/W, age 39, wife, born Tenn.
Aylene, F/W, age 16, daughter, b. Tenn.
Christine, F/W, age 14, daughter, b. Tenn.
Carl, M/W, age 9, son, born Tenn.
Olive, F/W, age 8, daughter, born Tenn.
Basil, M/W, age 6, son, born Tenn.
Nolan, M/W, age 3, son, born Tenn.
145. BRAZELTON, WILSON, M/W, age 61, married 32 yrs., born Tenn.
Charlotte, F/W, age 51, wife, b. in Iowa.
Abbie, F/W, age 26, daughter, born Tenn.
Grace, F/W, age 16, daughter, born Tenn.
Mabel, F/W, age 14, daughter, b. in Tenn.
Pearson, M/W, age 10, son, born Tenn.
146. ANDERSON, WILLIAM, M/W, age 29, married 9 yrs., born Tenn.
Ida, F/W, age 25, wife, born Tenn.
147. CUNNINGHAM, CHARLEY, M/W, age 48, married 2 yrs., born Tenn.
Rachel, F/W, age 50, wife, born Tenn.
O'DEAR, JACK, M/W, age 15, step-son, born Tenn.
Sara, F/W, age 13, step-daughter, b. Tenn.
148. HAWKINS, HARRY, M/W, age 27, married 4 yrs., born Tenn.
Annie, F/W, age 20, wife, born Tenn.
Irene, F/W, age 3, daughter, born Tenn.
Walter, M/W, age 2, son, born Tenn.
RAY, LOVISER, F/W, age 52, widowed mother, born Tenn.
149. GIPSON, IDA, F/W, age 48, widow, born in Alabama.
Rebecca, F/W, age 20, daughter, b. Tenn.
Knoble, M/W, age 17, son, born Tenn.
Homer, M/W, age 15, son, born Tenn.
DORSEY, REBECCA, F/W, age 75, widowed mother, born N.C.
150. HAWKINS, SALLIE M., F/W, age 61, widow, born Tenn.
Sallie, F/W, age 25, wife, born Tenn.
Addie, F/W, age 22, daughter, born Tenn.
Jeanette, F/W, age 18, daughter, born Tenn.
COOPER, RUTH, F/W, age 37, daughter married 10 yrs., born Tenn.
Morgan, M/W, age 8, grandson, b. Tenn.
151. LUTSINGER, RUDOLPH, M/W, age 64, widower, born Switzerland.
SUTHERLAND, MARY, F/W, age 17, daughter, born Illinois.
Andrew, M/W, age 23, son-in-law, born Tenn.
152. GOSSAGE, THOMAS, M/W, age 70, widower, born Tenn.
HOLLAND, LESTIA, F/W, age 39, daughter, born Tenn.
Samuel, M/W, age 42, son-in-law, born Tenn.
153. BROOKS, PRESTON S., M/W, age 56, married 35 yrs., born S.C.
Maria P., F/W, age 54, wife, born Tenn.
Preston S., M/W, age 30, son, born S.C.
Robert, M/W, age 26, son, born Tenn.
Catherine, F/W, age 24,
daughter, born Tenn.
Ray, F/W, age 21, daughter, born Tenn.
Annie, F/W, age 16, daughter, b. in Tenn.
154. NAUTS, WILLIAM, M/W, age 50, married 8 yrs., born Kentucky.
Clara, F/W, age 42, wife, b. in New York.
William B., M/W, age 7, son, b. in Tenn.
Richard L., M/W, age 5, son, born Ky.
JOHNSON, ROBERT, M/B, age 33, servant, born Tenn.
Ida, F/B, age 30, servant, born Tenn.
Ernest, M/B, age 8, servant, born Tenn.
155. MANSFIELD, ANDERSON, M/W, age 58, married 40 yrs., born Tenn.
Mary, F/W, age 57, wife, born Tenn.
Hallie, F/W, age 19, daughter, born Tenn.
Grace, F/W, age 14, daughter, born Tenn.
DARNELL, LIZZIE, F/W, age 32, daughter, born Tenn.
Mary, F/W, age 13, granddaughter, born Tenn.
Preston, M/W, age 10, grandson, born Tenn.

156. GRAHAM, ELIZABETH, F/W, age 64, single, born at sea.
Annie J., F/W, age 54, sister, born South Carolina.
CLARE, HAREY, M/W, age 6, companion, born Tenn.
GRUETTER, PEARL, F/W, age 18, servant, born Tenn.

157. HUNT, JOHN B., M/W, age 39, married 14 yrs., born Tenn.
Mary, F/W, age 39, , wife, born Tenn.
Martha, F/W, age 13, daughter, b. Tenn.
John B., M/W, age 12, son, born Tenn.
Mary C., F/W, age 10, daughter, born Tenn.
Thomas L., M/W, age 9, son, born Tenn.

158. WADHAMS, ELIZABETH, F/W, age 48, born New York.

159. BEASLEY, HARRY, M/W, age 27, married 5 yrs., born Alabama.
Jennie, F/W, age 21, wife, born Georgia.
Jeanette, F/W, age 4, daughter, born Tenn.

160. JUDD, SPENCER, M/W, age 54, married 25 yrs., born Tenn.
Hallie, F/W, age 47, wife, born Tenn.

161. GREEN, JOHN, M/B, age 55, married 26 yrs., born Tenn.
Annie, F/MU, age 44, wife, born Tenn.
Willie, M/MU, age 18, son, born Tenn.
Texas, M/MU, age 8, son, born Tenn.
Lena, F/MU, age 4, daughter, born Tenn.

162. TURNER, ALBERT, M/MU, age 26, married 2 yrs., born Tenn.
Mattie, F/MU, age 27, wife, born Ala.

163. ROBINSON, JOE, M/B, age 25, married 7 yrs., born Alabama.
Olive, F/MU, age 21, wife, born Alabama.

164. GREEN, LILLIE, F/W, age 63, born North Carolina.
Ella, F/W, age 68, sister-in-law, born Ga.
Paulina F/W, age 50, sister-in-law, born Tenn.
Kate, F/W, age 31, daughter, born Tenn.
MAYHEW, AUGUSTA, F/W, age 68, boarder, born New Jersey.

165. TIDEWALL, THOMAS, M/W, age 68, widower, born Virginia.
DAUGHERTY, KATE, F/W, age 38, servant, born Pennsylvania.
BONFIELGER, MARGARET, F/W, age 25, servant, born Tenn.

166. WOODS, HERVEY, M/MU, age 47, married 6 yrs., born Tenn.
Sallie, F/MU, age 44, wife, born Tenn.
Elick, M/MU, age 5, son, born Tenn.
BRAZELTON, EVA, F/MU, age 24, daughter, born Tenn.
Anderson, M/MU, age 2, grandson, born Tenn.
Carrie M., F/MU, granddaughter born 1910, in Tenn.
REESE, MARY, F/MU, age 15, step-daughter, born Tenn.
Wilfred, M/MU, age 18, step-son, born Tenn.

167. COLYAR, JOHN, M/MU, age 43, married 9 yrs., born Tenn.
Daisy, F/B, age 26, wife, born Tenn.
Garrett, M/MU, age 5, son, born Tenn.
Effie, F/MU, age 2, daughter, born Tenn.
Sarah, F/MU, daughter, born 1910, Tenn.
Lorine, F/MU, age 18, sister-in-law, born Tenn.
Roxie, F/MU, age 26, sister-in-law, born Tenn.
Elberta, F/MU, age 14, sister-in-law, born Tenn.
Mabel, F/MU, age 9, sister-in-law, born Tenn.

168. HUDDLESTON, WILLIAM, M/B, age 50, married 25 yrs., born Tenn.
Rose, F/B, age 59, wife, born Tenn.
Egie, F/B, age 14, daughter, born Tenn.
Ruth, F/B, age 21, daughter, born Tenn.
William, M/B, age 18, son, born Tenn.
Louis, M/B, age 16, son, born Tenn.
Bell, F/B, age 13, daughter, born Tenn.
Walter, M/B, age 10, son, born Tenn.
Bennie, M/B, age 8, son, born Tenn.

169. CARLCHER, HOLLAND, M/MU, age 21, married 1 yr., born Tenn.
Zian, F/MU, age 25, wife, born Tenn.

170. SIMS, RUFUS, M/MU, age 29, married 1 yr., born Tenn.
Lizzie, F/MU, age 32, wife, born Tenn.

171. SHARPE, SAMUEL, M/W, age 57, married 20 yrs., born England.
Florence, F/W, age 57, wife, born England.
Catherine, F/W, age 25, daughter, born Texas.
HINDALE, CATHERINE, F/W, age 68, boarder, born Wisconsin.
THOMPSON, ANNIE, F/W, age 69, boarder, born Wisconsin.
Surname illegible, JOSEPH, M/W, age 13, boarder, born Tenn.
PHILLIPS, MENTOR, M/MU, age 21, servant, born Tenn.

Rose, F/B, age 21, servant, born Tenn.
Myrtle, F/MU, age 2, companion, born Tenn.

172. TAYLOR, JAMES, M/MU, age 36, married 3 yrs., born Tenn.
Lena, F/MU, age 21, wife, born Tenn.
James, M/MU, age 8, son, born Tenn.
Robert, M/MU, age 12, son, born Tenn.

173. STEPHENS, CATHERINE, F/W, age 50, widow, born Mississippi.
FRIEST, POWER, M/W, age 18, son, born Mississippi.
Rosalie, F/W, age 24, daughter, born Mississippi.
Robert, M/W, age 16, son, born Miss.
Harrelson, M/W, age 10, son, born Miss.
CAMPBELL, CHARLOTTE, F/B, age 97, servant, born Tenn.

174. THOMAS, JAMES, M/W, age 43, married 27 yrs., born Tenn.
Fannie, F/W, age 42, wife, born Tenn.

175. LEACH, FLORA, F/W, age 24, married 3 yrs., born Tenn.
Fannie, F/W, age 7, daughter, born Tenn.
Thulena, F/W, age 5, daughter, b. Tenn.
THOMAS, DEAN, M/W, age 18, brother, born Tenn.
Esther, F/W, age 16, sister, born Tenn.
Eva, F/W, age 14, sister, born Tenn.

176. ADAMS, HARRY, M/W, age 24, married 3 yrs., born Tenn.
Claudia, F/W, age 19, wife, born Georgia.
Ola, F/W, daughter born 1910, in Tenn.
?Donnie, M/W, age 16, brother, born Tenn.

177. HOSKINS, HENRY, M/W, age 40, married 19 yrs., born Tenn.
Ada, F/W, age 39, wife, born Tenn.
Charley, M/W, age 16, son, born Tenn.
Ruby, F/W, age 12, daughter, born Tenn.
BRAZELTON, GLADYS, F/W, age 20, daughter, born Tenn.
Henry, M/W, age 3, grandson, born Tenn.
James, M/W, grandson born 1910, in Tenn.

178. SMEDES, SUSIE, F/W, age 67, widow, born Mississippi.
DABNEY, LELIA, F/W, age 57, sister, born Mississippi.

179. COLMORE, ROBERT, M/W, age 60, widower, born England.
Theodora, F/W, age 29, daughter, born Tenn.
Eva, F/W, age 24, daughter, born Tenn.

180. BARTON, SAMUEL, M/W, age 50, widower, born Virginia.
Mary, F/W, age 11, daughter, born Va.
Helen, F/W, age 9, daughter, born Tenn.
TIDWALL, SUSAN, F/W, age 60, mother-in-law, born Virginia.

181. MOONEY, CHARLES, M/W, age 25, married 6 yrs., born Tenn.
Martha, F/W, age 24, wife, born Tenn.
Catherine, F/W, age 5, daughter, born Tenn.
Irene, F/W, age 1, daughter, born Tenn.

182. O'DEAR, GEORGE, M/W, age 21, married 2 yrs., born Tenn.
Bettie, F/W, age 23, wife, born Tenn.
Preston, M/W, age 5, son, born Tenn.
Ora, M/W, son, born 1910, in Tenn.

183. PLYROM, STUART, M/W, age 37, married 14 yrs., born Pennsylvania.
Katie, F/W, age 31, wife, born Penn.
Catherine, F/W, age 13, daughter, born Wisconsin.
Stephen, M/W, age 12, son, born Wisconsin.
Paul, M/W, age 10, son, born England.
Edward, M/W, age 9, son, born England.
Philip, M/W, age 8, son, born England.
Hugh, M/W, age 7, son, born England.
John, M/W, age 6, son, born New Jersey.
Elizabeth, F/W, age 5, daughter, born England
James, M/W, age 4, son, born England.
Mark, M/W, age 1, son, born Illinois.
Mary, F/W, daughter, born 1910, Tenn.
MOSELY, FRANCIS, F/MU, age 16, servant, born Tenn.
JONES, BARBARA, F/MU, age 40, servant, born Tenn.
KINLEY, MARY, F/B, age 37, servant, born Tenn.
LONG, MARY, F/W, age 32, servant, born Pennsylvania.
GROVE, GRACE, F/W, age 29, governess, born Illinois.
JAMES, ANNA, F/W, age 19, governess, born Tenn.

184. GALLIHER, LETHA B., F/W, age 64, widow, born Kentucky.
Elizabeth, F/W, age 12, sister-in-law, born Kentucky.
SCOTT, ROSE, F/B, age 21, servant, born Tenn.
LOWE, CAPILATA, F/MU, age 25, servant, born Tenn.
THOMAS, MARY, F/MU, age 20, born Tenn.

185. KIRBY SMITH, ELIZABETH, F/W, age 36, born Tenn.
186. COLLYAR, EDWARD, M/MU, age 30, married 4 yrs. born Tenn.
Hallie L., F/MU, age 21, wife, born Tenn.
Johnnie, F/MU, age 3, daughter, born Tenn.
187. WILLIS, ?ALLEN, M/MU, age 21, born in Tenn.
Ella, F/MU, age 18, wife, born Tenn.
MCBRIDE, PRATER, M/MU, age 23, boarder, born Tenn.
188. MCBRIDE, J. JOHN, M/W, age 40, married 8 yrs., born Virginia.
Flora, F/W, age 30, wife, born Texas.
Jack, M/W, age 4, son, born Virginia.
Webster, M/W, age 2, son, born Virginia.
189. CHACKLEY, LYMAN, M/W, AGE 45, married 12 yrs., born Virginia.
Ellena, F/W, age 36, wife, born Kentucky.
Lyman, M/W, age 11, son, born Virginia.
Issa D., F/W, age 10, daughter, born Virginia.
NEVILS, TERRI, F/B, age 21, servant, born Tenn.
Fred, M/MU, age 8, servant, born Tenn.
MALADA, SALLIE, F/MU, age 65, servant, born Tenn.
190. HILL, HUGH, M/MU, age 30, married 3 yrs., born Tenn.
Willie, F/MU, age 28, wife, born Tenn.
191. COPE, ARTHUR, M/MU, age 24, married 4 yrs., born Tenn.
Jessie, F/MU, age 23, wife, born Tenn.
Johnnie, F/MU, age 1, son, born Tenn.
HOOTER, LILLIAN, F/MU, age 8, sister-in-law, born Tenn.
192. HANLEY, PRISCILLA, F/MU, age 60, widow, born Tenn.
HAND, IRENE, F/MU, age 14, granddaughter, born Tenn.
Priscilla, F/MU, age 11, granddaughter, born Tenn.
SIMS, ROSA, F/MU, age 62, sister, born Tenn.
Clara, F/MU, age 11, niece, born Tenn.
Armland, M/MU, age 15, nephew, born Tenn.
193. ANDREWS, WILLIAM, M/W, age 45, married 12 yrs., born Tenn.
Eva, F/W, age 32, wife, born Tenn.
Edwin, M/W, age 11, son, born Tenn.
Pattie R., F/W, age 9, daughter, born Tenn.
William, M/W, age 6, son, born Tenn.
194. KENNEDY, WILL, M/W, age 23, married 3 yrs., born Tenn.
Katie, F/W, age 25, wife, born Tenn.
Clifford, M/W, age 2, son, born Tenn.
COLLINS, BIRD, M/W, age 29, brother-in-law, born Tenn.
Jennie, F/W, age 19, sister-in-law, born Tenn.
GARNER, WILLIAM, M/W, age 55, boarder, born Tenn.
BUCHANAN, JENNIE, F/W, age 29, boarder, born Tenn.
195. JOHNSON, ALBERT S., M/W, age 37, married 11 yrs., born Tenn.
Bessie, F/W, age 36, wife, born Tenn.
Hazel, F/W, age 10, daughter, born Tenn.
William, M/W, age 8, son, born Tenn.
Lizzie, F/W, age 6, daughter, b. Tenn.
Lionel, M/W, age 4, son, born Tenn.
Elsie, F/W, age 1, daughter, born Tenn.
196. DOUGLAS, ELIZABETH, F/W, age 40, born Mississippi.
Ethel, F/W, age 38, widowed sister, born Tenn.
Taylor, M/W, age 16, nephew, born Louisana.
Elizabeth, F/W, age 13, niece, born Tenn.
John, M/W, age 12, nephew, born Tenn.
Richard, M/W, age 10, nephew, b. Tenn.
MORENO, ANNIE, F/W, age 39, sister, born Tenn.
197. MOSELEY, RUFUS, M/MU, age 57, married 17 yrs., born Tenn.
Mollie, F/MU, age 47, wife, born Tenn.
Wilford, F/MU, age 12, daughter, b. Tenn.
Katie, F/MU, age 10, daughter, b. Tenn.
Rufus Jr., M/MU, age 7, son, born Tenn.
George A., M/MU, son, born 1909, Tenn.
198. LOONEY, WILLIAM, M/W, age 52, widowed, born Tenn.
Leona, F/W, age 22, daughter, born Tenn.
Bernice, F/W, age 18, daughter, b. Tenn.
Lillian, F/W, age 16, daughter, born Tenn.
Irene, F/W, age 13, daughter, born Tenn.
199. HOGE, SARAH, F/W, age 67, widow, born Alabama.
Nellie, F/W, age 35, daughter, born Tenn.
Nannie, F/W, age 30, daughter, b. Tenn.
Lyman, M/W, age 10, son, born Tenn.
200. GRUBENSTEIN, FLATE, M/W, age 70, married 38 yrs., born Germany.
Alaga, F/W, age 64, wife, born Germany.
201. POWELL, JOSEPH, M/W, age 60, married 36 yrs., born Tenn.
Emma, F/W, age 57, wife, born Penn.

202. CAMPBELL, WILL, M/W, age 22, married 1 yr., born Tenn.
Cora, F/W, age 23, wife, born Tenn.
Lorine, F/W, daughter, born 1909, Tenn.
HOPKINS, Mamie, F/W, age 20, sister-in-law, born Tenn.
Pearl, F/W, age 10, sister-in-law, born Tenn.
203. BUCKNER, ROBERT, M/MU, age 26, born Tenn.
TRIGG, POSS, M/MU, age 19, partner, born Tenn.
204. SIONSOAT, ST. GEORGE L., M/W, age 32, married 3 yrs., born Maryland.
Alma, F/W, age 31, wife, born Texas.
DANIELS, SELDON, M/MU, age 17, servant, born Tenn.
205. DUBOSE, WILLIAM, M/W, age 39, married 13 yrs., born North Carolina.
Dean S., F/W, age 38, wife, born Missouri.
MURPHY, JULIA, F/B, age 25, servant, born Tenn.
206. JOHNSON, SOPHIA, F/W, age 60, widow, born Georgia.
Florine, F/W, age 25, daughter, born Georgia.
MCFARLAND, JULIA, F/MU, age 30, servant, born Tenn.
207. MCKER, MARY, F/W, age 45, widow, born Tenn.
208. GRAG, ARTHUR R., M/W, age 34, married 9 yrs., born New York.
Laura, F/W, age 34, wife, born Alabama.
John C. A., M/W, age 8, son, born NY.
PERRY, CHARLES, M/MU, age 35, servant, born Tenn.
FOSTER, FARRAR, M/MU, age 45, servant, born Tenn.
Jennie, F/MU, age 21, servant, born Tenn.
BURN, MARY, F/MU, age 21, servant, born Tenn.
HARLAND, BEN, M/B, age 60, servant, born Tenn.
209. EWING, A.C., F/W, age 65, widow, born Tenn.
210. PERRY, SAMUEL, M/W, age 40, born 16 yrs., born Tenn.
Mary, F/W, age 34, wife, born Tenn.
Robert, M/W, age 13, son, born Tenn.
Mary, F/W, age 9, daughter, b. Virginia.
John, M/W, age 7, son, born Tenn.
211. JONES OR JAMES, JIM, M/MU, age 36, married 17 yrs., born Tenn.
Barbara. F/MU, age 35, wife, born Tenn.
Jessie, F/MU, age 16, daughter, b. Tenn.
Barbara, F/MU, age 14, daughter, born Tenn.
Charley, M/MU, age 10, son, born Tenn.
212. HULLIHER, WALTER, M/W, age 35, married 3 yrs., born Virginia.
Maud L., F/W, age 29, wife, born Massachusetts.
Louis S., M/W, age 2, son, born Tenn.
213. BONHOLZER, JOHN, M/W, age 54, married 30, yrs., born Switzerland.
Armia, F/W, age 52, wife, born Switzerland.
Katie, F/W, age 22, daughter, b. Tenn.
Fred, M/W, age 21, son, born Tenn.
Annie, F/W, age 16, daughter, b. Tenn.
John, M/W, age 14, son, born Tenn.
Albert, M/W, age 12, son, born Tenn.
Andrew, M/W, age 10, son, born Tenn.
MCFARLAND, JOHN, M/W, age 18, servant, born Virginia.
214. CLAIBORNE, WILLIAM S., M/W, age 39, married 8 yrs., born Virginia.
Minnie M., F/W, age 44, wife, born Missouri.
Alice V., F/W, age 3, daughter, born Tenn.
215. MCBEE, JOSEPH C., M/W, age 58, married 30 yrs., born Tenn.
Mary, F/W, age 49, wife, born Tenn.
Henry, M/W, age 23, son, born Tenn.
John, M/W, age 21, son, born Tenn.
Harvey, M/W, age 18, son, born Tenn.
Walker, M/W, age 13, son, born Tenn.
Gertie, M/W, age 6, daughter, born Tenn.
216. GUDGER, WILLIAM F., M/W, age 60, married 21 yrs., born Georgia.
Jane, F/W, age 40, wife, born Illinois.
William H., M/W, age 18, son, born Tenn.
Carrie B., F/W, age 16, daughter, born Tenn.
James G., M/W, age 14, son, born Tenn.
Lillie, F/W, age 12, daughter, born Tenn.
Lawton, M/W, age 9, son, born Tenn.
John, M/W, age 7, son, born Tenn.
217. GUDGER, JOHN, M/W, age 60, married 28 yrs., born Georgia.
Nancy J., F/W, age 50, wife, born Tenn.
Mary, F/W, age 25, daughter, born Tenn.
Frank, M/W, age 19, son, born Tenn.

218. PARKER, WALTER, M/W, age 38, married 9 yrs., born England.
Gennie M., F/W, age 31, wife, born Alabama.
WALL, JOSHUA C., M/W, age 73, father-
in-law, born Alabama.
Nannie, F/W, age 70, mother-in-law, born in Alabama.

219. CASTLEBERRY, FRANCIS, F/W, age 54, widow, born Tenn.
Marion, M/W, age 23, son, born Tenn.
Theodore, M/W, age 17, son, born Tenn.
Frank, M/W, age 13, son, born Tenn.
Katherine, F/W, age 14, daughter, born Tenn.
Lucile, F/W, age 11, daughter, born Tenn.

220. JACKSON, MARY C., F/W, age 57, widow, born Tenn.

221. HAWKINS, IRA, M/W, age 30, born Tenn.
Susie, F/W, age 27, wife, born Tenn.
Horace, M/W, age 5, son, born Tenn.
Warrier, M/W, age 3, son, born Tenn.
Lawrence, M/W, age 1, son, born Tenn.

222. HAWKINS, JOHN, M/W, age 73, married 51 yrs., born Tenn.
Virginia E., F/W, age 57, wife, born Tenn.
Hattie, F/W, age 16, niece, born Tenn.
GRANT, SALLIE, F/W, age 36, daughter, born Tenn.
Aubrey, M/W, 14, grandson, born Tenn.

223. ROCHIELLEN, JAMES E., M/W, age 49, married 22 yrs., born Tenn.
Florence, F/W, age 50, wife, born Ala.
Ora, F/W, age 21, daughter, born Ala.
Lillian, F/W, age 17, daughter, born Ala.

224. HAWKINS, LUKE, M/W, age 32, married 9 yrs., born Tenn.
Maggie, F/W, age 37, wife, born Tenn.
Roberta M., F/W, age 8, daughter, born Tenn.
?Eva A., F/W, age 6, daughter, born Tenn.
Lyle A., M/W, age 3, son, born Tenn.
HAWKINS, NEVILLE E., M/W, age 4, son, born Tenn.
SNIDER, HARVEY, M/W, age 32, boarder, born Switzerland.

225. POWELL, JOHN B., M/W, age 56, married 17 yrs., born Tenn.
Mattie C., F/W, age 49, wife, born Tenn.

226. RILEY, LOUIS, M/W, age 30, married 7 yrs., born Tenn.
Blanche, F/W, age 30, wife, born Tenn.
Herschel, M/W, age 5, son, born Tenn.

227. RILEY, Sophia, F/W, age 64, widow, born Tenn.
Joe, M/W, age 38, son, born Tenn.
Ed, M/W, age 27, son, born Tenn.
Tom, M/W, age 23, son, born Tenn.

228. DARDIS, FRANK, M/W, age 53, married 4 yrs., born Tenn.
Josie, F/W, age 41, wife, born Tenn.

229. CASTLEBERRY, MARTHA, F/W, age 57, widow, born Tenn.
Maria, F/W, age 27, daughter, born Tenn.
Mizie, F/W, age 24, daughter, born Tenn.
Hattie, F/W, age 21, daughter, born Tenn.

230. HAMILTON, THOMAS, M/W, age 40, married 9 yrs., born Ireland.
Laura, F/W, age 34, wife, born Tenn.
William, M/W, age 8, son, born Tenn.
Juanita, F/W, age 6, daughter, born Tenn.
Gordon, M/W, age 4, son, born Tenn.
Hayden, M/W, age 2, son, born Tenn.
HOPKINS, ALICE, F/W, age 16, companion, born Tenn.
?STEWARD, PETER, M/MU, age 40, servant, born Tenn.

231. WINN, JOHN R., M/W, age 49, married 29 yrs., born Tenn.
Martha F., F/W, age 51, wife, born Tenn.

232. SHERILL, THOMAS, M/W, age 22, born in Tenn.
Ida, F/W, age 24, wife, born Tenn.

233. WINN, SAM, M/W, age 28, married 6 yrs., born Tenn.
Maud, F/W, age 25, wife, born Tenn.
Pauline, F/W, age 4, daughter, born Tenn.
Leon, M/W, age 1, son, born Tenn.

234. WINN, GRITT, M/W, age 25, married 4 yrs., born Tenn.
Mahaley, F/W, age 22, wife, born Tenn.
Robert, M/W, age 3, son, born Tenn.
Lila M., F/W, age 1, daughter, born Tenn.

235. RUEF, JOHN, M/W, age 30 married 12 yrs., born Tenn.
Winnie, F/W, age 27, wife, born Tenn.
FARRIS, ELIZABETH, F/W, age 64, mother-in-law, born Tenn.

236. GILLIAM, MITCH, M/W, age 40, married
17 yrs., born Tenn.
Malinda "Sis", F/W, age 37, wife, born Tenn.

Bob, M/W, age 16, son, born Tenn.
Andy, M/W, age 14, son, born Tenn.
Delia, F/W, age 12, daughter, born Tenn.
George, M/W, age 10, son, born Tenn.
Lindy, F/W, age 8, daughter, born Tenn.

237. SHORT, JULIANN, F/W, age 63, widow, born Tenn.
Edward, M/W, age 20, son, born Tenn.

238. SHORT, DAVE, M/W, age 30, married 9 yrs., born Tenn.
Lythia, F/W, age 25, wife, born Tenn.
Marvin, M/W, age 7, son, born Tenn.
Reece, M/W, age 5, son, born Tenn.
Lawrence, M/W, age 3, son, born Tenn.
Vernon, M/W, son, born 1909, in Tenn.

239. SOUTHERLAND, ROBERT, M/W, age 29, married 7 yrs., born Tenn.
Sallie, F/W, age 26, wife, born Tenn.
Lizzie, F/W, age 5, daughter, born Tenn.
Albert, M/W, age 3, son, born Tenn.
MORRIS, IDA, F/W, age 17, sister-in-law, born Tenn.

240. MONTGOMERY, LUTHER H., M/W, age 55, widower, born Tenn.
Stuart, M/W, age 65, brother, born Tenn.
Bettie E., F/W, age 47, sister, born Tenn.
PATTERSON, ANNIE, F/W, age 33, sister, born Tenn.
Arthur, M/W, age 24, brother-in-law, born in Tenn.
Brosie, M/W, age 4, nephew, b. in Tenn.

241. HARRIS, JOHN, M/W, AGE 48, married 24 yrs., born Tenn.
Sallie, F/W, age 40, wife, born Tenn.
Mary, F/W, age 22, daughter, born Tenn.
Will, M/W, age 20, son, born Tenn.
Lena, F/W, age 17, daughter, born Tenn.
Albert, M/W, age 14, son, born Tenn.
Florence, F/W, age 12, daughter, b. Tenn.
Arthur, M/W, age 8, son, born Tenn.
Hast, M/W, age 3, son, born Tenn.

242. CROWNOVER, THOMAS P. M/W, age 38, married 14 yrs., born Tenn.
Tennessee, F/W, age 32, wife, born Tenn.
Leonard, M/W, age 8, son, born Tenn.
Bessie, F/W, age 5, daughter, born Tenn.

243. GARNER, SAMUEL, M/W, age 37, married 17 yrs., born Tenn.
Mary, F/W, age 35, wife, born Tenn.
Tom, M/W, age 15, son, born Tenn.
Grace, F/W, age 13, daughter, born Tenn.
Reece, M/W, age 11, son, born Tenn.
Theodore, M/W, age 8, son, born Tenn.
Felix, M/W, age 6, son, born Tenn.
Eleanor, F/W, age 4, daughter, born Tenn.
Etta, F/W, age 2, daughter, born Tenn.

244. SHORT, RUBE, M/W, age 28, married 5 yrs., born Tenn.
Lena, F/W, age 23, wife, born Tenn.
Walter, M/W, age 3, son, born Tenn.
Louise, F/W, age 1, daughter, born Tenn.

245. LIGHT, JOSEPH W., M/W, age 46, married 18 yrs., born Indiana.
Delila, F/W, age 42, wife, born Indiana.
Esther, F/W, age 16, daughter, born Indiana.
Caroline, F/W, age 14, daughter, born Indiana.
Georgia, F/W, age 12, , daughter, born Indiana.
Lila, F/W, age 8, daughter, born Indiana.
Zada or Gada, F/W, age 6, dau. born Ind.

246. RUEF, CHRIS, M/W, age 62, married 33 yrs., born Switzerland.
Agnes, F/W, age 58, wife, born Switzerland.
Agnes, F/W, age 30, daughter, born Tenn.
Louise, F/W, age 18, daughter, born Tenn.
Martha, F/W, age 11, daughter, b. Tenn.
Helen, F/W, age 15, daughter, b. in Tenn.
BREWER, MARY, F/W, age 60, companion, born Switzerland.

247. HALPERN, DAVE, M/W, age 21, born Russia.

248. TERRILL, ERNEST, M/W, age 21 born Tenn.
Pearl, F/W, age 22, wife, born Tenn.

249. PIGGOT, CAMERON, M/W, age 38, married 28 yrs., born Maryland.
Annie, F/W, age 38, wife, born Maryland.
Charley, M/W, age 17, son, born Tenn.

250. BRYAN, FRED, M/MU, age 30, married 11 yrs., born Tenn.
Annie, F/MU, age 26, wife, born Tenn.
John, M/MU, age 10, son, born Tenn.
Lena, F/MU, age 8, daughter, born Tenn.
George, M/MU, age 6, son, born Tenn.

251. BLANTON, LIVY, M/W, age 32, married 10 yrs., born Tenn.
Martha, F/W, age 22, wife, born Tenn.
Herbert, M/W, age 8, son, born Tenn.
Ed, M/W, age 5, son, born Tenn.

252. PACK, JOHN, M/W, age 43 married 20 yrs., born Tenn.
Ellen, F/W, age 39, wife, born Tenn.
Susie, F/W, age 16, daughter, born Tenn.
Bruce, M/MU, age 14, son, born Tenn.
Wallace, M/W, age 12, son, born Tenn.
Alice, F/W, age 7, daughter, born Tenn.
Joseph, M/W, age 4, son, born Tenn.

253. O'DEAR, SARAH, F/W, age 65, widow, born Tenn.
Alise, F/W, age 17, granddaughter, born Tenn.
Robert, M/W, age 15, grandson, b. Tenn.
Carl, M/W, age 11, grandson, born Tenn.
Jim, M/W, age 2, grandson, born Tenn.
254. LAPPIN, JESSE, M/W, age 21, born Tenn
Carrie, F/W, age 19, born Tenn.
255. GREEN, BENTON, M/W, age 49, married 28 yrs., born Tenn.
Mary, F/W, age 48, wife, born Tenn.
Martha, F/W, age 27, daughter, born Tenn
Jim, M/W, age 25, son, born Tenn.
Thomas, M/W, age 20, son, born Tenn.
Becky, F/W, age 16, daughter, born Tenn.
Lou, F/W, age 14, daughter, born Tenn.
Andy, M/W, age 6, son, born Tenn.
Irene, F/W, age 3, daughter, born Tenn.
Martha, F/W, age 68, mother, born Tenn.
256. STIGER, EMIL, M/W, age 52, married 20 yrs., born Switzerland.
Lilia, F/W, age 45, wife, born Germany.
Lena, F/W, age 19, daughter, born Tenn.
John, M/W, age 17, son, born Tenn.
Lizzie, F/W, age 15, daughter, born Tenn.
Elmer, M/W, age 12, son, born Tenn.
Mary, F/W, age 9, daughter, born Tenn.
257. GREEN, JOHN, M/W, age 27, married 7 yrs., born Tenn.
Leathy, F/W, age 25, wife, born Tenn.
John, M/W, age 6, son, born Tenn.
Mary, F/W, age 3, daughter, born Tenn.
258. GARNER, ALFRED, M/B, age 56, married 14 yrs., born Tenn.
Charity, F/B, age 42, wife, born Tenn.
Mary, F/B, age 14, daughter, born Tenn.
Lulu, F/B, age 12, daughter, born Tenn.
259. GARNER, TOM, M/W, age 32, married 14 yrs., born Tenn.
Rose, F/W, age 32, wife, born Tenn.
Thuesdy, F/W, age 12, daughter, born Tenn.
Hobert, M/W, age 10, son, born Tenn.
Louis, M/W, age 6, son, born Tenn.
Della, F/W, age 4, daughter, born Tenn.
Edith, F/W, age 3, daughter, born Tenn.
Gladys, F/W, daughter born 1909, Tenn.
260. PERSHINO, IDA, F/W, age 80, widow, born South Carolina.
FINLEY, LOUISE, F/W, age 35, daughter, born South Carolina.
261. ROSE, GEORGIA W., F/W, age 60 widow, born Missouri.
262. BRUTRELL, WILL, M/W, age 25, born Tenn.
Lizzie, F/W, age 21, wife, born Tenn.
263. KING, PAUL, M/MU, age 35, married 5 yrs., born Tenn.
Dilsey, F/MU, age 35, wife, born Tenn.
264. SWIGGETT, GLENN L., M/W, age 42, married 16 yrs. born Indiana.
Emma, F/W, age 40, wife, born Indiana.
Levin, M/W, age 15, son, born Indiana.
Walker, Savanna, F/MU, age 28, servant, born Indiana.
265. ANDERSON, WILL K., M/W, age 65, married 8 yrs., born Tenn.
Mary, F/W, age 26, wife, born Tenn.
John, F/W, age 6, son, born Tenn.
Mary, F/W, age 3, daughter, born Tenn.
Frank, M/W, age 1, son, born Tenn.
266. MILHAIDIE, SALLIE, F/W, age 43, born Tenn.
267. SHOUP, MARY, F/W, age 65, widow, born South Carolina.
ELLIOTT, SALLIE B., F/W, age 50, born Georgia.
NICHOLS, SAM. M/W, age 12, grandson, born Georgia.
Jennie, F/W, age 6, granddaughter, born Georgia.

PEOPLE LIVING IN MARION COUNTY SECTION OF SEWANEE IN 1910

268. TATE, ELIJAH D., M/W, age 32, married 7 yrs., born Tenn.
Mary K., F/W, age 25, wife, born Tenn.
Janey E., F/W, age 5, daughter, b. Tenn.
John D., M/W, age 4, son, born Tenn.
Brice R., M/W, age 1, son, born Tenn.
No name , M/W, son, born 1910, Tenn.
269. LADD, JESSE, M/W, age 24, married 4 yrs., born Tenn.
Martha, F/W, age 20, wife, born Tenn.
Oscar, M/W, age 2, son, born Tenn.
James W., M/W, son b. in 1909, Tenn.
270. SARGENT, SAMUEL, M/W, age 31, married 9 yrs., born Tenn.
Olive, F/W, age 25, wife, born Tenn.
George, M/W, age 9, son, born Tenn.
Lola, F/W, age 6, daughter, born Tenn.
Mattie, F/W, age 3, daughter, born Tenn.
Ethel, F/W, daughter, born 1909, Tenn.
271. LAPPIN, GRANT, M/W, age 44, married 13 yrs., born Ohio.
Elizabeth, F/W, age 44, wife, born Tenn.
Fred, M/W, age 14, son, born Tenn.
Albert, M/W, age 17, son, born Tenn.
Mary, F/W, age 15, daughter, born Tenn.
Elizabeth, F/W, age 14, daughter, b. Tenn.
Hobert, M/W, age 12, son, born Tenn.
Emmie, F/W, age 10, daughter, b. Tenn.
Allie, F/W, age 9, daughter, born Tenn.
272. SMITH, CHARLES, M/W, age 24, married 6 yrs., born Tenn.
Annie, F/W, age 21, wife, born Tenn.
Althie, F/W, age 5, daughter, born Tenn.
Katie, F/W, age 3, daughter, born Tenn.
Howard, M/W, age 2, son, born Tenn.
273. LAPPIN, JESSE, M/W, age 56, married 34 yrs., born Ohio.
Martha E., F/W, age 56, wife, born Tenn.
Mattie E., F/W, age 18, daughter, b. Tenn.
Bertha, F/W, age 16, daughter, born Tenn.
William M., M/W, age 12, son, b. Tenn.
LOWE, FRANCIS P., F/W, age 75, widowed mother, born New York.
274. SULLIVAN, SAMUEL, M/W, age 40, married 15 yrs., born Tenn.
Elizabeth, F/W, age 30, wife, born Tenn.
Estelle, F/W, age 14, daughter, born Tenn.
Ethel, F/W, age 11, daughter, born Tenn.
Madie, F/W, age 9, daughter, born Tenn.
Margie, F/W, age 8, daughter, born Tenn.
Mark, M/W, age 5, son, born Tenn.
Anna, F/W. age 3, daughter, born Tenn.
Grant, M/W, son, born 1909, Tenn.
275. MORRIS, JAMES, M/W, age 32, married 7 yrs., born Tenn.
Carlee, F/W, age 23, wife, born Tenn.
Prince E., M/W, age 6, son, born Tenn.
Mason R, M/W, age 4, son, born Tenn.
James M., M/W, age 2, son, born Tenn.
Albany E., M/W, son, b. in 1909, Tenn.
276. SMITH, WILL, M/W, age 28, married 8 yrs., born Tenn.
Josie, F/W, age 27, wife, born Tenn.
Eddie, M/W, age 7, son, born Tenn.
Irene, F/W, age 6, daughter, born Tenn.
Walter, M/W, age 3, son, born Tenn.
Samuel, M/W, son, born 1909, in Tenn.
LEMONS, MALINDA, F/W, age 67, mother-in-law, born Tenn.
277. STATOM, JOHN, M/W, age 63, married 36 yrs., born Tenn.
Nancy, F/W, age 64, wife, born Tenn.
278. HEAD, WILLIAM, M/W, age 53, married 34 yrs., born Tenn.
Jane, F/W, age 54, wife, born Tenn.
William C., M/W, age 18, son, b. in Tenn.
279. SMITH, WADE, M/W, age 35, married 15 yrs., born Tenn.
Fanny, F/W, age 32, wife, born Alabama.
Luther, M/W, age 14, son, born Tenn.
Herbert, M/W, age 10, son, born Tenn.
Almer, F/W, daughter, born 1910, Tenn.
280. MCBEE, ROBERT, M/W, age 51, married 32 yrs., in Tenn.
Elizabeth, F/W, age 48, wife, born Tenn.
Obediah, M/W, age 18, son, born Tenn.
Churchville, M/W, age 13, son, born Tenn.
Della, F/W, age 10, daughter, born Tenn.
Susie, F/W, age 8, daughter, born Tenn.
Vera, F/W, age 5, daughter, born Tenn.
281. MCBEE, WILLIAM, M/W, age 30 yrs., born Tenn.
Anna B., F/W, age 47, wife, born Tenn.
James M., M/W, age 26, son, born Tenn.
Charles W., M/W, age 20, son, born Tenn.
Robert P., M/W, age 19, son, born Tenn.
Mary J., F/W, age 17, daughter, b. Tenn.
Nancy J., F/W, age 14, daughter, b. Tenn.
William L., M/W, age 13, son, born Tenn.

ST.MARY'S SCHOOL AND CONVENT

1. SISTER HUGHETTA, F/W, age 60, head Nun, born South Carolina.
2. SISTER HANNAH, F/W, age 40, assistant, born South Carolina.
3. WASHER, GLADYS, F/W, age 35, assistant, born Tenn.
4. GRIGESBY, NETTIE, F/W, age 30, assistant, born Tenn.
5. FISHER, ELLEN, F/W, age 35, pupil, born Tenn.
6. BOWEN, ESTHER, F/W, age 17, pupil, born Tenn.
7. GRACE, F/W, age 13, pupil, born Tenn.
8. HENLEY, MYRTLE, F/W, age 17, pupil, born Tenn.
9. MORRIS, , name illegible, F/W, age, 16, pupil, born Tenn.
10. KENNEDY, OLA, F/W, age 12, pupil, born Tenn.
11. IVES, FRANCES, F/W, age 12, pupil, born in Tenn.
12. GOURLETTE, PEARL, F/W, age 18, pupil, born Arkansas.
13. GOURLETTE, JESSIE, F/W, age 9, pupil, born Arkansas.
14. EDEN, ISABELLE, F/W, age 10, pupil, born Tenn.
15. WOOTEN, ANNIE, F/W, age 6, pupil, born in Tenn.
16. TAYLOR, MAY, F/W, age 10, pupil, born in Tenn.
17. HARRIS, JULIET, F/W, age 17, pupil, born in Tenn.
18. HARRIS, ELLEN, F/W, age 15, pupil, born in Tenn.
19. GRIGSBY, BELL, F/W, age 13, pupil, born in Tenn.
20. GRISBY, MAUD, F/W, age 11, pupil, born in Tenn.

There were 281 households in Sewanee. There was 20 students and faculty listed at St. Mary's Episcopal School during 1910 census. Students at the University of the South were not listed in 1910 census in Franklin County. They were probably counted in their home states.

PEOPLE LIVING AT SEWANEE DURING THE 1920 CENSUS

The following data was taken from the 1920 census records of the 18th District of Franklin County, Tennessee. All heads of household are listed in capital letter. Individuals living within the same household with different surnames are also capitalized.

1. O'DEAR, SARAH, F/W, age 72.
James, M/W, gr-son, age 11.
George, M/W, gr-son, age 10.
2. PACK, JOHN, M/W, age 53.
Elen, F/W, age wife, 45.
Susie, F/W, daughter, age 26.
Walace, M/W, son, age 21.
Alice, F/W, daughter, age 16.
Joe, M/W, son, age 13.
Mattie, M/W, daughter, age 8.
Sarah, F/W, daughter, age 8.
Josephine, F/W, dau-in-law. age 17.
3. GREEN, THOMAS A., M/W, age 30
Jeanetta, F/W, wife, age 23.
Richard, M/W, son, born in 1920.
Mary A., F/W, daughter, born in 1920.
4. MCBEE, JOSEPH C, M/W, age 63.
Walker, M/W, son, age 23.
Gertrude, F/W, daughter, age 15.
5. STEIGER, EMIL, M/W, age 61
Elizabeth, F/W, wife, age 53.
6. GREENE, JOHN M. M/W, age 36
Litha, F/W, wife, age 33.
Francis, M/W, son, age 12.
Maria, F/W, daughter, age 10.
Walter, M/W, son, age 8.
Mamie, F/W, age 6, daughter
Geraldine, F/W, age illegible
7. STEIGER, JOHN, M/W, age illegible
8. GARNER, SAMUEL, M/W, age 46
Mary J., F/W, age 44
Felix, M/W, son, age 16.
Eleanora, F/W, daughter, age 15.
Letha, F/W, daughter, age 12.
Maud, F/W, daughter, age 9.
Geraldine, F/W, daughter, age 7
Mamie, F/W, daughter, age 5.
Margret, F/W, daughter, age 1.
9. SIMMONS, JIM, M/W, age 22
Dottie, F/W, wife, age 23.
Addie Mae, F/W, daughter,
Willie Ruth, F/W, age 3, daughter
Hazel, F/W, daughter, age 5.
10. BATESMAN, HENRY, M/W, age 45.
Marie, F/W, wife, age 42.
Viaster, M/W, son, age 8.
Sophia, F/W, daughter
11. MCBEE, WILLIAM, M/W, age 62
Julia, F/W, wife, age 46.
JOHNSON, ?, M/W, step-son, age 20.
all information illegible.
all information illegible.
all information illegible.
12. INFORMATION ILLEGIBLE.
13. INFORMATION ILLEGIBLE
14. SHORT, REUBEN, M/W, age 39
Lena, F/W, age 34, wife
Walter, M/W, age 13, son
Louise, F/W, age 11, daughter
Eleanor, F/W, age 9, daughter
Ernest, M/W, age 7, son
Rubin, M/W, age 1, son
15. MCBEE, all information illegible
GRACE, all information illegible.
FRED, information illegible.
ERNEST, information illegible.
16. SHORT, EDWARD, M/W, age 31
Mary, F/W, age 23, wife
Charles Preson, M/W, age 5, son
Paul, M/W, age 3, son
Mary Esther, F/W, age 1, daughter
Julia Ann, F/W, age 72, mother
17. SUTHERLAND, ROBERT, age 39.
Sallie, F/W, age 36, wife
Alma E., F/W, age 15, daughter
Albert, M/W, age 13, son
Beatrice, F/W, information illegible.
Marion, M/W, information illegible.
Robert, M/W, information illegible.
18. INFORMATION ILLEGIBLE.
19. GREEN, BENTON, M/W, age 59.
Mary, F/W, age 58, wife
Jennie Lee, information illegible.
Feby, information illegible.
Andy, all other information illegible.
Irene, all other information illegible.
Charlies, grandson, illegible
20. GARNER, REECE, M/W, age 21
Martha, F/W, age 18, wife

21. SHORT, DAVID W., M/W, age 45
Litha, F/W, age 37, wife
Marvin, M/W, age 17, son
Short, Reece, M/W, age 15, son
Lawrence, M/W, age 13, son
Dorotha, F/W, age 5, daughter
22. VAUGHN, CHARLIE, M/W, age 54.
Mary, F/W, age 30, wife.
Ema, F/W, age 10, daughter.
23. HALEY, SALLIE, F/W, age 43.
GIPSON, GEORGE, M/W, age 16, son.
Jennie, F/W, age 15, daughter.
Earnest, M/W, age 13, son.
Berry, M/W, age 9, son.
Walter, M/W, age 7, son.
GREEN, MARTHA, age 79, mother.
24. MONTGOMERY, FRED H. , age 39.
Sallie C., F/W, age 34, wife.
James, M/W, age 13, son.
Mary, F/W, age 10, daughter.
Elen, F/W, age 7, daughter.
Sarrah, F/W, daughter, born in 1920.
Kenneth, M/W, son, born in 1920.
25. CROWNOVER, THOMAS, age 47.
Tennie, F/W, age 42, wife.
Lenard, M/W, age 18, son.
Mary E., F/W, age 14, daughter.
Maud E., F/W, age 9, daughter.
Dorie May, F/W, age 6, daughter.
26. HAWKINS, LUKE, M/W, age 52.
Maggie, F/W, age 47, wife.
Roberta M., F/W, age 18, daughter.
Clifford, M/W, age 15, son.
Lyle, M/W, age 13, son.
Nevill, M/W, age 11, son.
Vivian, F/W, age 5, daughter.
27. THOMAS, JAMES, M/W, age 55.
Fanny E., F/W, age 51, wife.
Felare, F/W, age 36, daughter.
Deon, M/W, age 25, son.
LEACH, Thelma, age 13, granddau.
28. CAMPBELL, JAMES W., age 58.
Elen, F/W, age 58, wife.
Nanie, F/W, age 30, daughter.
Dessie, F/W, age 30, daughter.
Elsie, F/W, age 21, daughter.
Gertrude, F/W, age 15, daughter.
29. CAMPBELL, WILLIAM, age 32.
Cora M., F/W, age 33, wife.
Lorene, F/W, age 10, daughter.
James W., M/W, age 5, son.
Ernest, M/W, age 6, son.
Mamie, F/W, born in 1919, daughter.
30. GUDGER, WILLIAM F., age 65.
Jane, F/W, age 50, wife.
Harrison, M/W, age 36, son.
Galiton, M/W, age 26, son.
Lawton, M/W, age 19, son.
John A., M/W, age 16, son.
Pressie, F/W, age 12, daughter.
31. GUDGER, ROBERT, M/W, age 67.
Nancy, F/W, age 65, wife.
MCBEE, MARY A., age 34, daughter.
Lenard, M/W, age 9, grandson.
Allan, M/W, twin son, born in 1920.
Ronal, M/W, twin son, born in 1920.
32. PRINCE, SARAH, F/W, age 52.
J. D., M/W, age 11, son.
33. DYER, ROBERT, M/W, age 42.
Magie, F/W, age 33, wife.
Lucile, F/W, age 14, daughter.
Mildred, F/W, age 11, daughter.
Charles, M/W, age 9, son.
Linard, M/W, age 5, son.
Leon, M/W, age 5, son.
Marshall, M/W, age 2, son.
34. ANDERSON, ANNIE, F/W, age 52.
Roy or Ray, M/W, age 25, son.
Ike, M/W, age 22, son.
John, M/W, age 18, son.
Anna L., F/W, age 10, daughter.
SAMSON, ERA, F/W, age 10, niece.
WATTY, Raymond, age 7, grandson.
35. ANDERSON, J. W., M/W, age 71.
Elizabeth, F/W, age 69.
36. REED, LOUIS, M/W, age 33.
Ida, F/W, age 39, wife.
Roberta, F/W, age 11, daughter.
Johnie, F/W, age 7, daughter.
Virginia, F/W, age 1, daughter.
37. TEAGUE, RACHEL, F/W, age 73.
Nancy, F/W, age 50, daughter.
Edward, M/W, age 6, grandson.
38. ROLLINS, GEORGE W., age 34.
Barbara, F/W, age 26, wife.
Edward, M/W, age 6, son.
Frances, F/W, age 3, daughter.
Virginia, F/W, age 1, daughter.
39. BENNETT, information illegible.
WEST, RUTH, F/W, age 51, cousin.
40. CALDWELL, FRANK W., age 29.
Rhoda, F/W, age 27, wife.
Zuela, F/W, age 7, daughter.
William, M/W, age 6, son.
Annie M., F/W, age 2, daughter.

41. CALDWELL, D. W., age 22.
Margret, F/W, age 20, wife.
Mamie, F/W, daughter, born in 1920.

42. GREEN, JAMES W., M/W, age 26.
Flora, F/W, age 28, daughter.
Charles, M/W, age 4, son.
Green, James, M/W, age 1, son.
USERY, THOMAS, age 91, uncle.

43. ?CHURCH, WILLIAM, M/W, age 76.
Mahaley, F/W, age 67, wife.

44. GREEN, WILLIAM A., M/W, age 46.
Sina, F/W, age 40, wife.
Roy Z., M/W, age 21, son.
Gertrude. F/W, age 15, daughter.

45. BUCHANAN, IZRA C., M/W, age 59.
Jennie, F/W, age 54, wife.
ANDERSON, ANDREW, age 26, step-son.
MOONEY, HALLEY, age 6, boarder.

46. JAMES, LAWRENCE, M/W, age 34.
Minnie, F/W, age 22, wife.
Berry, M/W, age 84, father.
REEVES, JULIA, F/W, age 40, sister.
Pearl, F/W, age 16, niece.

47. HOBACK, CHARLES E., age 37.
Beulah, F/W, age 30, wife.
Everet, M/W, age illegible, son.
Grace, F/W, age 7, daughter.
Dollie M., F/W, age 3, daughter.
Charles, M/W, age 1, son.

48. FOSTER, FRANK S., M/W, age 46.
Sallie, F/W, age 44, wife.
Flora, F/W, age 23, daughter.
CLARK, LUCINDA, age 65, mother-in-law.

49. CLARK, JAMES W., M/W, age 22.
Allie M., M/W, age 20, daughter.
Alvah, M/W, age 1, son.

50. FOSTER, JAMES C. M/W, age 39.
Sara, F/W, age 37, wife.
Martha, F/W, age 18, daughter.
Annie, F/W, age 13, daughter.
James, M/W, age 11, son.
May, F/W, age 7, daughter.
Ed., M/W, age 1, son.

51. GILLIAM, ROBERT, M/W, age 21.
Beatrice, F/W, age 20, wife.
John F., M/W, age 1, son.

52. BARRY, JOSEPH, M/W, age 38.
Sallie, F/W, age 34, wife.
Ida, F/W, age 15, daughter.
Eulis, F/W, age 11, daughter.
illegible name, son.
RICKETT, JESSIE M., age 12, step-daughter.
Angeline, F/W, age 11, step-daughter.
Mary A., F/W, age 9, step-daughter.

53. HUNZIKER, EMIL, M/W, age 54.
Virginia, M/W, age 39, daughter.
John, M/W, information illegible.
Lottie, F/W, age 18, daughter.
Veda, F/W, age 16, daughter.
Grace, F/W, age 14, daughter.
Elise, F/W, age 12, daughter.
Paul, M/W, age 8, son.
Alma, F/W, age 6, daughter.
Emil Jr., M/W, age 4, son.
Nellie, F/W, age 2, daughter.

54. LADD, WILLIAM E., M/W, age 29.
Ellie R., F/W, age 28, wife.
J. W. , M/W, age 1, son.
ANDERSON, DAVID, age 62, father-in-law.

55. KIMBRO, GLEN W., M/W, age 64.
Judith, F/W, age 64, wife.
Annie L., F/W, age ?, daughter.
Charles W., F/W, age 31, son.

56. RICKETT, JOSEPH, M/W, age 40.
Jane, F/W, age 34, wife.
Egbert, M/W, age 12, son.
Mary, F/W, age 9, daughter.
Rutha, F/W, age 5, daughter.

57. ROBERTSON, LENA, F/W, age 55.
BRADFORD, ELEN, age 38, boarder.
Lusy, F/W, age 13, boarder.
Mary, F/W, age 11, boarder.
Albert, M/W, age 7, boarder.
Lawrence, M/W, age 3, boarder.

58. LACKEY, JOSEPH S., M/W, age 24.
Beulah, F/W, age 24, wife.
Joseph Jr., M/W, age 2, son.

59. ?GORDIN, LEON H., M/W, age 50.
Mary, F/W, age illegible, wife.
Mary, F/W, age illegible, daughter.

60. FLYE, JAMES H., age 35.
Grace, F/W, age 42, wife.

61. ?AGEE, LAURA T, F/W, age 35.
James R., M/W, age 10, daughter.
Ema F., F/W, age 7, daughter.

62. GREENE, JOSEPH R., M/W, age 59.
Carrie, F/W, age 58, wife.
Addie L., F/W, age 18, daughter.
Josephine, F/W, age 16, daughter.
Jack, M/W, age 14, son.

63. COOPER, ANA, age 55.
BERLINA, ANA, age 50, boarder.

64. CAMPBEL, ROBERT, HEAD, age 5?,
WITEALL, EDWIN E., ASST., age 41.
LEROY, LEWIS, CHAPLAIN, 58.
WRIGHT, ERSKIN, ASST., age 43.
NEELY, THOS, EMPLOYEE, age 38.
TAILTON, CHAS., HELPER, 46.
EDWARDS, C.M., EMPLOYEE, 52.
SLOAN, C. D., EMPLOYEE, age 45.
STILWELL, R.J., EMPLOYEE, age ?.
STRAPP, EDITH, EMPLOYEE, 53
MARTIN, SAMUEL, EMPLOYEE, 38
MEDFORD, CLYDE, EMPLOYEE, 30
ANTHONY, ?, EMPLOYEE, age 26.
GROVE, LAWRENCE, EMPLOYEE.
ROOTEN, W.H., EMPLOYEE, age 27.
DEALOG, J.D., EMPLOYEE, age 23.
BURNS, ALLAN, EMPLOYEE, age ?.
REED, J. E., EMPLOYEE, age 26.

65. HUNZIKER, MARY, F/W, age 84.
Adolph, F/W, age 47, son.
MILLER, CLARA, gr-daughter, 31.
Dartha E, gr-granddaughter, age 2.
John C., M/W, gr-grandson, age 1.

66. CLARK, JOHN, M/W, age 63.
Alice, F/W, wife, age 50.
George W., M/W, son, age 10.

67. HARRISON, WILLIAM, M/W, age 41.
Frankie, F/W, wife, age 33.

68. YATES, BENJAMIN, F/W, age 62.
Urtie, F/W, wife, age 43.
WALKER, ELIZABETH, mother-in-law, age 67.

69. YATES, LECIL, M/W, age 25.
Mattie L., F/W, wife, age 23.
Lecil R., M/W, son, age 7.
Florence, F/W, dau., age 6.
Bert R., M/W, son, age 5.
J. D., M/W, son, age 1.

70. STATUM, JOHN, M/W, age 50.
Sarah, F/W, wife, age 45.
Mary, F/W, daughter, age 18.

71. HAWKINS, THOMAS, M/W, age 20.
Ethel, F/W, wife, age 19.
Charles, M/W, son, age 1.

72. HAWKINS, MARGARET, age 59.
Jackson, M/W, son, age 24.

73. CANTRELL, WILLIAM R., age 42.
Elizabeth, F/W, wife, age 36.
Walter P., M/W, son, age 7.

74. TERRILL ERNEST, M/W, age 34.
Eliza, F/W, wife, age 32.
Charles, M/W, son, age 1

75. HUNZIKER, JOHN C., age 35.
Bertha M., F/W, wife, age 20.
Ruby L., F/W, daughter, age 9.
Mary, F/W, daughter, age 7.
Annie W., F/W, daughter, age 5.

76. KENNEDY, GEORGE P., age 48.
Ardena, F/W, wife, age 37.
Nancy, F/W, daughter, age 17.
Ina R., F/W, daughter, age 5.

77. RUSSELL, JAMES L., age 59.
Maggie, F/W, wife, age 71.

78. POWELL, EMILY, F/W, age 66.
RUPLE, ANDREW P., boarder, age 26.
Mary, F/W, age 35. W, boarder's wife.

79. ANDERSON, ALBERT S., age 35.
Elizabeth, F/W, wife, age 27.
Irvin, M/W, son, age 9.
Mildred, F/W, daughter, age 1.

80. NEEDY, WARRICK, F/W, age 55.
Annie L, F/W, wife, age 30.
Howard, M/W, son, age 8.
Earlin, F/W, daughter, age 4.
Randall, M/W, son, age 2.

81. ROLLINS, WILLIAM J., age 35.
Eva, F/W, wife, age 34.
Erma L., F/W, daughter, age 11.
J. W., M/W, son, age 8.
Earl, M/W, son, age 4.

82. CAMP, EDWARD G., age 35.
Dollie, F/W, wife, age 26.
Inez, F/W, daughter, age 7.
Sarah, F/W, daughter, age 6.
Joseph, F/W, son, age 3.

83. PRINCE, JAMES P., age 55.
Emma, F/W, wife, age 50.
Walter, M/W, son, age 21.
Haden, M/W, son, age 17.
Laurine, F/W, daughter, age 16.
Susie, F/W, daughter, age 15.

84. DURIM, JOSEPH H., age 29.
Lilian, F/W, wife, age 21.

85. SIMS, ROSE, F/B, age 70.
BORNIE, CLARA, niece, age ?1.
Mira, F/B, niece, age 1.
HANDLEY, CILLA, sister, age 69.

86. MEAD, JAMES R. , M/W, age 36.
Rose, F/W, wife, age 27.
Mildred R., F/W, daughter, age 6.
Jeanette C., F/W, daughter, age 5.
MCPETERS, BERTHA, servant, 20.
Charles, M/W, boarder, age 18.
Henry, M/W, boarder, age 15.
Gaines, M/W, boarder, age 12.
FORE, ANDREW, boarder, age 21.
HESTER, ROBERT, boarder, age 25.
HICKSON, ANDREW, boarder, 18.

87. FARRIS, WILLIAM, M/W, age 78.
Nancy, F/W, wife, age 40.
Darrie, F/W, daughter, age 10.
Charlie, M/W, son, age 6.
Samuel, M/W, son, age 1.
NICKENS, WILLIE, daughter, age 21.
MEADOWS, TAMMIE, dau., 16.

88. FARRIS, BALTIMORE, M/W, age 59.
Annie, F/W, wife, age 42.
Thelma, F/W, daughter, age 10.
Ethel, F/W, daughter, age 7.

89. FAIRBANKS, FLORIDA, age 71.
LOUALTA, AGNES, companion, 50.

90. HOGE, SARAH T., F/W, age 76.
Nannie, F/W, daughter, age 41.
Lynman, M/W, grandson, age 19.

91. ARNOLD, WILLIAM G., age 67.
Mattie, F/W, wife, age 58.

92. KNOTT, WILLIAM S., age 26.
Irene, F/W, wife, age 23.
William Jr., M/W, son, age 2.

93. YATES, JOHN, M/W, age 52.
Nannie, F/W, wife, age 43.

94. REASON, HENRY I., age 53.
Lemay, F/W, daughter, age 17.
Ed., M/W, son, age 15.
Cleo, M/W, son, age 13.
Raymond, M/W, son, age 10.
John K., M/W, son, age 8.
Ellis, M/W, son, age 3.

95. RILEY, LOUIS R., age 40.
Blanche D., F/W, wife, age 40.
Hershell, M/W, son, age 14.
Nellie M., F/W, daughter, age 6.

96. YATES, WALTER, M/W, age 30.
Nora, F/W, wife, age 27.
Flora, F/W, daughter, age 7.
Rubie, F/W, daughter, age 4.

97. SCHNEIDER, LAURA, F/W, age 39.
Katie, F/W, daughter, age 14.
Henrietta, F/W, daughter, age 5.

98. POTTS, MAGGIE, F/W, age 57.
Gertrude, F/W, daughter, age 20.
John L., M/W, son, age 16.

99. SEWELL, HENRY M., M/W, age 66.
Rosa., F/W, wife, age 57.
Marie, F/W, daughter, age 27.
Ross, M/W, son, age 25.

100. POTTS, GEORGE, M/W, age 34.
Lou, F/W, wife, age 33.
Maggie, F/W, daughter, age 14.
Frank, M/W, son, age 11.
J. D., M/W, son, age 9.
Elmer, M/W, son, age 6.
Lylie, F/W, daughter, age 4.

101. CASTLEBERRY, JOHN H., age 39.
Bertha, F/W, wife, age 37.
John P., M/W, son, age 11.
Elizabeth, F/W, daughter, age 9.
Nannie, F/W, daughter, age 8.
Ralph, M/W, son, age 6.

102. SUTHERLAND, JAMES O., age 51.
Mary E, F/W, wife, 50.
Samuel W., M/W, son, age 25.
Earine, M/W, son, age 23.
Annie, F/W, daughter, age 21.
Alvin, M/W, son, age 19.
Earl, M/W, son, age 17.

103. TOMES, CHARLES W., age 59.
Georgia, F/W, wife, age 47.
Willie F., M/W, son, age 28.
Beulah, F/W, daughter, age 16.
Lula M., F/W, daughter, age 12.
DAVIS, LEANA, F/W, dau., age 26

104. HAMILTON, THOMAS, M/W, age 50.
Laura, F/W, wife, age 42.
William J., M/W, son, age 17.
Gorden, M/W, son, age 14.
Haden, M/W, son, age 11.

105. DONEY, ANN, F/W, age 62.
Katheline, F/W, daughter, age 19.

106. TOMES, ROBERT L., M/W, age 28.
Willie F., F/W, wife, age 25.
Ernest, M/W, son, age 3.
Virgil, M/W, son, age 1.

107. TUCKER, GREEN, M/W, age 46.
Minthey, F/W, wife, age 36.
Bessie, F/W, daughter, , age 19.
Mable, F/W, daughter, age 15.
Ethel, F/W, daughter, age 13.
Edward R., M/W, son, age 11.
Irene, F/W, daughter, age 7.
Clyde, M/W, son, age 4.

108. CASTLEBERRY, JAMES, age 54.
Lillie, F/W, daughter, age 51.
James H., M/W, son, age 13.
Velma, F/W, daughter, age 12.
Rebecca A., F/W, mother-in-law age 84.

109. PRINCE, JENNIE, F/W, age 52.
Lillie, F/W, daughter, age 28.
Harry, M/W, son, age 25.
Earnest, M/W, son, age 21.
Robert, M/W, son, age 19.
VAUGHN, LUCY, F/W, servant.

110. MYERS, THERON, M/W, age 27.
Margaret, F/W, wife, age 21.
Mignonne, F/W, daughter, age 1.

111. STEWMAN, ELIZABETH, age 54.
May, F/W, daughter, age 19.
GARNER, WILLIE, gr-daughter, 16.
BRINKLEY, HENRY, brother, age 58.
112. TERRILL, LUSURNIS, M/W, age 45.
Mahaley, F/W, wife, age 41.
Albert K., M/W, son, age 19.
Velma, F/W, daughter, age 17.
Thomas W., M/W, son, age 14.
Eva P., F/W, daughter, age 12.
Joseph L., M/W, son, age 7.
Martha, F/W, daughter, age 5.
Isaac H., M/W, brother, age 36.
113. SHERIL, THOMAS, M/W, age 33.
Ida, F/W, wife, age 41.
114. COLLINS, GEORGE W., age 25.
Florance M., F/W, wife, age 22.
Sarah M., F/W, daughter, age 1.
115. ROSS, WILLIAM D., M/W, age 75.
Mary C., F/W, wife, age 37.
Lucille, F/W, adopted-dau., age 6.
116. BENNETT, WILLIAM W,, age 44.
Rindy, F/W, wife, age 38.
Samuel , M/W, son, age 23.
Mack S., M/W, son, age 15.
Sarah A., F/W, daughter, age 13.
David, M/W, son, age 11.
George, M/W, son, age 8.
SWAN, MYRTLE, daughter, age 18.
117. SMITH, LAWRENCE, M/W, age 42.
Laura, F/W, wife, age 42.
Nellie, F/W, daughter, age 20.
Beulah, F/W, daughter, age 18.
John, M/W, son, age 16.
Elmer H., M/W, son, age 14.
Albert, M/W, son, age 12.
Joseph C., M/W, son, age 9.
Alice C., F/W, daughter, age 8.
LIMMON, MALINDA C., mother-in-law, age 77.
118. HARRISON, ANNIE, F/W, age 42.
Haze, F/W, son, age 21.
James O., M/W, son, age 19.
Floyid, M/W, son, age 16.
Benjamin F., M/W, son, age 14.
Grace, F/W, daughter, age illegible.
119. GIPSON, LEE, M/W, age illegible.
?Alene, F/W, wife, age illegible.
DOTSON, WILLIAM, step-son, age ?.
Calvin, M/W, step-son, age 4.
120. LONG, JOSEPH B., M/W, age 45.
Nora, F/W, wife, age 41.
John, M/W, son, age 15.
Joseph, M/W, son, age 11.
121. TATUM, JOSEPH S., M/W, age 43.
Mattie S., F/W, wife, age 31.
Gussie, F/W, daughter, age 12.
Clara B., F/W, daughter, age 11.
Helen, F/W, daughter, age 10.
Glatis, F/W, daughter, age 8.
Sanford, M/W, son, age 2.
Douglas, M/W, son, age 1.
Nathen, M/W, son, born in 1920.
122. CRICK, ED, M/W, age 52.
Alonia, F/W, wife, age 36.
Glen O., M/W, son, age 12.
Paul, M/W, son, age 10.
123. HILL, JOHN, M/W, age 36.
Otsie, F/W, daughter, age 14.
Rosie, F/W, daughter, age 12.
Vivian, M/W, son, age 8.
BARNES, NANCY, mother, age 66.
Margie L., F/W, sister, age 30.
124. MITCHELL, ROBERT L., age 52.
Jeane, F/W, wife, age 50.
Oliver B., M/W, son, age 15.
Leslie, M/W, son, age 8.
125. YATES, WARNER, M/W, age 31.
Doshia M., F/W, wife, age 17.
126. TERRILL, JAMES M., age 39.
Rachel, F/W, wife, age 36.
Claude L, M/W, son, age 18.
Walter, M/W, son, age 16.
Auther, M/W, son, age 15.
James E., M/W, son, age 11.
Andrew J., M/W, son, age 9.
Charles H., M/W, son, age 6.
Earnest, M/W, son, age 2.
127. MCCREARY, ALLEN R., age 29.
Irene, F/W, wife, age 22.
Allen L, M/W, son, age 2.
Dartha, F/W, daughter, age 1.
128. GIPSON, ALLEN, M/W, age 57.
Lora, F/W, daughter, age 17.
Layton, M/W, daughter, age 15.
Clarance, M/W, son, age 9.
129. BARNETT, ROBERT, M/W, age 35.
Joyce, F/W, wife, age 28.
Denis, M/W, twin-son, age 2.
Denton, M/W, twin-son, age 2.
130. RENALDS, SAMUEL D., age 38.
Maud L, F/W, wife, age 35.
Howard, M/W, son, age 11.
Lora M., F/W, daughter, age 9.
Rubie L., F/W, daughter, age 7.
131. POWELL, MATTIE C., F/W, age 59.

132. JOHNSON, ALBERT, M/W, age 47.
Bettie M., F/W, wife, age 46.
Hazel M., F/W, daughter, age 19.
Joseph W., M/W, son, age 17.
Elizabeth, F/W, daughter, age 16.
Leland, F/W, daughter, age 13.
Elsie, F/W, daughter, age 11.

133. RUSEL, GEORGE W., M/W, age 51.
Minnie, F/W, wife, age 42.
Carrie, F/W, daughter, age 16.
Nonie R., F/W, daughter, age 14.
James, M/W, son, age 8.
Julia H., F/W, daughter, age 5.
Lilian J., F/W, daughter, age 2.
PRINCE, MARGARET, gr-daughter, born in 1920.

134. FRANK, JAMES H., M/W, age 61.
Della, F/W, wife, age 34.

135. RILEY, SOPHA, F/W, age 73.
Joseph R., M/W, son, age 46.
Edward, M/W, son, age 37.
SHERILL, MOLLIE, F/W, age 35, servant for the Rileys.

136. WILSON, WILLIAM R., M/W, age 41.
Willie B., F/W, wife, age 35.
Lela, F/W, daughter, age ?.
Bobbie, F/W, daughter, age ?.
Louise, F/W, daughter, age ?.

137. BEAKLEY, WILLIAM J., age 22.
Fannie, F/W, wife, age 16.

138. HUNT, JOHN B., M/W, age 49.
Mary, F/W, daughter, age ?.
Mattie, F/W, daughter, age ?.
Mary, F/W, daughter, age 20.
Thomas, M/W, son, age 19.
WASHINGTON, MARY, F/W, mother-in-law, age 73.

139. WASHINGTON, WM. L., age 32.
Ethel P., F/W, wife, age 33.
William, M/W, son, age 13.
Juliann, F/W, daughter, age 11.
Gayle, F/W, daughter, age 2.

140. HELL, BILFORD, M/B, age 31.
Annie, F/B, wife, age 29.
Bessie, F/B, daughter, age 12.

141. JUDD, SPENCER, M/W, age 64.
Hallie R., F/W, wife, age 57.

142. FARRIS, HENRITA, F/B, age 49.
KEITH, JACOB, M/B, gr-son, age 19.

143. NAFF, JOHN J., M/W, age
Ruth R., F/W, wife, age 26 or 36.

144. REED, FREDRIE, M/W, age 38.
Bubbie, F/W, wife, age 20.
Clarance, M/W, son, age 1.

145. ADAMS, JOHN, M/W, age 43,
Emma, F/W, wife, age illegible.
Norwood, M/W, son, age illegible.
Mary, F/W, daughter, age 11.

146. SCHMITTE, HENRY A., age 35.
Grace, F/W, wife, age 34.

147. WADE, FRANCIS .K, F/W, age 55.
Francis, F/W, daughter, age 17.
M. L., son, age 13.

148. VAUGHN, DOUGLAS L., age 36.
Abbie, F/W, wife, age 36.
Douglas, M/W, son, age 8.
Charlotte, F/W, daughter, age 6.
Elizabeth, F/W, daughter, age 4.

149. BAILY, THOMAS P., M/W, age 52.
Minnie O., F/W, wife, age 48.
Thomas L., M/W, son, age 22.
James P., M/W, son, age 20.
Minnie O., F/W, daughter, age 17.
Mary B., F/W, daughter, age 14.
DAVIS, ANNA L, F/W, sister-in-law, age 44, single.

150. HICKERSON, JOSEPH R., age 37.
Mauree, F/W, wife, age 37.
Joseph R., M/W, son, age 2.

151. MADDUX, KENSHAW, M/W, age 29.
Beaulah M., F/W, wife, age 30.
Robert L, M/W, son, age 6.
Louise, F/W, daughter, age 4.
Ralph, F/W, son, age illegible.
Louis W., M/W, son, age illegible.

152. KENNEDY, JOHN, M/B, age 48.
Gertrude M., F/B, wife, age 33.
Julia, F/B, wife, age 16.
Ova, F/B, daughter, age 1.

153. PHILIPS, MINTER, M/B, age 34.
Madeline, F/B, wife, age 36.
Cleveland, M/B, son, age 5.

154. PHILIPS, NOBLE I., M/B, age 32.

155. PHILIPS, CALVIN, M/B, age 46.

156. SIMS, CHARLES, M/B, age 23.
Ectar O., F/W, wife, age 17.
BARNES, LUCY, F/B, age 32.

157. NOLEN, L.C., F/W, age 30.

158. WADAMS, ELIZABETH, age 53.

159. LANTENHISER, FRANKLIN, age 52.
Eva M., F/W, wife, age 49.
Renea, F/W, daughter, age 24.

160. BROOKS, PRESTON S., M/W, age 64.
Mariah, F/W, wife, 63.
Preston, M/W, son, age 40.
Robert, M/W, son, age 32.
Catherine, F/W, daughter, age 32.
Elen, F/W, dau-law, age 32.

161. MORTON, WILLIAM C., age illegible.
Pollie L., F/W, wife, age 24.
162. BECKLEY, JOHN P., M/W, age 53.
Mary M., F/W, wife, age 47.
Nellie, F/W, daughter, age 18.
Clara, F/W, daughter, age 14.
Robert, M/W, son, age 11.
Emit, M/W, son, age 7.
163. ANDREWS, WILLIAM, age 57.
Eva N., F/W, wife, age 40.
Edwin, M/W, son, age 20.
Pattie R., F/W, daughter, age 18.
William, M/W, son, age 15.
164. HARDING, FRANK, M/W, age 37.
Judy M., F/W, wife, age 35.
Jackson, M/W, son, age illegible.
165. RUEF, AGNES B., age illegible.
Agnes Jr., F/W, daughter, age 38.
Helen, F/W, daughter, age 24.
Martha, F/W, gr-daughter, age 11.
Dartha, F/W, gr-daughter, age 3.
BLUER, MARY, F/W, servant, age 78.
166. GLOVER, JOHN H., M/W, age 45.
Oriann, F/W, wife, age 20.
167. KENNEDY, WILLIAM, M/W, age 37.
Katie, F/W, wife, age 32.
Clifford, M/W, son, age 11.
Lorine, F/W, daughter, age 9.
Raymon, M/W, son, age 7.
J. illegible, M/W, son, age 3.
168. BLOCTON, L. A., M/W, age 45.
Martha, F/W, wife, age 32.
Herbert, M/W, son, age 18.
Edward, F/W, son, age 15.
169. CASTLEBERRY, MARTHA, age 67
Minzie, F/W, daughter, age 32.
Hattie, F/W, wife, age 30.
170. PRINCE, RENEAU , M/W, age 24.
Annie, F/W, wife, age 21.
Edward R., M/W, son, age 1.
171. BEASLY, HARRY, M/W, age 37.
Jennie, F/W, wife, age 32.
Jenanett, F/W, daughter, age 14.
Edward, M/W, son, age 8.
Harry, M/W, son, age 6.
172. HUDDLESON, WALTER, M/B, age ?.
Inez, F/B, wife, age 17.
173. KNUCKLES, JESS, M/B, age 38.
Willie, F/B, wife, age 37.
Aron, M/B, son, age 16.
MOSLEY, MARY, daughter, age 18.
Mary E., F/B, gr-granddaughter, age ?.
174. BRYANT, ANNIE, F/B, age 28.
Walter, M/W, son, age 15.
175. BOGER, JOHN, M/B, age 25.
Mary B., F/B, wife, age 24.
Sarah, F/B, daughter, age 1.
176. REECE, WILLIAM, M/B, age 27.
Annie, F/B, wife, age 28.
Georgia A., F/B, daughter, age 1.
HILL, GEORGE, M/B, bro-in-law. age 24.
177. WEST, EFFIE, F/W, age 42.
178. HARDGG, O., M/W, age 50.
Mary, C, F/W, wife, age 48.
Oscar., M/W, son, age 15.
Marie, F/W, daughter, age 48.
Eleanor, F/W, daughter, age 10.
Anna, F/W, daughter, age 5.
George W, M/W, son, age 1.
179. ?COOPER, JOSEPH, M/W, age ?.
180. TATBALL, H.A., M/W, age 72.
?ROE, ANNIE, F/W, age 36.
?PRICE, JAMES, F/W, age 14.
181. DECKER, JOHNNIE, F/W, age 41.
182. RICE, WILLIE W., F/B, age 19.
Martha G, F/B, wife, age 18.
MCFARLAND, JULIA, age 30.
DAVIS, THERMON, M/B, age 20.
184. ELLIOTT, SARAH, F/W, age 55.
?CHITCHIN, CLARA, servant, age ?
185. DABNEY, LELA, F/W, age, A69.
EGGLESTON, SARAH, sister, age 81.
186. COLMORE, ROBERT L., age 70.
Lizzie, F/W, daughter, age 39.
E. illegible, F/W, daughter, age 33.
187. CUNNINGHAM, PIERCY, age 55.
Roberta C., F/W, wife, age 47.
George, M/W, son, age 13.
188. HODGSON, TELFAIR, M/W, age 43.
Medora, F/W, wife, age 41.
Alice, F/W, daughter, age 1.
ROBERTSON, HETTIE, F/W, aunt, age 50.
PALMER, SALLIE, F/B, servant, age 80.
189. CASTLEBERRY, MARION, age 33.
Annie, F/W, wife, age 32.
Marion, M/W, son, age 6.
John, M/W, son, age 3.
Albert A., M/W, age 1.
190. MACKELLAR, WILLIAM H., age 52.
Elizabeth, F/W, wife, age 52.
Juliet, F/W, daughter, age 25.

191. WARE, SEDLEY, M/W, age 51.
Alice, F/W, wife, age 45.
William L., M/W, son, age 17.
John, M/W, son, age 16.
Mary, F/W, daughter, age 12.
Elizabeth, F/W, daughter, age 8.
Alice, F/W, daughter, age 6.
?, Madeline, illegible.
MILLER, MAGGIE, F/B, servant, age 24.

192. BENEDICT, T?illegible, age 55.
Lydia, F/W, wife, age 51.
Samuel, M/W, son, age 17.
Cooper P., M/W, son, age 12.
CRADYTON, ELIZABETH, illegible.
MCALLAH, WILLIAM, son-in-law, age 21.
Oliver, M/W, age 1.
HAWKINS, MARGUERITE, servant age 26.
GARNER, WILLIE M., F/W, servant, age 16.
FAURET, MARY, F/W, servant, age 60.

193. HULLIHEN, WALTER, M/W, age 44.
Madell, F/W, wife, age 38.
Louise W, F/W, daughter, age 11.
Frances H., F/W, daughter, age 8.

194. MYERS, ERNEST R., M/W, age 35.
Ranee D., F/W, wife, age 33.
Vernon B., M/W, son, age 14.
An illegible, F/W, dau., age 10.

195. BATEMAN, JANE, F/W, age 55.
Long, Dortha, F/W, gr-illegible.

196. BONHOLZER, JOHN, M/W, age 64.
Margrett, F/W, daughter, age 38.
Katie, F/W, daughter, age 36.
John W., M/W, son, age 32.
Andrew, M/W, son, age 26.

197. STUDENT NURSES:
SUDDITH, CARRIE H. head nurse. F/W, age 37.
Hayes, Sarah, F/W, age 21.
Griffith, Hazel A., F/W, age 15.
Luitman, Ruth E, F/W, age 20.
O'Dell, Mary, F/W, age 19.
Brooks, Lois L., F/W, age 15.

198. SIMMONS, GEORGE W., age 48.
Doris, F/B, wife, age 41.
Robert, M/B, son, age 17.

199. ?JAMES, HENRY A., M/W, age 53.
Agnes, F/W, wife, age 46.
Emilie N., F/W, daughter, age 11.
Elishie, F/W, daughter, age 11.
Margaret, F/W, daughter, age 9.
NATHEAST, EMILY L, F/W, age 60, sister-in-law.
SIMMONS, KITTY, F/W, age 32.

200. ?LEAR, ALLEN, M/W, age 32.
Mary A., F/W, wife, age 25.
James, M/W, son, age 4.
SIMMONS, BERTHA, F/W, 48.

201. ANDERSON, GEORGE P., age 28.
Willie A., F/W, wife, age 25.
Clara, F/W, daughter, age 6.
John, M/W, son, age 4.
George, M/W, son, age 1.

202. FINNEY, LEE A., M/W, age 50.
Sallie, F/W, wife, age 32.
Burford, M/W, son, age 10.
Josephine, F/W, daughter, age 4.

203. KIRBY SMITH, L. M/W., age 45.
Maude T., F/W, wife, age 37.
Reynolds M., M/W, son, age 15.
Henry, M/W, son, age 12.
Elizabeth, F/W, daughter, age 9.
John S., M/W, son, age 5.
Edwin, M/W, son, age 3.
Catherine, F/W, daughter, age 1.
SHEARD, BESSIE, F/B, age 38.
MANN, ALMA, F/B, servant, age 22.

204. LACKWOOD, EMMA, F/W, age 29.
Randolph, M/W, son, age 6.
DEWEY, EMMA S., F/W, mother, age 68.

205. NUGENT, GEORGE W., age 57.
Manerby, F/W, wife, age 50.
Dara W., F/W, daughter, age 21.
Livey, F/W, daughter, age 17.
George, M/W, son, age 14.
William B., M/W, son, age 10.
Avilda, F/W, daughter, age 6.

206. STEPHENS, WILLIAM, M/W, age 48.
Dellah, F/W, wife, age 37.
Rainey, M/W, son, age 18.
Cara, F/W, daughter, age 16.
Ema, F/W, daughter, age 14.
Howard, M/W, son, age 13.
Andy, M/W, son, age 12.
Arrie, M/W, son, age 8.

207. STEPHENS, NANCY, F/W, age 66.

208. SCOTT, ?IRV, M/W, age 33.
Eline, F/W, wife, age 24.
Ervin, M/W, son, age 2.
Walter, M/W, son, age 1.

209. MOONEY, RICHARD, M/W, age 72.
Catherine, F/W, wife, age 62.
Flora, F/W, daughter, age 21.
Preston, M/W, gr-son, age 14.
Annie, F/W, gr-daughter, age 3.

210. MOONEY, CHARLES W., M/W, age 36.
Martha, F/W, wife, age 35.
Catherine, F/W, daughter, age 15.
Irene, F/W, daughter, age 11.
Gloria, F/W, daughter, age 8.
Gladis, F/W, daughter, age 6.
Charlene, F/W, daughter, age 4.

211. PHILLIPS, HARRY, M/W, age 36.
Ella, F/W, wife, age 25.
Ella P., F/W, daughter, age 11.
Nancy, F/W, daughter, age 8.
Henriette, F/W, daughter, age 1.
SMITH, MINNIE L., F/MU, age 40.
MCBEE, DELLA, F/W, age 19.

212. NICHOLSON, JOHN P., M/W, age 30.
Gladys, F/W, wife, age 26.
John H., F/W, son, age 1.

213. EDWARDS, GEORGE, M/W, age 26.
Virginia, F/W, wife, age 30.
Ann B., F/W, daughter, age 4.
John M., M/W, son, age 2.

214. WELLS, CHARLES, M/W, age 47.
Marrie, F/W, wife, age 45.
GODDARD, WILLIAM W., M/W father-in-law, age 83.

215. MONLEY, GEORGE M., age 38.
Elizabeth, F/W, wife, age 29.
MINNS, MARGARET B., F/W, grandmother, age 81.

216. MARE, ANDREW M., M/W, age 60.
SONTARAN, MARY, F/W, daughter, age 36.
Cynthia, F/W, gr-daughter, age 7.
Charles A., M/W, gr-son, age 5.
FINLY, LOUISE, boarder, age 42.

217. SIMS, HUBERT, M/W, age 43.
Eloise, F/W, wife, age 43.
Peter M., M/W, son, age 8.

218. HUDDLESTON, WM. H., age 28.
Lila, F/B, wife, age 23.
KIRBY G. K., M/W, age 35.
Leon D., M/W, son, age 16.
Eleanor, F/W, daughter, age 10.
Mary G., F/W, daughter, age 9.
John G., M/W, son, age 8.

219. KIRBY, LEON D., M/W, age 45.

220. KNIGHT, ALBION, M/W, age 60.
Marian, F/W, wife, age 42.
RICHARD, ADA K., F/W, daughter, age 26.
Elza, F/W, gr-daughter, age 3.
YATES, POWELL, step-son, age 15.
SHARK, SINA, F/B, servant, age 49.
ALOGE, EVA, F/B, servant, age 14.
HARRIS, LENA, F/B, servant, age 28.

221. DUBOSE, WM. H., M/W, age 49.
Deane S., F/W, wife, age 48.
William H., M/W, son, age 9.
Suzie P., F/W, sister, age 53.
May P., F/W, sister, age 51.
TODD, LAURA, F/W, servant, age 18.

222. WEST, ANNA, F/W, age 67.
STOCKDALE, MARGRET E., F/W, sister, age 65.
Florance, F/W, niece, age 38.
FOSTOR, BESSIE, F/W, age 32.
Virginia, F/W, boarder, age 9.

223. HOLLAND, EMMA, F/W, age 49.

224. UNDERWOOD, CHARLES, age ?
Annie, F/W, wife, age 57.
Carlis, M/W, son, age 8.

225. RODGERS, ILLEGIBLE, age 43.
C., F/W, wife, age 40.
W. H., M/W, son, age 14.
Mary K., F/W, daughter, age 10.
SCHNEIDER, WILLIAM, boarder, 21.

226. OSBORNE, FRANCIS M., age 40.
Mary W., F/W, wife, age 38.
Francis, F/W, daughter, age 19.

227. EGGLESTON, MARY M, age 38.
Jack, M/W, son, age 14.

228. WARE, JOHN, M/W, age 37.
Dora, F/W, wife, age 33.
Dora, F/W, daughter, age 3.

229. SELDEN, MARY, F/W, age 68.

230. MCCRADY, SARAH, F/W, age 79.
Catherine, F/W, daughter, age 43.

231. WICK, CELESTE, F/W, age ?4.

232. KNEATFEL, WM., M/W, age 47.
Emma, F/W, wife, age 39.
Rudolph, M/W, son, age 13.
Evelin, F/W, daughter, age 9.

233. BOWMAN, FLORENCE A., age 45.
LEWIS, FLORENCE A., dau., age 20.
ALEXANDER, MARY P., mother, age 86.
DALLENRY, ROBRT W., boarder, age 23.

234. BAKER, GEORGE M., age 40.
Grase, F/W, wife, age 38.

235. SNEED, ALBERT C., M/W, age 52.
Mary E., F/W, wife, age 48.
Virginia, F/W, daughter, age 37.

236. LONG, LEM T., M/W, age 37.
Elizabeth, F/W, wife, age 38.
Gertrude, F/W, daughter, age 15.
Gladis, F/W, daughter, age 11.
Haden, M/W, son, age 7.

237. ANDISON, LOUISE P., F/W, age 47.
Lomax, M/W, son, age 13.
238. ARLEDGE, AND?, M/B, age 38.
Anna, F/MU, wife, age 36.
239. COLYAR, JOHN, F/B, age 50.
Daisy, F/B, daughter, age 37.
Garrett, M/B, son, age 14.
Eslie, F/B, daughter, age 12.
Sarah, F/B, daughter, age 8.
Carline, F/B, daughter, age 5.
Virginia, F/B, daughter, age 3.
David, M/B, son, age 1.
240. HILL, HUGH, F/B, age 41.
Lula, F/B, wife, age 36.
Robbie, F/B, daughter, age 10.
A.C., M/B, son, age 8.
241. GARNER, GEORGE W, M/MU, age 76.
Rachel, F/B, wife, age 40.
242. MARE, FLOYD, M/B, age 46.
Litha, F/B, wife, age 42.
Addie, F/B, daughter, age 13.
Hellen, F/B, daughter, age 6.
Floyd, M/B, son, age 5.
COOLEY, HAZEL, ?/B, age 14.
243. WINN, LEMMEL C., M/W, age 35.
Mahaly J., F/W, wife, age 30.
Robert, M/W, son, age 12.
Lila M., F/W, daughter, age 10.
Raymond, M/W, son, age 8.
Mary, F/W, daughter, age 5.
Robert, M/W, father, age 57.
Francis, F/W, mother, age 60.
244. HUNZIKER, THOMAS A., age 35.
Stella, F/W, wife, age 26.
Virginia, F/W, daughter, age 10.
Edgar, M/W, son, age 7.
Howard, M/W, son, age 3.
Aimy, F/W, daughter, age 1.
245. MYERS, WILLIAM L., M/W, age 68.
Elizabeth, F/W, wife, age 70.
William C., M/W, son, age 31.
Beatrice J., F/W, daughter, age 29.
246. ANDERSON, WILLIAM P., age 38.
Ida M., F/W, wife, age 29.
247. HOSKINS, HENRY, M/W, age 50.
Ada, F/W, wife, age 48.
James, M/W, gr-son, age 10.
Henry J., M/W, gr-son, age 13.
WILLIAMS, FIATE, M/MU, servant, age 38.
248. HILL, LILLARD J, M/MU, age 33.
Bell R., F/B, wife, age 22.
Laura, F/MU, daughter, age 4.
William, M/ Mu, son, age 3.
249. POSLEY, JANE, F/B, age 26.
James, M/B, son, age 10.
250. NEVELS, JAMES V., age 37.
Tersa, F/B, wife, age 37.
Fred, M/B son, age 18.
Matilda, F/B, mother, age 77.
Louise, F/B, dau-in-law, age 17.
251. CHILDRESS, ALPHERD, age 52.
Engie, F/B, wife, age 32.
252. HUDDLESTON, WILLIAM S., age 60.
Louis, M/B, son, age 25.
Benjamin, M/B, son, age 14.
253. GREEN, JOHN W, M/B, age 63.
Annie, F/B, wife, age 53.
Lena, F/B, daughter, age 13.
254 BROWN, MARY, F/B, age 97.
COLYAR, CASSIE, F/B, granddaughter, age 21.
GRAY, C?, F/B, boarder, age 24.
255. COWAN, JOHN, M/B, age 30.
Esmer, F/B, wife, age 28.
256. CHILDRESS, ROBERT, F/B, age 34.
Ada, F/B, wife, age 30.
257. BRYAN, BENJAMIN, M/MU, age 38.
Amia, F/MU, wife, age 24.
Lucile, F/MU, daughter, age 7.
Dabney, M/MU, son, age 4.
258. PATTON, RUFUS, M/B, age 31.
Eliza, F/B, wife, age 22.
Tommie R., M/B, son, age 3/
Sammie, F/B, daughter, age 2.
259. KENERLY, JOHN B., F/B, age ?6.
MILLER, OTSIE, F/B, dau., age 22.
Edward, M/B, son-in-law, age 22.
John, M/B, grandson, age 3.
260. KEITH, JOHN H., F/B, age 38.
Birdie, F/B, wife, age 35.
Arledge, Lucill, F/B, step-dau, age 20.
261. CHEATHAM, WILL, M/MU, age 50.
Carrie, F/B, wife, age 38.
TRAVIS, ALLIN, step-dau., age 19.
LANE, MARY L., boarder, age 37;
262. SMITH, SALLIE, F/B, age 66.
Huston, M/B, son, age 29.
Simon, M/B, son, age 25.
Lillie, F/B, dau.-in-law, age 21.
263. BRYAN, TAILOR Z., M/B, age 70.
Oscar, M/B, son, age 41.
264. DAVIS, THOMAS, M/B, age 32.
Leora, F/B, wife, age 22.
Christine, F/B, daughter, age 13.
Scott, M/B, brother, age 39.

265. SIMS, WILLIE, M/B, age 45.
Mollie, F/B, wife, age 28.
Lula B., F/B, daughter, age 12.
Frana, F/B, daughter, age 10.
Nevada, M/B, son, age 8.
John H., M/B, son, age 7.
266. WOOTTON, WALTER, M/B, age 32.
Eila, F/B, wife, age 30.
OSBORNE, SAMUEL, M/B, brother-in-law, age 38.
267. WINTON, HARRETT, F/B, age 56.
268. TRIMBLE, JOSEPH W., M/B, age 23.
Fannie, F/B, wife, age 22.
Elzabett, F/B, daughter, age 6.
RUTLEDGE, LYDIA, F/B, age 41, mother-in-law.
269. ROWE, WILLIAM, M/MU, age 40.
Azzie, F/B, wife, age 40.
270. MOSLEY, RULFES, M/B, age 65.
Mollie, F/B, wife, age 56.
Amos, M/B, son, age 17.
George, M/B, son, age 11.
Augstine, M/B, gr-son, age 6.
271. HAWKINS, HELARIS L., age 30.
Mary E, F/W, wife, age 29.
Hellen E., F/W, daughter, age 3.
272. HOPKINS, Mamie, F/W, age 24.
Pearl, F/W, sister, age 19.
273. GIPSON, THOMAS A., M/W, age 22.
Sallie, F/W, wife, age 21.
J. L., M/W, son, age illegible.
Annie M., F/W, daughter, age 1.
274. PRINCE, WILLIAM J., M/W, age 31.
Bessie, F/W, wife, age 28.
Leon, F/W, son, age 4.
275. SIMMONS, JAMES H., M/W, age 47.
Mary O., F/W, wife, age 42.
Vina, F/W, mother, age 72.
MCBEE, BEUFORD W., M/W, step-son, age 15.
Irene, F/W, step-daughter, age 13.
Hayden, M/W, step-son, age 10.
276. FOSTER, RAINEY, M/W, age 20.
Wallie, F/W, wife, age 21.
277. RILEY, ROBERT, M/W, age 51.
Viola E., F/W, wife, age 47.
Carl G., M/W, son, age 19.
Christine, F/W, daughter, age 20.
Olive, F/W, daughter, age 17.
Patric, M/W, son, age 16.
Nolan, M/W, son, age 12.
278. PERRY, SAMUEL M., M/W, age 55.
Mary, F/W, wife, age 48.
Robert W., M/W, son, age 22.
Mary, F/W, daughter, age 19.
John W., M/W, son, age 16.
279. BRATTON, ROSCOE L., F/W, age 33.
Flora, F/W, wife, age 29.
Gordon, M/W, son, age 3.
280. HAWKINS, HARRY, M/W, age 37.
Irene, F/W, daughter, age 12.
Walter E, F/W, son, age 11.
Paul, M/W, son, age 9.
Louise, F/W, daughter, age 7.
Annie, F/W, dau., age 6.
RAY, LOUISER, mother-in-law, 63.
281. GREEN, GEORGE W., M/W, age 39.
Lena, F/W, wife, age 38.
Maxey, M/W, son, age 16.
Herman, M/W, son, age 11.
John, M/W, son, age 10.
Albert, M/W, son, age 8.
Aimy, F/W, daughter, age 3.
Una, F/W, daughter, age 1.
Mary L., F/W, daughter, age 1.
ARN, MARY, F/W, mother-in-law, 67.
282. BIERY, SAMUEL, M/W, age 65.
Mary, F/W, wife, age 55.
283. POWELL, HOMAR, M/W, age 39.
Kathryn, F/W, wife, age 35.
284. HOLDEN, SAMUEL, M/B, age 62.
285. MCKAY, MARY S., F/W, age 52.
Earnest, M/W, son, age 20.
William, M/W, son, age 14.
286. NAUTS, WILLIAM B., M/W, age 59.
?Look C. H., wife, F/W, age 50.
William B. Jr., M/W, age 17.
Richard L., M/W, age 15.
KEITH, JAMES R., M/B, age 39.
Luela, F/B, Wife, age 38.
Seargie L., F/B, daughter, age 14.
Clarence, F/B, son, age 12.
Johnnie M., F/MU, niece, age 4.
287. WOODS, HENRY, M/MU, age 55.
Sallie A., F/MU, wife, age 53.
Alexander, M/MU, son, age 15.
TAYLOR, CARY M., F/MU, gr-daughter, age 10.
288. BONHOLZER, FRED J., M/W, age 36.
Florence, F/W, wife, age 35.
289. KNOTT, MARION F., M/W, age 52.
Alice, F/W, wife, age 44.
Sterlin, M/W, son, age 17.
James H., M/W, son, age 15.
Sherill, F/W, daughter, age 13.
Bessie M., F/W, daughter, age 10.
Francis R., M/W, son, age 6.

290. KNOTT, ROBRT L., M/W, AGE 24.
Dorivil, F/W, wife, age 21.
Francis, M/W, son, age 2.
SUTHERLAND, ROXANA, F/W, grandmother, age 77.

291. FRY, JESSIE, M/W, age 58.
Martha J., F/W, wife, age 62.

292. TRIPP, ROBERT A., M/W, age 28.
Lena, F/W, wife, age 26.
Sarah E., F/W, daughter, age 3.
Ruthie, F/W, daughter, age 1.
John W., F/W, brother, age 20.
Sarah, F/W, mother, age 66.

293. REED, JOHN, M/W, age 60.
Charlie, M/W, son, age 15.
Effie, F/W, daughter, age 12.
Speaker, M/W, son, age 10.

294. SUTHERLAND, JAMES C., age 59.
Mary D., F/W, wife, age 56.
George, M/W, son, age 29.
Cara, F/W, daughter, age 23.
Lillie, F/W, daughter, age 20.
John, M/W, son, age 18.
Katie, F/W, daughter, age 15.

295. OWENS, CHARLES, M/W, age 36.
Jessie, F/W, wife, age 38.
William, M/W, son, age 9.
Philip, M/W, son, age 7.
Mary E., F/W, daughter, age 3.
WALKER, RANEE, step-dau., age 15.
PIERCE, JAMES E., M/W, father-in-law, age 63.

296. SIMMONS, GEORGE, M/B, age 50.
Davis, F/B, wife, age 35.
Robert, M/B, son, age 17.

297. CHILDRESS, WILLIAM, MB, age 41.
Grace, F/B, wife, age 39.
Alexander, M/B, son, age 19.
William, M/B, son, age 16.

298. TRIGG, POSS, M/B, age 29.
Laura, F/B, daughter, age 1.

SAINT'S MARY SCHOOL

SNOWDEN, HUETTA, HEAD NUN. age 71.
GALT, HERBERTA, age 69.
CUNNINGHAM, AGNES, age 59.
SEARCY, MARTHA, age 59.
WINNE, SUSAN, age 55.
MACKAY, ERMAN, age 52.
WASHER, GLADYS, age 39.
WASHER, JULIA, age 20.
PEYTON, MARGRIT, age 26.
RUTHERFORD, MARY, age 38.

According to the 1920 census records, the Sherwood Road was called the Sewanee and Lost Cove Road. Families living on this road are numbered from 1 through 32 in the above census records. The families starts with Sarah O'Dear and ends with Sarah Prince. Families living on Harrison Chapel Road are listed from 33 through 42 in the census records. The Harrison Chapel Road families starts with Robert Dyer and ends with James Green.

People living on the Monteagle Road are numbered 43 through 49 in the census. Starting at William Church's house and ending at James Clark's house. People living on the Monteagle Road starts again with number 53 and goes through 64. The houses on the Monteagele Road starts with Emil Hunzikers's and ends with Robert Campbell and his group of employees. I think Robert Campbell was living at the Sand Cut and the employees were working there.

People living in the railroad section houses on the side of the mountain going to Cowan, at numbered from 50 through 52 in the census records. These families starts at James Foster's house and ends at Joseph Barry's house. People living on the Jump Off Road are numbered from 65 to 86 in the census. Starting at Mary Hunziker's house and ending at James Mead's house. People living on the Hawkins Cove Road starts with number 87 and ends at 90. Starting at William Farris' and ending at Sarah Hoge's house.

People living on the Dixie Highway (41A/64) are numbered 91 through 108, in the census records. Starting at William Arnold's and ending with James Castleberry's house. Bob Town Road starts with number 109 and ends with 129, in the census records . Beginning at Jennie Prince's house and ending at Robert Baronet's house. People living on Main Street (University Avenue) starts with number 130 and ends with 195. Beginning at Samuel Reynolds' house and ending at Jane Bateman's house. Families living on Morgan Steep Road starts with 196 and ends with 198, in the census. Starting at John Bonholzer's house and ending at George Simmons' house.

Families living near Main Street numbered from 199 through 229, in the census Starting at Henry James' house and ending at Sarah McCrady's. People living on Alabama Avenue number from 230 to 240. Starting with Celeste Wicks' house and ending at Floyd Mare's house.

People living on Alabama Avenue, near the railroad starts with number 241 and ends with 262. People with homes located in this area begins with Lemuel Winn and ends with Thomas Davis. Numbers 263 through 279, on the census records, are for people living off the road leading to Monteagle. Starting with census number 280 and ending with 282. These families lived from Harry Hawkins' house to Homar Powell's house. People living near the Monteagle Road went from census number 283 to 298. Beginning at Samuel Holden's house and ending at Poss Trigg's house. The Nuns and facility were located at St. Mary School, off the Sewanee Lost Cove Road.

All the above information was taken from the 1920 Franklin County, Tennessee, 18th District, census records. There were 298 heads of hold listed in the 1920 census. There were nuns and their assistants listed at St. Mary's Episcopal School totaling 10 people. The students at St. Mary's and the University of the South were not listed in 1920 census. They were probably counted in their home states.

ADDITIONAL INFORMATION

The following data is on people who were found in the 1870, 1880, 1900, 1910, and 1920 census records. The 1890 census records were destroyed. Various records were checked to provide more information than was found in the census records. The same numbering system that was used for each individual census year is also being used to present the data. If no additional information was found concerning a family or individual, their number will be left out of the sequential numbering order. The names are printed as they appear on the various census records or other records. Many times names were not spelled the same. To better understand the data, a comparison of the corresponding census records may be helpful.

The information listed within this section was extracted from the following books in order to further expand the census information:

Marriage Records of Franklin County, Tennessee 1838-1875, Transcribed by Billie and Hall Burks. (Winchester 1979)

Marion County Tennessee Cemetery Records, Compiled by Mary S. Harris and Euline Harris (Evansville 1987)

Franklin County, Marriages 1884-1903, Compiled by Shirley Russell Conn and Robert W. Conn (1991)

Franklin County, Tennessee Family Histories, 1807-1996, by thr Franklin County Historical Society (Paducah 1996)

Men Who Made Sewanee, by Arthur Ben and Elizabeth N. Chitty (Sewanee 1981)

Cemetery Records of Franklin County, Tennessee, Compiled by the Franklin County Historical Society (Baltimore 1984)

Purple Sewanee, by Lily Baker, Charlotte Gailor, Rose Duncan Lovell, and Sarah Hodgson Torian (Sewanee 1932 Reprint 1961)

A Journey Through History With The Short and Barnes Families, Compiled and Written by Patricia Short Makris (Rolla 1992)

DATA FOR PEOPLE LIVING AT SEWANEE DURING THE 1870 CENSUS

1. THOMAS A. MORRIS was a minister who at one time lived in Winchester, Tennessee.
2. GEORGE FAIRBANKS was one of the original trustees at the University of the South.
4. SARAH COTTON ran a boarding house for students in early Sewanee.
5. JOHN PHELAN was a judge who lived in the University of the South.
6. BISHOP WILLIAM MERCER GREEN was the Bishop of Mississippi.
7. ELIZABETH POLK is probably related to Bishop Leonidas Polk.
8. FRANK PRATT was one of the early carpenters at Sewanee.
9. JOHN PRATT was an early carpenter at Sewanee.
10. JOHN H. BURKS was an early merchant in the village of Sewanee.
14. J. M. COTTON was the son-in-law of Bishop William Mercer Green. J. M. was born on February 2, 1842, and died on December 31, 1915. He served in the Confederate Army. His wife was Sarah "Sally" Green born 1845, and died 1817.
16. JOHN BERRY also known as John Barry was born on August 5, 1840, and died September 10, 1914. His wife, Rachel, was born October 20, 1842, and died February 10, 1920. John was an early railroad boss at Sewanee.
21. BIRD ANDERSON'S real name was Albert. Albert was born March 15, 1815, and died February 21, 1885. Mary Anderson was born April 5, 1818, and died July 20, 1888.
22. JOHN ANDERSON married Elizabeth Winford on January 7, 1869.
24. JOHN GARNER married M. J. Kelly on April 24, 1866.
26. WILLIAM G. HILL married Martha M. Sansom on September 4, 1865.
27. F. B. FARRIS married Martha Henley on July 11, 1838. Fletcher B. Farris was born June 29, 1813, and died February 18, 1879. Martha Farris was born September 12, 1818, and died April 15, 1900.
28. PERNEGY PACK was born June 28, 1835, and died October 23, 1903.
31. FRANCIS MARION HILL married Sarah Ann Gipson on December 14, 1860.
33. T. S. SEVIER was the head master and commandant of the cadets. SAMUEL HOGE was an early merchant in the village of Sewanee.
34. WILLIAMSON TOMLINSON was born in 1828, and died on January 9, 1878. He was the first postmaster at Sewanee, an early merchant, and ran the first hotel. He served in the Confederate Army.
36. CLAIBORNE C. ROSE married Amanda S. Crownover. C. C. Rose was born April 6, 1818, and died December 6, 1887. Amanda was born July 6, 1814. Claiborne was a Justice of Peace at Sewanee. He married a man claiming to be John Wilkes Booth.
37. REBECCA CASTLEBERRY.
38. ALLEN GIPSON was born in 1804, in Laurens County, South Carolina. His first wife was Annie Long. His second marriage to Minerva Garner took place on January 3, 1855. He was a merchant and a Justice of the Peace. He was an early settler in Rowarks Cove. He gave land for the University of the South.
39. ANDREW GIPSON married Elizabeth "Betsy" Hill on March 2, 1849.
44. HANSFORD H. ROBERTS married Mary E. Lynch on March 7, 1851. Hance died January 9, 1875, at age 55. Hance's mother, Julia Roberts, died January 4, 1875, at age 82. Hance was living at Sewanee when the bishops arrived in 1858.
45. JAMES O'DEAR was born May 6,1797, and died March 19, 1883. He was the first person buried in the cemetery that now bears his name on Sherwood Road. He was a blacksmith and a veteran of the War of 1812.
49. PATTON WEAVER married Mary Gibson McKnight on August 23, 1859. Patton was a railroad worker and a veteran of the Civil War. Mary Gibson McKnight is the daughter of David and Nancy Morris Gibson. The Gibsons were early settlers in Rowarks Cove and early residents of Sewanee.
50. WILLIAM BOHANNON married Nancy Ann Smith. William was a railroad worker.
51. Nancy McKnight was born January 10, 1854, and died January 5, 1941. She was the daughter of James and Mary Gibson McKnight. She married Allen Hill on August 24, 1867. Their daughter

Margaret "Peggy" Hill was born February 10, 1869, in Rowarks Cove. Peggy married Robert McCreary on February 3, 1889. Allen McCreary, a long time resident of Sewanee, was their son. Robert was born in January 1869, and was killed by a train in the 1930's. Robert was half Cherokee Indian

52. ANDREW JACKSON SHORT married Americas Elizabeth "Lizzie" Lindsey on November 1, 1869. Andrew was better known as General Short. He was born on May 11, 1851, and died April 10, 1922, at Bridgeport, Alabama. Lizzie was the adopted daughter of Mr. and Mrs. Lindsey. Andrew was the youngest son of Jesse and Mary Evans Short of Georgia. Andrew was an early stone mason at Sewanee.

53. FRANKLIN SHORT was born in 1843, in Chambers County, Alabama. He was the son of Jesse and Mary Evans Short. Frank was a master stone mason at Sewanee during the early years. He was the major builder of the first sandstone depot at Sewanee. He and his wife, Alice, along with Alice's son, Columbus, lived near the depot in Sewanee. Frank died in Decherd and is buried in the University of the South Cemetery with Alice and Columbus. He helped build many of the original rock buildings in the University of the South. His brother is the above Andrew and Reuben Boaz Short who married Julia Ann Austin. The Shorts now living at Sewanee descend from Reuben. Some of Reuben's descendants were also stone masons that helped build many of the rock buildings in the University of the South.

56. PLEASANT GILLIAM was the son of Thomas and Elizabeth. He owned the first store in Sewanee. At one time he was a post master in Grundy County.

59. CHARLIE PORTER was an engineer for the train called the "Mountain Goat."

61. JAMES SERGEANT married Serena Cowan on October 28, 1868.

62. LENT WILLIAMS married Violet McIlherron on December 31, 1840. Lent was the son of Sherrod and Polly Looney Williams. Lent probably lived on land at Sewanee that was part of his father's land grant.

DATA FOR PEOPLE LIVING AT SEWANEE DURING THE 1880 CENSUS

1. SAMUEL C. HOGE married Sarah Temmie Holland. He was an early merchant and Justice of Peace at Sewanee. Sarah ran a boarding house.
2. FANNIE MOORE PRESTON was born on May 18, 1837, and died May 5, 1930. She ran a boarding house for students at the University of the South.
3. CHARLES H. WADHAMS was born March 11, 1828, and died December 12, 1897. He was born near Edinburgh, Scotland. Elizabeth Gibson Wadhams was born May 27, 1827, died March 7, 1899. Elizabeth W. Wadhams was born in 1858, and died in 1938. They are all buried in the University of the South Cemetery.
7. CASKIE HARRISON taught Latin and Greek at the University of the South.
9. JOHN GIPSON married Virginia Ellen Reed on March 14, 1872.
12. JAMES H. HARRISON married Sallie A. Gipson on December 23, 1867. James was born March 6, 1845, and died April 12, 1896. Sallie died in 1911.
13. FRANKLIN SHORT was an early stone mason at Sewanee. He helped build many of the early stone buildings at Sewanee.
15. MELMUTH COKER married Milly Gipson on November 1, 1841. She was the daughter of David and Nancy Morris Gipson of Laurens County, South Carolina. Their children were: James C.; Sarah; Amanda; and Nancy J. Coker who married a Stephens.
16. J. L. ARNOLD married Sallie Davis on October 6, 1874.
18. WILLIAM L. MYERS married Elizabeth J. McBride.
21. W. H. JOHNSON was born December 20, 1847, died May 7, 1890. Sarah E. Johnson was born November 1, 1852, and died November 11, 1936.
23. RICHARD MOONEY was born 1850, and died July 4, 1920. Catherine Mooney was born February 16, 1857, and died February 4, 1936. John S. Mooney was born April 6, 1874, and died April 12, 1963. Sarah A. Mooney, wife of John S. Mooney, was born June 27, 1879, and died June 27, 1967.
26. WILLIAM FREDERICK FISCHER was a well-known German cabinet maker at Sewanee.
27. ANDREW JACKSON SHORT married Elizabeth Lindsey. Their children were: David Sylvanes; Reuben John; George; Joseph Andrew; William; Rose; Alice; Frank; and Edward. Andrew was a railroad worker and stone mason at Sewanee.
31. CHRISTIAN RUEF owned a meat market at Sewanee. He was from Switzerland. He killed animals at the slaughter pen rock in Bob Town on a daily basis, so that, his customers would have fresh meat.
32. SARAH "SALLY" CASTELBERRY was born in March 1809, and died November 15, 1887. She was the wife of John Castleberry.
40. LEON PILLET was a French tailor at Sewanee. He was buried on December 31, 1907. His daughter was Alice Mariette Pillet born January 10, 1878, and died February 26, 1878.
41. CAROLYN WILDER LIDE GILLIAM was the wife of Pleasant Gilliam. She was born August 7, 1826, and died August 31, 1889. Her children were: Thomas D.; Mary E.; and James P. who was born November 18, 1860, and died November 18, 1910. James P. married Elizabeth Nolan who was born March 6, 1869, and died May 1898.
42. BARTLEY SUTHERLAND was a Confederate veteran. James C. Sutherland was born October 21, 1859, and died April 13, 1927. James' wife, Mary Miller Sutherland, was born November 21, 1858, and died February 27, 1935.
43. D. C. RICE married Martha Jane Crabtree on September 14, 1860.
44. NANCY AUSTIN MONTGOMERY was born September 10, 1821, and died March 19, 1887. She married Milton Montgomery on January 19, 1843. Milton was born April 2, 1811, and died September 30, 1879. Milton's family were among the earliest settlers in Franklin County. He was featured in a book titled "Sam Tag" that can be found in the Franklin County Historical Society in Winchester, Tennessee. Milton had strong ties to the Confederate Army during the Civil War. John Austin Montgomery was born April 18, 1863, and died March 7, 1894. Luther High Montgomery was born February 18, 1855, and died March 18, 1926.

46. MISOLYN "MARY" SHORT married William Thomas on December 30, 1865. William "Buck" Thomas was the son of John and Matilda Morgan Thomas. Mary was the daughter of Jesse and Mary Evans Short. The Shorts and Thomas's were early members of Saint-Pauls-on-the-Mountain Episcopal Church. William was an early stone mason at Sewanee.
47. RICHARD JEFFERSON MESSICK was born October 10, 1866, and died September 20, 1904.
48. P. TATE STATUM married Elizabeth J. Hiles on March 5, 1858.
49. MARY ANN PRINCE was born March 1, 1825, and died August 11, 1883. She was the mother of W. J. Prince, and Robert H. Prince who was born April 27, 1861, and died November 27, 1901.
56. ELIZABETH OWENS was born October 2, 1842, and died May 5, 1901.
58. JOSEPH AMSTUTZ was born December 23, 1823, in Engilberg, Switzerland, and died May 22, 1916. Joseph was a founder of the Swiss Colony of Gruetli, Tennessee. Anna was born April 16, 1840, and died January 18, 1898. Charley Amstrutz was born May 22, 1883, and died June 18, 1889. Emma Armustrutz married J. P. Price on June 16, 1889. Lena Armstutz married J. H. Fischer on January 14, 1886. Joe Arnstutz married Jennie Walker on October 5, 1892.
61. JENNIE BELLE SUTHERLAND died November 22, 1900, at age 21. James Owden was born March 17, 1868, and died March 4, 1942. Jennie and James were the children of Samuel and Roxanne Sutherland. Cemetery records have James Owden as being Roxanna's husband instead of her son.
62. ALMENDA CASTLEBERRY. James Castleberry married Lillie Castleberry on November 6, 1889.
65. MARY EASTER was the wife of Reverend Harry Easter. Their daughter, Nellie, was born in 1865, and died June 11, 1955, in Washington, D.C. She was the wife of Reverend John Harris. Henry Easter, son of Henry and Mary, was born in 1858, and was buried July 23, 1922.
68. WILLIAM HARLOWE was the first editor of the University News, Free, Frank, and Fearless. He was the editor on May 10, 1876.
88. CARRIE V. JUNY was born March 14, 1832, and died March 23, 1897. Carrie was the widow of Frederick Augustus Juny.
90. WILLIAM PORCHER DUBOSE was born April 11, 1836, and died August 18, 1918. He was the founder, professor and dean of the Theological Department. Maria Louisa Yerger DuBose was born April 14, 1836, and died September 25, 1887. Their daughter, May Peronneau DuBose, was born January 1, 1868, and died October 28, 1960. Maria was the founder of Fairmont College in Monteagle. May was in charge of the college.
91. CHARLOTTE B. B. ELLIOTT died June 27, 1895. She was the daughter of John and Sarah Bull Barnwell. Her husband was Bishop Stephen Elliott, the first Episcopal Bishop of Georgia. Sarah Bull Barnwell, their daughter, was born in 1848, and died in 1928. She and Flora Fairbanks were the first two school teachers in the Sewanee Village. She taught at St. Paul's on the Mountain.
97. JOHN BARNWELL ELLIOTT was in the Confederate Army. He was born in 1841, and died in 1921. He was a teacher, philosopher, and physician. He was the son of Bishop Stephen and Sarah Barnwell Elliott.
98. M. E. HUGER. Mary Esther Huger was born September 13, 1820, and died June 17, 1898. She was the wife of Joseph Alston Huger of South Carolina. Their daughter, Hariott Lucas Huger, was born in 1848, and died in 1931. She married John Barnwell Elliott. Mary Esther, daughter of Mary and Joseph Huger, was born in 1862, and died on August 15, 1902.
99. CLAY BUCHANAN married Agnes Peters on October 2, 1873.
105. JOHN BERRY married Rachel Garner on August 23, 1858.
106. DR. JAMES SEVERIN GREEN was born in 1825 and died in 1900. His wife, Ella Philou W. Green, was born 1842, and died in 1925. Otey Polk Green was born May 10, 1866, and died February 23, 1939. He was married to Virginia Alice Crump. Alice died in 1942, at the age of 73.
107. WILLIAM LESLIE YARWORTH was born September 23, 1861. George W. Yarworth was born January 26, 1865.
108. THOMAS PERRY married Sarah Coker on September 1, 1865. Mary Jane Perry married John Berdin McKnight.
109. WILLIAM TOMLINSON married Delia Jones on December 6, 1871. He ran a hotel at Sewanee.
113. WILLIAM AND EMILY ROSE.

116. MATTIE A. DUBOSE was born May 3, 1836, and died September 14, 1882. She ran a boarding house at Sewanee.

118. PROFESSOR JOHN MCCRADY died in Nashville on his 50th birthday.

119. GENERAL EDMUND KIRBY SMITH was a mathematics teacher at Sewanee. He was born May 16, 1824, and died March 26, 1893. His wife was Cassie Selden. She was born on September 26, 1837, and died November 3,1907.

121. GEORGE RAINSFORD FAIRBANKS was born July 5, 1820, and died August 3, 1906. He was born in Watertown, New York, and served in the Confederate Army. He was a scholarly gentleman who preserved Sewanee's history in his book titled, "History of the University of the South." Much of what is known about early Sewanee was learned from reading his book. His house called the "Rebel's Rest" is still standing proudly in the University of the South. George was first married to Sarah Catherine Wright. His second wife was Susan Beard who was first married to Reverend Benjamin Wright. Susan was born September 8, 1826, and died November 25, 1931. George and Sarah's daughter, Florida, better known as Flora Fairbanks, was born on July 24, 1848, and died November 25, 1931. She and Charlotte Elliott were the first teachers for the Sewanee Village children. They taught at St. Pauls on the Mountain.

125. ALFRED H. ANDERSON married Margaret Finney on November 5, 1855. Their children were: Sarah E.; Mary J.; Nancy E.; Frances C.; Lucy Ann; and Margaret B. Anderson.

131. SOLOMON ROSE married Lucinda Lynch on November 4, 1869. Their oldest son was named Thomas.

132. MARY HUNZIKER was born July 15, 1835, and died September 2, 1927. She was born in Switzerland. Mary's husband was Frederick Hunziker. He died August 10, 1871. Their daughter Emma was born one month after her father's death. She was born on Sept 18, 1871.

133. SAMUEL GOODE JONES was born September 20, 1815, and died October 4, 1886. His wife, Aurora S. Elmore Jones, was born February 1, 1831, and died June 14, 1912. Samuel was the treasurer for the University of the South, ran their coal mines and took care of their hotel business. He was a Colonel in the Confederate Army. His coal mine was on land previously owned by Allen Gipson. His family moved to Montgomery, Alabama.

136. MARIA L. PORCHER was born November 26, 1828, and died November 4, 1910. Maria ran a boarding house at Sewanee. Mary E. Eggleston was born August 16, 1848, and died December 14, 1893.

138. ROBERT MARION DUBOSE was born September 18, 1841, and died October 30, 1907. Elizabeth Egleston DuBose was born November 1, 1849, and died February 25, 1918. Robert M. DuBose Jr. was born August 29, 1874, and died November 19, 1905. Marion Porcher DuBose was born in November 21, 1879, and died July 26, 1911. Robert Marion DuBose served in the Confederate Army.

144. CHARLES TODD QUINTARD was the main driving force behind getting the University of the South rebuilt after the Civil War. He went all over soliciting funds to accomplish the work that had been started by the founders of the University of the South. Bishop Quintard planned and organized the village depot area. He brought business people to the village to provide jobs. Elizabeth Catherine Hand Quintard was Bishop Quintard's wife. His daughter was Clara E. Quintard and his son was George W. Quintard. Bishop Quintard was the first doctor for the village depot people and other people living in the surrounding coves. He was well respected by the mountain residents.

148. JOHN M. COTTON was born February 2, 1842, and died December 13, 1915. He served in the Confederate Army. He married Sarah Green, daughter of Reverend William Mercer Green.

152. R. J. GILLASPIE married Delitha Gipson on April 20, 1872. R. J. was born December 13, 1840, and died December 10, 1868. He served in the Confederate Army. A. D. Gillespie died August 30, 1882. George Gillaspie was born December 23, 1883, and died July 18, 1885. George was the son of R. J. and A.D. Gillaspie.

156. ALLEN GIPSON was born 1851, and died 1898. Lucinda Gipson was born 1836, and died 1899.

157. ANDERSON JOHN NORTHCUTT was born May 3, 1836. Martha Jane Northcutt was born November 13, 1845, and died March 19, 1875. Rebecca Frances Northcutt was born September 8, 1863; Laura Ann Northcutt was born May 4, 1866; Fanny Northcutt was born February 1,

1871; John Robert was born August 18, 1873; Maggie Leila Northcutt was born August 1, 1875. Martha Jane Northcutt's maiden name was Swetton.

159. REUBEN BOAZ SHORT'S wife was Julia Ann Austin Short.
163. JAMES O'DEAR was born May 6, 1797, and died March 19, 1883. James' wife was Sarah O'Dear.
164. JAMES M. GREEN was a miller. James' wife was Martha A. Green. His children were Richard C.; James B.; Martha J; and Joseph Green.
165. WILLIAM R. GREEN married Rebecca Muse on April 21, 1849.
168. HENRY SEWELL was born February 28, 1818, and died August 14, 1881.
170. WILLIAM STEVENS was born 1851, and died 1924. Sallie Stevens was born February 15, 1854, and died March 27, 1947. Lucy was born July 20, 1876, and died February 8, 1893.
176. TAYLOR STEPHENS was married to Martha Bennett on March 18, 1870.
182. IKE W. ANDERSON was born 1848 and died 1935. Lizzie B. was born 1850, and died 1940.
184. TOM WALKER was born 1843, and died 1895. Tom's wife was Nancy Crownover.
191. TELFAIR HODGSON was born March 14, 1840. He married Frances Glen Potter who was born April 16, 1865, and died September 11, 1893. Telfair Jr. was treasurer for the University of the South.
196. JOHN H. BURKS was an early merchant in Sewanee.

DATA FOR PEOPLE LIVING AT SEWANEE DURING THE 1900 CENSUS

1. JAMES C. COLLINS was born July 31, 1852, died December 28, 1938. James married Sarah C. Garner on October 16, 1873. Sarah was born November 20, 1855, and died September 2, 1905. James may be the son of William and Catherine Collins. Jim was one of the founders of the Cumberland Presbyterian Church in Bob Town.
2. SAMUEL BLACK married Josephine "Josie" Posey on May 14, 1895.
3. JAMES 'WHITE' CAMPBELL married Ellen Riley on December 25, 1884. White died 1931, and Ellen died 1922. White was a master stone mason for University of the South. His son Ernest was one of two soldiers from Sewanee to die in World War I. Ernest is buried in the Argonne Forest in France.
5. ANDREW JACKSON "JACK" O'DEAR is the son of James and Sarah O'Dear. He was born August 16, 1836, and died June 17, 1904. He was married to Catherine Mary Garner.
6. JULIA ANN SHORT was born November 1848. She was the daughter of Washington and Mary Gibson Austin. Julia Ann married Reuben Boaz Short on December 1, 1866. He was a Civil War veteran and is buried in the University of the South Cemetery.
8. STEWART, WILLIAM, AND LIZZIE MONTGOMERY are children of Milton and Nancy Austin Montgomery who were early settlers in Franklin County. Stewart was born in 1845, and died 1916. William was born 1847, and died in 1829.
9. HENRY SCHNEICHE was born February 11, 1857, in Switzerland. He was married to Currie maiden name unknown. Henry died November 29, 1916. Currie was born February 29, 1856, and died March 25, 1909. Their name was also spelled Schneider. Henry was a well know cabinet maker.
11. WILLIAM A. GREEN married Sina O'Dear on November 29, 1897. Sina was born August 6, 1879, and died July 13, 1924.
13. THOMAS DYER married Bettie Weaver on January 5, 1896.
14. WILLIAM A. MCCOY was born December 2, 1846, and died November 18, 1908. Mary Lou was born February 25, 1856, and died April 18, 1938.
16. ALLEN GIPSON was born March 20, 1859, and died September 3, 1926. He married Emma Short on June 28, 1890. Emma was the daughter of Reuben B. and Julia Ann Austin Short. She was born August 10, 1869, and died March 22, 1918. Allen was the son of John L. and Mary Jane Hill Gipson. Grandson of Allen Gipson Sr. who gave property to the University of the South. Allen was a deaf mute
17. NANCY MCKNIGHT BARNES was born January 10, 1854, and died January 5, 1941. She married George Barnes on August 31, 1885. She is the half sister to Julia Ann Austin that married Reuben B. Short. She is the daughter of James and Mary Gibson McKnight.
19. JOHN S. HENLEY married Mary Smith on July 21, 1894.
20. ROBERT MITCHELL married Jeanne Ives on May 12, 1889. Irene Mitchell, daughter of Robert and Jeanne, married Allen McCreary.
21. JOHN STATEM was born June 4, 1860, and died in 1925. He was the son of Dean and Mary Downum Statem. His first marriage was to Barbara Zoppi on December 18, 1885. His second marriage was to Sarah "Saidee" Elizabeth Biddle on December 17, 1891. Sarah was born June 18, 1864, and died 1928. John and Saidee were the parents of Mary who married William Hamilton and Blanche who married Theron Myers. Mrs. Mary Hamilton wrote the beautiful story about her memories of the town of Sewanee and the people who lived there. It was first published in my family book titled, "A Journey through history with the Short & Barnes family."
22. WILLIAM FOSTER married Tennie Williamson on January 27, 1894.
25. ELIZABETH BRINKLEY STEWMAN died in 1934. She was married to Robert E. Stewman who was born October 14, 1865. Bob Town was named in honor of Elizabeth's husband. Their daughter, Mamie, was married to Henry Garner.
26. C. H. TERRILL was born February 18, 1875. He married Mahala Smith on June 8, 1894. Mahala was born September 27, 1878.
27. ELIZABETH "BETTIE" MCBRIDE MYERS was the wife of William L. Myers. William was a founder of the Cumberland Presbyterian Church at Sewanee.

30. JOHN O. PACK was born February 16, 1867, and died August 26, 1928. Ellen was born February 22, 1870, and died November 1949.
32. SAMUEL GARNER was born December 4, 1872. He married Mary Jane O'Dear on January 23, 1892. Mary Jane was born June 29, 1876, and died June 16, 1946. Samuel died February 23, 1960. Samuel was the son of Henry Griffith and Mary Ann Barnes Garner of Lost Cove. Mary Jane's parents were Andrew Jackson and Catherine Mary Garner O'Dear.
33. WILLIAM GUDGER died in 1921. Jane died in 1933. Carrie Bell married Raleigh McBee. Harrison died in 1960, Carrie died November 10, 1965, Gailton died June 5, 1965, and Lillie died October 28, 1939.
37. THOMAS HARRISON married Annie Farris on September 27, 1896. Hays died July 7, 1975, and James Oliver died in 1954.
38. JAMES GRANT IVES married Martha Crownover on October 2, 1893.
39. GEORGE PERRY married Sarah Finney on March 22, 1871. George was born July 25, 1850, and died July 11, 1912. Sarah was born July 26, 1850, and died May 11, 1921. George's parents were Jeremiah and Mary Garner Perry.
40. ISAAC 'IKE' ANDERSON married Elizabeth Doney. Ike died in 1935. Elizabeth died in 1940.
43. JOHN JEFFERSON ROLLINS married Martha Ann Margaret Anderson. She was the daughter of Albert Spencer Anderson. John died in 1923. Martha died in 1919. Their son, John William, married Eva Pyle.
45. JOSLIN S. DYER was born August 15, 1835, and died January 5, 1900. Margaret was born April 25, 1833, and died May 5, 1917.
46. THOMAS HARRISON was the son of Jerry and Elizabeth Harrison.
48. FRANCIS "FRANK" MARION ROLLINS married Tilpha Gilliam on October 1, 1892.
49. JOSEPH LEWIS married Mary M. Godfry on February 3, 1895.
51. THOMAS GODBEY married Sarah "Sally" Perry on February 8, 1871. Sally was born January 21, 1850, and died December 23, 1919. Their son, Francis, married Martha Ellen Green. Their daughter, Lizzie, married John Collins.
52. JEANNIE ANDERSON was born March 13, 1866, and died March 17, 1955. She was first married to John Anderson who was born August 1, 1859, and died August 2, 1896. Her second marriage was to Iziah C. Bohannen. Her son, Alfred Anderson, married Bell Cates on October 10, 1901.
53. EMILE HUNZIKER was first married to Lottie Tucker.
54. GABRIEL J. DISHROOM married Amanda "Amady" A. Farris on June 5, 1867. Their daughter, Martha "Kallie" Dishroom, married J.A. Gipson on April 18, 1894.
55. PEGGY PERRY married Samuel Norwood on October 6, 1873.
57. DAVID ANDERSON was born March 22, 1852, and died October 28, 1934. Annie was born June 7, 1866, and died July 17, 1825. Their daughter, Edna, married a Watley.
58. MACK GILLIAM married Bettie A. Church on August 17, 1891.
59. JOE CHURCH married Susie Lewis on February 24, 1895.
60. JAMES ELLIS married Margaret "Maggie" Finney on August 21, 1886.
63. JOHN ARN married Mary Ann Bluer. Mary Ann died in 1929. John was the first sexton (maintenance man) at the University of the South. He came to Sewanee from Belvidere, Tennessee. John and Mary Ann's daughter, Lenah, married George W. Green.
64. FRANCIS "MARION" KNOTT married Alice Southerland on August 26, 1892. Alice was born October 17, 1875, and died July 21, 1934. Marion died August 4, 1938. Their son, Oscar, married Carrie Long. They lived at Midway. Alfred married Flora Long, and Francis L. married Bertha Cecil Martin.
66. W. R. STEPHENS married Adelle Walker on January 6, 1897.
68. JOHN MOONEY was born April 6, 1874, and died April 12, 1963. Sarah was born June 27, 1879, and died June 27, 1967. Their daughter, Bessie, married a Tucker.
69. DAVID MYERS married Susan Miller on January 31, 1889.
73. JOE BARRY was born October 11, 1871, and died April 1, 1925. Martha was born February 26, 1871, and died August 13, 1916.
75. RICHARD MOONEY died July 4, 1920. Catherine was born February 16, 1857, and died February 4, 1936.
76. WILLIAM MOONEY married Martha Cook on August 31, 1895.

77. W. D. COLLINS married Sarah "Fannie" Guthrie on March 3, 1894.
79. CHARLIE WESTLAND married Mary Ives on January 12, 1888.
80. PATSY J. RILEY married Sophia Anderson on August 2, 1868. Their son, Joseph Riley, owned the livery stable. Their son, Louis, was the father of Nellie Mae Riley, a school teacher at Sewanee Public School for many years. Louis was an undertaker and he also worked at the livery stable. Louis Riley's house is still standing. Tate Realty is now located in it.
81. ROBERT W. JACKSON married Mary C. Arnold on May 18, 1873.
82. LEE FINNEY married Minnie Gillespie on November 12, 1891.
83. MATTHEW "MATT" J. FINNEY married Julia Gillespie on February 23, 1900.
84. J. MARION CASTLEBERRY married Frances "Franny" Wiley on July 4, 1872. Marion died April 20, 1907.
85. WILLIAM "WILL" T. GIPSON married Kate M. Carson on January 5, 1896. Will died in 1960. Kate died in 1932.
86. SAMUEL PRINCE married Edna Haffor on February 15, 1892.
87. JAMES CASTLEBERRY married Lillie Castleberry on November 6, 1889. James' mother was Almeda Castleberry. His mother-in-law was Rebecca Castleberry.
88. ROBERT H. PRINCE was born April 27, 1861. He married Jenny Lee on November 27, 1901. Jenny was born May 8, 1866, and died April 6, 1944. Their son, Edward Reneau, was born on November 10, 1895, and died March 10, 1940.
89. JOHN O. SUTHERLAND was born March 17, 1868, and died March 4, 1942. John was the son of Samuel and Rosanna Sutherland. Mary died July 6, 1930. They are buried in the University of the South Cemetery.
90. J. H. FISCHER married Lenz Armstutz on January 14, 1886.
91. FRANK SHORT was born in Chambers County, Alabama. He was the son of Jesse and Mary Evans Short of Georgia. Frank was the a master stone mason. He built the first sandstone depot at Sewanee.
92. MARGUERITE L. HAWKINS died in 1939. Marguerite's maiden name was Luchsinger. She was the daughter of Barbara Trumpy Luchsinger who was born on November 4, 1835, in Switzerland, and died March 7, 1915, in Sewanee.
93. J. M. HARRISON married Minnie May Johnson on February 21, 1898.
94. WILLIAM RICKETTS died in 1915.
95. DORA J. GILLESPIE died in 1960.
96. GEORGE P. KENNEDY married Martha Gipson on October 30, 1895. He was born May 20, 1870, and died September 22, 1940. Martha was born September 27, 1877, and died November 3, 1908.
97. JOHN POWELL married Nancy Ellis on February 2, 1845. He was born August 24, 1823, and died March 13, 1911. Nancy was born February 4, 1826, and died March 2, 1908.
99. ROXANNA W. SUTHERLAND was born January 6, 1848, and died August 16, 1925. She was the wife of Samuel Sutherland.
100. W. T. GARNER married Nancy A. Hendley on July 6, 1874.
101. Z. H. RICE was born December 15, 1852, and died April 10, 1910. Nancy was born March 11, 1852, died March 7, 1907.
103. LEE THOMAS married Estelle Sharp on November 17, 1892.
105. ROBERT RILEY married Viola Ives on September 16, 1892. Robert died in 1939. Viola died in 1920.
106. TAYLOR O'DEAR married Malinda Long Hendly on October 30, 1897. Malinda was previously married to John Henley.
107. MINERVA GARNER married Allen Gipson on January 3, 1855. John Clark was married to their daughter, Dollie Gipson Hunziker. Dollie was previously married to Jacob Hunziker. She and John were married on February 1, 1889.
108. HENRY LONG married Bettie Gibson on August 7, 1895.
109. IDA DORSEY GIBSON was born March 26, 1861.
110. EMET KUNTZ married Della Morris on November 14, 1891.

111. EMMA VAN VLECK was born August 24, 1829, and died December 17, 1914. She went by the name of Emily. She was married to Abraham Van Vleck who commanded a unit from Franklin County during the Civil War.
113. SAMUEL HOLLAND married Listy Gossage on August 3, 1887. Celestie L. Gossage was born June 20, 1870, and died August 6, 1915.
114. ABBEY BRAZELTON was born February 28, 1884, and died October 15, 1945. She was married to Douglas Loughmiller Vaughn.
115. JAMES PRINCE died in 1936. Emma Prince died in 1955.
116. JAMES T. THOMAS died in 1932. Fannie Statem Thomas was the daughter of Dean and Mary Downum Statem.
117. GOTTFRIED GRUETTER married Risti Brewer on December 1, 1886. Gottfried was born January 11, 1866, in Berne, Switzerland. He died October 22, 1916, in Sewanee. He owned a shoe shop in the village of Sewanee. He built his own house in Bob Town. The house was later owned by Nancy Barnes.
118. MARTHA CASTLEBERRY died in 1925.
119. GEORGE TUCKER married Jeannie Brewer on September 3, 1891. George and Gennie Tucker were buried in Mountain View, Red Hill Cemetery in Sherwood.
121. H. H. HOFFOR married Martha Dugger Fischer on August 14, 1895. Martha Dugger was first married to William M. Fischer on February 11, 1886.
122. J. B. POWELL married Mattie C. Corn on October 27, 1893.
123. E. FISCHER was the wife of William Frederick Fischer. Mr. Fischer was a well-known cabinet maker from Germany.
124. CHRISTIAN RUEF was born in Berne, Switzerland. He died in 1919. He was married to Agnes Bollinger. He owned a meat market in the village of Sewanee. He was also a Justice of the Peace.
125. JOHN RUEF was the son of Christian and Agnes. He married Winnie E. Morris on August 4, 1898. John owned a store in the village of Sewanee.
127. ABRAHAM "BENNY" LEVOVITZ was Jewish. He owned a dry goods store in Sewanee.
128. A. WHITLOCK married Florence Alexander on February 13, 1898.
129. S. C. HOGE married Temmie Holland on November 19, 1872. Samuel C. Hoge was born April 10, 1839, died July 29, 1902. Sarah Temmie Hoge was born April 14, 1843, and died February 11, 1933. Samuel was a merchant at Sewanee.
130. WILLIAM C. LOONEY married Elna Dorsey on June 28, 1885. William died in 1926. Ettie Dorsey Looney was born March 26, 1861, and died March 11, 1901. W. C. Looney was a medical doctor at Sewanee.
132. ELIZABETH OWENS was born October 2, 1842, and died April 5, 1901. She was the mother of S.W. and J.M. Owens.
134. RUFF MOSELY married Mollie Chappell on January 31, 1893.
135. HENRY HUNT married Lena Handly on April 24, 1895.
137. P. B. HAWKINS married S.M. Sewell on February 6, 1871. Sallie Merritt Hawkins was born April 6, 1849, and died November 26, 1936. Phillip B. Hawkins was in the 1st Tennessee Infantry, Company I in the Confederate Army.
142. EMMA SUTTON CARTER was born September 6, 1890.
143. WILLIAM GULHAIR married Isabella Wright on October 5, 1896. William's surname was probably misspelled in the marriage records.
145. JANE OAKLEY died April 4, 1906, at age 57.
147. BURR RAMAGE was born July 1, 1858, and died March 23, 1914. Harriett Page Ramage was born August 13, 1874, and died March 4, 1937. Burr was a professor.
148. WALTER O. HARRIS married Lizie Bennett on August 20, 1899.
150. GEORGE PRICE married Annie Hunt on January 11, 1899.
151. WILL SANDERS married Birta Hunt on August 25, 1895.
152. PINK SIMS married Megg Colyar on May 23, 1893.
153. S. F. FOSTER married Sallie Clark on June 26, 1898.
154. JAMES MESSICK married Minnie Wade on July 11, 1889.

155. JAMES SEVERIN GREEN died in 1900. Ella Philoura W. Green died in 1925. James was a medical doctor at Sewanee.
156. ADAM FINCH married Jessie Sims on March 18, 1890.
157. FRANK PHILLIPS married Tina Myers on August 30, 1898.
158. GEORGE SIMMONS married Davis Trigg on December 29, 1895.
162. SPENCER JUDD was buried on November 2, 1920. Hallie Rodgers Judd died January 22, 1949. Spencer was a photographer at Sewanee.
173. CALVIN CLARK married Susie Nuckles on December 20, 1888.
174. BILLY CHILDRESS married Grace Dardin on July 16, 1899.
175. CALVIN CHILDRESS married Hallie Sharp on December 9, 1899.
179. GEORGE GARNER married Rachel Turner on April 3, 1899.
180. WILLIAM SHARP married Ella Arledge on December 30, 1886.
181. JACK WISEMAN married Missouri Custer on August 16, 1897.
183. DOCK FARRIS married Annie Bowan on August 31, 1894.
184. HUSTON AND SIMON SMITH were written about in Ely Green's book titled, "Ely." They were friends of Ely.
185. ANCE ROWE married Jennie Chinn on February 19, 1900. Ance is short for Anderson.
186. WILLIAM ANDREWS ran the railroad station at Sewanee.
193. RICHARD JEFFERSON MESSICK was born October 10, 1866, and died September 20, 1904. Mattie J. Messick was born April 22, 1858. Pernegy Pack was born June 28, 1835, and died October 23, 1903.
194. JACK F. PRINCE was born January 14, 1864, and died November 25, 1949. He married Mary Alice Pack on March 13, 1890. In the book titled "Ely" by Ely Green, Jack Prince was said to be a bounty hunter. Jack descends from Dr. William Prince who came to Sherwood, Tennessee, between 1820 and 1830. Dr. Prince married Isabel "Ebbie" Roberts. The Prince family came to Tennessee from North Carolina. Jack's parents were Nathan and Sarah Ann Garner Prince. Nathan was the son of Dr. Prince and his wife, Isabel. Sarah is the daughter of Henry and Elizabeth Catchings Garner. Dr. Prince delivered many of the babies in Sherwood. Jack was considered by Ely to be one of his heroes. Jack gave Ely a job and taught him how to shoot a gun and hunt. He and his family were always kind to Ely.
202. DEANE SPENCE DUBOSE was born October 16, 1871, and died January 19, 1960. William Haskell DuBose died in 1936. He was a priest at the University of the South.
203. SAM BIERY SR. was born December 10, 1851, and died January 1, 1926. Mary Hunziker Biery was born July 4, 1860, and died August 28, 1941.
206. CARITA VAN NESS ROGERS died in 1937. She is buried in the University of the South Cemetery.
207. ROBERT MARION DUBOSE was born September 18, 1841, and died October 30, 1907. Elizabeth Egleston DuBose was born November 1, 1849, and died February 25, 1918. Maria L. Porcher was born November 26, 1828, and died November 4, 1910. Maria ran Magnolia Hall boarding house. Maria Louisa Finley died June 28, 1949. She was a librarian at the University of the South.
208. CATHERINE MCCRADY was born June 5, 1876, and died December 20, 1960. John McCrady was a professor at the University of the South.
211. FLORENCE O'NEILL BARNWELL died October 18, 1922. Bower W. Barnwell died in 1895. He served in the Confederate Army. Florence made the caps and gowns for the students and teachers at the University of the South.
213. MARY A WILMERING was born April 19, 1851, and died April 7, 1909.
215. SALLY GREEN COTTON died in 1917. She was the daughter of Reverend William Mercer Green and wife of J. M. Cotton. She ran Otey Hall boarding house and her sister, Lillie, ran Kendall Hall.
217. W. J. PRINCE married Mariah Sewell on April 16, 1891. William J. died in 1939. Mariah died in 1936.
219. PRESTON SMITH BROOKS SR. was born July 1, 1854, and died July 6, 1928. He was born in Edgefield, South Carolina. Maria Porcher Brooks was born November 4, 1855, and died April 14, 1940. Maria was born in Winnsboro, South Carolina. Preston was a merchant. At one time,

his store was the largest in the village of Sewanee. The Brooks Store is still standing. Mr. Taylor has a flower shop in it. Thomas Hamilton, who was a boarder at the Brooks' home, married Laura Castleberry on November 25, 1900.

222. HENRY HOSKINS married Mrs. Ada Phillips on July 15, 1893. Ada M. Hoskins was born June 29, 1870, and died November 29, 1921. J. Henry Hoskins was born March 26, 1868, and died September 14, 1943. He was a hack driver in Sewanee.

225. CHARLOTTE B. E. PUCKETTE died June 1, 1902. She was the daughter of Rev. Stephen and Charlotte Bull Barnwell Elliott. Charlotte's husband was Charles Puckette. She and Flora Fairbanks were the first two school teachers for the public school at Sewanee. It was called St. Pauls on the Mountain.

227. WILLIAM ALEXANDER GUERRY was born July 7, 1861. He married Anne McBee on November 27, 1885, in Lincolnton, North Carolina. He died June 9, 1928, in Charleston, South Carolina. Anne was the sister of Silas McBee who was born November 14, 1853, and died September 3, 1924. William Alexander was a chaplain and professor. Silas made the original design for All Saints Chapel. Silas married Louise Post who was born February 8, 1860, and died March 9, 1933. The McBees were from Lincolnton, North Carolina.

230. WILLIAM PETERFIELD TRENT was a professor of English. He was the first editor of the Sewanee Review. The Sewanee Review is the oldest literary quarterly in the country. Most writers and publishers know about the Sewanee Review.

231. ROBERT COLMORE took over the operation of the University farm at St. Andrews. He did various jobs for the University of the South. Robert Lionel Colmore was born February 25, 1876, and died at age 73. He was born in Warwickshire, England, His wife, Priscilla Diana Colmore, was born June 13, 1852, and died August 13, 1904. He was affectionately known by the students as General Colmore.

232. FRANCES GLEN POTTER was married to Telfair Hodgton. She was the daughter of Mr. and Mrs. James Potter of Savannah, Georgia.

235. ALBERT BONHOLZER died in the Argonne Forest of France in 1918. He was one of two soldiers from Sewanee to die during World War I.

237. CAMERON PIGGOT was born September 4, 1855, and died August 30, 1911. He was married to Anne Cockey. Cameron is the son of Aaron and Margaret Moore Piggot of Baltimore, Maryland. Cameron was a medical doctor and professor at Sewanee.

238. SUSAN SMEDES died July 4, 1913. She was the wife of Lyell Smedes. Lelia J. Dabney was born April 29, 1852, and died May 28, 1927.

239. CHARLOTTE GALLEHER was the wife of John N. Galleher, a Bishop at the U. of the South.

240. BENJAMIN LAWTON WIGGINS was born September 11, 1861, at Sand Ridge, South Carolina. He died June 14, 1909. He was a professor of Greek and Vice Chancellor of the University of the South. He married Clara Quintard, daughter of Bishop Charles and Kate Quintard. Clara Quintard Wiggins died February 4, 1915. Elizabeth Katherine Hand Quintard died March 16, 1905. Bishop Charles Todd Quintard was born December 22, 1824, and died February 15, 1898. He was the second bishop of Tennessee. He was a surgeon during the Civil War and the first medical doctor at Sewanee. He planned and directed the construction of the town of Sewanee and the University of the South.

241. HENRY SEWELL was born August 11, 1865, and died January 22, 1930.

242. SALLIE MILHADO lived at Sewanee for 40 years. Sallie was said to be eccentric.

244. CASSIE SELDEN KIRBY SMITH was the wife of the famous Confederate General, Edmund Kirby Smith. Cassie was born September 26, 1837, and died November 3, 1907. She was born at Lynchburg, Virginia. General Kirby Smith was born May 16, 1842, and died March 26, 1893. The general was born at St. Augustine, Florida. He won more battles for the South during the Civil War than any other Confederate general. He was a professor of mathematics at the University of the South. Members of the Kirby Smith family said he never actually surrendered, but that his army deserted him.

DATA FOR PEOPLE LIVING AT SEWANEE DURING 1910 CENSUS

4. T. J. REID born 1858 died 1925. Lulu Reid born 1869 died 1952.
5. MARY HUNZIKER born July 15, 1835 died September 2, 1927. Mary was the wife of Frederich Hunziker. Adolph Hunziker born 1866 died 1943.
6. WILLIAM COLLINS. W. D. Collins married Fannie Guthrie on March 4, 1894.
7. IKE ANDERSON born 1848 and died 1935. Lizzie B. Anderson born 1850 and died in 1940.
8. TOM HARRISON married Annie Farris on September 27, 1896.
9. RICHARD BIDDLE died October 30, 1918. Richard was one of Sewanee's hermits. Another hermit was Jim Walker. Richard was born in Pennsylvania in 1850. His house in Sewanee was in the woods with a fence surrounding it. He died at age 68, and is buried in the University of the South Cemetery.
10. REYNOLDS MARTIN KIRBY SMITH was born in 1882, and died July 31, 1861. Maude Bethune Tompkins died in Nashville in 1961. Reynolds M. Jr. was born 1904, and died in 1982, in the Philippines. Henry Tompkins Kirby Smith was born April 30, 1907, and died April 4, 1974. He was a surgeon at Sewanee. Dr. Elizabeth was born 1910. She was a medical doctor at Sewanee. She delivered many of the babies born at Sewanee, during her tenure as a doctor.
12. HENRY F. COULSON was born October 6, 1896, and died May 19, 1973.
13. WILLIAM STEPHENS married Adelle Walker.
14. RICHARD MOONEY born 1850, died July 4, 1920. Catherine Mooney was born February 16, 1857, and died February 4, 1936.
15. JOSEPH "JOE" BARRY married Martha "Mollie" Bishop on July 14, 1889. Joe was born October 11, 1871, and died April 3, 1925. Martha born February 26, 1871, died August 13, 1916.
16. MEREDITH MARLOW born 1881, and died 1928. Elizabeth "Lizzie" born 1891, died in 1920.
17. JOE RICKETTS born July 6, 1874, died December 24, 1962. Janie born October 11, 1884, died December 26, 1972.
20. EMIL HUNZIKER born 1865, and died 1925. Virginia M. Hunziker born 1882, died 1925. Veda Hunziker born 1903, and died 1926.
21. S. FRANK FOSTER married Sallie Clark on June 26, 1898. Sallie's mother was Lucinda Clark.
22. JENNIE ANDERSON born March 13, 1866, died March 17, 1955. Jennie was the wife of John Anderson born August 1, 1859, and died August 2, 1896.
25. CHARLIE E. HOBACK born October 8, 1883, and died January 25, 1980. Dollie Hoback born March 1, 1882, died September 21, 1910. Charlie's 2nd wife was Beulah E. born September 29, 1893, and died October 28, 1975.
26. JOHN BARRY married Rachel Garner on August 23, 1858.
28. WILLIAM E. LADD was born June 7, 1888, and died January 1, 1968. Rebecca Elliott Ladd was born April 11, 1890.
29. GEORGE W. JENNINGS married Sally Phillips on May 31, 1894.
30. JAMES W. CLARK born February 5, 1888, died October 31, 1931.
32. DAVID ANDERSON born March 22, 1852, and died October 28, 1934.
34. JOHN ROLLINS born December 25, 1859, died August 3, 1923. Martha born March 19, 1961, died January 5, 1919.
36. THOMAS GREEN married Sarah Dyer on February 2, 1891.
39. CASEY FOSTER married Dora Clark on July 4, 1900. James C. Foster born July 24, 1880, died April 7, 1946. Dora M. Foster was born March 5, 1881, died March 25, 1949.
40. SARAH E. JOHNSON was born November 1, 1852, died November 11, 1936. Sarah's husband was W. H. Johnson born December 20, 1847, and died May 7, 1890.
42. MARGARET 'PEGGY' PERRY married Samuel Norwood on October 1, 1873.
43. ANN DISHROON born January 8, 1846, died January 20, 1917.
46. JOHN STATEM born 1860, died 1925. Sarah Biddle Statem born 1864, died 1928.
47. THOMAS NELSON BIDDLE born November 7, 1859, died March 7, 1940.
49. GODFRIED GRUETTER married Myrtle Reavis on June 22, 1902. This was Gotfried's 2nd marriage. Godfried was born January 11, 1866, died October 22, 1916.
50. JAMES RUSSELL married Maggie Butler on July 14, 1889.

51. GEORGE P. KENNEDY born May 20, 1870, died September 22, 1940. Tennie R. Kenney born March 13, 1881, died April 30, 1934.
52. WILLIAM T. GARNER married Nancy Hendley on July 6, 1874.
55. W. A. SULLIVAN married Sophia J. Anderson on December 28, 1901.
56. MATTHEW TERRILL married Rachel O'Dear. Matthew was born March 22, 1880, died June 5, 1962. Rachel was born July 13, 1884, died March 6, 1961.
57. CATHERINE GARNER O'DEAR was the wife of Andrew Jackson O'Dear.
59. CURGE TERRILL married Mahala Smith on June 8, 1894. Mahala Terrill born September 27, 1878, died November 5, 1959.
60. ALEXANDER TRIPP married Sarah Campbell on August 27, 1874.
61. ROBERT MITCHELL married Jeannie Ives on May 12, 1889.
62. WALLIS HAWKINS married Maggie Luchsinger on December 25, 1881, Gruetli.
63. FRANK SHORT was the son of Jesse and Mary Evans Short. Frank was a master stone mason at Sewanee from the 1870's.
64. WILLIAM L. MYERS married Elizabeth McBride.
65. ROBERT STEWMAN'S date of death is listed as November 4, 1899, however, he was still living during the 1910 census year. Elizabeth Brinkley Stewman was listed as being born in 1866, and died in 1934. In the census Robert is listed as being a widower in 1910. Elizabeth was still living in 1900 census. Robert was born October 14, 1865. Bob Town is named for Robert "Bob" Stewman. He was a house builder.
66. JAMES P. PRINCE married Emma Armstrutz on June 16, 1889. James Prince was born 1868, died 1936. Emma Prince born 1868, died 1955.
68. J. C. PIERCE was born 1855, died in 1921. Mary Pierce was born October 16, 1854, died June 27, 1917.
69. JOHN WESLEY MCBEE born September 30, 1856, died September 4, 1917. John was the first chief of Police of Sewanee. Mary Hoggest McBee was the chief's wife.
70. NANCY BARNES, daughter of James and Mary Gibson McKnight. She married George W. Barnes. George's ancestors were the first known settlers on the Sewanee Mountain. Margie Lee Barnes born November 9, 1889, died November 6, 1961. She is buried in Eastern Star Cemetery. Jack Hill's real name is John Johnson. He changed his own name. Jack was born July 4, 1881, died December 12, 1968. He owned the store where Joe David McBee now has an antique shop. His first wife was Adell Williams born July 27, 1889, died November 23, 1968, Fort Myers, Florida. His second marriage was to Mary Woodson.
71. JOSEPH "BUD" LONG was first married to Nora Hobbs on January 22, 1899. Bud's second marriage was to Rosie Hill, daughter of the above Jack Hill. J. B. Long born February 22, 1908, and died March 31, 1966. John F. Long born August 31, 1904, and died August 8, 1979. Rosie Dell Hill Long was born May 20, 1907, and died in 1996.
73. ALLEN GIPSON was born March 20, 1859. He was a deaf mute. His wife was Emma Short. Joice married Robert Barnett, Lois married Noble Gipson, Sylvester married Sarah Smith, Austin married Sally Yokley, Zella married Jack Hawkins, Lora married Charles Barnett, Layton married Evelyn Heike, Clarence married Dorothy Reikowski, Hayden married Gertrude Reikowski. Lora, Layton, Clarence and Hayden moved to Chicago, Illinois. The last three married there.
74. J. H. FISCHER married Lena Armstrutz on January 14, 1886. Joseph Amstrutz was born December 23, 1823, and died May 22, 1916.
75. JENNIE LEE PRINCE was born May 8, 1866, and died April 6, 1944, wife of Robert H. Prince.
76. JAMES CASTLEBERRY was born June 10, 1868, died February 16, 1922. Lillie Castleberry was born December 20, 1869.
77. FREELAND G. JOHNSON was born December 3, 1884, and died October 20, 1970.
78. J.M. HARRISON married Minnie May Johnson on February 21, 1898.
79. JAMES C. SUTHERLAND born October 21, 1859, died April 13, 1927. Mary Miller Sutherland born November 21, 1858, died February 27, 1935.
81. WILLIAM GREEN married Sina O'Dear on November 29, 1897. William was born in 1873, died in 1948. Sina was born August 6, 1879, died July 13, 1924.
82. WHITE CAMPBELL was born 1861, died 1931. Ellen Riley Campbell was born 1861, died 1922.

83. JOHN H. CASTLEBERRY died March 5, 1964, at age 84. Bertha T. Castleberry was born in 1882, and died in 1982.
84. JAMES MATTHEW FINCHUM was born September 10, 1884, died October 25, 1959. Susan E. "Lena" Finchum was born September 5, 1888, died September 12, 1973. Wesley Lee Finchum was born May 20, 1910, died July 14, 1974. Clarence Finchum was born January 25, 1905, died September 30, 1968.
86. ANDY J. GOFF was born March 7, 1882, died March 20, 1951. Flossie B. Goff born January 18, 1892, died May 26, 1960. Fay Goff married Jim Short, son of John and Bettie O'Dear Short.
90. JAMES L. PACK married Florence Goff on July 28, 1897.
92. JACK F. PRINCE. See 1900 data .
94. EMMA JONES VAN VLECK was born on August 24, 1829, wife of Abraham.
96. F. MARION KNOTT was born August 3, 1869, died August 4, 1938. Alice Knott was born October 17, 1875, died July 21, 1934.
99. JOHN C. SUTHERLAND was born 1902, and died 1978.
100. NEVA GIPSON. MINERVA GIPSON, was wife of Allen Gipson. Flora Clark is daughter of John and Dollie Gipson Clark.
103. WILLIAM CHILDRESS was born 1874, died 1953. William C. Childress born February 3, 1903, died December 22, 1927. Elexander Childress was born 1900, died in 1953. Grace Childress died October 4, 1957.
104. MARY BROWN died in 1933.
107. CARL D. RANKINS was born September 7, 1896, died March 3, 1961.
109. WILLIE SIMS was born on December 10, 1886, died January 12, 1950. He was a athletic trainer at the University of the South. Mollie Sims born 1890, died 1960. Willie was called "Willie Six."
110. GREEN TAYLOR married Allice Hines on April 7, 1887.
114. GEORGE GARNER married Rachel Turner on April 3, 1899.
116. WILLIAM ROWE married Azie Arledge on January 9, 1902.
117. WILLIAM CHEATMAN was born 1868, died January 1, 1950.
121. ELY GREEN wrote the book titled, "Ely", which tells about his life at Sewanee. His great-aunt, Mattie Davis, raised him after his mother died.
123. SALLY SMITH born 1850, died 1948. Houston Smith born 1885, died 1969. William R. Smith married Sallie Cheatham on November 1, 1888.
124. CALVAN CHILDRESS married Hallie Sharp on December 9, 1899.
125. NED GREEN was Ely Green's grandfather.
126. B. H. BOYCE married Minnie Sherwood on June 9, 1900.
128. WILLIAM J. PRINCE was born 1855, died 1939. Maria S. Prince was born 1858, died 1936.
129. MARY SELDEN ran a boarding house in Sewanee.
130. JOHN MCCRADY died on October 16, 1881, at the home of his friend, Felix De Violle, in Nashville, Tennessee. John was a Professor of Science and Biology at the University of the South. Two weeks before his death on September 27, 1881, Otey Hall burned. His home was located at Otey Hall.
131. Frank L. Lautzenheiser born February 13, 1867, died September 20, 1953. May Newell Lautzenheiser was born January 14, 1870, died July 17, 1928. Frank was a bookkeeper at the University of the South.
132. MARY CUNNINGHAM WICKS. Celeste Lasater Wicks died April 21, 1947.
133. T. M. TIDWELL married Mary Crabtree on October 26, 1889.
135. MARIANNE B. ARN was born 1852, died 1929. She was born in Switzerland. George Green was born 1880, died 1971.
136. THOMAS ALLEN HUNZIKER was born August 24, 1886, died June 24, 1950. Stella Hunziker was born December 19, 1894, died February 12, 1927.
137. SAM BIERY SR. was born December 10, 1851, died January 1, 1926. Mary Hunziker Biery was born July 4, 1860, died April 28, 1941. Sammie W. C. Biery was born June 1, 1895, died February 26, 1913.
141. JOHN CLARK was born 1866, died 1943. Alice was born 1858, died 1959.
143. FRED MONTGOMERY was born 1880, died 1944. Sally Campbell Montgomery was born 1885, died 1974.

144. ROBERT RILEY was born 1866, died 1939. Viola Ives Riley was born 1871, died 1920.
148. HARRY HAWKINS was born October 12, 1882, died April 1, 1970. Annie K. Hawkins was born May 9, 1885, died July 3, 1914.
149. IDA GIPSON was born March 26, 1861, died March 18, 1927, wife of Thomas D.
150. SALLIE M. SEWELL HAWKINS born April 6, 1849, died November 26, 1936.
152. T. J. GOSSAGE born March 20, 1840, died March 20, 1923. Celestie L. Gossage born June 20, 1870, died August 6, 1915, wife of S. L. Holland.
153. PRESTON SMITH BROOKS was born July 1, 1854, died July 6, 1928. Maria Porcher Brooks was born November 4, 1855, died April 14, 1940.
157. JOHN B. HUNT was born July 6, 1870, died March 13, 1953. Mary Love Washington Hunt born 1871, died 1934.
158. ELIZABETH WADHAMS, daughter of Charles and Elizabeth Gibson Wadhams.
160. SPENCER JUDD was born in 1855, died in 1920. Hallie Rodgers Judd born 1863, died January 22, 1949.
164. LILLIE GREEN was the daughter of Reverend William Mercer Green.
167. JOHN COLYAR married Dosia Colyar on January 13, 1900.
168. WILLIAM S. HUDDLESTON was born December 8, 1859, died April 11, 1923. Rose Huddleston was born December 25, 1865, died January 24, 1912, Ben Huddleston was born March 1905, died May 23, 1924.
177. J. HENRY HOSKINS married Mrs. Ada Phillips on June 6, 1893. Ada was born June 29, 1870, died November 29, 1921. J. Henry Hoskins was born March 26, 1868, died September 14, 1943. Henry was a hack driver at Sewanee.
178. SUSIE SMEDES was born in 1840, died in 1913, wife of Lyle Smedes.
179. ROBERT LIONEL COLMORE died on December 2, 1922, at age 73. Priscilla Diane Colmore was born June 13, 1852, died August 13, 1904. Lizzie Theodore Colmore was born October 28, 1880, died March 1, 1863. Lionel Henry Colmore was born February 25, 1876, died August 14, 1902. Evelyn Quintard Colmore was born June 15, 1886, died October 19, 1948. William Briscoe Colmore was born June 21, 1877, died September 5, 1882.
185. ELIZABETH KIRBY SMITH died November 25, 1917, daughter of General Edmund Kirby Smith.
186. EDWARD COLYAR married Hattie Lee Douglas. Edward was a servant for Dr. Henry Kirby Smith. He also worked at Mrs. Hale's boarding house. Edward was a barber and a dry cleaner at Sewanee. Hattie was from Coffee County, Tennessee.
194. KATHERINE COLLINS KENNEDY was born 1887, died 1971. W. M. Kennedy was born May 15, 1885, died October 27, 1957. Clifford E. Kennedy was born 1908, died 1940.
195. ALBERT JOHNSON married Bessie Miller on May 31, 1899. Albert was born 1872, died 1920. Bettie M. Johnson born 1873, died April 7, 1951.
197. RUFUS MOSLEY married Mollie Chappel on January 21, 1893. Rufus worked for the Sewanee hermit, Richard Biddle.
198. DR. W. C. LOONEY born 1857, died 1926.
199. SARAH HOGE ran a boarding house. She was the wife of Samuel Hoge.
202. WILL CAMPBELL was born July 16, 1886, died 1924. Cora Hopkins Campbell born 1886, died 1924. Will's second wife was Lizzie Gipson Sherill.

DATA FOR PEOPLE LIVING AT SEWANEE DURING 1920 CENSUS

1. See 1900 or 1910 data.
2. See 1900 or 1910 data.
3. THOMAS A. GREEN born 1891, died 1943. Jeanette born 1897, died 1964. Litha R. Green born September 26, 1884, died December 31, 1956.
6. JOHN GREENE born May 24, 1882, died September 4, 1972.
8. SAMUEL GARNER born December 4, 1872, died February 23, 1960.
14. REUBEN SHORT, son of Reuben and Julia Ann Austin Short, was born April 16, 1881, died August 25, 1956. Lena E. Morris Short born September 12, 1886, and died February 17, 1966.
15. FRED MCBEE born October 18, 1915, died May 1, 1977, married Willow M. McBee. She was born September 4, 1922, died December 16, 1973. Ernest "Buster" H. McBee was born August 1, 1917, died April 11, 1978. Ernest married E. Lucille D. McBee born September 9, 1915, died January 15, 1981.
16. EDWARD PRESTON SHORT, son of Reuben and Julia Ann Austin Short. Edward was born April 7, 1889. His first marriage was to Esther Bowen, a student at St. Mary's. Esther Bowen was born December 25, 1891, died December 28, 1911. Second marriage was to Darthy Mary Cline born March 23, 1897, died November 28, 1940.
17. ROBERT L. SUTHERLAND born November 6, 1881, died January 18, 1924. Sally Morris Sutherland born 1884, died 1964.
19. J. BENTON GREEN born February 11, 1861, died June 26, 1937. Mary King Green. Jennie Lee Green born March 8, 1884, died December 27, 1947. Andrew J. Green born May 5, 1911, died August 29, 1974. Irene Minor Green born September 3, 1906, died October 31, 1981. Mary A. Green born June 2, 1860, died February 13, 1962. Mary died at 102 years of age.
20. SAMUEL "REECE" GARNER, son of Samuel and Mary Jane Barnes Garner, born August 18, 1898, died May 3, 1942. Martha Henley Garner born September 21, 1903, died June 23, 1933.
21. DAVID WASHINGTON SHORT, born January 4, 1875, married Litha Barnes on June 3, 1883. David died October 4, 1951. Litha died December 31, 1951. David was the son of Reuben and Julia Ann Austin Short. Litha was the daughter of George W. and Nancy McKnight Barnes. Her ancestor were the first known settlers at Sewanee. Marvin Lee Short born November 28, 1903; Joseph Reece Short born December 6, 1905, died September 13, 1996; William Lawrence was born November 7, 1907, died January 8, 1986; Alfred Vernon was born September 27, 1909, died February 20, 1911. Dorothy Lorene Short was born April 24, 1914. She is now living in Charlestown, Indiana.
23. SARAH E. GREEN was first married to Bud O'Dear. She was married to John Franklin Gipson. Her parents were James and Martha James Green. Berry Gipson was a stone mason at the University of the South.
24. See 1900 or 1910 data.
25. THOMAS CROWNOVER married Tennessee "Tennie" Payne on September 29, 1895. Thomas Crownover was born 1872, died 1945. Tennie born 1877, died 1960.
26. LUKE HAWKINS married Maggie Fisher on January 28, 1901. Luke was born June 10, 1877, died July 2, 1945. Maggie M. Fischer born June 18, 1872, died May 20, 1950.
27. JAMES T. THOMAS born 1861, died 1932. Fannie born 1866, died 1954.
28. See 1900 or 1910 data.
29. See 1900 or 1910 data.
30. See 1900 or 1910 data
31. See 1900 or 1910 data.
32. See 1900 or 1910 data.
36. LOUIS F. REED SR. born August 26, 1885, died September 24, 1966. Ida Bell Reed born December 28,1880, died January 27, 1938.
38. GEORGE ROLLINS born 1886. Barbara Rollins born 1893, died 1951.
40. W. FRANK CALDWELL born June 8, 1889, died May 6, 1962. Rhoda born December 3, 1891, died February 2, 1974.
41. DEWITT CALDWELL born March 5, 1897, died April 14, 1953. Margaret D. Caldwell born June 9, 1899.

44. JAMES GREEN born 1892. Flora H. born 1891, died 1939. Sina Green was born August 6, 1879, died July 13, 1924. William Green married Sina O'Dear on November 29, 1897.
46. LAWRENCE JAMES born 1884 died 1953. Minnie L. James born January 18, 1973. Julia Ann Reeves on January 22, 1880, died December 12, 1977.
47. CHARLES E. HOBACK born October 8, 1883, died January 25, 1980. Beulah E. Hoback born September 29, 1893, died October 28, 1975.
48. S. F. FOSTER married Sallie Clark on June 26, 1898.
49. JAMES W. CLARK born February 5, 1888, died October 31, 1931.
50. JAMES C. FOSTER born July 24, 1880, died April 7, 1946.
52. SALLY RICKETTS BARRY born February 1, 1886, died August 2, 1964. Angeline Ricketts died November 5, 1871, at age 62.
53. See 1900 or 1910 data.
54. WILLIAM E. LADD born June 7, 1888, died 1968. Rebecca Elliott "Ellie" born April 11, 1890.
56. JOE RICKETTS born July 6, 1874, died December 24, 1962.
60. REVEREND JAMES H. FLYE was at St. Andrews. Grace Houghton Flye born 1875, died 1954.
65. See 1900 or 1910 data.
66. See 1900 or 1910 data.
67. WILLIAM P. HARRISON born 1880, died 1949. Francis L. Harrison born 1894, the cemetery records have her death date as 1919, but she was still living in 1920 census.
70. See 1900 or 1910 data.
71. THOMAS E. HAWKINS born 1899, died 1967. Ethel R. born 1900, died 1967.
72. MARGARET L. HAWKINS born 1860, died 1939. Jackson H. Hawkins born October 8, 1895, died February 5, 1969.
73. WILLIAM CANTRELL married Lizzie Farris on October 24, 1900. Walter P. Crabtree. born May 12, 1910, died June 5, 1965.
74. ERNEST TERRILL born August 12, 1888, died June 8, 1943. Eliza Pearl Terrill born December 12, 1887, died April 9, 1967.
75. JOHN HUNZIKER born November 22, 1874, died February 8, 1889. Bertha Pierce Hunziker.
76. GEORGE P. KENNEDY born May 20, 1870, died September 22, 1940.
77. JAMES RUSSELL married Maggie Butler on July 14, 1889.
83. JAMES P. PRINCE born 1868, died 1936. Emma Prince born 1868, died 1955.
84. JOE HARDY DURRUM born September 27, 1891, died February 16, 1966.
89. FLORIDA "FLORA" FAIRBANKS, daughter of George Fairbanks, one of first teachers at St. Paul's-on-the-Mountain.
90. See 1900 or 1910 data.
95. LEWIS R. RILEY born 1879, died 1942. Blanche Riley born 1879, died 1955. Nellie May Riley born 1913, died 1963. Hershall Riley born February 16, 1905, died June 22, 1981.
96. W. H. YATES. Nora Lee Yates born March 15, 1894, died July 11, 1966.
99. HENRY SEWELL born August 11, 1865, died January 8, 1935.
101. See 1900 or 1910 data.
104. See 1900 or 1910 data.
106. ROBERT L. TOMES born August 30, 1891, died September 23, 1952. Willie Florence Tomes born 1894, died 1979. Ernest Tomes born May 10, 1916, died February 28, 1983.
108. See 1900 or 1910 data.
110. THERON MYERS was born August 25, 1892, died July 17, 1981. Blanche Statem Myers born April 14, 1898, died June 5, 1968.
111. See 1900 or 1910 data.
112. L. C. TERRILL born October 28, 1875, died November 10, 1952. Mahala A. Terrill born September 27, 1878, died November 5, 1959.
113. THOMAS A. SHERILL born September 22, 1885, died September 7, 1943. Ida Kennedy Sherill born July 21, 1881, died July 31, 1975.
114. GEORGE HANNUM COLLIN born September 11, 1894, died November 30, 1966. Florence Gilbert Collins born May 4, 1897, died December 3, 1959.
115. W. D. "BONE" ROSS was born December 19, 1852, died October 19, 1924. Mollie born August 10, 1862, died June 24, 1956.

116. WILLIAM W. BENNETT. Mack S. Bennett born May 28, 1904, died April 20, 1956. ?David H. Bennett born June 5, 1910, died July 4, 1973.
118. See 1900 or 1910 data.
120. See 1900 or 1910 data.
121. See 1900 or 1910 data.
123. See 1900 or 1910 data.
124. See 1900 or 1910 data.
125. WARNER YATES. Dosha Mae Timbs Yates was born March 10, 1902, died March 25, 1930. Their children were Flossie, John "Jay Bird", and Dorothy Yates.
126. See 1900 or 1910 data.
127. ALLEN R. MCCREARY born January 4, 1890, died June 26, 1977. Irene Mitchell McCreary born October 26, 1897, died 1971.
128. See 1900 and 1910 data.
129. ROBERT BARNETT was born January 5, 1885, married 1909, Joice Gipson, daughter of Allen and Emma Short Gipson. Joice died November 12, 1928.
130. D. S. REYNOLDS born September 14, 1881, died July 15, 1941. Maude Stewman Reynolds born March 3, 1884, died December 25, 1961.
132. See 1900 or 1910 data.
135. See 1900 or 1910 data.
138. Mary Love Washington born 1871, died 1935, wife of John B. Hunt.
141. See 1900 or 1910 data.
148. DOUGLAS LOUGHMILLER VAUGHAN born February 28, 1884, died January 11, 1931. Abbey Brazelton Vaughn born died October 15, 1945.
150. J. ROY HICKERSON born March 18, 1893, died February 15, 1962. Maurice G. Hickerson born April 2, 1882, died August 18, 1965.
158. See 1900 or 1910 data.
159. See 1900 or 1910 data.
160. See 1900 or 1910 data.
163. See 1900 or 1910 data.
165. See 1900 or 1910 data.
167. See 1900 or 1910 data.
169. See 1900 or 1910 data.
170. EDWARD RENEAU PRINCE was born November 10, 1895, died March 10, 1940.
184. See 1900 or 1910 data.
185. See 1900 or 1910 data.
186. See 1900 or 1910 data.
187. ERCY CUNNINGHAM born December 20, 1865, died August 10, 1921. Roberta Clarkson Cunningham born December 3, 1869, died November 7, 1939. Roberta ran Hoffman Hall.
188. TELFAIR HODGSON born September 18, 1876, died September 16, 1952. University Treasurer. Medora Cheatham Hodgson born May 20, 1878, died March 14, 1969. Medora was the daughter of General B. Cheatham, Confederate Army.
189. See 1900 or 1910 data.
190. WILLIAM HOWARD MACKELLER born 1863, died October 1, 1946. Elizabeth Hall MacKeller born 1865, died March 10, 1950. Elizabeth was the granddaughter of Bishop Cobb of Alabama. Juliet MacKeller was born December 17, 1944. William was the author of "Chuwalee" which was chronicles of Franklin County. This book contains a wealth of information on early Franklin County.
191. SEDLEY LYNCH WARE born November 15, 1868, died December 21, 1951. Professor at the University of the South. Alice Turner Porter Ware was born 1874, died April 28, 1959.
194. RANEE DALE MYERS born September 24, 1886, died May 9, 1960, wife of Everett B. Myers.
195. JANE BATEMAN born 1866, died 1942.
196. See 1900 or 1910 data.
201. GEORGE P. ANDERSON born February 7, 1891. Willie Ann born December 23, 1895, June 2, 1973.
202. See 1900 or 1910 data.

209. CATHERINE MOONEY born February 16, 1857, died 1936. Richard born 1850, died July 4, 1920.
210. MARTHA MOONEY born February 20, 1885, died May 29, 1964. Charles W. Mooney born May 10, 1884, died August 18, 1927.
218. LEON DAVIS KIRBY born December 30, 1874, died September 30, 1944. Eleanor Gildersleeve Kirby born September 13, 1884, died March 31, 1954, wife of Leon.
220. See 1900 or 1910 data.
223. CHARLES W. UNDERWOOD born December 4, 1884, died December 28, 1948. Ann T., born September 23, 1892, died August 12, 1967.
226. See 1900 or 1910 data.
228. JOHN NOTTINGHAM WARE born 1882, died 1959. Professor Dora Von Turckheim Ware was born 1886, died 1952.
228. See 1900 or 1910 data.
229. See 1900 or 1910 data.
230. See 1900 or 1910 data.
236. LEM TOM LONG born 1883, died 1948. Elizabeth Long born 1881, died 1963.
241. See 1900 or 1910 data.
242. See 1900 or 1910 data.
243. See 1900 or 1910 data.
244. See 1900 or 1910 data.
245. See 1900 or 1910 data.
250. WILLIAM S. HUDDLESTON born December 8, 1859, died April 11, 1923. Ben Huddleston born March 1905, died May 23, 1924.
252. See 1900 or 1910 data.
256. Rufus Patton born January 8, 1888, died June 21, 1948.
261. WILLIAM CHEATHAM born 1868, died 1950.
260. See 1900 or 1910 data.
263. See 1900 or 1910 data.
268. See 1900 or 1910 data.
271 HILARIUS L. HAWKINS was born 1889, died 1941.
274. WILLIAM J. PRINCE born July 31, 1888, died December 14, 1954. Bessie L. Prince 1891, died 1966.
276. RAINNIE W. FOSTER born March 5, 1898, died July 25, 1958. Willa F. Foster born August 28,l 1898.
277. See 1900 or 1910 data.

FOOTNOTES

(1) *Allan Gipson's Recollections* , written by H. M.. Huse, Principal of the Grammar School.
(2) "Daniel Boone," Purple Sewanee , (Sewanee, 1932, Reprint 1962), p. 4.
(3) James McCague, The Cumberland.
(4) "Tennessee", American Peoples Encyclopedia by Groliers (N.Y. 1965), Vol. 18, p. 56.
(5) David Williamson, "Great Britain", Debrett's Presidents of U.S. of the America, (Webb & Bower, 1989), p. 8.
(6) *Tennessee Historical Magazine*, published by the Tennessee Historical Society, Series II., Vol. III, No. 2, January, 1935, p. 111-113, p. 117-119.
(7) Ibid, p. 111-113, p. 117-119.
(8) Ibid, p. 111-113, p. 117-119.
(9) "In Memoriam -- Allen Gipson's Death Notice", The Sewanee Purple, April 18, 1896.
(10) Charles E. Thomas, Charlotte Gailor, and Sarah Hodson, Purple Sewanee , (Sewanee, 1932), p. 3.
(11) Ibid, p. 4.
(12) A letter to Pat Makris from Mrs. Mary Hamilton, from Sewanee, Tennessee, dated May 12, 1983.
(13) Franklin County Tennessee Deeds, Book Z, p. 25, reg. 8-25-1859.
(14) From various land grants for people living on the Cumberland Mountain.
(15) State of Tennessee Land Grant #2160, p. 37. Found in Tennessee State Archives, Nashville, Tennessee.
(16) State of Tennessee Land Grant #336, p. 335.
(17) "Land Distribution," Family Histories, Franklin County, Tennessee 1807-1996, Franklin County Historical Society (Paducah 1996), p. 13.
(18) State of Tennessee Land Grant #1716, p. 483.
(19) State of Tennessee Land Grant #849, p. 86.
(20) State of Tennessee Land Grant #7117, supplement #1014, p. 772.
(21) State of Tennessee Land Grant # 7113, supplement #1017, p. 768.
(22) State of Tennessee Land Grant #7116, p. 771.
(23) State of Tennessee Land Grant #1139, Dennis Barnes, dated 4-16-1827.
(24) State of Tennessee Land Grant #9982 p. 501.
(25) State of Tennessee Land Grant # 9972, p. 490.
(26) State of Tennessee Land Grant #8342, p. 77.
(27) State of Tennessee Land Grant #8346, p. 74.
(28) State of Tennessee Land Grant # 8347, p. 78
(29) State of Tennessee Land Grant #87864, entry #24, p. 94-95.
(30) State of Tennessee Land Grant #9306, entry #2877, p. 84.
(31) State of Tennessee Land Grant #9985, entry #2993, p. 503

(32) Deed Records, Franklin County, Book Y, p 332-336, 456-458.
Deed Records, Davidson County Notebook A, p.234.
Deed Records, Franklin County, Book Z, p. 349-350
Deed Records, Franklin County, John Hendley to U.S., dated 5-26-1860.
Deed Records, Franklin County, W.H. Tomlinson, Book 7, p 467.
Deed Records, Franklin County, A.E. Gibson, Book 8, p. 21
(33) Arthur Ben Chitty, Sewanee Sampler, (Sewanee, Tennessee-1978).
(34) Franklin County Deeds, Book 5, p. 172.
(35) State of Tennessee Land Grant #7113, p. 768.
(36) Deed Records, Franklin County, Henry Garner to University of the South, registered 8-10-1859.
(37) Goodspeed's History of Tennessee, (Nashville, 1886), p. 796.
(38) Deed Records, Franklin County, Book Z, p. 52.
(39) Ibid, p. 29.
(40) Beatrice Alexander Collins, "Winchester Female Academy," Franklin County Historical Review, IX #2 (1978), p. 80.
(41) Goodspeed's History of Tennessee, (Nashville, 1886), p. 798.
(42) State of Tennessee Land Grant #9306, entry #2877, p. 84
(43) Goodspeed's History of Tennessee, (Nashville, 1886), p. 798.
(44) Deed Records, Franklin County, A.M. Ruthledge, Book Z, p. 60.
(45) State of Tennessee Land Grant #559 for Wood Moreland.
(46) Proceedings of the Executive Committee of the University of the South, July 19, 1860. Found in Jessie Ball duPont Library at the University of the South.
(47) Erick D. Montgomery, "The Montgomery Family of Franklin County," Franklin County Historical Review, IX #2 (1978), p. 102.
(48) "In Memoriam -- Allen Gipson's Death Notice", The Sewanee Purple, April 18, 1896.
(49) Deed Records, Franklin County, Book Y, p 332-336, p. 456-458.
Deed Records, Davidson County Notebook A, p. 234.
Deed Records, Franklin County, Book Z, p. 349-350
Deed Records, Franklin County, John Hendley to U.S., dated 5-26-1860.
Deed Records, Franklin County, W.H. Tomlinson, Book 7, p 467.
Deed Records, Franklin County, A. E. Gibson, Book 8, p.21
(50) Deed Records, Franklin County, Allen Gipson, Book Y, p. 413.
(51) J.H. Otey, University of the South Board of Trustee's Meeting 1857-68, p. 13. Located in the Jessie Ball duPont Library at the University of the South.
(52) "Allen Gipson," Family Histories, Franklin County, Tennessee 1807-1996, Franklin County Historical Society (Paducah 1996), p. 205-206.
(53) Deed Records, Franklin County, W.B. Shepard, Book Z, p. 349-350.
Deed Records, Franklin County, W.B. Shepard Sr. Book H, p. 55-56.
(54) Deed Records, Franklin County, A.M. Rutledge, Book Z, p. 60.
(55) 1860 Franklin County, Tennessee Census Records.
(56) State of Tennessee Land Grant #26633 for W.S. Bennett, p. 462.
(57) William H. Kellar, Chuwalee (Chronicles of Franklin County), (Winchester 1973), p. 77.

(58) Erick D. Montgomery, "The Montgomery Family of Franklin County," Franklin County Historical Review, IX #2 (1978), p. 100 & 102.
(59) Deed Records, Franklin County, Dennis Barnes, Book 18, p. 628.
(60) Deed Records, Franklin County, S.W. Houghton & Hines, Book Z, p. 29.
(61) Goodspeed's History of Tennessee, (Nashville, 1886), p. 797.
(62) "Free Taxable Inhabitants: Voter Enumeration of 1812, Franklin County," Franklin County Historical Review, XIX #1 (1988), p. 55.
(63) Deed Records, Franklin County, Allen Gipson, Book Y, p. 43.
(64) Plat Record, Franklin County, Rubin C. Short, Book 89, p. 126, envelope 117A.
(65) George Reynolds, Sewanee and the Cumberland Plateau in the Civil War, undated, p. 9
(66) State of Tennessee Land Grant #9982, entry #1970, p. 501.
(67) State of Tennessee Land Grant #8346, entry #1926, p. 74.
(68) William Ray Turner, "Kennedy Told World of Coal," *Grundy County Herald*, 9-2-1976, p. 10A.
(69) Deed Records, Franklin County, Book Y, p. 332-336.
(70) Thomas E. Bailey, "Storm on Cumberland Mountain, The Story of the Cowan Pusher District," Tennessee Historical Quarterly, Fall 1975, p. 6.
(71) George R. Fairbanks, History of the University of the South, (Jacksonville 1905), p. 11.
(72) "Unmarked Historical Spots of Franklin County, University of the South," *Tennessee Historical Magazine*, Series II., Vol. III #2, dated January, 1935, p. 119
(73) George R. Fairbanks, History of the University of the South, (Jacksonville 1905), p. 1.
(74) Ibid, p. 12.
(75) Ibid, p. 29.
(76) Ibid, p. 29-30.
(77) Ibid, p. 30.
(78) Ibid, p. 30-31.
(79) Ibid, p. 34.
(80) Proceedings of the Executive Committee of the University of the South, July 19, 1860. Found in Jessie Ball duPont Library at the University of the South.
(81) Ibid.
(82) Deed Records, Franklin County, Book Y, p 332-336, 456-458.
Deed Records, Davidson County Notebook A, p.234.
Deed Records, Franklin County, Book Z, p. 349-350
Deed Records, Franklin County, John Hendley to U.S., dated 5-26-1860.
Deed Records, Franklin County, W.H. Tomlinson, Book 7, p 467.
Deed Records, Franklin County, A. E. Gibson, Book 8, p. 21
(83) Ibid.
(84) Ibid.
(85) Ibid.
(86) Deed Records, Franklin County, W.B. Shepard, Book Z, p 349-350.
(87) Deed Records, Franklin County, A.M. Ruthledge, Book Z, p 60.

(88) Deed Records, Franklin County, S.W. Houghton & Robert Hines, Book Z, p 29.
(89) State of Tennessee Land Grant #559, Wood Moreland & J.B. Hawkins.
(90) Deed Records, Franklin County, Abraham Bowers, registered 8-8-1859.
(91) Deed Records, Franklin County, Allen Gipson, Book Y, p 413.
(92) Deed Records, Franklin County, Henry Garner, registered 8-10-1859.
(93) Deed Records, Franklin County, Dennis Barnes, Book 18, p. 628.
(94) Beatrice Alexander Collins, "Winchester Female Academy," Franklin County Historical Review, IX #2 (1978), p. 80.
(95) Goodspeed's History of Tennessee, (Nashville, 1886), p. 796-797.
(96) Family Histories, Franklin County, Tennessee 1807-1996, Franklin County Historical Society (Paducah 1996), Estill, p. 185.
(97) Elizabeth Chitty, "How the University of the South Came to be in Franklin County," The Way We Were, Franklin County Historical Review, Vol. XXVI (Winchester 1996). p. 98.
(98) George R. Fairbanks, History of the University of the South, (Jacksonville 1905), p. 29 and 39.
(99) Ibid, p. 44.
(100) Deed Records, Franklin County, A.M. Rutledge, Book Z, p. 60.
(101) "Progress," Purple Sewanee , (Sewanee, 1932, Reprint 1962), p. 38
(102) Arthur Ben Chitty, Sewanee Sampler, (Sewanee 1978), p. 9-10.
(103) "Progress," Purple Sewanee , (Sewanee, 1932, Reprint 1962), p. 38
(104) 1860 Franklin County, - 1880 Marion County, Tennessee Census.
(105) Deed Records, Franklin County, A.M. Rutledge, Book Z, p. 60.
(106) "Progress," Purple Sewanee , (Sewanee, 1932, Reprint 1962), p. 20
(107) Conversations between family descendants and Pat Makris.
(108) "Progress," Purple Sewanee , (Sewanee, 1932, Reprint 1962), p. 19
(109) George R. Fairbanks, History of the University of the South, (Jacksonville 1905), p. 40.
(110) Ibid, p. 19-21.
(111) Mike Foreman, "The Secession of Franklin County," The Way We Were, Franklin County Historical Review, Vol. XXVI (Winchester 1996). p. 63-68.
(112) George Reynolds, Sewanee and the Cumberland Plateau in the Civil War, undated, p. 1-15
(113) Ibid, p. 1-15
(114) Ibid, p. 1-15
(115) George R. Fairbanks, History of the University of the South, (Jacksonville 1905), p. 263-264.
(116) Edgar Legard Pennington, "Battle of Sewanee," Tennessee Historical Quarterly, Vol. IX #3, September 1950, p. 232-241.
(117) George R. Fairbanks, History of the University of the South, (Jacksonville 1905), p. 61.
(118) Ibid, p. 82-85.
(119) Ibid, p. 91.

(120) Moultrie Guerry & Arthur Ben & Elizabeth N. Chitty," George Rainsford Fairbanks, The Last of the Founders" Men Who Made Sewanee, (Sewanee 1981), p. 50.
(121) Ibid, p. 156.
(122) Ibid, p. 71.
(123) "Education - Sewanee, How I Love You," *Time Magazine*, April 4, 1983.
(124) George R. Fairbanks, History of the University of the South, (Jacksonville 1905), p. 100.
(125) Deed Records, Franklin County, University Mining Company, Book Y, p. 332-336, p. 456-458.
(126) George R. Fairbanks, History of the University of the South, (Jacksonville 1905), p. 99-100.
(127) Ibid, p. 100 & 195.
(128) Ibid, p. 123-125.
(129) Ibid, p. 130 & 140.
(130) Ibid, p. 99-100.
(131) Ibid, p. 131.
(132) Franklin County Records, University of the South To Charles W. Hayes, Book Y, p. 374-376 .
(133) George R. Fairbanks, History of the University of the South, (Jacksonville 1905), p. 150.
(134) Franklin County Historical Review, XVII #1 (1986), p. 13.
(135) George R. Fairbanks, History of the University of the South, (Jacksonville 1905), p. 150.
(136) "In the Beginning," Purple Sewanee , (Sewanee, 1932, Reprint 1962), p. 38-39.
(137) Ibid, p. 38.
(138) Franklin County, Tennessee 1870 Census Record.
(139) George R. Fairbanks, History of the University of the South, (Jacksonville 1905), p. 156.
(140) Ibid, p. 167-169.
(141) Ely Green, Ely, An Autobiography, (University of Georgia 1966), p. 69.
(142) Ibid, p. 3
(143) Ibid, p. xxviii.
(146) "Charles Wadhams," Goodspeed's History of Tennessee, (Nashville, 1886).
(147) "Bishop Wadham," Purple Sewanee , (Sewanee, 1932, Reprint 1962), p. 46.
(148) Franklin County, Tennessee 1870 Census Record
(149) Ibid.
(150) Herman Green notes, provided Pat Makris by Mrs. Hayden McBee.
(151) Information provided by a family member.
(152) "Mr. Judd," Purple Sewanee , (Sewanee, 1932, Reprint 1962), p. 136.
(153) "C.S. Judd Opens Photography Studio," *The University News*, Vol. 2 # 17, May 3, 1876.
(154) Letter to Pat Makris from Mary Hamilton, 1983.
(155) Recollections of Reece Short.

(156) John Wilson, "Did Lincoln's Assassin Booth Escape, Live in Tennessee?," Chattanooga News Free Press, June 14, 1992, p. A11-A12.
(157) Moultrie Guerry & Arthur Ben & Elizabeth N. Chitty," Edmund Kirby-Smith Biography in Outline," Men Who Made Sewanee, (Sewanee 1981), p. 72.
(158) Sister Mary Hilary C.S.M., Ten Decades of Praise, p. 125-126.
(159) Information provided by Sister Kiara and Family Histories, Franklin County, Tennessee 1807-1996, Franklin County Historical Society (Paducah 1996), Ghost, p. 332
(160) Recollections of Pat Makris.
(161) Recollections of Reece Short.
(162) "Rededication of the Cross: A Story of the Community," *The Sewanee Purple*, April 28, 1983, p. 7.
(163) Ibid.
(164) David Littler, "Designer Tells About Erection of the Cross," *The Sewanee Purple*, April 16, 1958, p. 1.
(165) Ibid.
(166) Ibid.
(167) Ibid.
(168) "Rededication of the Cross: A Story of the Community," *The Sewanee Purple*, April 28, 1983, p. 7.
(169) Ibid.
(170) Ibid, p. 6.
(171) Ibid.
(172) "President Taft," Purple Sewanee , (Sewanee, 1932, Reprint 1962), p. 131-132.
(173) Ely Green, Ely, An Autobiography, (University of Georgia 1966), p. 220.
(174) Franklin County Court Records, University of the South vs. Franklin County, Tennessee, October 21, 1887.
(175) Sewanee & Cowan Church Directory of Past & Present Ministries, p. 46.
(176) Recollections of Pat Makris and William "Bug" McBee.
(177) "Jump Off," Purple Sewanee , (Sewanee, 1932, Reprint 1962), p. 4-5
(178) Recollections of Pat Makris.
(179) 1870 Franklin County Tennessee Census and Lost Cove Baptismal Records. Baptismal records found in the Jessie Ball duPont library at the University of the South.
(180) Ibid.
(181) "Sewanee Now and Then, Air Fields," *Sewanee Mountain Messenger*, , May 16, 1996, p. 3
(182) Provided by Dr. Harold Jackson, brother of M. F. Jackson Jr., and son of M. F. Sr.
(183) "Sewanee Now and Then, Air Fields," *Sewanee Mountain Messenger*, , May 16, 1996, p. 3
(184) Recollections of Pat Makris.
(185) Recollections of Lucia Green Yates, Benton Green, Polly Pack Green, Reece Short, Margaret Garner Short, and Patricia Short Makris.
(186) "Progress," Purple Sewanee , (Sewanee, 1932, Reprint 1962), p. 38

(187) Howard Malcolm Hannah, "At the University of the South," Confederate Actions in Franklin County, Tennessee, (Winchester 1963), p. 31.
(188) Information provided by Annie Armour, Archivist in Jessie Ball duPont Library at the University of the South.
(189) Recollections of Pat Makris.
(190) "In the Beginning," Purple Sewanee , (Sewanee, 1932, Reprint 1962), p. 39.

(191) Telfair Hodgson, "The Report of the Chancellor," dated June 30, 1882. Deposition of Hodgson & Sam G. Jones filed 12/88 Clerks Ledger. Located in Franklin County Loose Records, Winchester, Tennessee.
(192) "President Taft," Purple Sewanee , (Sewanee, 1932, Reprint 1962), p. 132.
(193) Provided by Mrs. Una Green McBee, wife of Chief Hayden McBee.
(194) Provided by Dr. Harold Jackson, son of Sheriff Jackson.
(195) Ibid.
(196) Recollections of Reece Short.
(197) Information provided by Sister Kiara and Family Histories, Franklin County, Tennessee 1807-1996, Franklin County Historical Society (Paducah 1996), Ghost, p. 332.
(198) Stories handed down in Short family by Reece Short and his father David W. Short.
(199) "Headless Gownsman; Shades & Shadows; Sewanee Ghost; The Townsman; Crying Baby," Purple Sewanee , (Reprint of Sewanee, 1932), p. 144-150.
(200) "American Legion Bonholzer - Campbell Post 51 Resolutions," passed March 17, 1949.
(201) War Memorial Committee of the Woman's Club letter dated March 16, 1949 to Acting Vice-Chancellor Henry Gass, University of the South.
(202) Recollections of Pat Makris after visiting American cemetery in Argonne Forest, France with her father Reece Short.
(203) Recollections of Pat Makris.
(204) 1870 Franklin County, Tennessee Census.